MOVING AND RESTING IN GOD'S DESIRE:

A Spirituality of Peace

Andrew Marr, OSB

St. Gregory's Abbey Press
Three Rivers, Michigan

Moving and Resting in God's Desire: A Spirituality of Peace

c St. Gregory's Abbey Press

ISBN 978-0-9862485-2-8 (softcover)
ISBN 978-0-9862485-3-5 (eBook)

Cover art and design by Ricky Gunawan
Formatting by Polgarus Studio

In memory of René Girard and Raymund Schwager, for the stimulation of their thought and their personal encouragement to me.

NOTES ON TRANSLATIONS

All quotations from the Bible are from the New Revised Standard Version.

All quotations from *The Rule of St. Benedict* (RB) are from *RB 1980: The Rule of St. Benedict in Latin and English with Notes*. Timothy Fry, ed. Collegeville, MN: Liturgical Press, 1981.

ACKNOWLEDGEMENTS

I wish to give a special thank you to Angela Borda for her expert editing and, even more, for her challenging suggestions that goaded me on to probing some difficult subjects further than I otherwise might have. Another special thank you goes to J. Samuel Hammond for composing the index to this book and for making many constructive suggestions for improving the text. Any remaining errors are my responsibility. I also wish to thank my fellow monks of St. Gregory's Abbey for the supportive social atmosphere they provide for me.

Contents

Introduction

Spiritual writing often places a strong emphasis on obeying God's will. That is good, but I think we can deepen our relationship with God by shifting the emphasis from trying to do God's will to sharing God's desire. The two seem to amount to the same thing: if God desires something, then God wills it. But the differing connotations of these two words resonate differently within us. The phrase "obey God's will" suggests that God's will is something we should allow God to impose on us. The phrase "share God's desire" has a much gentler connotation. It suggests that God has a certain desire that God wishes to share. Sharing a desire is a very different thing than giving marching orders. God's desire extends an invitation to enter into a great mystery. I purposely use the singular form of desire for God because, although God could be said to have many desires, they all converge into one all-encompassing desire for the well-being of all Creation.

Thinking and praying in terms of God's desire is attractive in the sense that it opens up a collaborative relationship with God, such as what Abraham and Moses had when they bargained with God on behalf of God's people. But our desires are complex, stimulating, and troubling. The problematic aspect of our desires makes us want to exert our own wills against these desires and then ask God to take the same dictatorial approach with them as well. But if God shares God's desire with us instead, then exerting our own will against our desires when God does not do that to us is not likely to work. That God shares a desire with us rather than imposes it on us tells us that desire is always shared by two or more people.

The French polymath thinker René Girard has suggested that the desires within us do not originate within ourselves, but rather they originate from the desires of others. When our desires are shared, they are contagious and this contagion can become an epidemic. We see this when a firestorm of rage flares up throughout a social network. Shared desire can also be as contagious as a gentle smile that floats around people like a soft breeze. Girard calls this shared desire "mimetic desire." That is, desire that imitates the desires of others. Mimetic desire is not imitation in the sense of an external copying such as mimicking the actions of others. Rather, our desires are shared through a deep resonance that connects us with other people and with God. When we think of desires as our own, we are likely to treat them like weapons in battles with the will. But the more we try to assert our desires as our own, the more they are governed by the desires of others. If we try to control the desires of others by trying to make them imitate us, we are organizing our lives around their desires all the more. Meanwhile, the people who have lured us into imitating their desires are just as trapped into imitating ours.

This phenomenon of shared desire is like a worm that boars through an intricate route to the depths of our personhood. This is why trying to control our own desires as if they were strictly our own is "beating the air." (1 Cor. 9:26) On a broad social scale, this labyrinth of mimetic desire can lead to meltdowns, culminating in collective violence such as the crucifixion of Jesus of Nazareth. For his part, Jesus nailed this persecutory meltdown to the cross, to quote Paul creatively. (Col. 2:14)

God's desire enters into this dizzying matrix of human mimetic desire more deeply than the devouring worm ever could, so as to save us from being overrun by these desires. The amazing thing about God's desire is its spaciousness, contrasting greatly with the cramped nexus of human mimetic desire. In God's desire, there is all the room in the world. That is not surprising since God created all of the room in the world. While human mimetic desire creates scarcity through conflict, God's desire provides abundance such as the abundance that flowed from five barley loaves and two fishes to a multitude of people in the wilderness. (Jn. 6:1–14) The gentleness of sharing God's desire might make it look like an easy option, but I find it highly challenging. Sharing God's desire asks of us nothing short of a total transformation of ourselves as we open our hearts to embrace the expansive desire of God.

In bringing the shared aspect of desire to our attention, Girard and his colleagues have opened up a powerful avenue for spiritual and social renewal. This small insight may not look like much, but it has the power to help us understand how violence, especially violence connected with religion, occurs. This is especially true with the Paschal Mystery of Christ. More importantly, this small insight can help us learn how we can become living stones in the temple of God that grow into God's Kingdom like a mustard seed growing into a large tree. (Mt. 13:31–32) In the pages that follow, I will explore these ideas as means of hearing God's Word and making it flesh in our acts of service and prayer. I will touch on the most fundamental aspects of Christian living but not everything. Ways of reading scripture will be stressed throughout. Practices of liturgical prayer and contemplative prayer will be examined. I shall probe the fundamental attitudes of respect and humility and the process of forgiveness. Indeed, as the greatest of challenges, forgiveness will be a running thread throughout this book. These are the areas of Christian practice that most benefit from insights into mimetic desire and that are most helpful for resting and moving in God's desire.

Chapter 1
Nailed to the Cross

Tongues Speaking the Word

A strange gathering took place about two thousand years ago in Jerusalem. Jews had gathered from many nations to celebrate *Shavuot*, the spring harvest festival occurring fifty days after Passover, hence the name Pentecost. Within this gathering a group of Jews heard some Galileans speaking in their different tongues. In their perplexity over this new and exciting gift of understanding languages in their midst, some of them mocked the Galileans, thinking they were drunk.

Peter responded by mocking the mockers for losing track of what time in the morning it was. Then he quoted Joel's prophesy: "In the last days it will be, God declares, that I will pour out my Spirit upon all flesh, and your sons and your daughters shall prophesy, and your young men shall see visions, and your old men shall dream dreams." (Acts 2:17) Unlike Joel's prophecy, the sun was not turning into darkness and the moon into blood, but Peter's message was about to be enough to make them feel as if that was exactly what was happening. The cosmic applecart was being upended, and nothing would ever be the same.

In this exciting and mysterious gathering, Peter redirected his listeners' attention to a very different gathering that had taken place fifty days earlier. At that time, the people gathered to have a man named Jesus handed over "according to the definite plan and foreknowledge of God" and killed "by the hands of those outside the law." (Acts 2:23) That Jesus was killed unjustly, by those outside the law, indicates that God's plan and foreknowledge should not be equated with God's will. Quite the contrary. Peter's next announcement was even more startling: "God raised him up, having freed him from death." (Acts 2:24) The risen victim, "sitting at the right hand of God," poured out the Holy Spirit that everybody was seeing and hearing. In declaring that the crucified and risen Jesus was the Messiah, Peter was claiming that a radically new understanding of life was being given through the Holy Spirit.

At these words, Peter's listeners were "cut to the heart," and they asked what they should do. It seems odd that it would be news to them that Jesus of Nazareth was killed in this city just fifty days before. Quite possibly some of them were in the crowd crying out to Pilate to crucify him. What was new was that Peter persuaded the people to see that their act of mob violence had been perpetrated against a victim who did not deserve to suffer at their hands. A new miracle, greater than speaking in tongues, was making it possible for them to *hear* Peter tell them what had happened fifty days ago, to hear Peter deeply enough to be cut to the heart and ask what they should do. The Tower of Babel was being reversed in two ways: 1) by replacing the scattering that occurred when all languages were confused with a gift of understanding languages that gathered people back together, and 2) by people gathering *with* God rather than against God. The reversal of confounding languages communicated in plain words the truth that the confused languages had hidden: collective violence is ultimately directed at God. This revealing truth was delivered not in accusation but in the astounding spirit of forgiveness.

Peter's advice to these people, who were cut to the heart, was to repent and be baptized in the name of Jesus for the forgiveness of their sins. A brief, bare-bones look at the story narrated in the Gospels and proclaimed by Peter in Acts tells us what they, and we, are called to repent of. A charismatic preacher and healer named Jesus arose from a backwater where, Nathanael suggested, nothing good could come. (Jn. 1:46) As this preacher gathered a following, the authorities formed another circle around the preacher to spy on everything he did and question his every move. Jesus came to Jerusalem for the Passover at a time when Jerusalem was filled with partisan tensions: the Pharisees against the Sadducees, the insurgent zealots against the Roman occupation, to mention the most serious ones. These people, who were at loggerheads over pretty much everything, suddenly and miraculously came to an agreement to put Jesus of Nazareth to death for being a disturber of the peace. Luke highlights this banding together of enemies when he notes that after Pilate sent Jesus to Herod, the two enemies became friends from that day forward. (Lk. 23:12) First, we see the persecuting circle close in on Jesus as they question him in the temple by asking questions transparently designed to entrap him. Jesus' cleansing of the temple was the last straw. Jesus was arrested, and the whole city was incited against Jesus to cry out for his crucifixion. Pilate showed some reluctance to sentence Jesus to death, but he did it anyway. In essence, the crowd gathered around a victim who was blamed for a society's ills, and the victim was put to death. At no time is God portrayed as the agent of any of these events. Everything that preceded nailing Jesus to the cross and then taking him down was done by human beings who chose to do what they did. All of this tells us that we are called to repent of collective violence.

Astoundingly, the crucifixion of Jesus was followed by his Resurrection. *Here* is where God enters the picture. *This* is what *God* does. That is, God vindicates Jesus as innocent, a victim of rank injustice on the part of human beings. There is nothing in the Gospels or the apostolic preaching recorded in Acts to suggest that *God* willed the murder of Jesus. Moreover, there is not the slightest trace of the notion that God *needed* to punish somebody for the sins of humanity and that God was willing, even *wanted* to vent that wrath on Jesus. The question of God's alleged wrath will be examined at length below. The only way the Gospels and apostolic preaching allow room for God willing, or being willing to allow, the crucifixion of Jesus, is in the sense that *humanity's* wrath could not be cured in any other way, and curing humanity's wrath was so important to God that God was willing suffer a painful death on a cross if that is what it took. Most important and most astounding of all, Jesus returned in peace to gather all who had been scattered at the time of his death. He did not come to punish any of the people who had murdered him. On top of that, he sent the Holy Spirit to gather the people of Jerusalem and embrace the people with forgiveness. It was this forgiveness that gave them the courage to face what they had done and receive the divine life of the Spirit that was already forming the foundation for their renewed life even before they knew it was happening. Any notion that God's wrath was somehow appeased by the murder of God's son makes no sense in the light of the forgiveness preached by the apostles. Explain

A crucial word in the Greek text used in reference to the death of Jesus is a small one with huge implications: *dei.* (cf. Lk.24:26) This word means roughly "it was necessary" or "it had to happen." We have to be very careful about how we understand the notion that the collective murder of Jesus was "necessary." There is a tendency to think that somehow it was "necessary" to God that Jesus suffer and die. But the apostolic proclamation suggests, on the contrary, that it was "necessary" for *humans* that Jesus die. We see this human human act! "necessity" in the words of Caiaphas when he said: "It is better for you to have one man die for the people than to have the whole nation destroyed." (Jn. 11:50) If we are going to repent of the collective violence that led to Jesus' death, we have to understand what made it seem so "necessary" at the time. John goes on to say that Caiaphas was not saying these words on his own accord but was inadvertently being a prophet. That is, although Caiaphas did not understand the full impact of what he was saying, he was exposing the truth of collective violence. Not only that, but he was exposing the truth of the *sacralization* of collective violence.

A few days later, Peter and John strengthened the gathering in the Holy Spirit by healing a cripple at the temple gate in the name of "the Holy and Righteous One," "the Author of life" whom these people had killed while preferring to release a murderer. (Acts 3:14–15) The priests and the Sadducees, normally at enmity with each other, cooperated enough to bring the apostles in for questioning. While affirming, yet again, that the cripple had been healed by the man *they* (the Jewish authorities) had rejected, Peter refers to Psalm 118: the stone rejected by *them*, the builders of the temple, had been made the cornerstone by God. (Psalm 118:22) The context of the psalm strengthens the power of this verse. The Psalmist is surrounded by enemies, "surrounded on every side," "surrounded like bees," and yet the Psalmist is delivered by God. It is during his thanksgiving for deliverance that the Psalmist sings out the verse about the rejected stone, suggesting that he himself had been a rejected stone that God had chosen to be a cornerstone for a whole new way for society to form. This very verse was quoted by Jesus as his conclusion to the Parable of the Evil Workers (Mt. 21:33–45), a parable of collective violence that foreshadows what would soon happen to him at the hands of the authorities. After Peter and John were released from prison, the prayer of the apostles reached a climax with a quote from Psalm 2 that succinctly summarizes the apostolic witness: "Why do the nations conspire, and the peoples plot in vain? The kings of the earth set themselves, and the rulers take counsel together, against the Lord and his anointed." (Ps. 2:1–2) That is, discord among rulers was resolved by gathering against the victim, the rejected stone who has been made the cornerstone. This verse tells the whole story of the passion and death of Jesus in an explosive nutshell.

There are several more instances in the Gospels and Acts where verses from the Psalms are interpreted as prophecies of Christ's death and Resurrection. When, after dividing Jesus' garments after nailing him to the cross, they cast lots for the seamless robe, John quotes from Psalm 22: "They parted my garments among them and for my clothing they cast lots." Earlier, the Psalmist was surrounded by "strong bulls of Bashan," dogs, and "a company of evildoers." (Ps. 22:12, 16) Jesus' cry "I thirst" that prompted a bystander to give him some vinegar is an allusion to Psalm 69: "They gave me poison for food, and for my thirst they gave me vinegar to drink." Previously, the Psalmist had cried out: "more in number than the hairs of my head are those who hate me without cause." (Ps. 69:4) Like the Psalmist, most of the prophets were either victims of collective violence or were threatened with it. Jeremiah was persecuted by the crowds and even his own family. He was thrown into a dry cistern, where he would have perished if he had not been saved by a sympathizer. The "Suffering Servant" of Isaiah 53 is a particularly poignant example of a person persecuted and executed by the community under the belief that he was "stricken, struck down by God." (Isa. 53:4) Only after they had cut him off from the land of the living did they realize that the servant was actually stricken by humans, namely themselves. Isa. 53:8) Moses, also a prophet, (Deut. 34: 10) was persecuted so many times during the desert journey by the people he led that it's a wonder he got as close to the Promised Land as he did. His death is mysterious enough to raise suspicions. Maybe the crowd finally got him in the end. In Matthew 23:35, Jesus defines a prophet as a victim of the people when he calls his own persecutors to account for "the righteous blood shed on Earth, from the blood of innocent Abel to the blood of Zechariah the son of Barechiah, whom you murdered between the sanctuary and the altar."

Although these psalms and stories of the prophets were understood as prophecies of the Passion and Resurrection of Jesus by the apostles and generations of theologians following, they are not prophecies in the sense that somebody gazed into a crystal ball and saw the passion of Jesus several centuries later. The psalms of persecution were complaints of a horror that happened again and again. What these psalms and prophecies reveal is that the collective violence that Jesus suffered was not a new story but an *old* story. What happened to Jesus was what had happened to countless victims before him. Moreover, just as the Suffering Servant was seen to be vindicated by God, the Suffering Servant was also vindicated by God through the gift of new life. (Isa. 53:10–12) In this confidence, the Psalmist cries out: "You will not abandon me to the realm of the dead, nor will you let your faithful one see decay." (Ps. 16:10) It is fortuitous that in the Latin alphabet, Abel to Zechariah has the comprehensiveness of A to Z. By starting with Abel as the first of the prophets in this sense, Jesus is making it clear that such persecution goes back to the dawn of civilization.

A look at a disturbing story about collective violence that takes place in Joshua Chapter 7 gives us another example of this incipient disclosure of the truth of collective violence. In his analysis of the story, James Alison notes that Joshua followed a stirring victory at Jericho with a stunning defeat at Ai. (Alison 2013, 93–117) Like most good generals and government officials, Joshua cast lots to find somebody else to blame. The lot fell on Achan, who was found responsible for stirring God's anger by taking some of the loot for himself. Never mind the great unlikelihood that Achan was the only one who committed this crime. Achan and his family were killed by stoning and, with the public morale boosted through this grisly activity, Israel soundly won their next battle. Enough information is given in this narrative to suggest that the real reason for the military defeat was a military blunder and not God's anger over somebody taking some loot. In fact, God never gets a word in this story. Casting lots to assess blame was going to have a result pointing to somebody regardless of what God willed in the matter. Achan may or may not have been guilty, but his execution is shown to be unjust, a resolution of social tension through collective murder. The author probably believed that Achan was guilty and deserved to be killed, but instead of inventing a myth, this author told the story for what it was so that later readers, alerted by the Forgiving Victim, can see the truth. (I will discuss myth as a means of covering up the truth in the next section.) The violence of this story and many others like it horrifies many modern readers for good reason. However, it is important to realize that the Bible is *revealing* the truth of violence rather than covering it up with a "nice" myth. In short, the Hebrew Bible was gradually, over time, revealing the basic truth that Jesus would reveal in a definitive way.

Since the Foundation of Human Culture

René Girard has explored at length how old the story of collective violence is. In several books, most especially *Violence and the Sacred* and *Things Hidden Since the Foundation of the World*, Girard argues that in archaic society, social tensions fueled by rivalry reached a boiling point that led to the chaotic warfare of everybody against everybody. (Hobbes also imagined the same scenario.) Some societies that have not been preserved in the historical record may have imploded from this kind of violence. In at least most of the societies we do know about, peace suddenly and mysteriously emerged out of this chaos when, at the crucial point of teetering on the brink of destruction, all of the collective rage focused on one person or a small group of people. This one person or group was deemed responsible for all of the social chaos.

Everybody who was caught in reciprocal violence was just as suddenly caught in the collective accusation against the person on whom all blame was cast. This responsible person was then killed through spontaneous mob violence. Girard and his colleagues commonly refer to this phenomenon as the Scapegoat Mechanism. Here, the word "scapegoat" is not being used in its original sense of referring to a cryptic Jewish ritual but in its popular sense of referring to a single person or group of persons being unjustly blamed for a society's ills. This common meaning of the term is in itself a strong testimony to the commonality of this scenario. In *Flesh Becomes Word*, David Dawson charts the etymology of the word from its origins to present usage.

The immediate relief of peace and order that followed the collective murder would have been dramatic. The shattering awe experienced through the violence and the sudden peace that ensued turned the victim into a deity. The person who was totally responsible for the social violence suddenly became totally responsible for the peace. This is where Girard locates the origins of religion. Rudolf Otto is famous for articulating the fascinating and frightening mystery experienced by early humanity that inspired religious awe. I think Girard scoffed too much at the idea that early humanity tried to probe the mysteries of the world about them, but I am inclined to think that much of this tremulous awe did result from the intensity of the primal collective murders. (Palaver 2013, 154) This "solution" to social meltdown was not the result of human ingenuity. Rather, the escalation of the flood of violence itself triggered the mechanism of singling out a victim who was then promptly dispatched. In order for collective violence to stabilize a society, it was essential that *nobody* suffer a moral hangover as a result of the event. One dissenting voice would have spoiled everything. This collective murder was a *binding* of the people together. Of course, there was somebody—a corpse— at the bottom of the pile of stones who might have had a different point of view. Girard habitually calls this scenario "unanimity minus one." To preserve the unity, the lynching of the victim *must not* be seen for what it was. There must be a total forgetting of what actually happened. We will soon look at the ways this forgetting happens. It is important to note that Girard's anthropological theory of the origins of religion speaks about humanity; it is not a theory about God. We have already seen how the apostolic preaching about the risen, Forgiving Victim is the climax of God's revelation of the truth about Godself.

At the heart of the mechanism of collective violence is accusation. The victim was blamed for everything that was wrong with society. Accusation is what we saw at the heart of the apostolic proclamation about Jesus: he was falsely accused. In scripture, Satan was the accuser. That means that all crowds caught up in collective false accusation leading to collective murder are possessed with the spirit of Satan. When Satan was booted out of Heaven in Revelation 12, he was *not* called the tempter as in popular thought, but the accuser. There does not need to be a supernatural element to this collective possession of accusation. In essence, everyone in the crowd is possessed by one another's rage with each other and then everybody is possessed by rage against the designated enemy who must be eliminated. So it is that every accuser is obsessed, if not possessed, by the accused person. It is no wonder that the truth of what is happening during a crisis of accusation must be suppressed. John captures this combination of mendacity and violence with Jesus' charge that the devil "was a murderer from the beginning and does not stand in the truth, because there is no truth in him." (Jn. 8:44)

These primordial acts of collective violence across the globe, though spontaneous and chaotic, would have re-established order for a time. Such order is inherently unstable as social tensions are sure to rise again, requiring the same "solution." From the point of view of Girard's thesis, we can see that the rhythmic reversion to primordial chaos discussed in many of Mircea Eliade's books would be such a rhythm of renewed crisis and violent resolution. As societies developed greater complexity, it was necessary for this spontaneous "solution" to be institutionalized. Girard argues that societies tended to impose roughly the same structures to limit such outbreaks in the future: myth, ritual, and prohibition.

Girard argues that myth retains the narrative shape of collective violence but garbles it. That is myths reveal the truth in a way that hides it. This is how Satan buries accusation in lies. Myths are told by the murderers, not the victims. The more alert one is to these traces, the more of them one will find when examining myths. Many deities created the world through a process of their own dismemberment. Purusha was sacrificed by the gods and the dismembered parts of his body were used to create the cosmos. These body parts of Purusha became the castes that structured Indian society. Dionysus was another dismembered deity whose devotees, in turn, dismembered a victim when consumed by mania caused by their god. Other myths tell of strife at the dawn of creation, such as Marduk's dismemberment of the sea monster Tiamat to win the cosmic battle against her. In a myth of the Yahuna Indians, Milomaki, a singer who enchants the populace with his music, is deemed responsible for numerous deaths through fish poisoning. He is cremated on a funeral pyre and from his body grows the first paxiuba palm tree in the world (Hamerton-Kelly, ed. 1987, 79–80.) Oedipus is deemed responsible for the plague that has stricken Thebes because he is the one who killed Laius and then married his mother, so he is expelled from the city. There is no question of giving a fair trial to the likes of Tiamat, Milomaki, or Oedipus. To question the total guilt of any of these victims would spoil the mechanism of collective violence. It is essential that the victim have no voice. Gil Bailie points out that the root of the Greek word "mythos" is "mu," which means to close or to keep secret. (Bailie 1995, 33) Aeschylus understood the importance of silencing. When Agamemnon is about to sacrifice his daughter, Iphigenia, he orders that his daughter's mouth be gagged. (Bailie, 31)

The "choice" of the victim is usually arbitrary, a lottery, to use the title of a famous story by Shirley Jackson. (Jackson 1991, 291–302) However, many of the myths that have come down to us suggest that any little or not-so-little thing that causes a person to stand out makes that person particularly vulnerable in a time of social crisis. Being lame like Oedipus or blind in one eye like Woden will do it. Being talented like Quetzalcoatl or Orpheus also makes one a target as we still see today in the way we treat celebrities. Being the chief or the monarch has the same effect, to the extent that Girard defined a monarch as "a sacrificial victim with a kind of suspended sentence." (Girard 1987, 52) The arbitrariness of the chosen victims attests to the mendacity of the accusations leading to their deaths or expulsion.

Girard's take on myths brings to mind the memorable phrase coined by

C.S. Lewis: Christ is myth made fact. The notion kind of sneaked up on Lewis during the process that led to his conversion to Christianity. An offhand remark by his friend T. D. Weldon, a fellow Oxford don and, like Lewis at the time, an avowed atheist, made a deep impression on him over the years: "Rum thing, that stuff of Frazer's about the Dying God. It almost looks as if it really happened once." (Lewis 1955, 223–224) Of course, that is precisely the claim of the Gospels. Girard, of course, also studied James Frazer's writings about deities, most of them vegetation deities who were in the habit of dying and rising. Frazer seems to have absorbed Jesus into the other myths, blurring the distinction between them.

For Girard, all myths in their origins derive from fact even as they distort it. For Girard, the Gospel narrative of Jesus dying and rising is not an abstract cosmic truth, but a real scenario that has been happening in reality since the dawn of humanity. As a Christian, Lewis retained sympathy for the myths of dying and rising deities, regarding them as great poetry. Girard, of course, is not so affirming of mythology, as he sees it as obscuring the truth. However, Girard's point of view does not necessarily mean that myths are bad poetry. Moral goodness and ascetic goodness are not equivalent. There is a deeper reason though for being open to Lewis's sympathy. The pathos of a deity like Balder who was killed through collective violence moved Lewis, and that same sensitivity eventually made the Passion of Jesus deeply moving for him as well. There is a still deeper reason for sympathy for myth. Deplorable as the countless acts of collective violence were and continue to be, Girard's thesis also demonstrates how profoundly people are caught up in this mechanism so that they cannot escape without an intervention from God. It is precisely this intervention from God to free humans in bondage that Paul celebrates time and again in his epistles. If we need this intervention from God in Christ, then we are hardly in a position to be judgmental against the first humans that fell into the same traps we do.

The institutionalizing of sacrifice is another pillar of order to prevent outbreaks of chaotic violence. Gil Bailie explained this pillar in an oral presentation: "Sacrifices renew the camaraderie of the collective violence but in a less lethal form." Usually animals and/or plants were used as substitutes for human beings, but the ante would be raised for humans during times of severe crisis. Evidence of recurring human sacrifice has surfaced in just about every known culture. (Davies 1981) These sacrifices took on different meanings in different cultures, and they hooked into some of the more generous aspects of human nature, such as the desire to share with others and to show reverence to higher beings. Sacrifices also, of course, connected with more questionable traits such as making offerings to a deity either in hope of receiving at least as much value in return or trying to stave off divine wrath.

The sacrificial rites of the Aztecs at the time of their conquest give a rich example of the institutionalizing of sacrifice. The horrific quantity of children sacrificed to bring on rain with their tears, and the men whose hearts were cut out to keep the sun alive lead us to dismiss them as uncivilized human beings, but Girard argues that sacrifice is one of the principle institutions of civilization. In their articles in *Sacrifice and Modern Thought*, Laura Rival and David Brown help us sympathize with the Aztecs as human beings. Rival points out that human sacrifice was modeled on the deities who threw themselves into the primordial fire to create the fifth sun and set it in motion. This myth points to a noble disposition behind the sacrifice, but it is also not hard to see it as a typical myth that hides the collective violence that laid the foundations of culture. Brown argues that the wars they fought were as highly ritualized as the sacrifices performed on the top of the pyramids. The whole purpose of these wars was to capture sacrificial victims in fair fights. This is one example of a typical alternative to collective violence against a victim within a society. The violence would be directed outwards to neighboring tribes who became the source for designated victims. As happened with the Aztecs, captives were often adopted by the tribe but kept on the margins and then sacrificed later. The initial chaos leading to the myths and sacrificial rites had led to a complex, highly restrained structure of warfare. Brown quotes a moving statement by an Aztec leader who says that the Spaniards did not understand "how vital it is for us to give blood to the gods." (Meszaros, ed., 185) As selfless as the sacrifices were, and the Aztecs believed they were rewarded in the afterlife, they were convinced that if they failed to continue these sacrifices, the gods would become angry and turn away from them. Here we have it: as with so many other early cultures, the Aztecs were caught in a sacrificial system that allowed no escape. If the gods are subject to anger and capriciousness, one does not dare turn away from the only rites that have a chance of deflecting the divine wrath. Cortés justified his imperialistic measures out of revulsion for the sacrifices carried out by the conquered people, but in a cruel irony, the Spanish inflicted a holocaust on the sacrificers.

One telling example of institutionalized sacrifice is the treatment of twins. During times of primordial chaos, indifferentiation was precisely the problem as differences between people melted in the heat of conflict, as we shall see below. It is no surprise, then, that sometimes the mimetic doubling in a community is portrayed in a myth of two brothers who fight to the death, such as the slaying of Remus by Romulus, who then founded the city of Rome. Out of fear of this sort of conflict, twins were killed. Lois Lowry's chilling dystopia *The Giver* has a modern-day-futurist twin killing. The society is peaceful but colorless with every human trait that could lead to conflict excised. For example, there is no courtship and no sex, just artificially inseminated babies. Matthew is a boy being trained to be the "giver," that is someone with a broad view of how society works who mostly will be ignored but consulted in an emergency. During his training, he sees on the Giver's monitor his own father kill one of two twin babies with a lethal injection because this modern society, too, believes that twins are a potential cause of conflict. The authors of Genesis had no illusions about the danger of mimetic doubles. Brothers paired off against each other are the driving force of the book, starting with Cain and Abel and culminating in Joseph's brothers.

The third pillar, prohibition, spreads sacrifice to the whole society, where some expendable people become perpetual victims. This is accomplished by creating a hierarchical structure that allows only a few to compete for the top positions and the best resources. So it is that institutions spawned from primordial collective violence inevitably institutionalize sacrifice not only ritually but in the structure of society. Eli Sagan recounts this process of institutionalizing violence in his book *The Rise of Tyranny*. The creating of the casts in Vedic society in India out of the parts of Purusha's body is a particularly clear example of society's structures emerging out of myth. The castes, which didn't even give a place for the outcasts, the Dalits, created a social structure that made millions of people permanent sacrificial victims. As a social meltdown blurs the differences between people, differentiation is created by singling out a victim from the rest of society. Victims continue to be singled out in the ensuing sacrificial structure that to this day finds a way to enslave human beings.

It stands to reason that any social structure with its origins in spontaneous collective violence will perpetuate that violence in its mythology, ritual, and structure. The *Pax Romana* wasn't so peaceful for the countless men who were crucified, one of whom was Jesus of Nazareth. The "peaceful" society envisioned in *The Giver* made every person in it a sacrificial victim to maintain that peace. The Aztecs were convinced that not only would the gods turn against them if they stopped their sacrifices but that the whole world would unravel. Myth, ritual, and institutionalized violence make a tight triad that keeps everybody in thrall. In this triad, religion is the core ingredient. The myths tell stories of the gods, sacrifices are made to these gods, and the laws have divine sanction that makes them unquestionable. The collective violence at the dawn of civilization has become what Girard calls "sacred violence." Although this sacralization can be credited with restraining violence enough to save society from catastrophe, it has become a problem that makes violence all the more difficult to overcome.

Since the Greeks, especially the Athenians, are great forerunners of democracy and rational thought, one might think they were a less sacrificial society. Unfortunately, their advances in intellectual endeavors did not make any inroads into the problem of collective violence, and so they hardly prove to be an exception to the rule. Girard writes at some length about the institution of the *Pharmakoi*. (Girard, 1977) These men, considered useless to society, were rounded up and permanently imprisoned. They were fed and clothed at state expense, but when there was a social crisis, one of them was executed. The word *pharmakos* means both medicine and poison, suggesting that the problem and the solution were embodied in one person, as was the case with mythological victims. Then there is also the matter of the judicial offer of a cup of hemlock to Socrates.

Unraveling the Primitive Sacred

If the institutionalization of collective violence is old news and bad news at that, what is the good news? In his preaching, Peter told the old bad news in the context of the forgiveness offered by the Risen Victim. This good news is an invitation for humanity to gather in a radically new way, a way that does not require a victim to keep people together but rather a way that embraces the victim. Exciting as this good news is, violence filled with a sacred aura continues to happen frequently up to the present time, with no end in sight. Girard's theory of sacred violence goes a long way toward explaining this problem. The longstanding habituation to sacred violence would make it very difficult for humanity to give it up, no matter how powerful a jolt it receives from Jesus' Resurrection and forgiveness. Moreover, as we shall see, it proved to be very easy for Christians to backslide into the primitive sacred. So, has anything changed? Quite a lot has changed, but we need a lot more to change. Let's take a look at some of the changes that have taken place.

The biggest change is that Jesus' death and Resurrection announced by the apostolic preaching have blown the cover of sacred violence. The murders shrouded in myth and ritual have been revealed for exactly what they are. As we have seen, Jesus is not the only innocent victim of mob and institutionalized violence. If Jesus was innocent, what about all victims before him? If the accusations against Jesus were false, what about our accusations against others who were killed? We now know that we must be skeptical about these accusations, and we need to be just as skeptical of accusations that swirl through social media today. There is, unfortunately, a frightening side effect of this revelation of the truth of sacred violence. Although it is good news that sacred violence no longer works, the bad news is that we still try to make it work, even though these attempts always fail. This means that the violence that was contained by the killing of one victim is no longer contained. Our attempts to perpetuate sacred violence will intensify the violence until it spins out of control. As Revelation puts it, Satan, the Accuser, has been set free for a time. (Rev. 20:7)

Luke offers the first hint that the crucifixion of Jesus didn't "work" when he says that "the crowds that had gathered to watch the spectacle returned home, beating their breasts." (Lk. 23:48) Acts goes on to show how continued attempts to solve social tensions by collective violence continue to fail, starting with the murder of Stephen. Given the self-righteous accusations Stephen leveled against the Jews, one can argue that he wasn't a totally innocent victim, but when he was being stoned, he saw Heaven open, revealing Jesus at God's right hand and he forgave his persecutors. (Acts 7:69) It is significant that it was the vision of Jesus that inspired Stephen's forgiveness. This is a powerful example of how a new level of forgiveness has been unleashed in humanity. When Paul and Barnabas healed a cripple in Lystra, the mob tried to worship them in the old way, and Paul and Barnabas had to stop them from sacrificing garlanded oxen. The reaction of the Jews in the area was quite different. They turned the adoring crowd against the healers, and they stoned Paul and Barnabas. (Acts 14:8–19) In Ephesus, the idol carver Demetrius, fearing economic loss, roused the crowd against Paul with the slogan: "Great is Artemis of the Ephesians!" (Acts 19: 28) The climax, of course, is the riot in Jerusalem inflamed by misinformation alleging that Paul had brought a Gentile into the temple. (Acts 21:27–36) After Paul's arrest, there is the comical incident where Paul is brought before a group consisting of Pharisees and Sadducees. By proclaiming himself to be a Pharisee, Paul plunged the two groups into an argument that made the tribune afraid they would pull Paul to pieces if they didn't get him out of there. (Acts 23:10) So much for the unity that the crucifixion of Jesus was supposed to have created. What is new about these narratives is that they show people still trying the same old ways with the same old lies, but this time, the truth is being told. We also see how the rioting gets more and more out of hand as collective persecution fails to bind the people back together. Note that both Jews and Pagans are implicated in these attempts to maintain the old ways of collective violence.

In Acts, the persecutors are outside the nascent church. It wasn't long, unfortunately, before the Church backslid into the persecution business. Persecution of Jews (putting church leaders in the position of Pharisees), persecutions of heretics (real and imagined), and the Inquisition are among the more notorious examples. The Church wasn't all persecution by a long shot. The new sympathy for victims showed itself in many ways, not least in the building of hospitals and the urgent preaching on behalf of the poor. Important as these outreaches to marginal people are, I will concentrate on the persistence of the persecutory mechanism in Christianity because we need to better understand how it works.

In the opening chapter of his book *The Scapegoat,* Girard gives us a good example of this persecutory trend in Christianity with an analysis of *Judgment of the King of Navarre* by Guillaume de Machaut. (Girard 1986, 1–11) During the time of the Black Death, Guillaume writes of stones raining from the sky and entire cities destroyed by lightning. More plausibly, he writes of large numbers of people dying of the plague. He blames the plague on the Jews and those who had tolerated their presence in the town. The Jews had poisoned the river and destroyed the town's drinking water. When "heaven" revealed what the Jews had done, the townspeople rose up and massacred them. Suddenly life was good again with people dancing in the streets. There seems little reason to doubt that Guillaume firmly believed in the Jews' guilt, yet today, hardly anyone can read the text and believe what Guillaume believed. Partly that is because we know more about sanitation, but more importantly, we can see in the text a city that resolved its crisis through collective violence. As with the story of Achan, there is no myth requiring detective work to speculate on the real events behind it. We can now read this text and know exactly what happened.

Being a Frenchman, Girard is clearly haunted by the notorious Dreyfus affair. In 1894, Alfred Dreyfus, a man of Jewish background, was imprisoned after being falsely accused of espionage. In the days of the primitive sacred, his persecution would have been unanimous and his guilt unquestioned. In modern France, however, Dreyfus's conviction *was* questioned. The poet Charles Péguy was one of the first to start a collective movement in the opposite direction. In Girard's impassioned retelling of the affair, one can sense the psychic pain of all France and Girard himself over what occurred in his country. He ends his recount with the ringing question: "Was Dreyfus really guilty? Yes or No?" This is the question that the Gospel's unraveling of the primitive sacred has unleashed, a question that arises, if only in a few voices, every time accusation overcomes a mob. As an American, I will look briefly at two prolonged instances of scapegoating in this country.

The Salem witch trials are so ingrained in the American psyche that they have given us the expression "witch hunt" for scapegoating activity. The story of Samuel Sewall, a good, generous, and devout man, told by Eve LaPlante in *Salem Witch Judge: The Life and Repentance of Samuel Sewall*, is not as well-known as it should be. He was appointed to the panel of judges that sat on the witchcraft trials in Salem Village, a community beset with disputes between neighbors over land boundaries, crops, and grazing rights. Successive ministers had habitual battles with the community over compensation owed their work. Not surprisingly, the witchcraft accusations started in the home of the incumbent minister, Samuel Parris. Many of those accused were involved in the various ongoing disputes and many of the accusers were servant girls who were suddenly empowered to get back at their social betters. All of those condemned were convicted on what was called "spectral evidence," which consisted of one or more witnesses seeing a spectral image of another person committing foul deeds with the devil.

In the days of the primitive sacred, one death was enough to reconcile a community. In Salem, twenty deaths and counting wasn't nearly enough. This is one of the indications that these judicial murders weren't "working." Furthermore, there was not unanimity over the witches' guilt. One judge resigned early in protest and Sewall's own minister at Third Church was among the clergy who opposed the persecutions. Then Sewall publically repented. His journals don't explain the process but he did record that at a service for a dead child, his son read Matthew 9:13: "I will have mercy and not sacrifice." This is a key verse for the unequivocal love of God and total rejection of persecutory violence.

Through this sobering experience, Sewall went on to show insight into two major issues far beyond that of almost all of his contemporaries. In spite of the Native American attacks that continued to be the scourge of the colony, he wrote of the inherent dignity of Native Americans as worthy of salvation on an equal footing with his own race. More farsightedly, Sewall wrote the first anti-slavery treatise composed on North American soil, using the story of Joseph and his brothers as his proof text. (LaPlante, 2007)

Then there is lynching. Bob Dylan's masterpiece "Desolation Row" begins with:

They're selling postcards of the hanging
They're painting the passports brown.

When he first came out with that song in the late Sixties, few listeners knew that Bob Dylan was singing about a lynching. James Cone's book *The Cross and the Lynching Tree* elucidates these lines when he refers to the custom of spectators at a lynching taking pictures and making postcards out of them to send to their friends. Cone argues that the lynching tree was a series of grisly re-enactments of the crucifixion of Jesus. As with lynchings from the primitive sacred, it has been very difficult for most Americans to see this truth. In "Desolation Row," "the circus is in town." The image is literal in that the victim of the lynching was a member of a circus troop. Circus imagery continues to permeate the rest of this epic song about the downfall of Western civilization with its connotations of jaded human folly. The "blind commissioner" caught "in a trance" suggests both the blindness of collective violence and its mesmerizing effect. The fight "in the captain's tower" between Ezra Pound and T. S. Eliot while "the Titanic sails at dawn" further suggests that culture cannot hold civilization together and it is about to sink like the Titanic. (Dylan 2004, 181–183) Although Cone builds a strong argument about our cultural blindness to lynching, Dylan proved to be an exception when he wrote "The Ballad of Emmett Till" which tells in stark terms the story of what is considered the last lynching. Dylan accentuates the implication of all humanity in such tragedies by singing that the human race has fallen "down so god-awful low." Earlier than Dylan, Mark Twain showed much the same lucidity in his essay "The United States of Lyncherdom," in which he called out lynching for what it was. In *The One by Whom Scandal Comes*, René Girard contrasts the fundamental way Satan works in archaic cultures and in modern cultures where some awareness of the Gospel has occurred. Among many ancient peoples, Satan was the transcendent principle of order. That is, the Satanic action as accuser worked through the established social system. But with Satan cast out of the sky by the ministry of Jesus, the Satanic action of accuser occurs *within* human cultures as a disrupter. (Girard 2014, 97) That this level of sacred violence continues to happen without the brake that the primitive sacred exerted to it indicates the high price we pay for the dismantling of the sacrificial system by the Gospels.

One might be inclined to think that in our secular society, sacred violence and the cover-ups that myths provided would be a thing of the past even if ongoing conflicts between religious groups provide relics of earlier times. Actually, myth is very much alive. Contemporary myth isn't about Thor or Zeus, but the myth of the state is full of thunder and lightning bolts. In *Theopolitical Imagination*, William T. Cavanaugh traces the development of the myth of the liberal state that claims to have freed us from religious conflict only to spawn far more frequent and destructive wars than ever. He demonstrates that the actual alignments in the religious wars of the sixteenth and seventeenth centuries were not along religious lines but rather were comprised by the self-interests of the emerging warring states. The state constantly seeks to unify its people through focusing on external enemies, but it also focuses on the "enemy within" who always seems to pop up in times of warfare.

Highly publicized arrests and prosecutions of perpetrators for crimes committed almost always have a sense of scapegoating about them. Both the movie and the book *Dead Man Walking* highlight this element. Many times the prosecuted person is finally proven innocent, but even when the person is manifestly guilty, such as the murderer in the movie, all of the guilt of a much more massive social problem is visited on the one who was caught and arrested. It makes sense that police officers who abuse their authority in the violent treatment of people they arrest should be held accountable, but in those instances where such an officer is persecuted, the larger ambience of violence is ignored so that the same acts of violence continue to repeat themselves.

That scapegoating continues on a massive scale today is evident to everyone who has eyes to see. Crowd phenomena have been studied many times with Elias Canetti being among the most perceptive. Just as Orpheus and Quetzalcoatl were persecuted in mythic times, celebrities of all kinds are persecuted in the press. The tragic death of Princess Diana makes it clear that frenetic hounding of celebrities can spill blood. Celebrities are both adored and hated, sometimes by the same people. Scandal papers don't write about ordinary people, no matter how scandalous their lives might be. They write about celebrities, with little or no reference to what is true, because it is the rich and famous who must be sacrificed when the time is ripe.

The combination of adulation and denigration in relation to the victim is revealed by the New Testament's use of the Greek word *doxa*. This is sometimes translated as "glory," sometimes with "shame." How can one word mean two opposite things? James Alison says that is because the word means "reputation." (Alison 2000, 181–183) What kind of reputation? Any kind of reputation. The implication is that bad reputation is a common flip side to good reputation. That is, praise and acclamation of someone tends to inspire others to denigrate that same person. Moreover, the very people who acclaim an idol will turn on that idol at the drop of a hat if that person doesn't do what the acclaiming crowd wants.

In his Gospel, John plays with both sides of the meaning of *doxa* in relation to Christ. Jesus seeks *doxa* from his Abba while the people who put him to death or hide their sympathy for him seek *doxa* from other people. So it is that *doxa* inevitably falls into sacrificial violence if reputation is sought from people instead of from God. The raising of the cross *is* Jesus' *doxa*. That is why God has such a bad reputation nowadays. This raises the question for us: Where do we look for our own reputations?

Bob Dylan is an interesting example of this dialectic of honor and shame. He has been praised as one of the greatest poets and songwriters of our time, but he has also been the object of ignominy at every turn in his career. He did

24

not receive ignominy for any drugs or sex he may have indulged in, but rather for using electric guitars instead of a simple acoustic guitar like a "true" folk singer. Then he was excoriated for living an ordinary life, as if living an ordinary life is a scandal! The worst ignominy heaped on Dylan was for turning to Christ and recording Gospel albums. The problem with idols is that they have to stay the same, stuck in place. If an idol shows signs of life, the idolater reacts with rage. Dylan complains in "Idiot Wind" that "they're planting stories in the press" and warns us that "you'll find when you've reached the top/You're on the bottom." (Dylan, 236–237)

In *The Ambivalence of Scarcity*, Paul Dumouchel, a longtime colleague of Girard, traces the transformation of collective violence from the primitive sacred to the social violence that we experience in our time. He suggests that early societies were affluent in the sense that they had enough material goods to survive. Their social bonding was close enough that they shared what they had among themselves. Nobody was left to starve unless the whole group starved. But, as Girard hypothesized, the very social bonds that led the members to provide for one another also bound them together against enemy groups. This social bonding caused mimetic tensions to escalate. The obligation to feed the members of one's group was bound with the obligation to fight for the group. Even in earlier times, there was just enough unease about this kind of violence for some people to instinctively seek another solution. Dumouchel suggests that the typical way to diffuse this violence was to loosen the social bonds that obligated everybody in the group to fight. In so loosening these bonds, the violence became more sporadic. Not everybody joined a bloody feud. The violence still did a lot of harm but, with far fewer participants, society as a whole was not engulfed in the feuding and the crises leading to the scapegoating mechanism occurred much less often. Unfortunately, the loosening of the social bonds that reduced the scale of violence also created scarcity. The bonds that loosened the obligation to fight also loosened the obligation to provide for others in the group. Those who could not provide for themselves were left out in the cold—literally. Indifference also kills. Nobody in particular causes the system to leave some people to starve. Therefore, nobody is responsible for it any more than any one person is responsible for collective violence except the victim. To this day, economically marginalized people are routinely blamed for their plight. It is the same scapegoating mechanism that has more than one way of working its magic. (Dumouchel 2014, 33–48)

This schema of Dumouchel is valuable for connecting the scapegoating mechanism in early societies posited by Girard with the modern style of exclusions that leave large numbers of people on the margins and outside of them. Frenzied scapegoating actions continue to happen but with a difference. In *The Barren Sacrifice*, Dumouchel analyzes the mob attack on a nobleman at the Hautefaye Fair in France in 1870. The violent mob consisted of about a quarter of the people there. The rest allowed it to happen. This is very different from the unanimous mob hypothesized by Girard in the primitive sacred. Likewise, the scapegoating of Jews during the Nazi persecution could not have been so destructive without the acquiescence of a large majority of the people. (Dumouchel 2015, 5–20) This goes hand in hand with the individualism that creates economic scarcity. Dumouchel illustrates this whole process of scarcity in his analysis of the land enclosures in England that culminated in the closing off of lands in the eighteenth century, creating scarcity where there had once been adequate resources for everybody. All this happened without any change in the quantity of material goods. It was the arrangement of goods made by those with the political and economic power to do it that caused the scarcity. The loosening of social ties facilitated the enclosure movement, and enclosure led to further loosening of social ties. (Dumouchel 2014, 84–96) This second scheme of scapegoating suggested by Dumouchel is very much with us in the economic systems of today. Dumouchel's insights show us that merely trying to avoid violence is not anywhere near enough. There is also the need for increased sensitivity to others. That is, we need to dissolve the borders between us in a way that social bonds grow stronger rather than weaker. We will see below that this is the primary mission of the Church.

There is a certain amount of speculation on Girard's part in this theory of the primitive sacred rooted in collective violence. The case is not air-tight but the circumstantial evidence is heavy enough to make it worthy of serious consideration. The continuation of the scapegoating mechanism in our time shows no signs of abating. Moreover, for those of us who believe that the Bible attests to truth revealed by God, the centrality of Jesus' death by collective violence and his Resurrection in the Gospel message suggests that understanding and repenting of our participation in persecutory violence is fundamental to the Christian life. The Christian view is grounded foremost in the reality of the victim *as* victim. I say this advisedly because if a victim acts out of rage and creates victims, then those victims move to the center where Jesus is and the victim-become-oppressor moves to the periphery where the stone throwers are. There are many books on epistemology, the philosophical discipline that explores how and if humans attain knowledge. The Gospels show us that the place of the victim is the fundamental locus for knowledge and the prerequisite for any other knowledge. Insofar as we persecute others, our minds are darkened. Insofar as we sympathize with the victim *as* victim and, if necessary, enter that place and suffer persecution ourselves, we have the beginning of the knowledge that opens our hearts to God. Moreover, the contrast between a *group* mechanism of scapegoating and a gathering of community based on forgiveness makes it clear that a sound Christian spirituality is not an individual matter but is a matter of relationships. Relationships with people are inextricably bound with relationship with God. We are not alone with God; we are together with God.

The scapegoating mechanism has much to say about human desire, but it conceals at least as much as it reveals. When everybody agrees to gang up on one vulnerable person or one vulnerable group, it seems that the group is united in *and possessed by* this one desire. And yet this unification of desire has been spawned by systemic conflict. In this conflict, did everybody have a different desire, or was there already a unified desire that could not be shared as handily as the desire to focus on a victim who is blamed for the discord? Girard suggests the latter. We will take a close look at how Girard understands shared desires that lead to conflict. More importantly, the outpouring of the Holy Spirit at Pentecost suggests that God is seeking to gather us in a shared desire that does not require a victim. This will be a gathering of peoples seeking to do away with victimization for the sake of God's desire.

Chapter 2
Desiring Through the Other

Desire as Social

At a child's birthday party that a friend described to me, the children were happily playing with balloons that filled the house. Suddenly, one child grabbed one of the balloons and yelled: "This balloon is *mine*!" Suddenly, all the children forsook the other balloons they were enjoying up to that moment and fought over the one balloon. It is hard to imagine one balloon being so much better than the others as to merit this sudden unanimous desire for it. What happened is that once a child expressed a desire for a particular balloon, the value of that balloon—pardon the pun—ballooned. Desire for the one balloon increased exponentially simply because one person wanted it, and then suddenly everybody wanted it.

Can this little tempest in children's teacups be written off as childish behavior that these children will outgrow? Girard says no. On the contrary, this scenario is a classic example of what he calls "mimetic desire." We all know that we tend to imitate each other in actions, dress, mannerisms, and much more. What is less well-known at a conscious level is that we imitate each other's desires. This anecdote shows us how arbitrary mimetic desire can be. When one person wants something, that desire suddenly becomes contagious. This contagion can lead to the kind of societal meltdown discussed in the first chapter. If there were no adults around, this little squabble over the balloons might easily have escalated to a *Lord of the Flies* kind of situation. Girard commonly illustrates his theory with the example of one child in a nursery reaching for a toy in a room full of toys. Much more often than not, the other children then reach for the same toy until they are all fighting over it. (Girard 1987, 9) Girard notes that, far from outgrowing this sort of thing, adults continue to act like children with the same result except that there aren't super-adults around to stop the fighting. As these children grow up, many a youth will desire a certain girl that another youth, quite possibly a friend, also desires even though he had paid little attention to that girl until his friend did. Many girls will experience the same thing in relation to boys when other girls get a crush on one boy or another. Girard calls these configurations of two people entering conflict over an object a "mimetic triangle." Mimetic desire is not about small children, it is about all humans.

The exploration of mimetic desire is often referred to as mimetic theory, but I prefer the less cerebral and more embodied term coined by Robert Hamerton-Kelly: "mimetic realism." Mimetic desire is similar to imitation but differs from it in subtle ways. Imitation refers primarily to external actions: monkey see, monkey do. (Ironically, monkeys don't imitate the way humans do.) It is through imitation, for example, that we learn to talk and how to act in our particular culture. This is why modeling good behavior to small children is important. Parents and guardians who act like children should not be surprised if their children fail to grow up emotionally. Mimetic desire is copying the *desires* of other people. That is what happened at the children's party with all the balloons. Once one balloon was deemed desirable, everybody wanted it. This is how fads gets started and then reach a certain peak of madness before quickly dying out. I can remember a brief period during my childhood when everybody simply *had* to have a hula hoop to twirl around one's waist. Then just as suddenly, the hula hoops disappeared. A quick phrase for mimetic desire is: Human see, human want. The desire of some people for a certain cut of jeans tends to awaken the desire for the same cut of jeans on the part of others in a social group. A common trivial example is the person looking at a book on the sale table of a bookstore, then putting it down while a nearby person looks on. This person will often pick up the same book. That in turn will often make the first person more interested in that book than before. These little circles of mimetic desire can be little perpetual motion machines if nothing intervenes to stop them. Girard purposely uses the term "mimetic" for the tendency to copy the desires of others because the desires of other people get under the skin. By getting under the skin, mimetic desire also gets under our consciousness as well. That is to say, the desires of others affect our own desires, whether we realize it or not and usually we don't. In "The Gates of Eden," Bob Dylan expresses mimetic desire succinctly and precisely in these lines:

> The kingdoms of experience
> In their precious winds they rot
> While paupers change possessions,
> Each one wishing for what the other has got. (Dylan 2004, p154)

The fight over the one balloon at the children's party is a clear example of how mimetic desire leads to what René Girard calls "mimetic rivalry." At the moment one child claimed one balloon as "mine," all other balloons disappeared as if a magician had waved a wand to whisk them out of existence. Balloons, so abundant a moment ago, have suddenly become scarce. The same thing will happen to these children later in life when girls become scarce for boys because they are copying one another's desires. There is such a thing as real scarcity. All of the material goods in the world are finite and scarcity can happen, as it does in times of famine. But much more often, scarcity is created through mimetic desire leading to mimetic rivalry. If only one balloon matters, then there is only one balloon for all of the children, in spite of the many other balloons surrounding them. On a larger scale, the enclosure movement analyzed by Dumouchel is another example of the creation of scarcity. Advertisers understand the creation of scarcity instinctually. They show people desiring the object they wish to sell, hoping to evoke the same desire in those who see the ad. They then imply subliminally that everybody wants the object but not everybody can have it, but *you* can have it—if you are in the right and desirable social set. These items may be flooding the market, but the advertisers have created an illusion of scarcity.

There is a distinction between appetite—our bodily needs and gut reactions to various things—and desire, which is mainly socially constituted. Pinpointing the distinction in our ongoing experience is sometimes tricky. We need food to survive. The actual food that we eat may depend on what is available, but when there is a choice, the desires of other people tend to make some foods more desirable than others. In my case, my father shared his love of pizza and butterscotch sundaes with me when I was little and I desire them to this day. This is one reason people of different cultures tend to desire some available foods and not others. A shoe is a shoe is a shoe and most of the time, in most places, we need to wear them. But some shoes are fashionable while others are not. Not wearing the fashionable shoe, which is usually more expensive than others, can be a social problem. Hormones make sure that the biological urge for sexual relations is part of our makeup. However, the particular partners that we desire are, again, affected by mimetic desire. It is interesting, amusing, but also troubling that advertisers try to sell products like cars to men by coupling a particular car with a desirable female who, by some magic, will appear once the car is bought.

We also have many desires that have nothing to do with survival per se but have a lot to do with making survival worthwhile. My father shared his desire for Detroit Tigers baseball games, and I still like to see a good game when I can. Teachers and other mentors who desire the plays of Shakespeare, will try to instill the same desire in their students. Mimetic desire does not mean that we *always* desire what somebody else desires, but we are strongly influenced by these desires. As small children, our ability to desire independently is very limited, and it is the desires modeled by those around us who first teach us to desire anything at all. As we get older, our desires gain some independence but they always remain strongly connected to the desires of others.

Mimetic desire ensures that we live in a web of personal desires. The individualism that is so highly prized in modern Western civilization takes a serious blow that threatens to enrage us if we aren't willing to come to terms with this reality. Far from being individual blocks of personality shooting personal desires out at the world, our desires resonate with the desires of others and vice versa. Our individualism inclines us to claim ownership of our desires and deny that they derive in any way from anybody else. The more our desire is derived from that of another, the more adamant we are that the desire belongs to us individually and the harder we fight not only for any object in contention but for the priority of the desire as well. Struggling against this reality locks us all the more tightly into rivalry with the desires of others.

Although these conflicts may seem to suggest that mimetic desire is a bad thing, we can see that mimetic desire is part of human nature, instilled in us by God. Conflict is by no means the only way mimetic desire plays out, common as it is. In the earlier stages of his thought, Girard and his colleagues tended to stress the problematic aspects of mimetic desire, its potential for conflict and violence, culminating in the scapegoating mechanism. If mimetic desire always went smoothly, there would be no need to worry about it or think about it. But since mimetic desire is often a rocky road, we do well to give it our attention. It is possible for mimetic desire to be constructive and I will explore this possibility at length below. We have to make efforts to live constructively with mimetic desire because of our fallen nature. The story of the children's party is a story of the Fall in miniature. There was an Eden, relatively speaking, of peace among the children and then a sudden and silly conflict blew up, destroying the peace. What blew up into rivalry was a social system that became infected by mimetic rivalry. Mimetic rivalry, as we shall see, is highly contagious. It can spread like a plague until the whole social system is engulfed in an epidemic. In the example of the Black Death striking the medieval French town, the medical plague became a social plague of persecution against an unpopular minority. The children fighting over the balloons may look like a tempest in a teacup compared to the wars and other outbreaks of social unrest exploding across the globe, but it is the same dynamic that resulted in the crucifixion of Jesus and of the prophets who came before him.

Mirror Neurons

An important discovery in neurology adds some scientific backing to the concept of mimetic desire and also gives us added insight into how it works. Neuro-scientists have known for a long time that neurons fire inside the brain when we decide to pick up a banana and even more so when we actually pick one up. It turns out there is more. A serendipitous discovery during research on a macaque monkey led to the discovery that when the scientist picked up a banana, the monkey's neurons fired the same neurons that fired when the monkey itself picked up a banana. Further investigation showed the human neurons also fire in response to the intentional activities of others, such as picking up a piece of fruit.

The important thing here is that the neurons' firing responds to intention. The neurons don't wait until somebody actually picks up a banana to fire. All it takes is for somebody to reach for the banana in such a way as to convey the intention of picking it up. If a person draws the hand away at the last second or tries to pick it up and drops it, the same neurons have fired. However, when one is shown a cartoon stick figure reaching for a banana, these neurons do not fire. The action has been portrayed but the live *intention* has not. Scientists call the neurons that fire under these circumstances "mirror neurons" because the neurons are mirroring the displayed intentional behavior. (Iacoboni, 2008)

In his book *The Myth of Mirror Neurons*, Gregory Hickock cautions us against some of the hype over this discovery, most particularly the notion that mirror neurons explain human linguistic ability and imitation. These broader claims, however, were never aspects of mirror neuron theory that are taken to confirm the reality of mimetic desire. Hickock argues that it is the computational power in the human brain that makes these traits possible, but this computational power, far from being disembodied, is now known to be grounded in our mirror neurons. This evidence seems to confirm that our bodies are wired to respond to the intentions and desires of other people whether our computational minds realize it or not. A disconnect between mind and body is clearly possible as Girard's analysis suggests it can and does occur. A lot depends on connecting our minds with our bodies at this motor level.

This discovery seems to confirm, or at least add credence to, Girard's concept of mimetic desire. This neural mirroring of others' intention does not, in itself, indicate that we imitate the desires of others. But it does indicate very strongly that we automatically resonate with the intentions of other people at a deep physiological level, and these intentions are grounded in desire. It follows that the likelihood of imitating the desires that our mirror neurons react to is strong. The interaction of mirror neurons means that mimetic desire tends to arise spontaneously where not only do we pick up the faintest signal that somebody else wants something, but we project our own desire for something on somebody else. Our projections often lead us to make pre-emptive strikes to get the objects we want. The problem is that when we deny this derivation, we become puppets of the desires of others and lose what agency we really could and should have to act responsibly.

Mimetic Desire and Freedom

We need to pursue further the question: Are we the puppets of other people's desires? My short answer is: sometimes. But not necessarily all the time. Mirror neurons seem to work by resonating with the visible intentions of others. These intentions are fueled by desires. This resonance happens on a preconscious level. That is, we resonate with the desires of others before we know it is happening, and often we never realize that it's happening. To this extent, we have no control over mimetic desire, but at this stage, mimetic desire has not determined any of our actions. Mimetic desire is usually explained by imaging two people wanting the same thing, such as two children wanting the same toy. In reality, environments are complex. We don't usually resonate with the desire of just one person; we resonate with many desires of many people around us all the time. An analogy often used for mimetic desire is with the gravitational field in Einsteinian physics. Just as moving objects exert forces on other moving objects, desires in a field move other desires in that field. I have already used the word "resonance" several times, particularly while discussing mirror neurons. When we are dealing more with a field of desires resonating with one another, we are not yet dealing with imitation of another's desire. With this in mind, I suggest that we use the term "mimetic resonance" for this stage of interacting with the desires and intentions of others. This phrase captures the reality of these desires exerting an influence on us. Our desires are influencing them in return, but without determining the outcome of the constellation of desires within us or within anybody else in the field. I will continue to use the term "mimetic desire" when it refers more specifically to the specific desires resonating between two people in a focused way. If we are resonating with the desires of others as others resonate with ours, then there is some room for freedom. The more aware we are of this resonance, the more freedom. The more we are in denial, something individualism tends to foster, the less freedom we have.

Let us recall the small scenario of two people in a bookstore converging on the same book on the sale table. Were both determined by mimetic desire beyond any free will? Often, observing another person's desire for a book increases one's desire for it at least a little. How strongly the observer's desire is heightened can vary depending on how interested one is in the book's content. This desire, if any, will have been previously strengthened or weakened by the desires of other people, from friends and family to public opinion. Such a small scenario is so low-key to start with that each person has an element of choice as to what they do as they resonate with the desire on the part of the other. But if ever their resonance should take the form of conflict, they could become so caught up in rivalry that it might become very difficult for them to extricate themselves from it in a peaceful manner. The violent madness that consumes some shoppers at Black Friday sales confirms the possible end results of such a scenario.

The importance of other people's desires in one's social life points to how freedom and determinism can work with mimetic desire. In the broader scheme of things, people model so many different desires for us that we simply cannot imitate all of them all of the time. That is, there is a lot more going on than two people converging on the book sale table. Do we choose which model to follow when there are so many of them? It seems likely that in such cases we do make choices at least some of the time. To the degree that mimetic desire is deterministic (if it is at all), the desire modeled by the most people will likely win out, or the desire modeled by the person with the greatest impact, such as a parent or best friend will have the strongest pull. If most of my friends like Mozart, chances increase that I will like Mozart too. But then why do I hang out with a Mozart crowd? If our desires are affected by other people, are *their* desires affected by ours? Do the people in my crowd like Mozart because I like him or do I like Mozart because of them? This starts to look like a vicious circle with no beginning or end. This also begins to look like a hall of mirrors, not a surprise now that we know something about mirror neurons. There does, however, seem to be some freedom to maneuver in the constellations of desires that we all live with.

The many likes and dislikes that come naturally to us and their interactions with the field of mimetic resonance also affect our freedom. No amount of social pressure is going to make me like cola drinks or pickles. Although my family environment didn't include much in the way of classical music, I soon discovered an affinity for Bach, Mozart, and many other great composers when I joined the boys' choir at my church. Some resources were latent in my home in that my parents had gotten some classical records that they didn't listen to anymore. As I interacted with some friends and acquaintances who liked classical music, I was influenced by their opinions. With mimetic resonance running strong, it was frankly difficult at times to tell where their likes left off and my personal inclinations began.

We experience a similar mix of determination and choice with the models in our lives. In our youngest years, we have little choice of models as they assert themselves upon us for good and ill, and we are as inevitably overwhelmed by their desires as we are by our own bodily needs. The older we get, the broader the horizon of models and the more choices we have. The amount of choice depends to some extent on the luck of the draw. Parents and teachers and peers who basically present themselves as possible choices give us the most freedom, while those who assert themselves aggressively stifle our freedom. Some models are attractive while others are repellent, but we need to remember that repellent models keep us in their thrall more than positive ones. Being repelled by a parent who did not always manage anger well almost always leads to internalization of that very anger at a deep level. We can make wise choices that enhance freedom and foolish choices that constrict freedom. The latter is what happens, at an extreme, in cults that take over the entire personality.

This mimetic resonance tends to be preconscious, but it is possible to cultivate a greater awareness of this resonant mimetic field through self-discipline. Of course, the more people who model this self-discipline, the better the chances that I might also. These resonances may pull us primarily in one direction or they might pull us in many, depending on how homogeneous or heterogeneous the environment. Sooner or later, usually sooner, we have to act on some of these ambient desires and that is where it is more meaningful to speak of "mimetic desire," even if this mimesis is still not conscious. So when one person reaches for the book on the sale table that another has just looked at, and the first person becomes more interested in the book than before, we are seeing mimetic desire in action, even if neither believes they are imitating the other. Girard's theory of mimetic desire pushes the lack that leads to desire a step further. We don't just lack possessions or a girlfriend; we don't know what food or what girl to desire until we see what food and what girl somebody else desires. We don't necessarily desire what other people want because they want it or we think they want it. Rather our desires automatically resonate with the desires of others and we need to learn to navigate these resonances as part of human maturation. This prevents us from automatically copying every desire we see in others. But the less conscious we are of the impact others' desires have on us, the more likely we will be driven by others' desires and the more empty we will be as a result.

Mimetic Desire and Human Emptiness

In one way or another, human desire indicates something is lacking. My stomach is empty so I desire to fill it with food. I don't have as much money to get everything I want so I feel empty until I get enough money to get what I want. Only to want more, of course, since the emptiness doesn't go away. I lack the satisfaction of seeing my favorite baseball team win unless they win. If they should win the World Series, I'm not satisfied unless they win it every year. Not even the New York Yankees do that. I feel empty because I need more friends and companions but more isn't necessarily enough.

Mimetic realism helps us understand the nothingness, the lack that haunts every one of us. To begin with, mimetic realism takes us one step back from the objects we think will fill our emptiness and exposes the deeper lack of not even knowing what to desire without the help of human models. It is inevitable that, even in non-rivalrous situations, the desires we share with others will not lead to fulfillment. At most, they will give us some good moments such as enjoying a fish dinner or a good concert. When desire becomes rivalrous, then it instantly becomes profoundly insatiable. In such situations, the object of desire is usually unobtainable and, as we shall see below, if it is obtained, it will not be enough. If one reaches a point of needing to have at least as much as other people and preferably more, then it is impossible to have enough because such people are perpetually afraid of falling behind. When I was growing up, an apt phrase was in circulation: "Keep up with the Joneses." The intense craving of always wanting more is not a bottomless pit inside a human being; the intense craving is a crevice opening up in the *relationships* between people.

Paradoxically, the more intense the mimetic rivalry, the less value the object triangled by that rivalry has until it drops to zero. When more two or more rivals converge on a bone of contention, the more the rivals become preoccupied with each other, and in the heat of the rivalry the bone dissolves. Girard explains: "As rivalry becomes acute, the rivals are more apt to forget about whatever objects are, in principle, the cause of the rivalry and instead to become more fascinated with one another. In effect the rivalry is purged of any external stake and becomes a matter of pure rivalry and prestige." (Girard 1987, 26) When the heat of mimetic rivalry dissolves the original object of the rivalry, the rivalry degenerates into conflict for the sake of conflict. This is why the fundamental mimetic conflict is over power, which has no substance beyond the conflict between the rivals. As Macbeth found out too late, the quest for power is "full of sound and fury, signifying nothing." (*Macbeth* Act V, Scene 5)

When its ostensible object disappears, the emptiness opened by mimetic rivalry deepens into an abyss. When we are grappling with a rival, it is never enough to have what the rival wants. We need to *become* the other person. We believe (wrongly) that the other person has a certain fullness of being that we don't have because that person has—or seems to have—what we want but don't have. So it is that we don't just covet the ox or wife or car of another but the very *being* of another person. This is why we never have enough money or possessions or anything else as long as we are in rivalrous relationships. For Girard, this is not an ontological statement but an anthropological one. That is, it is about human relationships. The problem is that we can covet the being of another person until the end of the world and we'll come up empty. Since the alleged fullness of being on the part of another is illusory, we are only "chasing after wind" (Eccl. 1:14). More seriously yet, mimetic rivalry degenerates into idolatry. I define idolatry as allowing anything other than God to be the prime organizing factor in one's life. When mimetic rivalry takes over a person's life, it becomes that prime organizing factor that sucks everything else into it. Just look at how some people are consumed with revenge. Such a one can reach a point where revenge is the *only* thing that gives meaning to life and that doesn't leave much of a life.

Another thing that dissolves in mimetic rivalry is the sense of beginnings and endings. Just as mimetic desire loses this sense when each person desiring the same thing claims to be the *first* to desire it, everybody involved in a conflict assumes that the other person started it. The first punch is always thrown because of provocation from the other. One of Girard's maxims is: "Nobody starts a fight." By definition, a fight is a vicious cycle with no beginning and no end. The true beginning in God's Creation and true end in God's Kingdom disappear from the horizon for as long as the conflict continues.

It is important to remember that mimetic desire is not necessarily rivalrous, although it often becomes so. Mimetic desire can be expansive and enriching. There is a growing tendency to call this expansive, nurturing use of mimetic desire "good mimesis," while referring to rivalrous mimetic desire as "bad mimesis." C. S. Lewis points to a powerful example of "good mimesis" when he defines friendship as two or more people sharing the same interests so as to nurture each other's interest non-rivalrously. (Lewis, 1960) The most important instance of positive mimesis is that we are born into God's mimetic desire for us and for all other people. We are constantly faced with the choice of which direction we are willing to go in, given that we share mimetic desire with all others.

We cannot avoid mimetic desire. We are tied into a sea of mimetic desire as soon as we are born. Mimetic desire connects us with other people whether we like it or not. So much for individualism. In the last chapter, I discussed the social network of the sacrificial order that engulfs all of us. There are several layers of such networks, of which the political system and the economic system are among the most prominent on the large scale, and family and friends are most prominent close to home. At the basis of all these systems, fueling them, is the system of mimetic desire. The question is whether we will be connected through expansive sharing or constrictive conflict. Will our mimetic desire directed to the good of those in our families and towns and countries expand further, as Dante's love of Beatrice expanded to a love for everybody? (Dante 1969) Or will the mimetic desire for the good of those close to us *cause* us to close ranks and treat others as enemies?

There is an inherent instability in the human modeling of desires. Even when they are benign, there are many ways they can degenerate into discord. Left to human devices only, it is unlikely that we could build human communities even on a small scale without rivalry and contention intruding on the more expansive sharing of positive mimetic desire. Fortunately, we are not left to human devices alone. God's desire for the good of all people is a stable, if dynamic desire that will not change. This is not because God is somehow imprisoned in a certain desire, but because God freely and consistently desires the everlasting good of all. We would expect no less of the God preached by the apostles, who were forgiven for their betrayal of Jesus.

Christian thinkers have consistently averred that we are instilled with a longing for God that is a gift from God and that this longing means that we cannot be totally satisfied with anything other than God, no matter how wonderful. As the Psalmist says: our souls "thirst for the living God." (Ps. 42: 2) If we see mimetic desire as fundamental to humanity, it follows that this trait is willed by God and used by God in a fundamental way for our salvation. The emptiness caused by mimetic desire gives us an ongoing openness to God, an opening for God to enter into us and dwell within us as Jesus promised us in John's Gospel. We are created to resonate with the desires of others so that we can resonate with the desire of the God who is wholly Other. St. Augustine suggests that the phrase "deep calls from deep" (Ps. 42: 7) probes the mystery of humans reaching out to the depths of each other and, even more, reaching out to the depths of God. (Augustine 2000, 251) While it is an illusion to think that a human rival has a plenitude of being, God really does have such plenitude and is infinitely generous. If we open ourselves to God's desire, we participate in that desire in such a way that we can be equally generous with others.

Mimetic Desire and the Unconscious

Mimetic desire gives us vital clues as to what dwells in our unconscious. By definition, the unconscious is what we don't know about ourselves. I have noted several times how we often fail to realize how we are being affected by the desires of other people. When that is the case, the effects of their desires on us seep into the unconscious. There is surely much more to the unconscious than mimetic desire. Deep trauma lurks there when such has been inflicted on us. Mimetic resonance with the desires of others has infiltrated us since birth, gotten under our skin, and deep into our hearts. Hence the importance of the desires we present to small children to absorb. What keeps mimetic desire in our unconscious is our defiant, pig-headed conviction that our desires belong to each of us alone and to nobody else. The stronger this sort of conviction, the more likely the desire is entangled in serious rivalry with somebody else; probably a lot of somebodies. Somehow, we feel threatened at the idea that our desires are intertwined with the desires of everybody else, and we push these ideas away, only to have them manipulate us at ever deeper levels. This is how the unconscious can hamper and, in extreme cases, destroy our freedom.

What about Freud? I don't want to get sidetracked by discussing Girard's disagreements with Freud, but it is worth noting that mimetic desire is the big anthropological elephant that Freud fails to see. For Girard, insofar as there is such a thing as an Oedipus complex, it is one of many possible mimetic triangles that a child might experience in formative years. Most importantly, for Girard, mimetic desire is the primary content of the unconscious. (Girard 1987, 350–359)

There is a peculiar twilight zone between what is preconscious—what we fail to apprehend right in front of us and the unconscious—that which is buried. Freedom is still half intact and half gone in this state. Paul Dumouchel calls this *méconnaissance,* a French word that is hard to translate. The closest translation is misrecognition, but the English word suggests making a mistake in apprehension, while the French word includes a willful element in the failure to recognize a truth. That is, at some level, one does not want to see the truth of mimetic desire and so one fails to see it. It is one of many ways of having eyes that cannot see and ears that cannot hear. (Dumouchel 2014, 209–223) We see in the *méconnaissance* of mimetic desire the roots of a far more malign *méconnaissance* in the face of collective violence.

The impression that the unconscious is full of horrible monsters and some of them are us tends to push conflict into the individual person, which sets up something of a mimetic rivalry within the self. In the simple story *Where the Wild Things Are,* Maurice Sendak shows us what great friends the inner monsters can be if we get to know them. The "wild things" within may not be so much our own personal monsters but the monsters that grow out of the mimetic desires between us and others. The monsters aren't "me," they're "us." These considerations do not preclude the Freudian notion of repressed or suppressed memories influencing current behavior. Per Grande points out in his fine book *Mimesis and Desire* that we go through life interacting with the desires of others in our past just as much, if not more, than those in the present. (Grande 2009, 58–59) There is a sense in which we are possessed by the people we are currently entwined with, but we are also possessed by those people in our past who in some cases may have harmed us, thus putting us in bondage to the aggressive desires that invaded us. This is what happens in child abuse of all kinds. Coming to grips with the way we are possessed through the unconscious has a lot to do with the process of forgiveness, which we will examine at length below. On the brighter side, we are also possessed by the people who have affirmed and strengthened us. The importance of mimetic desire in the unconscious suggests that an overly individualistic approach to therapy has its drawbacks. There may be serious problems inside of each of us, but much of the sickness is not so much in ourselves as in our relationships, something that Jean-Michel Oughourlian has explored in some detail.

So much attention has been paid to monstrous wild things in the human unconscious that we don't realize that deeper in the unconscious than any wild desires flaring up is God's desire. So it is that these wild things may well take their romp to deeper levels of joy than we expect. The web of mimetic desire is not, in the hands of God, a set of elaborate chains to imprison us but links to connect us. No matter how entangled our mimetic desires with other people, God holds all of the links in unconditional love, all the while calling each of us to open our outer and inner eyes to see how wild divine love is. In God's desire we receive the gift of deep freedom that God is giving us, a gift that frees us from the entanglements of others' desires that hold us in thrall.

Mimetic Resonance and Christian Asceticism

Although there is a lot more than physiology to mimetic resonance, this trait, so important for a renewed spirituality, is grounded in our bodies. Given the fact that God took on human flesh and lived among us, we shouldn't need insights into mimetic resonance to alert us to the goodness of Creation, including its physicality. Unfortunately, Christianity, along with many other schools of thought, have sometimes denigrated physical reality in favor of some immaterial reality that is somehow much better, much cleaner than the nitty-gritty earth we walk on. This denigration highlights our tendency to scapegoat material reality for our own disordered desires. If we eat too much, it isn't really the fault of the food, though we quickly blame it for our own lack of self-control. It isn't the fault of the stomach, either. Gluttons keep on eating even when they are full. Women, of course, have been blamed for being "tempting" as if it is their responsibility to control the desires of men, while men need take no responsibility for themselves. The intertwining of our desires with the desires of others in a dense network of mutual imitation complicates the picture. If we become ensnared in desires for certain things or people because others desire them, we are in a frustrating situation and, again, it becomes convenient to blame the other people and other things for the bind we are in. Although we are more than our bodies, we are certainly not less than our bodies. That is another way of saying that we are stuck with the connections we have with the desires of others though our mirror neurons. A sound spirituality will be grounded in this fact.

Self-denial is admirable in many ways but it can have a paradoxical effect that we fall victim to if we are not careful. It is possible for self-denial to focus us upon ourselves in an unhealthy way. It is *I* who am fasting. *I* am giving up pleasures I normally indulge in. If we become so fixated on ourselves, we are puffing ourselves up rather than denying ourselves. Isaiah shows how such self-centered fasting leads to quarreling and fighting and striking others with their fists. (Isa. 58:4) If self-denial has made us so grouchy that we have to make up for what we are giving up by giving ourselves the alternate pleasure of striking out at other people and putting them down, then it is grouchiness and lashing out at others that we must fast from.

Likewise, Jesus warns us against putting on long faces so that others will admire our fasting while blowing trumpets to call attention to our almsgiving. (Mt. 6: 1–2) Once again, our self-denial is being compensated for by self-indulgence in other ways. When the admiration of others is filling our egos, then we need to fast from seeking such admiration. We may well find that this renunciation is harder than renouncing food and other pleasures. As we deepen renunciation, we become aware of deeper levels of our desires that need to be turned into a more positive direction.

Given this pitfall, I suggest that we emphasize the needs of other people and renounce ourselves by thinking of *them* rather than about ourselves. Isaiah suggests that a better fast would be to let the oppressed go free and loosen every yoke. (Isa. 58: 6) Jesus echoes Isaiah's sentiments at the beginning of his teaching ministry by proclaiming a Year of Jubilee that would free all people of their imprisonment to debt so as to give all a new start in life. (Lk. 4: 16–20) Instead of puffing ourselves up, we should build up other people. Perhaps we will find this to be a greater renunciation than cutting back on our eating habits. In any case, renunciation of food and other pleasures will help us grow spiritually only if they are the basis for reaching out to other people. When we really think of others, we have less room in our hearts to think about ourselves.

One possible way of understanding Jesus' warning that it is not possible to serve two masters, (Mt. 6: 24) is to acknowledge that it is not possible to follow both the mimetic desires of other people and God's desire. We can't escape the desires of other people and their effect on us, but the more we allow ourselves to be planted in God's desire, the more constructively we can prevent the desires from pulling us away from God. Of course, many other people are conforming to God's desire. When we discern that that is the case, we should follow their examples. We also want to be able to inspire others with God's desire. One of the things that mimetic realism makes clear is that Christian spirituality is not and cannot be a one-person show. Although our relationships with God are of capital importance, it is not possible to build a sound spirituality if it's just between me and God and nobody else. We are too involved with the desires of other people for that to be possible. This is why individual practices such as fasting must be directed towards the good of others. We must, with God's help, negotiate the relationships of our desires with those of other people along with our relationships with God's desire.

The notion of mimetic resonance may seem a small matter, but I hope I have indicated that this is a small matter that worms its way into the most important things having to do with living a human life well, or not so well. The scapegoating mechanism that I outlined in the first chapter might seem more dramatic and spectacular, but if mimetic resonance did not have the potential to act the way it does, there would be no scapegoating mechanism. I have already alluded to a few ways that mimetic desire can not only deepen our relationships with each other but also with God. I hope that what I have said about mimetic desire and mimetic resonance brings home the challenges they pose for us not only in daily living but for Christian spirituality. For the rest of this book I will discuss the fundamental aspects of spiritual practices to explore ways they help us live by the insights offered by mimetic desire now that Girard and his colleagues have made us more conscious of its dynamics. The practices and cultivation of virtues that I will discuss will not be new. As I will show in the next three chapters, great literature and the Bible reveal much about mimetic desire. Practices derived from scripture have given us tools for handling it for centuries. Our growing awareness of mimetic resonance gives us some fresh opportunities to make major breakthroughs, especially in appreciating the systemic social problems caused by mimetic rivalry and the resulting scapegoating activity that still goes on even in congregations founded in the name of the Forgiving Victim.

Chapter 3

Reading Mimetic Desire

Although Girard articulated the notion of mimetic desire in a powerful way, it is not a concept that Girard dreamed up himself. Neither is it accurate to say that Girard discovered mimetic desire. It is more accurate to say that Girard discovered *other people's* discovery of mimetic desire and pulled their perceptions into a compelling paradigm. Girard first found the discovery of others in some of the great works that he examined as a literary critic. In his first book, *Deceit, Desire and the Novel,* Girard uncovered the force of mimetic desire in the novels of Cervantes, Flaubert, Stendhal, Proust, and Dostoevsky. Shortly thereafter, he discovered a treasure trove of insights into mimetic desire in the plays of Shakespeare. I will comment on some of the novels and plays that Girard analyzed and add a discussion of the operas Mozart wrote with Lorenzo Da Ponte. These works comprise a set of case studies into the working of mimetic desire that will help us to both understand its destructive potential and learn how to use it in positive ways.

It is interesting that in two of the novels Girard analyzes, the protagonist's model for desire is not another live character in the novel but a fictional character. Don Quixote famously goes mad with a desire to imitate Amadis of Gaul, a knight errant described in several medieval romances. A century or so later, Emma Bovary's desires are fueled by the heroines of sentimental romance novels. The literature consumed by both characters gives them distorted visions of reality. Don Quixote mistakes windmills for evil giants and a barber's basin for a knight's helmet. Emma Bovary sees the lovers in her life through the lens of the romance novels and fails to see them as they really are until it is too late. Of the two, Don Quixote is much more removed from "reality" than Emma Bovary. Yet, although the novels that Emma Bovary reads seemed to mirror "real life" and so are more "realistic," she is the one who is even more confused about "reality" than Don Quixote. Don Quixote does repent of his fantasies and dies peacefully while Emma Bovary, so smothered by fantasy that what self she once had disappears, commits suicide. "Realistic" stories present models and stir up desires that seem realistic but are traps that catch the unwary reader.

Novelists such as Cervantes and Flaubert are faced with the enormous challenge of revealing the truth of mimetic desire in a medium that is normally used to reflect and fuel mimetic desire. After all, it is the latter tendency that makes huge profits for the producers in all media. In the second part of *Don Quixote,* Cervantes does not disguise his indignation over copycat offshoots of his work. Perhaps the main thrust of the second part was to mirror the misunderstandings of his readers in the Duke and the Duchess, who spend huge amounts of time and expense to incite Don Quixote's desires through theatrical fakery. Although they are ostensibly trying to "cure" the Don, they themselves seem to be caught up in Quixote's madness as much as their victim. It isn't enough to write novels revealing mimetic desire. Readers who can truly see what these novels reveal are also needed. If Cervantes was exasperated by the readers of his time, imagine what his apoplexy would have been if he had lived to see a musical featuring an inspirational song about following impossible dreams. Cervantes was showing us that successfully imitating fictional characters is truly impossible. Don Quixote could not live Amadis of Gaul's life any more than Emma Bovary could live the lives of heroines in the novels she read. They could only live their own lives, which they failed to do.

Dante showed the same degree of insight into mimetic desire fueled by bad reading in the story of Paolo and Francesca in *The Divine Comedy.* When Paolo was tutoring Francesca in literature, they read an account of Lancelot's falling in love with Guinevere. When they read the line describing Lancelot's kiss, Paolo kissed Francesca. It wasn't long until the book dropped to the floor. Francesca said: "We read no more that day." (*Divine Comedy* 5:138) The text had dropped into real life with tragic results that landed the two lovers in Hell.

Werther is another fictional person who was widely imitated by real people for a time. Heartsick and overwhelmed by his mimetic desire for a woman already promised to another man, Werther kills himself. The fact that the woman he loved, Lotte, was betrothed seemed to make her more desirable, and when Werther actually sees Albert's desire for Lotte, his desire becomes all the more passionate. The publication of Goethe's novella was followed by an epidemic of suicides throughout Europe. This phenomenon is still called the "Werther effect." These young readers were not just imitating the suicide; they were imitating the mimetic desire on Werther's part that led to his suicide in the novella. Many of them even copied the clothing Werther was described as wearing. Drowning in the mimetic desire of fictional characters can be deadly. I hasten to add that Goethe is not to be blamed for what some of his readers did. Goethe gained enough of a catharsis of his own frustration that he could move on with his life. Goethe learned, by writing, to let go of his idolatrous love. His readers could have imitated that.

So how do we read in a way that is life giving? Reading in a life-giving way is not primarily a matter of reading but of living; of how we read our lives. Don Quixote idolized Amadis of Gaul, Emma Bovary idolized her lovers, and Goethe's readers imitated Werther. If we are too embroiled in our mimetic desires to see what Cervantes, Flaubert, and Goethe saw, then we will only see what the deluded characters in these novels saw. That is, the way the readers of these novels were living their lives affected their reading, and their reading reinforced the way they were living their lives.

In his incisive study of *Don Quixote*, Cesáreo Bandera leads us to the heart of the Don's problem and ours: "God-like Amadis is not God. God transcends empirical reality but does not ignore it or make it irrelevant." The more we *look* at the world around us and interact respectfully with it, the less apt we are to be swept away by the fantasies of mimetic desire. God "demands an absolute act of faith beyond empirical reality, but such an act of faith does not obliterate the inherent rationality of the world 'out there.' The act of faith is essential only to prevent empirical reality from becoming a god unto itself, an idol." (Bandera 2006, 155) Bandera is alerting us to the problem of allowing our models to distort the world around us, making models like Amadis or Albert (Lotte's husband) the lens through which we interact with the world instead of making God the lens.

In analyzing mimetic desire, Girard draws a distinction between "external mediation" and "internal mediation." These terms are a bit bulky but their meaning is easily explained. "External mediation" refers to mimetic desire modeled by someone who is far from equal in social standing. Since Amadis of Gaul was a fantastical fictional character, Don Quixote could not be his rival. Likewise, Sancho Panza, being a peasant, could not compete with Don Quixote. The situation is very different in the interrelationships in Stendhal's *The Red and the Black*. In this case, M. de Rênal, mayor of his village, and M. Valenod are close enough in rank that they can easily become real rivals and they do. At the beginning of this novel, M. de Rênal assumes that M. Valenod covets the tutor, Julien, whom he has hired for his own children. M. de Rênal follows up his fantasy by resolving to offer his tutor more money. Suddenly, Julien has become more valuable simply because he is desired by a second person. This increase in value is delusionary because it has nothing to do with Julien's real merits (if any) as a tutor. Neither M. de Rênal nor M. Valenod give any thought as to which tutor might actually be the most suitable for their children. The triviality of this example of mimetic desire indicates its ubiquity. Mimetic desire is not about the object; it is about the rivals. The more two people compete for social standing, the more they will compete about anything at all. Once again, mimetic desire leads to delusion, but in the case of internal mediation where rivalry is possible and likely, the delusion becomes both more serious and more commonplace. The commonsense solution of looking for a tutor of equal value to the tutor hired by the rival does not enter into this any more than the commonsense solution of looking for another girl as attractive and desirable as Lotte enters the head of Werther.

The three operas Mozart composed to libretti by Lorenzo Da Ponte are also highly instructive about mimetic desire. *The Marriage of Figaro* incorporates the social insights of the French playwright Pierre Beaumarchais who scandalized the French aristocracy with his acute awareness of the increase of mimetic rivalry during the last days of the *Ancien Régime*. The opera centers on Count Almaviva's desire for his servant Susanna who is betrothed to the count's servant Figaro. For all of his chasing after women, the count seems not to have desired Susanna until Figaro desired her and wished to marry her. ✱ who is her half-brother

Meanwhile, Marcellina, a servant of Dr. Bartolo, wishes to marry Figaro. Dr. Bartolo wants revenge for Figaro's helping the count marry Rosina when he himself had desired her. To this end, he supports his servant's claim based on Figaro's unpayable debt to her. (This was the main plot of *The Barber of Seville* famously set to music by Rossini.) This triangle becomes farcical when it turns out that Figaro is Marcellina's son begotten by Dr. Bartolo himself, who has done with his servant what the count wants to do with Susanna.

The adolescent servant Cherubino provides a comical mirror image of the count in that he also desires all women, especially the countess, the only woman the count does not desire. This infatuation does not make him a serious rival to the count, but he becomes entangled with Rosina and Susanna's plot against the count.

The count only shows any desire for his wife when he believes that Cherubino has been flirting with her and is hiding in the closet (which he was until Susanna helped him escape). When it is Susanna who emerges from the closet, an uneasy forgiveness ensemble ensues that foreshadows the opera's finale, but this unravels when the gardener complains about somebody (Cherubino) jumping into the flower garden.

The abortive plans of Act 2 to trick the count come to fruition in the last two acts when Rosina and Susanna disguise themselves as each other and entrap him so that the count has no choice but to drop to his knees and ask his wife's forgiveness, which she freely gives in one of Mozart's most sublime musical moments.

The disguises and mistaken identities throughout the opera dissolve the characters into the indifferentiation of mimetic desire. At a deeper level, Mozart's music weaves a unity out of the passions of all these characters so as to unite them in their mimetic desires, a unity that transcends the class differences of the characters and creates a social vision more subversive than the play by Pierre Beaumarchais. The noble forgiveness scene is as fragile as it is beautiful; a fragile fleeting vision that can be blown away by the next breath of mimetic desire.

2. This fleeting vision is blown away in *Don Giovanni*. The Don is totally, hopelessly, consumed with mimetic desire. Like Count Almaviva, he desires every woman he sees, but in the opera he goes after two women, Donna Anna and Zerlina, who are betrothed, and Donna Elvira, a woman who desires her own (illusory) wholeness. Don Giovanni becomes the center of everybody's attention to the extent that he becomes their idol. He is also the center of their attempted collective violence that fails when Don Giovanni's servant Leporello, who was forced to disguise himself as his master, is the one who takes the blows after the peasant Masetto is beat up by Don Giovanni disguised as Leporello. As usual, it is the more vulnerable people who suffer from a collective rage for vengeance. Count Almaviva is really no better than Don Giovanni except for one thing: he has enough class consciousness to hold himself back. Don Giovanni has no such restraint and so is an agent of chaos, which is illustrated by his party that mixes the classes and features three orchestras playing three different dances at the same time. Don Giovanni is dragged into Hell, not because of divine vengeance, as he is given ample opportunity to repent, but because there is nothing left of him except mimetic desire.

The verdict on *Così fan Tutti* has traditionally been that it is an opera of sublime music set to an inane plot. However, once alerted to the phenomenon of mimetic desire, one finds that this is the deepest of the three Mozart-Da Ponte operas. The silly bet of the two men that their betrothed women will remain faithful under temptation becomes an ominous game when each man finds his desires for his friend's betrothed inflamed in the course of wooing her. At the same time, his jealousy for his own betrothed grows stronger because of his friend's increased desire for the woman he himself loves. If this sounds confused, it is because the desires and even the identities of the four people involved have become so confused that they hardly know who they are. Both men have become more involved in their rivalry than with the women they love. The opera ends happily with mutual forgiveness, but so uneasy is this forgiveness that one doubts that their relationships will ever recover from the trauma they have just suffered. The opera's title means "so are they all." Ostensibly this refers to women, but that strikes me as a projection. If two men agreeing to woo each other's betrothed for the sake of a bet isn't being fickle, nothing is.

The plays of William Shakespeare and the novels of Fyodor Dostoevsky offer many of the deepest and richest insights into mimetic desire that can be found in world literature. Shakespeare's *A Midsummer Night's Dream* is a particularly clear example of how unstable mimetic triangles can be. At the beginning of the play, Lysander and Demetrius both pursue Hermia, Helena having been forsaken by Demetrius. But halfway through the play, due to Puck's mix-up of enchantments ordered by the Fairy King Oberon, Lysander and Demetrius both forsake Hermia and chase after Helena. The fanciful setting of a forest where fairies play their pranks on the humans, while simultaneously acting out their own mimetic triangles, highlights the power of mimetic desire to enchant those who fall sway to it. Hermia herself pinpoints the dynamics of mimetic desire when she cries out, "Oh hell! To choose love by another's eyes!" (*Midsummer Night's Dream*, Act 1, Scene 1) The switching back and forth of the lovers while the rivalry between the two men remains constant until the end is a perfect illustration of the irrelevance of the object in the face of mimetic rivalry.

If desire is as mimetic as Girard suggests, then it follows that one person's love for another will often need to be validated by somebody else. This validation occurs if the second party's desire for one's beloved is inflamed to the same intensity as one's own. In fact, it may be that it takes the desire of another for the woman a man thinks he loves to inflame his own desire for her. Fyodor Dostoevsky illustrates this dynamic clearly in his novella *The Eternal Husband*. After the death of his wife, Pavel Pavlovitch Trusotsky searches out the men who had been rivals for his wife's affections. He finds Velchaninov and becomes his companion. Later, when Trusotsky decides to remarry, "he cannot hold to his own choice inasmuch as the appointed seducer has not confirmed it." (Girard 1997, 49) That is, his rival must desire the same woman he desires. Velchaninov does just that, and Trusotsky loses the woman to his rival. Understanding this dynamic of mimetic desire makes the otherwise puzzling opening scene of Shakespeare's *The Winter's Tale* not only intelligible but profound. Leontes urges his best friend, Polixenes, to admire his wife Hermione, but as soon as he does, Leontes becomes insanely jealous and sets off a wave of violent reaction that is only partially resolved at the end of the play.

    The Merchant of Venice gives us a slice of a society swamped in acquisitiveness that fuels the scapegoat mechanism. The first thing that usually pops into anybody's mind when Shakespeare's *The Merchant of Venice* is mentioned is the cardboard stereotyped Jew Shylock. After Auschwitz, we cannot slip into enjoying this caricature the way earlier audiences might have done, and now we are apt to dismiss the play because we realize how lethal such stereotyping can be. The second thing about the play that usually comes to mind is Portia's set of three boxes where it is not the gold or silver covers that hide her riches, but the unattractive lead cover. Appearances can be misleading and so perhaps it will be worth looking for value beneath the ugly stereotyping.

    It's hard to find any gold under the ugly exterior of Shylock's behavior, but it is equally hard to find any gold under the apparently more attractive exterior of Antonio's behavior. Antonio is noble in that he is willing to take the risk of giving surety to a loan for his friend Bassanio, but the way he treats Shylock is shameful. In one respect, Shylock is offering to do good to an enemy, but in another, he is hoping that the interest-free loan will lead to Antonio's downfall when he extracts a pound of his flesh. It is important to realize that both men are mimetic doubles, rivals in the quest for increasing wealth for the sake of wealth.

    In Shylock's famous speech, when he is taken to task for his vengeful terms, he insists he is exactly the same kind of man as any of his Gentile rivals: "If you prick us, do we not bleed?" Which is what would happen to Antonio if a pound of flesh is cut out of him. "If you wrong us, shall we not revenge? If we are like you in the rest, we will resemble you in that." (*Merchant of*

Venice, Act 3, Scene 1) Shylock's detractors try to distinguish themselves from Shylock by claiming to be merciful while he is not, but mercy is conspicuously lacking in their treatment of Shylock.

Meanwhile, Bassanio is often thought to have proven himself wise by choosing the lead casket, which wins him the hand of Portia in marriage. The speech he makes before making the choice, however, shows that he is not wise but cunning and calculating in his own desire for wealth. "Thus ornament is but the guiled shore/To a most dangerous sea." (act 2, scene 3) Bassanio is so used to disseminating that dissemination is what he expects of Portia. And he is right.

The famous trial scene features Portia's famous praise of mercy: "The quality of mercy is not strain'd,/It droppeth as the gentle rain from heaven." (Act 4, Scene 1) This is as golden a speech as any in Shakespeare. But—mercy is—again!—lacking in dealing with Shylock. By the end of the trial, he has lost his wealth, his livelihood, and his religion. Portia's words seem to echo Ecclesiasticus 35:20: "Mercy is seasonable in the time of affliction as clouds of rain in the time of drought." But her actions belie the beautiful words, thus proving Shylock right when he says that when wronged, Christians revenge— just like Shylock. Unfortunately, Portia's great speech is a golden casket with nothing inside. The words, however, really are golden and invite any of us who rejoice in Shylock's downfall to repent and open our hearts to accept this gift from Heaven. In general, Shakespeare presents us with characters who talk a good game but don't know how to play it. Arguably the greatest wizard of words in the English language, Shakespeare knew how empty language could be—and how violent.

Plays like *Midsummer Night's Dream* and *The Merchant of Venice* along with operas like *The Marriage of Figaro* and *Cosí fan Tutti* present a world full Bill! of mimetic desire and mimetic rivalry and nothing else. The plays and operas reflect the social changes that were opening up opportunities for more and more people to engage in rivalrous activity compared to the smaller number of nobility struggling for power, such as we see in Shakespeare's history plays and tragedies. The meltdowns presented in these works raise the question: What if the whole universe were like this? In these plays and operas, all the

What do they reflect.

players in the game are human, but mythology portrays worlds where it is nothing but mimetic rivalry throughout the universe from top to bottom. In Hindu mythology, for example, the Devas and the Asuras are mirror-image pairs of rivals. One group consists of "gods" and the other of "demons," but this only reflects our tendency to always think we are on the side of the "gods" and our enemies are on the side of the "demons." What do the "gods" and "demons" fight about? Nothing really, except for lordship over the universe. Greek mythology is likewise full of rivalry between the gods. Interestingly, a set of young adult novels by Rick Riordan portrays this sort of universe with uncanny accuracy. These books can be a fun way to learn about Greek and Roman mythology, but if ever these gods should turn out to be real and they really (mis)rule the universe, we're in trouble. The ruling positions of Zeus and the other Olympians, for example, are the result of earlier conflict. In Riordan's novels, Cronos and Gaia make comebacks that fuel the divine in-fighting. — Is This Life

The Mark of Athena is a good example where millennia-old resentments come alive in their tense paralysis. Arachne, who offended Athena by weaving a better tapestry than Athena could, is imprisoned under Rome as a giant spider with a monstrously bad attitude. Beth, a daughter of Athena and a human father, has to steal the Athena Parthenos that was stolen by the Romans from Arachne and restore it to the Olympians. We see frozen resentments such as Arachne's in human experience all the time. What if God really were like Athena instead of a God who generously brings us into being and even more generously saves us from follies such as that of Athena and Arachne?

Dostoevsky builds the plot of *The Brothers Karamazov* around the mimetic triangle created by Fyodor Karamazov and his son Dmitri with Grushenka. For her part, Grushenka not only actively fuels this rivalry, but she tries to Key stoke the fires further by drawing yet another Karamazov, Alyosha, into the fray. Alyosha, however, being a devout follower of the holy man Zossima, declines to play the game.

Alyosha's charitable behavior to Grushenka leads her to repent of her actions, and she no longer tries to fuel the rivalry between Dmitri and his

what motivates you from playing the game

father. Unfortunately, Fyodor and Dmitri Karamazov prove that the presence of Grushenka is no longer necessary for them to pursue their mimetic rivalry with each other, with tragic results. After delivering Grushenka from her involvement in the mimetic rivalry between Dmitri and his father, Alyosha, comes across a group of boys ganging up on their mate Ilyusha. Over time, he weans the boys away from their scapegoating behavior and binds them together into a deeper sense of brotherhood. It is important to note here that Dostoevsky is showing how mimetic desire can work for the good. The boys learn to imitate Alyosha's care for Ilyusha. These boys imitate Alyosha in the same way that Alyosha learned to imitate his elder Zossima. Zossima, in turn, had learned to imitate his saintly brother and turn away from the mimetic conflicts he had indulged in. Ultimately, all of these people are imitating Christ. With Dostoevsky, as well as with the Gospels that provide Father Zossima and Alyosha with their model, we have a vision contrary to the mythological vision of rivalry all the way down. Here, the rivalry empties out and disappears in the Divine Light.

Fyodor Dostoevsky portrayed the resentment of what he called "the Underground Man" with riveting, even seductive power. I experienced this seductive power myself when I first read *Notes from Underground* during late adolescence. I experienced the same thing in the alienated, resentment-filled criminal Rodya Rashkolnikov in *Crime and Punishment* and also the overwhelming force of Ivan Karamazov's personality. I was inclined to see them as models but the truth turned out to be that they were mirroring my own resentments against society, people, and God. That is, Dostoevsky showed the grotesqueness of my resentments in a mirror and I couldn't see how ugly it was until other factors in my life led me to repentance. Ivan Karamazov's resentment of God for allowing the suffering of innocent children seemed unanswerable when Alyosha could say no word in reply. It took years for me to realize how profound that silence really is. It is the silence of Christ in response to the Grand Inquisitor. Alyosha's answer was to invest time and energy with dealing with a group of boys who needed a mentor. Ivan, on the other hand, was big on words but he never lifted a finger to help even one child. I share all of this to illustrate the importance of learning to read well and that learning to read well is inextricably bound up with learning to act well and to see our resentments for the distortions of reality that they are.

Before I could understand Dostoevsky's last great novels, I had to repent. Girard says that the protagonists of the novels he analyzed in *Deceit, Desire, and the Novel* repented at the end. Cervantes renounced the medieval romances that had befuddled him. Dmitri Karamazov, who did not murder his father, but hated him enough to do so, repents while in prison, having been convicted of a murder he did not commit. In *The Red and the Black,* Julian "repudiates his will to power." In short, "all novelistic conclusions are conversions." (Girard 1961, 294) Girard goes on to argue that these great novelists understood mimetic desire, and their participation in it, and repented of it. Flaubert expressed his self-discovery when he cried out: "*Mme Bovary, c'est moi!*" ("I am Madame Bovary!") (Girard 1961, 300) All of which suggests that great novels that *reveal* mimetic desire are a call for repentance. The protagonists in the novel and the novelist both have to renounce the vanity of mimetic desire. This is a call to penance that romantic readers of these novels have been deaf to. They have expressed their incomprehension and scorn at these novelistic endings, taking their great hero Don Giovanni as their model. In this early work of his, where he explored other writers' discovery of mimetic desire, Girard gives a brief but powerful hint of the religious dimension of this novelistic conversion. He notes that Dostoevsky, the most religious of the novelists examined in this book, quoted John 12:24 several times in *The Brothers Karamazov* as a *leitmotiv*: "Very truly, I tell you, unless a grain of wheat falls into the earth and dies, it remains just a single grain; but if it dies, it bears much fruit."

This ties the novelistic conversion to the Paschal Mystery as Jesus' words come just before he is arrested and crucified. As he continued to explore the ramifications of mimetic desire, anthropological studies led to Girard's theory about sacred violence. Girard discovered that the insights into mimetic desire, gleaned from masterpieces of world literature were profoundly and clearly illuminated by Holy Scripture, as was the unveiling of the truth of sacred violence. It is to Holy Scripture's unveiling that we now turn.

Chapter 4

Blessings and the Word

Emmaus as a Lens for Reading Scripture

Prayerful reading of scripture is one of the fundamental practices that immerse us in God's desire. Reading scripture leads us into God's desire as embodied in Jesus, the Word made flesh. As many contemporary writers have asserted: we read scripture not for information but for formation. In his *Rule*, St. Benedict prescribed daily reading of scripture as a practice as important as manual labor. (RB 48:1) It is a monastic saying that one reads scripture as a cow chews its cud. To be formed by scripture, we need to read it prayerfully, slowly, so as to allow the Word to quicken our embodied being in the same way that food strengthens us. The Word comes from without to nourish us. Without the Word, we feed on ourselves as the body consumes itself when it receives no food. But we have to put the food in our mouths and chew it in order to be nourished. The Word cannot nourish us if we use it as a battering ram on people we don't like or agree with. Making a weapon of the Word starves everybody.

Traditionally, this practice of scripture reading is called *Lectio Divina*, the term used in the Rule of St. Benedict. It is good to have this as a daily practice either individually or in a small group. The practice gains much depth when one has a scheme for a comprehensive reading of scripture. This can be done by using a lectionary or reading the Bible or each testament in course.

"Reading in course" means starting at the beginning and continuing to read a bit each day until coming to the end and then starting over again. This practice goes better if either the time spent or the amount read is not limited and better still if neither is strictly limited. This open-endedness provides a leisurely quality to the reading. In this practice, we are often advised to ask ourselves what each passage of scripture reveals about God and what it reveals about ourselves. I agree, but a growing awareness of mimetic resonance leads me to suggest that we also give attention to what each passage of scripture reveals to us about our *relationships* with God, with other people, and with the world, and how our desires interact with those of other people and with God.

It is important to be constantly mindful of the communal dimension of reading and hearing scripture, especially at those times when we read it and reflect on it by ourselves. To begin with, scripture emerged out of community, with many people contributing to its final form. Moreover, the choices as to which writings would be considered canonical, that is, authoritative, were decided in council by the Jewish rabbis for the Hebrew Bible, or the Tanakh as Jews call it, and early Church councils for the New Testament. Most important of all, reading and listening to scripture is central to corporate worship. Church lectionaries, in those churches that have them, help keep us immersed in scripture comprehensively. Hearing the Word in the congregation and listening to preaching on that Word helps us with our own reflections and keeps our own reflections connected with those of others.

In his catechesis of Christian living, *Jesus the Forgiving Victim*, James Alison raises the question: Through whose eyes should we read scripture? He replies that we should read all of scripture through the eyes of Jesus. He explains how we can do this by discussing the powerful story of the journey to Emmaus in Luke 24. Here we are directed, within scripture, to this fundamental principle for interpreting scripture. The two disciples of Jesus who are journeying to Emmaus do not recognize the man who joins them and enters into a discussion of the scriptures with them. They are more than startled when this man suddenly becomes recognizable as Jesus in the breaking of bread, at which point he disappears. The two disciples remark on how their hearts had burned while this stranger talked to them on their journey. Alison says that in this story, Luke claims that Jesus is the "living interpretive principle" of scripture (Alison 2013, 49). In reading scripture through the eyes of Jesus, we realize that his story is the story of countless victims before and after him. Conversely, we can say that the story of all victims is Jesus' story. As Jesus said that those who did acts of mercy to the least of his little ones had done them to him, (Mt. 25: 40) so those who persecute his little ones have persecuted him, as Paul found out on the road to Damascus. It was by reading Joshua through the eyes of Jesus that I, with Alison, suggested it was Achan, the victim, who was the Christ figure in the story, not Joshua who cast lots that fell on Achan. Remember, it is the story of victims *as* victims whose story is Jesus's story. This gives us a firm anchor for hearing what God would have us hear as our hearts burn when we read and listen to scripture.

Many people insist that we have to accept the whole Bible and not pick and choose. That sounds good until we realize that even people who believe strongly in this principle end up picking and choosing. Moreover, when we look at how Jesus himself actually treated scripture, we find that he did a lot of careful picking and choosing to construct the way his Jewish inheritance would form his own outlook. Jesus' inaugural sermon in Nazareth is a ringing proclamation of God's desire. He reads from Isaiah: "The spirit of the Lord God is upon me, because the Lord has anointed me; he has sent me to bring good news to the oppressed, to bind up the brokenhearted, to proclaim liberty to the captives, and release to the prisoners; to proclaim the year of the Lord's favor. (Isa. 61:1—2) To broaden the context, we should note Isaiah's illusion to Leviticus 25:10 where Yahweh prescribes a year of jubilee to free all slaves and forgive all debts, a commandment that has been mostly ignored from the day it was first proclaimed up to the present day. This is an interesting and common example of picking and choosing. Jesus *picked* and *chose* what most people leave on the vine of the Bible. What is also important is the phrase from Isaiah that Jesus purposely did *not* choose: "and the day of vengeance of our Lord." (Isa. 61:2) I have seen some argue that it is typical for a quote of the first verse to stand for the rest of the utterance. Jesus' cry from the cross, being the first line of Psalm 22 is an example where that may be the case. But everything that Jesus proclaims here is contrary to any notion of God exercising vengeance. We shall find that this "edited" version of Isaiah is typical of what Jesus picks from the Hebrew scriptures and what he does not.

The way Jesus treated the scriptures he inherited makes it clear that he did not think they were self-interpreting. They do need to be interpreted, and Jesus gives us the model in his earthly life, death, and resurrected life for how to interpret them. Moreover, the very fact that the collective murder of Jesus and Jesus' vindication by God through the Resurrection is the center of God's revelation as to what/who God is tells us that revelation has to cut through huge amounts of human wrath that has been projected onto God. Girard's theory of sacred violence tells the same story. Lest one think that Girard's theory itself is the touchstone, I hasten to add that Girard would be the first person to insist that he could never have arrived at his theory if it were not for the Gospels. All of this makes a strong case for seeing in scripture a progressive revelation that would take time to undo the mimetic force of sacred violence and its projections. (This is not the first time that a progressive theory of scripture has been suggested. Such theories have abounded since the early Church.) It is not possible that the Jewish scriptures could have gotten everything right, given the challenge of overcoming their inheritance of sacred violence. Girard uses the term "in travail" to describe the struggle in scripture to arrive at the God revealed as the risen, Forgiving Victim who talked to the disciples on the Road to Emmaus. Jesus' treatment of his inheritance shows that Jesus saw the scripture and even the emerging movement he was putting into motion as also in travail. We ourselves have to enter the process of being in travail if we are ever to have hope of reaching the mind of Christ.

Jesus studied scripture and its many voices to discern what kind of a Messiah he was supposed to be. As we will see below, he chose the model based on the Suffering Servant and *not* a Davidic model of a conquering warrior. The fact that Jesus had to enter such a discernment process shows that Jesus did not find a monolithic message in scripture that clarified his mission. He found many voices in scripture arguing many contrary positions. One of the more prominent debates was the efficacy of sacrifice. Another was whether God's wrath was vindictive or remedial—or nonexistent. Jesus had to discern which side to take in the various debates. This need for discernment required that Jesus be personally and deeply involved in how he was going to interpret scripture. We need to be just as deeply involved if we are going to read scripture through Jesus' eyes.

St. Ignatius of Loyola provides a powerful model for this kind of involved reading that provides an instructive contrast to Don Quixote. According to his *Autobiography*, Ignatius was a soldier who liked to read the same sorts of chivalrous romances that Don Quixote did. While he was recovering from some serious battle injuries, he asked for this sort of literature. It turned out that only a life of Christ and a book of the lives of the saints was available, so he read those instead. These books changed not only *what* Ignatius read, but *how* he read. Not only did he stop to think about the things he was reading, he also stopped to think "about the things of the world that he used to think of before." That is, Ignatius was using what he read to connect him to real life, the life God had created rather than what life looks like through the lens of an idol like Amadis. During this time of struggle and repentance, Ignatius then confessed his infatuation with the *idea* (not reality) of going into the service of a "certain lady," oblivious to "how impossible it would be." (Ignatius 1991, 70)

But then Ignatius started to reflect on what it would be like to imitate Saint Francis or Saint Dominic who had imitated Christ. Such thoughts gave him consolations that thoughts of soldiering and chivalry did not give. Here were models that were challenging but not impossible. Ignatius was spurred to develop a spirituality based on the imitation of Christ, not an imitation of external actions only but, more important, of cultivating the inner disposition of Christ's charity for others that was to become the backbone of his *Spiritual Exercises*. It is reading scripture through the eyes of Jesus that leads us into Jesus' desire, which is God's desire. Bandera draws the contrast for us when he says that "unlike Christ, Amadis cannot give his follower what he wants without ceasing to be Amadis." (Bandera 2006, 157) That is, Amadis, if real, would be what Girard calls a model-obstacle whom Quixote would need to defeat in combat, which would change Amadis for the worse if Amadis was vanquished. Christ, on the other hand is a model without rivalry, who wishes to be imitated without rivalry. Ignatius discovered that Christ creates an abundance of charity that can only become more abundant through imitating him. Imitating Jesus led Ignatius to make a pilgrimage to Jerusalem and then to a spiritual pilgrimage of imitating Christ for the rest of his life.

In the rest of this chapter, I will emphasize what scripture reveals about the workings of mimetic desire and how mimetic desire escalates into mimetic rivalry.

Divine Abundance in Creation and the Fall

In the Bible, mimetic desire begins where one would expect it to, in the beginning. The roll call of Creation in Genesis 1 shows abundance that reveals God's desire to give generously. There is no holding back, no cutting back on benefits to balance the budget. Just giving for the sake of giving. God encouraged Creation to share the same generosity by saying: "Let the land produce vegetation: seed-bearing plants and trees on the land that bear fruit with seed in it, according to their various kinds." (Gen. 1:11) If the land is supposed to be generous, surely humans, created in God's image should be generous as well. This sort of generosity *is* God's image, as we shall see in the life of Jesus. We find this same overflowing generosity on God's part in Creation in Psalm 104 where God makes springs gush forth and flow between the hills, and gives air for the birds' habitation, grass for the cattle and plants for people to grow and wine to gladden human hearts.

The Creation narrative in Genesis can be read as a refutation of Babylonian mythology. The Babylonian exile was traumatic for the Jews. Those taken there had to live in an alien environment contrary to everything they believed in. But an interesting thing happened during this exile. The sages and prophets who were living in exile lived in close quarters with the mythology and sacrificial religion of their captors. The clash between the two taught them a few things about what the God they worshiped was all about. Back in Israel, when the prophets saw the sacrifices of children to Moloch, they knew that this was not the kind of sacrifice Israel's God wished, and they protested these sacrifices with all their might. In Babylon, the sages and prophets came up against a mythology of a violent creation that took place with the dismemberment of Tiamat, who was deemed the cause of all the problems among the deities and therefore had to be punished. Moreover, the reason that Marduk created humanity was to make slaves who would serve the gods. The Jewish sages and prophets learned from this mythology that this was *not* what their God was about. The God who had delivered them from the Red Sea was interested in freeing slaves, not making them. This God had created a people by delivering them *from* violence and *from* a violent culture. They were hoping their God would do it again, and God did just that when the Persians defeated Babylon and allowed the Jews to return to their home.

Isaiah proclaimed Israel's God to be far different, fully other, than Marduk and his pantheon. "With whom then will you compare me, or who is my equal?" asks Israel's God in a question so rhetorical that it stops all human mouths. (Isa. 40:25) The violence in Babylonian mythology mirrors the violence of Babylonian culture and other human cultures as both deities and humans live in the same system of retributive violence. But Israel's God "sits above the circle of the earth." (Isa. 40:22) That is, God is outside the system. From God's vantage point, we are all like little grasshoppers. This God is the creator "of the ends of the earth." Not only that, but God "gives power to the faint, and strengthens the powerless." (Isa. 40:29) Far from creating servants, God *serves* the creatures God has made, and God serves most especially the powerless, like a rabble of slaves in Egypt and an exiled people in Babylon. Grasshoppers may be small in size but they are great in God's care. God's act of Creation shows God to be so free of rivalry that whatever the command to not eat the fruit of one particular tree in the Garden of Eden is about, it is not about God trying to withhold anything from humanity over jealousy with humans.

Genesis says that Eve saw that the tree was "a delight to the eyes." (Gen.3:6) Was the fruit orange or yellow? Large or small? We don't know. What made this tree different from any other tree? Nothing, except that God had told Adam not to take the fruit from that tree. That was not a problem until the serpent insinuated to Eve that God was withholding the fruit of that tree in a rivalrous fashion. The illusory thought that God wanted that tree more than the others made it stand out. More important, where are all the other trees and plants that filled the garden just a moment ago? They're gone! We have here the classic symptom of rivalrous mimetic desire: the shrinkage of abundance. This boundless garden filled with everything humans and plants and animals need and much more has suddenly shrunken to one measly tree. Then comes the suggestion that the humans will become like God if they eat of this fruit: yet another illusion that is caused by moving into a rivalrous position towards God. Not only has the ostensible object of desire shrunk to nothingness, but the humans begin to desire the *being* of the one they have just made their rival, which, in Girard's analysis, is what happens between rivals. Desiring the *being* of the one who has given *them* (us) being is cutting off the limb we are sitting on. But this is what happens in the course of mimetic rivalry.

Oughourlian suggests that the serpent stands for rivalrous mimetic desire. (Oughourlian 2010, 54) In order to stand for rivalrous mimetic desire, the serpent really has to symbolize a human potential that is threatening to take over humanity. That is, just as Adam means "man," making him a symbolic figure of humanity who has not yet fallen into rivalrous mimetic desire, the serpent also stands for humanity that has fallen into rivalrous mimetic desire, and Eve is humanity on the cusp between the two. This brings us to the delicate question of freedom. Was the Fall absolutely inevitable? Raymund Schwager argues that at the dawn of humanity, there was a fundamental collective choice: whether to expand mimetic desire in the direction of good mimesis, or to shrink mimetic desire into rivalry. (Schwager 2006) Would humanity accept the world as gift and build on the natural tendency to gift their children with expansive mimetic desire? *Or* would humanity take the fruit from a tree that they believe is being withheld from them? If even one person should reach for the fruit in a rivalrous way, other humans would be more likely to desire the fruit from that very tree. In this way, rivalry becomes the model for how humans raise their children. Rivalry tends to create energy and excitement, and the anger and rage spurred on by this rivalry begets exponentially more energy, so it is not surprising that humanity fell into the rivalrous direction. Adam and then Eve show themselves highly energized by the blame game they play when God comes a-calling. This is why the news media arouses anger and fear more than it disseminates news. In any case, this fall into mimetic rivalry is what happened and once it happened, it was pretty much impossible for humanity to find its own way out of it.

It isn't until Adam has also eaten the fruit that he and Eve become alienated from God and from each other. Mimetic rivalry is a collaborative process that ties people together in blame. Once God is believed to be a rival the way human beings often are, then the trees in the garden cease to be free gifts and only one tree matters, the one tree that must be seized rather than received. Once this one tree has become the center of humanity's universe, humanity finds itself in a desert of humanity's own making. It isn't God who drove Adam and Eve out of the garden, rather *they* drove God out of the garden, at which point it ceased to be much of a garden. The prolog to John's Gospel confirms that it was not God who drove Adam and Eve out of Eden, it was humanity that expelled God: "He came to what was his own, and his own people did not accept him." (Jn. 1:11)

God said that if humanity ate of the fruit of the tree of good and evil, they would die. The serpent told Eve they would not die. At first, the serpent seemed to be right. The fruit did not explode in the stomachs of those who ate it and kill them on the spot. They were still alive after their little meal on the sly. But in the longer run, it was God and not the serpent who was proved right. When our eyes are open to good and evil, we see evil where we didn't see it before. Once our eyes open to good and evil, suddenly some people (ourselves, of course) are seen as good, as clean, and *other* people are seen as evil or unclean. It just so happens that the next tribe is unclean, and it just so happens that some people in our own social group are unclean. So it is that eating the fruit does indeed cause death.

Romans 5:12 posits sin's entry into the world through that act of one man (Adam), but this act promptly brings on a host of imitators, making the spread of sin a collective effort. The phrase "death came through sin, and so death spread to all" points to the subsequent violence in Genesis after Adam's sin: Cain killing Abel, the flood of social violence from which Noah was delivered, and the Tower of Babel. To quote Psalm 2 again: "Why do the nations conspire, and the peoples plot in vain? The kings of the earth set themselves, and the rulers take counsel together, against the Lord and his anointed." Once culture was founded on collective violence, these cultures were founded on death. Imitation doesn't seem to be that big a deal until we become aware of the force of mimetic resonance, a force that operates like a gravitational field. The closer two or more people are to each other in rivalry, the stronger the mimetic gravitational field. A gravitational field can become so strong that it is inescapable. That is why the planets in our solar system can't go west to look for a better solar system. The same is true of mimetic resonance. There is no mimetic resonance in an isolated individual. What Paul is suggesting is that at the dawn of humanity, a mimetic gravitational field of sacrificial violence was created in which humanity was trapped, until Jesus initiated a new mimetic gravitational field where "the abundance of grace and the free gift of righteousness exercise dominion in life through the one man Jesus Christ." (Rom. 5:17) The first chapter of Romans also famously depicts the Fall as a collective decision of humanity that soon spiraled out of control.

Brothers and Blessings

After the scattering of the builders of the Tower of Babel, God makes a new beginning of gathering humanity. God calls Abraham to leave his father's house, i.e. the scattered, rivalrous civilization he was born in, and move to a land God would show him. When Abraham leaves the entanglements of mimetic rivalry behind, whole new vistas of possibilities suddenly present themselves. God enumerates these possibilities by saying to Abraham: "I will make of you a great nation, and I will bless you, and make your name great, so that you will be a blessing" and by Abraham "all the families of the earth shall be blessed." (Gen. 12:1–3) We are so habituated to getting (or taking) blessings that we often fail to notice that God said Abraham would *be* a blessing, not just for himself and his household but for *all* households. The intervening verse that God will curse those who curse Abraham is discordant. If God really is in the business of blessings, then God is not in the business of cursing. After all, Jesus did not curse those who not only cursed him but put him to death. However, we could say that when we curse someone who *is* a blessing, and through Abraham *everybody* is a blessing, then we are consumed by our own cursing. God doesn't curse us, we curse ourselves. God promised Abraham that he would have as many descendants as the dust of the earth, (Gen. 13:16) the stars in the sky, and the grains of sand on the seashore. (Gen. 22:17) Much as I like the image of the stars in the sky, and I think of this verse every time a night is clear enough for me to see the stars, the image of dust ties in with the creation of humanity out of dust. This makes it clear that descendants of Abraham (like us) are part of God's ongoing Creation. That's how expansive God's blessing and *being* God's blessing can be.

When Abraham and his nephew Lot find that there is tension between their herdsmen, Abraham suggests that they separate. He gives Lot the choice of the land to the left or the land to the right. (Gen. 13:5–9) This is quite the opposite of what most of us do: first see what the other desires and then desire it for ourselves. Instead, Abraham renounces the desire for the land Lot wants and goes in the other direction. (The better-looking land turned out to have its liabilities, but that is another story.)

In the fraternal strife that runs throughout Genesis, the rivalry has nothing to do with romantic triangles as in many novels and plays. Neither is the rivalry over land or any other material entity. The disputes are over blessings. In Creation, God blesses humanity with all that God has created, but humanity rejects that blessing for the sake of one tree that withers, taking all the other trees with it, and leaving a barren landscape. Abraham didn't just *have* a blessing, he *was* a blessing. So why should anybody fight about blessings? That is the riddle that Genesis poses for us. We see this rivalry over blessings in the generations that followed Abraham, but this same rivalry had already occurred at the dawn of humanity between the first two sons of Adam and Eve.

Genesis does not tell us why God accepted Abel's sacrifice and not Cain's.

Girard's theory that culture is founded on collective violence leads me to suspect that tilling the ground was a factor. There could have been mimetic rivalry among nomadic sheep herders but tilling the ground like Cain was all the more conducive to rivalry as particular plots of land more quickly inspire mimetic rivalry. The proliferation of dying and rising deities in the mythology of early agrarian societies suggests that a landed economy intensified mimetic crises and their resolution through collective violence.

But that does not get us to the heart of the mystery of this story, particularly when we consider the alleged zero sum blessings in the fratricidal strife in the stories that follow. I suspect that Cain jumped to the conclusion that when Abel's offering was accepted, God could not also accept his offering. What is decisive is that when Cain's offering was rejected or, more likely, he thought it was rejected, he embroiled himself with Abel, considering him a rival, although there is no evidence that Abel thought the same of Cain. As usual with mimetic rivalry, Abel became an idol to Cain, which entailed exiling God. God called out to Cain, something God continues to do with violent humans to the end of time, but Cain would not let go of his preoccupation with his brother until he had killed him. As noted above, Abel's blood cried from the ground in marked contrast with the fratricidal myth of the founding of Rome, where the blood of Remus was silent. Like Romulus, though, Cain was a founder of culture, while Abel was the first prophet as defined by Jesus in Mt. 23:35, that is, a prophet is a victim. Abel's blood seems to have cried for vengeance. The author of Hebrews, however, says that the blood of Jesus "speaks a better word than the blood of Abel." (Heb. 12:24) Here is more proof that God is in the business of blessing and not cursing.

Although Abraham gave us a perfect example of renouncing mimetic rivalry in relation to Lot, he failed the challenge posed by his two sons from two different mothers, Ishmael and Isaac. In spite of being called to *be* a blessing and being promised by God that he would have as many descendants as the dust of the earth, Abraham fails to believe that *both* of his sons can inherit the blessing he had been given by God. Far from fighting each other, Ishmael and Isaac play well together, but they fall victim to the rivalry between their mothers. (Women are equal participants in the mimetic rivalry game in

Genesis.) Abraham casts Ishmael out so that his favorite son born of Sarah can inherit the blessing. The exiling of Hagar and Ishmael is heartbreaking. God, however, visits Hagar and makes it clear that there is a blessing for Ishmael, too, even if Abraham did not believe it.

Following his father's example, Isaac assumes that only one of his two sons can receive his blessing and, like Abraham, he wants to give it to his favorite son. It so happens that Rebekah has a favorite son as well. Perhaps tension between Rebecca and Isaac worked its way out through each championing a different son. As a result, Isaac's scheme misfires. This time, it is the son who receives (*takes*) the blessing who goes into exile, where Jacob spends many years in rivalry with his kinsman Laban. When Esau re-enters the story on Jacob's return, Esau has done well for himself and has no need to envy his brother's success. Apparently there was a lot more of a blessing left for Esau than Isaac thought.

Jacob stubbornly upholds the family tradition of disbelief in the scope of God's blessing and singles out his favorite son, Joseph, over/against his ten older brothers. This time the fratricidal strife has enough brothers to create a scenario of collective violence. In contrast to the primitive sacred, however, the unanimity is not complete. Both Reuben and Judah separately make plans to save Joseph, but they both fail. If they had stood up to their brothers together, the mimetic process would likely have been redirected in a peaceful direction. The upshot of the story is that Joseph ends up becoming a blessing to Egypt and to lands far beyond so that he saves his own family through his foresight in collecting food during the years of plenty. (Joseph as provider is sometimes seen as a type of Jesus feeding the multitudes and of the Eucharist. But his *taking* the food from the Egyptians and making them buy it back so that they fall into debt and slavery makes Joseph fall far short of Jesus.) Before he dies, Jacob blesses the two sons of Joseph: Ephraim and Manasseh. He crosses his hands to indicate that Ephraim will be greater than his elder brother, but he gives *both* boys the *same* blessing. Finally, through excruciatingly painful experience, Jacob has learned that God has blessings for *all* of Abraham's offspring.

Although these stories feature individuals, it is important to realize that throughout, mimetic rivalry is a corporate matter. That is, the mimetic rivalry over blessings is shown be to systemic throughout the family over three generations. These stories show mimetic rivalry to be a system and not just the hang-ups of a few individuals. That the individuality of the characters comes across in powerful ways only goes to show how particular people are caught up in rivalrous systems and perpetuate them. These strong personalities also help us see ourselves mirrored in them. That the rivalry is over blessings lays bare the absurdity of mimetic rivalry. There is really nothing to fight over, and yet Cain and Abel, Jacob and Esau, and Joseph and his brothers fight over this nothing anyway, even though blessings are as abundant as the dust of the earth and the stars in the sky.

We would do well to pause and reflect on this. I am afraid that the reason we don't think about blessings as nothing to fight over is because we are so used to claiming blessings at the expense of other people that we don't even notice it or think anything of it. We need to take note of our tendency to claim blessings for ourselves and try to wrest them away from other people. Often our group identities depend on this. If our group is blessed, other groups must be cursed. God just doesn't have enough blessings for everybody. But when Paul extolled Abraham as the progenitor of God's blessings, Paul was saying that Abraham is the progenitor of *all* people. Note also that Abraham is not the progenitor because he was blameless; he had his faults as I pointed out above. Being a blessing and always acting like it are two different things. We should take notice of how the two might differ within each of us and seek to *act* like the blessings we are meant to be.

The Ten Commandments

The Ten Commandments stress the importance of mimetic desire by concluding with: "You shall not covet your neighbor's house; you shall not covet your neighbor's wife, or male or female slave, or ox, or donkey, or anything that belongs to your neighbor." (Ex. 20:17) When we pair this commandment with the first: "You shall have no other gods before (beside) me," we have the spirituality of mimetic desire in a nutshell. I have already discussed how mimetic rivals become idols who take the place of God. The tenth commandment has a rather long list of things that one should not covet. Obviously, this list is not exhaustive. It is long enough to show that it is infinitely long; we should not covet *anything* that belongs to another. To place a "god" before or besides God *is* to covet. To covet *is* to place a "god" before or besides God. It is not enough to refrain from coveting. More accurately, we cannot rescind in this negative sense. If we try that, we become all the more consumed by what we are trying *not* to covet. This is perhaps at least part of what Paul was getting at when he said that the commandment "You shall not covet" *caused* him to covet. (Rom. 7:7–8) We must turn to God and God's desire if we are to have any hope of following this commandment.

Royal Rivals

Samuel, Saul, and David were embroiled in a deep web of mimetic rivalry. To begin with, Samuel was in rivalry with Saul, not because Saul was a bad person (although he had serious faults), but because Saul was the king. Samuel did not want Israel to have a king in the first place. Since Samuel's fear that being like the other nations would entail institutionalizing sacred violence did indeed happen, Samuel had a point. The end of the Book of Judges, however, shows the horror that ensues when each person does what is right in one's own eyes. (Judg. 21:25) Unfortunately, like Eli before him, Samuel had failed to pass on his desire to serve God to his sons, and that lead the people to ask for a king. Although Samuel had to give in to the people's request, he managed to retain his position as power broker for Israel. When Saul did not wait more than seven days for Samuel to come to a sacrifice, (1 Sam. 13:8) and then spared an enemy defeated in battle, (1 Sam. 15:9) Samuel took advantage of these actions to declare that God had taken the kingship away from Saul.

Saul's rash vow that threatened his son Jonathan (1 Sam. 14:24–46) shows that Saul had his problems and that he may have looked on his son as a potential rival. Even before lots were cast to see who had violated his ban on eating before a battle, he insisted that even if his son was the one at fault, that person should die. (Indeed, Jonathan was the one who had eaten some honey, not knowing about the ban until it was too late.) For his part, David was ambitious enough that he may have vied for the throne with no goading from anybody else. However, it is not until Samuel deposed Saul and looked for a new king, presumably one he thought he could better control, that David actually became a rival to Saul. The rivalry was fueled when, after a victorious battle, the women sang, "Saul has killed his thousands, and David his ten thousands." (1 Sam. 18:7) David was riding a mimetic wave of supporters who were fueling the rivalry between two men who supposedly were on the same side and should have been working together. This story shows us that a whole society can be caught in this kind of rivalry. Jonathan, for his part, supported David against his father. Saul's treatment of his son may have been a factor, but Jonathan also loved David "with his own soul." (1 Kings 18:1) Girard has noted the many close friends in Shakespeare's plays, such as *The Two Gentlemen of Verona,* who became bitter enemies as soon as something (or someone) they could not or would not share came along. Jonathan, however, renounced any potential rivalry for the crown in favor of his friend. Here is a rare biblical precedent for another man who would flee from a crowd that wanted to make him king.

I was startled when I first learned that Girard attached great importance to the Judgement of Solomon. (1 Kings 3:16–28) After all, it was one of the first Bible stories I learned in Sunday school. However, thinking about it with Girard's goading has convinced me that it is a powerful revelation of mimetic rivalry. The two women who are fighting over the baby are indistinguishable mimetic doubles. They echo one another exactly, and when Solomon responds, he can only echo their echoing. At this point, Solomon resorts to the time-honored method of differentiating the mimetically undifferentiated: he asks for a sword. Girard suggests that this command recalls the ancient custom of child sacrifice, a custom denounced by the prophets during and after Solomon's reign. (Jer. 32–35) (Girard 1987, 239) Whether or not this speculation applies here, the mimetic rivalry of the women threatens to have the result it always has: the creation of a victim. One of the women agrees to this solution but the other does something extraordinary: she begs the king to give the child to the other woman rather than kill the child. This woman has broken off her mimetic rivalry with the other woman out of concern for the child. This is the opposite of what usually happens in such cases, and children all over the world suffer for it. This is the decision that faces us time and again: will we renounce mimetic rivalry for the sake of those caught in the crossfire, or is our rivalry more important than anybody or anything else? Solomon's judgment did not solve the question of which woman was the biological mother. What was revealed is which woman was fit to be a mother.

Now for a story that doesn't end so well. First Kings 21 begins with a rivalry between King Ahab and Naboth. Ahab wants a vineyard that belongs to Naboth. When Ahab tries to make a deal for it, Naboth declines. The land had ancestral meaning to Naboth, but the king's desire seems to have heightened his own. Naboth's refusal seems to have intensified Ahab's desire for the vineyard, so that the king goes to bed in a full-blown pout. Jezebel steps in and "solves" the problem by sending letters to the elders in Naboth's town. Naboth is a civic leader, and Jezebel instinctively knows that other civic leaders are likely to covet Naboth's position and will welcome the chance to rid themselves of their rival. Such proves to be the case. They orchestrate a charge of blasphemy, the same charge that will later to be leveled against Jesus, and then everybody in the town stones Naboth to death. This time, the victim is shown to be innocent, unjustly murdered with the help of a royal abuse of power. This is a disturbing story that shows another example of the Hebrew Bible revealing the truth of violence rather than hiding it as mythology does.

The Epistle of James

The Epistle of James is full of acute observations about mimetic desire. Early on James debunks the notion that God tempts us to sin. Rather, it is we who tempt ourselves, enticed by our own desires. (Jas. 1:13–14) James goes on to say that when "desire has conceived, it gives birth to sin, and that sin, when it is fully grown, gives birth to death." In this way, James demythologizes the devil as an external force who tempts us. The devil is the mimetic rivalry that arises within the relationships between people. We don't need a supernatural creature goading us on; we stir up plenty of trouble among ourselves. James develops the connection between our rivalrous desires and their potential end in death at the beginning of Chapter 4. James says that our disputes come from the cravings that are at war within us. "You want something and do not have it; so you commit murder. And you covet something and cannot obtain it; so you engage in disputes and conflicts." (Jas. 4:2–3) Here is that tenth commandment again and, like the tablet given to Moses, James connects the commandment against coveting to the first commandment. We do not receive because we do not ask, and if we ask, we ask wrongly because we are acting out of the passions of mimetic desire. James then advises us to submit ourselves to God. (Jas. 4:7) Submitting to God means submitting our *desires* to God. Submitting in this way frees our desires from their mimetic entanglements so that we can realize that "every perfect gift, is from above, coming down from the Father of lights, with whom there is no variation or shadow due to change" (Jas. 1:17) James' many jibes against rich people warn us that wealth might be a sign of disobedience to God rather than of blessing, especially if we cheat workers of their wages (or fail to pay them fairly) and treat the poor shabbily. (Jas. 5:4)

James also warns us of the mimetic contagion of the tongue. Small as it is, it can cause much harm when it boasts of great things. These boasts take over and escalate with the desire to top other people. Other people, caught up in our boasting, swell with boasting as well. So it is that "the tongue is a fire" that can grow and set a whole forest afire. (Jas. 3:5–6) With the way destructive fires fueled by words can swarm through the Internet, we need to take care how our small fingers holding a pen or poised over a keyboard can also veer out of control. James says that the tongue is capable of blessing, and surely this is what God made it for, but when the tongue has set a fire gone amok, it is the instrument of cursing our brothers and sisters. Worse, the two can happen at the same time when we speak out of different sides of our mouths, both praising and blaming our brothers and sisters. (Jas. 4:11)

Principalities and Powers

Jesus wasn't killed by individuals, he was killed by a social network that converged on him. Surely James had the persecution of his Lord in mind when he warned how the contagion of mimetic desire in its rivalrous form can engulf a society. I think it is this social contagion that Paul is getting at when he warns us against the "principalities and powers." (The phrase is translated as "the elemental spirits of the universe" in the NRSV.) He has often been understood as referring to supernatural beings hostile to God, but mimetic realism gives us reason to see a powerful anthropological understanding of these powers. Paul is warning us of a whole social system fueled by sacrificial violence. He says that Jesus "disarmed the powers and authorities" and "made a public spectacle of them, triumphing over them by the cross." (Col. 2:15) Paul is saying that Jesus' death and the apostolic proclamation of his innocence has given us the possibility of becoming aware of these principalities and powers, the systemic dimension of sin. Paul goes on to ask the Colossians: "Since you died with Christ to the elemental spiritual forces of this world, why, as though you still belonged to the world, do you submit to its rules?" (Col. 2:20) That is, why do we fall back into a persecutory society filled with unproductive rules and regulations that have nothing to do with God?

The power of evil can be so overwhelming that we are tempted to think that evil is much more than the sum of its parts, that there is a transcendent dimension to it, a dimension of supernatural origin. I think evil *is* much more than the sum of its parts but, given how overwhelming mimetic rivalry running through a society can be, it is the exponential escalation of this mimetic process that creates the illusion of transcendence. That is to say, these principalities get their power from the collective cohesiveness of persecution. However, the principalities and powers have been dismantled and nailed to the cross by Jesus. The Forgiving Victim is gathering a radically different social system that not only does not require the sacrifice of a victim but totally precludes such a thing. Paul says that if the "rulers of this age" had known what Jesus was doing on the cross, "they would not have crucified the Lord of glory." (1 Cor. 2:8) But because they did just that, we have some ability, by the grace of God, to see the fundamental signs of a society that is still run, at least in part, by the principalities and powers, and for seeing the signs of the Kingdom that the risen and Forgiving Victim has opened up for us. Although the phrase "principalities and powers" is not used in Revelation, we see throughout the book images of empire run precisely on these same lines. (For an in-depth study of this approach to the principalities and powers, see Walter Wink's trilogy *The Powers.*) We shall list some of the chief characteristics.

A society run by the principalities and powers is punitive. Some people may think that is a good thing as it keeps order in society, but in a punitive society, somebody *must* be to blame whenever anything goes wrong or seems to go wrong, and that somebody *must* be punished. When a society *needs* to have somebody punished, this need takes precedence over justice. It is better for an innocent person to suffer than for the corporate rage of society to suffer for lack of an object. It follows from this that the Law of Tit for Tat reigns. There is no room for mercy. Every offense must be met in equal measure. As long as this law reigns, there is no end in sight to the spiral of retaliation. There is also no room for grace as a free gift from God.

The principalities and powers necessarily institute scarcity. I noted above Dumouchel's contention that scarcity, the founding dynamic of capitalism, was instituted as a second "solution" to collective violence. The basic argument, as I understand it, is that the scarcity gives humans an incentive to try to overcome scarcity by increasing production so that there will be more material goods than there were. This works in the sense that more material goods are produced that can be consumed by people. But scarcity is not overcome because the increase of production increases desire for goods. When this increased desire leads to more increased production, desires increase even more in a never-ending spiral. So it is that material goods can never catch up with desire. Mimetic desire, desiring things because other people desire them, further intensifies this frenzy. Whole inventories of perfectly wearable shoes disappear if only a few designs are in fashion. This is how this "peaceful" solution to violence leads directly to the quiet, hidden sacrifice of many people on the hidden altars of indifference. Collateral damage once again. Indifference is just as contagious as mimetic violence. The ennui of modern humanity analyzed by legions of philosophers and social commentators shows the extent of this contagion.

In a society run by the principalities and powers, somebody is *always* expendable. Caiaphas's dictum that it is better that one person die than that the whole nation should perish is "gospel." Collateral damage is an acceptable price to pay for objectives deemed good to those who are running the show. When the principalities and powers go to war, even for theoretically "good" reasons, collateral damage is just part of the price that has to be paid for the "good" that the war is intended to achieve.

A society of the principalities and powers is dualistic. There has to be an "in" group and an "out" group. There must be outcasts. The society's identity is based on what is wrong with *those* people, the enemy. The *other people* are always impure in some way. They contaminate what should be a "pure" society and so society must be "purified."

Most devastating of all, a society of the principalities and powers is mendacious. The need to cover up the truth of collective violence in primitive societies carries over to the most sophisticated of modern societies. Part of this mendacity is to blame the victim. The blame that many U. S. politicians cast on women who are raped is a particularly grisly example. Victims of lynching, too, were blamed for what happened to them. It is instructive that the psalms that complained of persecution also complained of lying. The Psalmist who is for peace while others speak for war prays to be saved from "lying lips and from deceitful tongues." (Ps. 120:2) Elsewhere, the Psalmist prays: "Let their lying lips be silenced, for with pride and contempt they speak arrogantly against the righteous." (Ps. 31:18) So bad is systemic mendacity that "everyone lies to their neighbor; they flatter with their lips but harbor deception in their hearts." (Ps. 12:2) Then, famously, in a state of alarm the

Psalmist cries out: "Everyone is a liar!" (Ps. 116:11)

Everything about the sacrificial system of the principalities and powers amounts to what we can call the anti-Church. What the Church *is* has been hinted at several times and will be explored in detail below. The apostolic preaching at Pentecost proclaimed the birth of the Church in the gathering of persecutors of the Forgiving Victim by the Holy Spirit. The Holy Spirit gave everybody present the gift of tongues, allowing people to *understand* one another. The Holy Spirit, then, is gathering everybody into God's desire. The essence of the Church, the essence of God's desire, is told by Jesus in the Parable of the Lost Sheep in Luke 15:3–7. Not surprisingly, Jesus tells this parable to the Pharisees and teachers of the Law who muttered about Jesus' table fellowship, a typical attitude fostered by the principalities and powers. This parable is a direct refutation of Caiaphas's conviction that it is better for one person to die than for the whole people to perish. In the parable, the shepherd leaves the ninety-nine and goes in search of the one sheep that has gone astray. When he finds the lost sheep there is great rejoicing, something that would never happen under the rule of the principalities and powers. Jesus has expressed God's desire as precisely the opposite of the "logic" of a sacrificial society.

The story of the woman caught in the act of adultery in John is poised between the mimetic movement towards scapegoating persecution and the mimetic movement that the Holy Spirit would move us toward. The scribes and the Pharisees pose a double-bind question to Jesus typical of the questions posed in the Synoptic Gospels. This time, the ganging up on Jesus is intensified by attempted collective violence against a woman who was caught breaking a law of Moses. There is a real possibility that both the woman and Jesus will be stoned before this is over. There are many speculations about what Jesus wrote on the ground but I think Gil Bailie's suggestion offered in an oral presentation is the most likely: "Jesus was stopping the show." When a crowd is building up steam to kill someone, creating a hiatus is one of the most effective ways of stopping the momentum. The period of silence then sets the stage for people to actually listen to what Jesus says: "Let anyone among you who is without sin be the first to throw a stone at her." (Jn. 8:7)

These words start a different mimetic process with the eldest among them being the model for how to follow these words until the crowd has all moved away.

In the greatest of all Jeremiah's prophecies, he declared that God would make a new covenant with God's people, not like the covenant God made when God delivered the people from Egypt, a covenant they broke. This time: "I will put my law in their minds and write it on their hearts. I will be their God, and they will be my people. No longer will they teach their neighbor, or say to one another, 'Know the Lord,' because they will all know me, from the least of them to the greatest . . . For I will forgive their wickedness." (Jer. 31:33–34) Note how forgiveness is wrapped up with the Law written in our hearts. In the same spirit, God promises through Ezekiel: "I will give you a new heart and put a new spirit in you; I will remove from you your heart of stone and give you a heart of flesh. And I will put my Spirit in you and move you to follow my decrees and be careful to keep my laws." (Ezek. 36:26–27) One can hardly imagine a more powerful statement of God infusing God's desire into us than this.

This infusion of God's desire into human hearts is deepened in John's Gospel, where Jesus affirms a close mimetic resonance with his Abba: "the Son can do nothing on his own, but only what he sees the Father doing; for whatever the Father does, the Son does likewise." (Jn. 5:19) Here, Jesus is expressing the deep familiar love between himself and the Father that is captured by the Aramaic word "Abba," the word a child used to address his or her father. This word even appears in Romans 8:15 when Paul says that it is by the Holy Spirit that we cry out: "Abba, Father!" Jesus goes on to say that he does whatever his Abba is doing. That is, Jesus and his Abba desire the same things and out of their shared desire they do the same things. Jesus also affirms his close mimetic desire with the Paraclete (Holy Spirit) when he says that the Spirit "will not speak on his own, but will speak whatever he hears and he will take what is mine and declare it to you." (Jn. 16:13–14) What we have here is a Trinitarian flow of mimetic desire between the Abba, the Son and the Holy Spirit. That is, the Trinity is filled with mimetic desire that is not at all rivalrous but rather resonates in perfect harmony. We can also see here that the Persons of the Trinity are not autonomous individuals but are comprised of their relationships.

In his high priestly prayer, Jesus includes all of humanity in the flow of the Trinity's mimetic desire: "As you, Father, are in me and I am in you, may they also be in us." (Jn. 17:21) Jesus says that he has given us everything that he has received from his Abba. That is, Jesus has gifted us with God's desire. In participating in God's desire, we are participating in the death and Resurrection of Christ, as Paul proclaims in several of his epistles. This mutual participation of persons in mimetic desire is the backdrop for Paul's admonition: "Be imitators of me, as I am of Christ" (1 Cor. 11:1). Imitation is not just external action but internal sharing of God's desire among all of us. In the next chapter, we will reflect on God's acts through Christ that bring us into the heart of God's desire.

Chapter 5
A Word from Above

This chapter will concentrate on the divine initiative, namely God's entry into humanity as Jesus, born of Mary, to destroy the principalities and powers from within. By concentrating on what God did through Jesus, we will take a narrative approach that has much in common with the dramatic theology of Raymund Schwager in his book *Jesus in the Drama of Salvation*. A dramatic theology stresses the *story* of redemption as it unfolds as a drama. Schwager used the dramatic theology of Hans Urs von Balthasar, although the two differ in some significant ways in how they understand this drama. In my presentation of dramatic theology, the Christian year as celebrated in many churches will be the framework

Creation

It is tempting to place Creation as the first act or the prolog of the story, but that would be a misunderstanding of Creation. Creation includes the creation of time, but Creation is not bound by time and certainly is not the beginning as far as God is concerned. To put human mimetic desire in context, I elaborated on the bounty and generosity of God. Far from the universe being filled with mimetic rivalry at all levels, as mythology would have it, God's Creation is filled with divine generosity at all levels, no matter how frantically we humans try to thwart that generosity. The most important thing about Creation is that it is not a one-shot deal. Creation is a continuous process. God renews the strength of those who wait on God so that we can "mount up with wings like eagles." (Isa. 40:31) When Jesus drives out demons and calms the stormy waters, Jesus is renewing Creation. Jesus echoes the Creation of humanity out of the earth when he moistens a handful of dust with spittle to heal the eyes of the man born blind. (Jn. 9:6) By being fruitful and multiplying through sexual reproduction and other acts of invention and nurturing, we renew the earth and participate in God's Creation.

A basic question for us as created beings is whether or not we, on our own, could have come to see the truth of sacred violence and effectively initiated a process of reversing the systems of principalities and powers without divine intervention. The short answer is that we don't know. It hadn't happened by the time that Jesus was born into our world, but that does not prove it couldn't have. Girard is quite adamant that humanity was not capable of seeing the truth about what it was doing until Jesus revealed the truth in his Passion and Resurrection. This is quite a sweeping judgment, but outside of the Hebrew Bible there is close to nothing that comes to mind to refute this generalization. Girard's theory would predict this to be the case, and Paul's assertions that humanity is too deeply enslaved by sin to escape it without the help of divine grace would also corroborate this position.

However, when we consider that we are all created by God with mimetic desire, and that mimetic desire can create wholesome connections between people, one might think that some people may have caught on to the truth of sacred violence at least to some extent. An interesting phenomenon that occurred between the eighth and third centuries BC clearly indicates some human ability to see the problem with sacred violence. This period of collective awakening in humanity is customarily called the Axial Age. In several cultures, there was a questioning of and withdrawal from sacrificial rites, especially where animals and humans were concerned. It was the Hebrew prophets who were by far the most articulate on the subject, and they coupled their critiques with oracles that revealed the truth about collective violence behind sacrifice. In India, the *Brahmanas* edged away from sacrifice as Girard pointed out (2011) and Brian Collins corroborated at greater length (2014). The Upanishadic tradition turned away from sacrificial practices to intense inward meditation. Jainism and Buddhism did the same. They all seem to have seen a smoking gun in sacrificial rituals. It is instructive that these new movements in India rejected the Vedic caste system, although Jainism created a caste system of its own that was relatively less hierarchal. In China, Lao Tzu and Chuang Tzu preached withdrawal from conflictive societies to seek union with the Tao. In all of these traditions, deep meditation and contemplation is the route to escaping from a sacrificial society and one's own participation in it. In Christianity, meditation and contemplation are also important means of moving out of the system of the principalities and powers and into the realm of Christ, but these practices come later in this tradition. Inner enlightenment has never been the focus of Christianity the way it is for Buddhism, for example. It is the prophetic call for repentance that is central, and meditation has evolved as a powerful way to repent deeply and change our lives. Confucius remained involved with society but sought to limit mimetic rivalry. It occurs to me that the ancestral rites in honor of ancestors were an extension of filial respect in this life that could limit conflict between generations. Many examples of insights into the problem of mimetic violence could be noted. I will confine myself to three powerful examples.

One of the most memorable teachings attributed to the Buddha is the "Parable of the Burning House" in the third chapter of the *Lotus Sutra*. A dilapidated house catches fire while the children are playing inside. They are so absorbed in their games that they do not want to come out of the burning house, no matter how urgently their father calls them. In the end, the father has to make extravagant promises of the rarest and greatest of toy chariots to entice them to come out. Once the children are outside the house and are safe, they wonder where the toys are. Their father, being very rich, gives them carriages of great size and beauty, way beyond their wildest, childish dreams. (*Lotus Sutra* 1976, 64–65) From the standpoint of mimetic realism, it is not difficult to see the burning of a dilapidated house as an image of a society engulfed in mimetic violence that threatens to destroy the society, much as the Flood in Noah's time threatened to destroy humanity. Meditation such as taught by Buddha and the Upanishadic sages and Christian mystics is often dubbed as escapist. However, most people don't think of escaping from a burning house to be a bad thing. Given the phenomenon of scarcity caused by mimetic rivalry, it is instructive that once the children are outside the burning house, there is mind-boggling abundance such as the abundance Jesus created in the wilderness for the four and five thousand people.

The second example is the Theban plays of Sophocles. *Oedipus the King* has been studied at length by Girard and Sandor Goodhart for the mimetic tensions and the scapegoating of Oedipus, who is blamed for the plague, another image of a society in mimetic crisis. Goodhart argues that Sophocles seems to have believed that Oedipus was innocent and gave clues covertly for the reader or watcher of a performance to see this, but he was carefully subtle about it. After all, plays in Athens were performed at the Festival of Dionysus, a highly sacrificial god who was torn to pieces and whose devotees tore people into pieces during their frenzies. (Goodhart 1996, 13–41) In *Intimate Domain*, Martha Reineke demonstrates that in *Antigone*, Sophocles takes his insights much deeper. Antigone shows a deep, self-sacrificing love by burying her brother's body against express orders from Creon. She dies a sacrificial death for her defiance, but she dies not as a sacrificial victim but on her own terms, as Jesus died on his own terms and not those of Pontius Pilate or Caiaphas. Since Antigone dies outside of the city, she has died outside of the system of the persecutory polis. In this way, Reineke suggests that she has become a figure of Christ. (Reineke 2014, 167–168)

The execution of Socrates is a well-known example of collective murder, one that has inspired comparisons with the execution of Jesus. William Blake Tyrrell (2014) analyzes the political and social dynamics in Athens at the time of the trial of Socrates and shows clearly how riddled the city-state was with rivalry. The sentence of death was not unanimous but it was a large majority, and nobody on the jury who voted against the death penalty went down in history as protesting the result. Interestingly, Tyrrell points out how Socrates himself acted in a rivalrous way in his debates, and to that extent, fueled the rivalries surrounding him. Socrates showed this same style of debate in his *Apologia* with the result that more people voted for the death penalty than had voted for a guilty verdict in the first place. Socrates's acceptance of the death sentence, however, as opposed to trying to escape, showed a clear intention to calm the strife about him through his death, something that would not have happened if he had gone into exile.

The relationship between Christianity and other religions as understood through mimetic realism is both important and complicated. Since this book is devoted to Christian spirituality, there is not enough space to explore the ways Christianity can be enriched and renewed with the help of other traditions, nor the ways that Christian spirituality can enrich and renew mimetic realism. In any case, I wouldn't want to presume to suggest how Buddhists, Hindus, or Muslims might use mimetic realism in their faiths. I leave it to adherents of these faiths to make these explorations.

Inter-faith dialogue these days is usually cordial, mainly because those who participate in it are inclined to listen to people of other traditions with respect and explain their own faiths with deep conviction. In this sort of approach, there is no blurring of distinctions between religions. The day when well-meaning people thought there was a religious melting pot that would make all religions one is, for the most part, well past. Brian McLaren presents a thought experiment where we imagine a meeting of inter-religious dialogue between Moses, Jesus, Buddha, and Muhammad. Would the four of them spend their time fighting over who was the greatest? McLaren, for one, cannot imagine such a thing. (2012, 3–4) In any case, it is important for each of us to be more attentive to abiding sacrificial aspects in our faiths rather than dwell on what we think is wrong with others. If I am right that we should take Jesus at his word when he quoted Hosea's oracle that God wants mercy rather than sacrifice, then we'd do well to listen to people of other faiths—and no faith—for what we can learn from them in this important matter. It is in this spirit that I continue to share the powerful revelation of a totally loving and forgiving God as proclaimed in the story and teachings of Jesus.

Advent

The season of Advent captures a sense of expectation that humanity was gradually catching on to the fact that it was living in a burning house, inundated by a flood, and overwhelmed by a plague, all of which were things beyond the grasp of humans to deal with. After centuries without a prophet, a wave of expectation flooded Judea and Galilee when a man named John, dressed the way Elijah had dressed, came along. He rode this wave of expectation and pushed it by proclaiming that something, *someone* was coming, although John did not know what or who. He was a voice crying in the wilderness, feeling as lost as anyone else save for the conviction that God, who had done great things in the past, was about to do something that would really turn the world upside down.

In this conviction, John the Baptist cried out with Isaiah's words: "Prepare the way of the Lord, make his paths straight." (Isa. 40:3; Mt. 3:3) Isaiah was referring to the return of God's people to their rightful home from which they had been uprooted by the Babylonians. Even today, we live in exile by not living our lives in God as we ought. In this way, we make the world a distortion of what God intended. The call to repentance (*metanoia*) in John's baptism means, literally, to turn our minds. This does not mean filling our minds with new ideas; it means turning our whole embodied selves in a new direction to see and live in a different way, a way that will be more in tune with the desires of our Creator.

Isaiah inspired many of the proclamations John made. The prophet prophesied a leveling process where the valleys will be filled in, the mountains brought low, and the crooked ways straightened. That is, the obstacles within ourselves and within our culture that prevent God from coming to us will be removed. The image of leveling seems to suggest a social upheaval where the mighty are brought low and the lowly are raised up, so that all come together on the same level. This would be to overlook the real obstacle to God: our tendency to compare ourselves with one another without reference to God. This leaves us preoccupied with being better than others or fretting that others are better than us. This preoccupation and the resentment it fosters maintain the isolating barriers of valleys and mountains and block the way to God.

Repentance takes the form of renouncing our rivalrous entanglement with others so that we can open ourselves to God's leveling process that holds everybody in the same regard without exalting some or lowering others. Unfortunately, while God is smoothing out the way for us, we prefer to maintain the barriers that we think protect us. Opening a highway for God makes us vulnerable, not only to God but to all of God's people. Take out the valleys and mountains and anybody could come deeply into our lives! Isaiah gives us fair warning of where this leveling process is going by declaring that "the glory of the Lord shall be revealed, and all people shall see it together." (Isa. 40:5) Note that we are to see God's glory *together*, not as isolated individuals.

Like all analogies, the analogy of smoothing out the landscape has its liabilities. Flat ground makes for boring scenery, while valleys and mountains take our breath away. God doesn't destroy the landscapes God has made. That means, if we turn our embodied minds around, we see that God's leveling process is to rejoice in the valleys and mountains and twists of the road without rivalry or resentment.

Two other astounding prophecies by Isaiah offer us intriguing, inspiring, but puzzling hints about what the Kingdom might be like. He urges us to turn "swords into plowshares" and "spears into pruning hooks" so that we will not "learn war any more." (Isa. 2:4) Then, he promises, "The wolf shall live with the lamb." (Isa. 11:6) So, now we have all of Creation at peace? Not quite. Isaiah tells us that the "shoot from the stump of Jesse" (Isa. 11:1) will "smite the earth with the rod of his mouth, and with the breath of his lips he shall slay the wicked." (Isa. 11:4) Apparently taming lions and tigers and bears is easier than taming predatory humans. The predatory lenders of today seem just as untamable. John seems to have thought that humans needed taming when he warned the people that another would be coming with a winnowing fork in his hand. He will "clear his threshing floor and will gather his wheat into the granary; but the chaff he will burn with unquenchable fire." (Mt. 3:12) As it turned out, John's successor didn't wield the kind of winnowing fork John expected he would.

Then the one John was proclaiming came to him. John sensed that Jesus was the one he was prophesying and seems to have been flummoxed when Jesus asked to be baptized by him. So begins an enigmatic relationship, one that provided the perfect recipe for mimetic rivalry. But that did not happen. The main reason it didn't happen is because, for all his following and popularity, John insisted that he was a forerunner for someone greater than himself. Far from competing with Jesus, John said that "he must increase, but I must decrease." (Jn. 3:30) It's no wonder then, that he was shocked when asked to baptize the man he thought was the one who would increase.

At first, Jesus imitated John by crying out the same words: "Repent, for the kingdom of heaven has come near," (Mt. 4:17) but it wasn't long before Jesus' path diverged from John's. The Sermon on the Mount was very different from warning people that God was about to thresh out the bad guys with a winnowing fork and burn them. One might argue that later Jesus himself had some choice words for the Sadducees and Pharisees, such as calling them whitewashed tombs filled with people's bones. (Mt. 23:27) But Jesus wasn't chopping off their heads or burning them up; he was warning them about how dead they were. By the time John was in prison, he seemed confused as to what his successor was about and he sent some followers to question Jesus. The reply Jesus sent back to John is: "Blessed is anyone who takes no offense at me." (Mt. 11:6) When the time came, John seems to have struggled with decreasing while Jesus increased, but clearly he was doing his best.

Christmas

When John says that the Word became flesh and dwelt among us, (Jn. 1:14) he is sharing a mystery so deep that we don't know what to say. What is more, the Word *was* God. Which is to say, the Word *is* God for all time. (Jn. 1:1–3)

So why would the Word enter into the Creation that the Word shaped? Isn't that ultimate downward mobility? Later in his Gospel, John says that

God so loved the world that God gave God's only begotten Son. (Jn. 3:16) This was a costly gift since God's only son died on the cross. Suddenly, the Word, who seems so abstract in the rarefied language of the opening words of John's Gospel, is much more concrete and understandable. Except why would God love us so much as to do such a thing? Looking around at ourselves, there seems to be no accounting for taste.

What is so amazing is that God, who we might think is the ultimate in invulnerability, chooses to be vulnerable. God's vulnerability is attested by the prophets who spoke of God's distress over human waywardness and infidelity, but even then, the Word was not vulnerable to the "boots of the tramping warriors." (Isa. 9:5) But once the Word was born in the flesh of a human mother and laid in a manger, the Word had become just as vulnerable to trampling boots and automatic rifles as the children at Sandy Hook School in Newtown, Connecticut, and the children slaughtered in and around Bethlehem by order of King Herod. (Mt. 2:16)

Here is where the mystery deepens so profoundly as to escape comprehension. It goes against what we think are our deepest instincts. We do everything to make ourselves less vulnerable, from putting on plated armor, to hardening our feelings, to buying weapons to defend us from the "slings and arrows of outrageous fortune," to quote Hamlet. If the Word, without whom nothing that was made was made, is willing to be so defenseless, then perhaps it isn't really our deepest instinct to defend ourselves so aggressively after all.

Perhaps if we, like Mary, ponder these things deeply in our hearts, we will find within ourselves a love created by God that loves so abundantly that it melts all our defenses and we need no longer worry about accounting for God's taste. Surely Mary started to ponder the mystery in her heart the moment Gabriel announced her conception of the Christ Child. What could the angel's greeting mean?

The number of deities begetting human children by human women in mythology are so legion that some people have noted scornfully that anybody who was anybody in the ancient world was born of a virgin. But the birth of Jesus was quite different. Hindu deities tended to use trickery, often disguising themselves by taking the form of the husbands of the women they wanted to seduce. (Doniger, 2000) Gods like Zeus used brute force, but Mary was *asked* if she would allow the Holy Spirit to overshadow her and when she said "Let it be with me according to your word," (Lk. 1:38) the impregnation was done with the fiery gentleness that is the Holy Spirit's character.

I discussed in Chapter 1 the Greek word *doxa*, often translated as glory but also meaning shame, and applied it to Jesus. The same applies to his mother Mary and his human father Joseph. Conceiving a child by the Holy Spirit put Mary in an awkward social situation. Since she was betrothed to Joseph, she was expected to be sexually faithful to him, as if they were already married. If Mary had been single, she would have been in an equally disgraceful position. In short, Mary was in a place of shame. Many medieval mystery plays emphasize Mary's disgrace. For example, there is the scene where she has to drink the water of bitterness in the temple to prove her innocence. (Num. 5:19) One of the things Mary surely pondered was the mystery of God choosing to become vulnerable by becoming a child conceived in her womb. This conception made her vulnerable as well, or rather the annunciation challenged her to participate in God's elected vulnerability.

Joseph, of course, was placed in an equally disgraceful position. Being a "just man," he resolved to divorce Mary privately. The Greek word *dikaios*, translated as "just," is rich in meaning. It suggests that Joseph was a follower of the Jewish Law, which required he divorce a betrothed woman who had proven to be unfaithful, but also that Joseph was "just" in the broader sense of being sensitive to Mary and doing what he could to minimize the embarrassment for all. In a dream, an angel told Joseph the truth of what had happened and Joseph solidified his relationship with Mary and the child-to-come. Their child would grow up to occupy places of honor and shame to a much greater degree than they did.

Other people in the Christmas story also occupied a place of shame. Shepherds were outsiders, distrusted by all. They were considered so untrustworthy that they were not allowed to testify in court. So why would the angel of the Lord show such bad taste by revealing the birth of the Savior to *them*?

The Magi were highly placed insiders in their own country, most likely top advisors of royalty. So why would they travel to another land where they were outsiders? If the star was there for all to see, why did these foreigners respond when others did not? The Magi, used to being insiders where they came from, went straight to the top by asking King Herod which newborn child the star was indicating. Ironically, Herod was an Idumean, not a full-blooded Jew. He had power, but he was an outsider. Herod's reaction to the Magi's inquiry showed him to be an outsider also to humanitarian feelings once he thought his power was threatened. He acted in the typical fashion of the principalities and powers. Mixed racial background aside, being rich and powerful pushes one to the margins of society as much as the poverty of the despised shepherds.

These days, we easily see Herod as an outsider, an intrusive foreign element entering the story only to stir up trouble and grief. The shepherds and the Magi are insiders, like us. How did that happen? There is a certain sleight of hand that turns us into insiders when it suits us. Not only do we not wish to be outsiders, we don't like to be challenged by outsiders. If we realize that the shepherds and Magi and the Holy Family were outsiders, our identities as insiders are shaken at a deep level. If it is outsiders who appreciated the richness of the Christ Child, maybe the same thing happens today. After all, some nonbelievers care more about the poor than rich Christians, and Mohandas Gandhi, a Hindu early in the twentieth century believed in the Sermon on the Mount more than many Christians of his time.

The ultimate insider in the Roman Empire was the emperor. But it was to the despised shepherds that the angels sang: "Glory to God in the highest heaven, and on earth peace among those whom he favors!" (Lk. 2:14) This sounds innocuous, but it is one of the most subversive verses in the Bible. Peace was the Emperor's prerogative, not anybody else's. Of course the emperor established peace on *his* terms, which entailed the subjugation of various peoples and the enslavement of many. The angels—and God—were turning this upside down. The emperor has become the outsider and the helpless child in the manger has become the insider, the one who will bring true peace. The greatest irony is that Christ was born to save all people, to make insiders of all of us. The problem is, we don't want to be insiders with those who are outsiders, and we certainly don't want outsiders to join us. After all, what would we do if there were no outsiders?

Baptism and Temptations

At his baptism by John in the Jordan River, Jesus heard a voice from Heaven saying: "This is my beloved Son with whom I am well pleased." (Mt. 3:17) Jesus must have experienced these powerful words, proclaimed by his heavenly Abba, as an assurance of unconditional love. He was going to need the strength of this assurance in the trials immediately ahead of him.

No sooner had he undergone baptism than Jesus was thrown out into the desert by the Spirit and tempted by Satan, the stumbling block that comes from mimetic rivalry. The affirmation of Jesus at his baptism was purely gratuitous, totally beyond any entanglement of mimetic rivalry. However, even for the best of us, temptations to entangle ourselves in rivalrous relationships abound. The author of Hebrews says that Jesus is a high priest who has sympathy for our human weakness because "he was tested as we are." (Heb. 4:15) The three temptations recorded in Matthew and Luke all have to do with mimetic issues. Turning stones into bread seems not to be a bad thing if you can do it, which Jesus presumably could. Otherwise it wouldn't have been much of a temptation. But if Jesus had followed the devil's suggestion, he would have been making bread on his own terms rather than on the terms of his heavenly Abba. The bread he later gave in the wilderness was a gift from the Abba through Jesus to the crowd. Throwing himself off the temple roof would have made a public spectacle of himself. He would have become quite a celebrity that way. That would have been quite the opposite of commending his spirit into his Abba's hands on the cross. Attempting to rule the kingdoms of the world would, of course, entail entering directly into the entanglements of the principalities and powers on the terms of those powers. Jesus presumably could have used his charisma to take control of the known world, but the world would have no way out of humanity's enslavements to empire if he had done so. The imperialistic rule of so many Christian powers proves this point beyond any doubt.

Acts of Healing

Right after his return from his testing in the desert, Jesus proclaims the Year of Jubilee: that we would give sight to the blind and let the oppressed go free. (Lk 4:18) Given the blindness and entrapment caused by mimetic rivalry, the two go hand in hand. Only if we let others be free do we release ourselves, and freeing others opens our eyes so that we can really see. I sense that this jubilee wasn't just to recur every seven years but was to be the norm for all time. Right from the start, Jesus suffers the fate of celebrities. Everybody is amazed at "the gracious words that came from his mouth" but immediately they begin wrangling among themselves since he is only the son of Joseph the carpenter. (Lk. 4:22) When Jesus tries to broaden their horizons by reminding them of the widow at Zarephath in Sidon whose son was cured and Naaman the Syrian whose leprosy was cleansed, they try to drive Jesus over a cliff. Jesus escapes this time, but the shape of his life and ministry has already been established. Jesus has discerned that one of the fundamental challenges in his life and teachings was to expand our sense of humanity so that the positive, nurturing mimetic desire we share with others in our group are extended to those outside the group.

After saying that he would give sight to the blind and let the oppressed go free, Jesus proceeded to do just that in healing the sick and casting out demons. This ministry is given the strongest emphasis in Mark's Gospel, where the first several chapters consist mainly of healings and exorcisms. Lest one think that gender inclusiveness is a modern invention, one should note Mark's inclusiveness in his healing narratives, where he shows the healings of men and women and boys and girls. Everybody matters to Jesus. Healings and exorcisms are difficult for many of us to take seriously because it is hard for many to accept the miraculous. The important thing is to realize that Jesus is creating a *climate* of healing, a social climate that *we* are invited to participate in. That is, Jesus is seeking to spread his desire that we be healed of our infirmities so that we also will desire it not only for ourselves and our loved ones but for everybody. Most of us do not have a gift of healing through the laying on of hands (though some do), but all of us can and should do what we can to promote healing. Doctors and medical researchers do much to bring about the healing of people who in former times would not have been healed and also do much to prevent diseases and other medical problems. Hospitals are a Christian invention as far as I can see, an institution inspired by the example of Jesus. On the other hand, we still have to fight against elements in our social climate and environment that are detrimental to our health. Doing everything we can do to make the air breathable for all is part of extending Jesus' healing ministry.

The healing of the paralytic in Mark's version is a particularly dramatic narrative illustrating the social dimension of healing. The crowd gathering in the house in Capernaum, where Jesus was staying, had become so great that it created an obstacle to the healing of the paralytic man. Nobody was letting him in! So, his friends carried him up to the roof, dug through the roof, and let him into the room through the hole they had made. Quite an effort to bring the man in range for the healing! This was also a sacrifice on the part of the owner of the house who had some repairs to make. Jesus said something we still find strange: "Son, your sins are forgiven." (Mk. 2:5) As we'll see below, Jesus was not equating sickness with sin but, but by saying that the paralytic's sins are forgiven, he was putting healing in the context of repentance. That is, the healing of society requires a whole new way of relating with one another, a way modeled by those who made such efforts to bring the paralytic to Jesus. The friends' efforts are an even greater contrast to the scribes who took umbrage at Jesus for taking what they thought should be God's prerogative to forgive sins. I would add that these scribes probably didn't think God gave forgiveness so freely. In healing the paralytic, we see that Jesus was doing battle not only with physical infirmities but social infirmities as well.

What makes Jesus' healing of the Man Born Blind in John's Gospel (Chapter 9) remarkable is that man would have needed a radical overhaul of his neurological system so that his brain could grasp what was being seen. John didn't know about neurology, but he did know that *really* learning to see involves at least as radical an overhaul of our human system to heal our deeper levels of blindness. John shows us the blindness in the social climate around the blind man when the disciples ask Jesus if it was the man's own sin or the sin of his parents that caused him to be born blind. (Jn. 9:2) The notion that the poor guy sinned before he was born should be enough to show us how blind this attitude is. This social blindness was compounded by excluding the blind man from the religious practices of Judaism. Neither the Jewish leaders nor even Jesus' disciples could see any potential worth in the blind man.

Jesus took the man's blindness as an occasion for revealing God's work rather than for blame. By daubing the man's eyes with mud, he was re-enacting, in miniature, the creation of humanity out of the moist earth. The Jewish leaders reacted to the healing with anger. They seemed determined from the start to discredit the healing rather than change their own way of seeing. Their search for blame was rewarded when they discovered that the healing was done on the Sabbath.

It is important not to let Gospel stories such as this discredit the Jewish practice of the Sabbath. It was a great gift for Jews and for Christians, who treat Sunday in a similar fashion, a day for renewal. That is the key: a day for renewal. The Man Born Blind is being recreated on the Sabbath. In sharp contrast to the paralytic in John 5, who remained as paralyzed as far as personal growth was concerned, no matter how much he carried his mat, the formerly blind man shows himself to be renewed at a very deep level. The clever way he handles the hostile questions from the Jewish leaders reveals a man with sharp intelligence and wit. Meanwhile, the Jewish leaders make it clear that their initial judgment that the blind man was a sinner and an outcast was immutable. As long as he was blind he was an outcast, and once he could see, he was cast out for being healed by the wrong person in the wrong way at the wrong time. There can, of course, be no renewal, no re-creation if we insist on being immutable in judgment, neither can we see renewal or re-creation even when it takes place right under our noses. As with Jesus' healing of the paralytic in Mark, Jesus is fighting against a social climate hostile to healing.

But the Man Born Blind shows that he sees even more. James Alison coined the phrase the "intelligence of the victim" to draw attention to the privileged point of view a victim has of reality as a result of being the victim. (Alison 1993) The Man Born Blind shows a deep insight into what life was about and also into what God was about because he was blind and an outcast. During the grilling he received from the Jewish leaders, (Jn. 9:13–34) he was given the opportunity of repudiating Jesus the way the paralytic did, which would have brought him approbation from the crowd and the authorities. Instead, he staunchly defended Jesus, which landed him in precisely the same place of blame and expulsion as Jesus himself. It is in this place, where he's always been, that the man really *sees*. That means that we also will *see* only if we also enter the place of the victim rather than that of the persecutors.

The disciples fade from the story after their question about who sinned, but far from really disappearing, their circle expands to include all of us who read and hear the story. This expansion forces us to choose: Will we let Jesus re-create us in the place of shame shared with the man born blind and Jesus himself, or will we hop out of the circle so that our lives will continue to be etched in stone as we remain fixed on persecution?

I have already noted in passing that one reason we have trouble believing in the stories about Jesus' healings is that miraculous healings don't happen very often. More to the point, we see people die all the time. We gain some perspective when we realize that every person Jesus healed and even those few he raised from the dead still died at a later time. The same is true of those today who are healed miraculously through prayer. A climate of health does not mean that people do not die, but it does mean that people do not die unnecessarily of curable diseases. A climate of healing also means that we do everything we can to comfort those with chronic illnesses that don't get better. Hospice care is an example of this ministry in a powerful way, a way that involves not only the professionals but the family of the dying person. Such a climate greatly increases the chances that God's light and love will become visible as the person dies.

The exorcisms are even harder to relate to, and the story of the Gerasene demoniac and the herd of pigs running off a cliff is particularly bewildering to modern readers. (Mk. 5:1–20) Girard helps us understand the story when he suggests that the people in the town are possessed by one another as a result of intense mimetic rivalry. (Girard 1985, 165–186) If one person stands out as being "possessed," that person is possessed by mimetic rivalries that have reached a crisis level. Those rivalries are absorbed by one victim, or the "designated patient," to use the term of Edwin Friedman. (Friedman 1985, 19–20) Girard points out that Matthew's version heightens the mimetic aspect of the story by having two demoniacs who mimic each other. When people possess other people in such destructive ways, they create an unhealthy climate.

When Jesus and his disciples arrive on the scene, they are not greeted by the mayor or any of the "normal" people; they are greeted by the demoniac, who begs Jesus not to torment him (them). That the demon(s) gives its name as "Legion" confirms that this man is possessed by the community, and is also possessed by the Romans, whose occupation surely increases the tensions within the local community. The demoniac is regularly chained but just as regularly breaks free, a pattern that mimics the repetition of ritual. That is to say, this pattern represents the town's sense of stability, much as the incarceration of multitudes of black youths from the ghettos gives the more powerful citizens of the U. S. a similar sense of stability today.

Jesus sends the demons into the herd of pigs that then runs off a cliff into the sea. We have here an interesting reversal of the scapegoating mechanism, since usually it is the town that drives a single victim off the cliff, a fate Jesus has narrowly avoided himself a few times. Upon seeing the formerly possessed man clothed and in his right mind, the townspeople ask Jesus to leave. One would think that they would be happy to see a sick person cured and would ask Jesus to stay and cure everybody else of whatever ails them. But they don't. Why? Because the people of the Gerasene region are not happy over being robbed of their victim. The demons requested that they not be expelled from the town because the people, possessed by their rivalries, wanted to remain possessed. When robbed of their victim, the possessed town implodes in its collective violence and becomes the sacrificial victim. When a community "needs" a victim, for somebody to be sick, then the community is toxic. It cannot stand.

The anthropological dimension of this story can be seen more clearly by comparing it with that of the Samaritan woman at the well, which has none of the mythological trappings. (Jn. 4:1–42) It is the woman at the well, and not any of the other people of Sychar, who greets Jesus. The woman is alone at the most social place in town and at the time of day when nobody else would want to be there, indications that the woman is the town's scapegoat. There is no exorcism, but the woman eventually becomes possessed by Jesus when she drinks the water he has to give, just as the Gerasene demoniac became possessed by Jesus once the demons were driven out. The woman goes to tell the townspeople about Jesus as the Gerasene demoniac was told to spread the word throughout his area of what Jesus had done for him. The story in Sychar has a happier ending than the story in Gerasa. The people come out to listen to Jesus, a mimetic process where they give up their collective victim in exchange for the water of rebirth that Jesus has to give. Perhaps this foretells a happier ending for Gerasa someday and a happier ending for our own society. In these two stories, we can see that the principalities and powers do not refer just to the empire, although that is part of it. Rather, the principalities and powers consist of people just like us. Ordinary people can easily contribute to an unhealthy climate that makes sure some people are sick and don't get well. But just as the Gerasene demoniac was healed, when everybody else in town was not, indicates that those who know they are sick and blind can be healed and those who think they are healthy and can see are really too sick and blind to be healed. Perhaps this is what Jesus was hinting at when he answered those who criticized him for calling the tax collector Matthew, which in Mark he does right after healing the paralytic: "Those who are well have no need of a physician, but those who are sick. I have come to call not the righteous but sinners." (Mk 2:17) Although Jesus bucked unhealthy social climates many times, it could get to be too much. In his home town Capernaum, "he could do no deed of power there, except that he laid his hands on a few sick people and cured them. And he was amazed at their unbelief." (Mk. 6:5)

Matthew was not the only enemy Jesus befriended. Zacchaeus was another. Both were tax collectors who made fortunes at the expense of their own people by colluding with their imperial bosses. When Jesus came to Jericho, he was famous, or notorious enough, that something of a hubbub arose as a result of his passing through the town. People gathered and crowded one another to gawk at the man and his followers. Why the stir? The mayor wasn't exactly giving him the key to the city. Throughout Jesus' journey to Jerusalem, Jesus was set upon by Pharisees and scribes and questioned in front of the crowd. Such questioning, of course, was made with the intention of publicly discrediting the freelance itinerant preacher who was becoming famous for his clever retorts. The result was bound to be entertaining. The scribes and Pharisees were surely on the prowl in a town that large. Zacchaeus's act of climbing a tree to get a look at Jesus need not be taken as an indication that he was inclined to have his life changed by this stranger. His eagerness to see and hear the duel is enough to account for his action. And yet the anticipated debate does not occur. Why? Because Jesus saw Zacchaeus up in the tree. The signs that Zacchaeus was a rich man hated by everybody in town were there to be seen by a person with eyes to see.

That Jesus had discerned the social matrix of Jericho rightly was immediately manifest when Jesus called out to the tax collector and invited himself to that man's house. St. Luke says that "*all* who saw it began to grumble and said, 'He has gone to be the guest of one who is a sinner.'" (Lk. 19:7) Here is another example of Luke's astute anthropological insight. It isn't just the Pharisees and scribes who grumble about Zacchaeus. *Everybody* grumbles about him. Like Simon when confronted with the Woman Who Was a Sinner, (Lk. 7:36–50) the people of Jericho were thinking that if this man were a prophet, he would have known who and what kind of man this was who was sitting up in a tree—that he was a sinner. One doesn't have to be a demonically possessed man or a sinful woman to be a communal scapegoat. A rich man who is a traitor to his people can hold the same position. And deserve it. After all, he was treading down the downtrodden. For scapegoating others, he deserved to be scapegoated. As it happened, Jesus *did* know what kind of man Zacchaeus was. It is through showing us that anybody can be the scapegoat and anybody can be a persecutor that Luke shows the communal scapegoating phenomenon for what it is. Given the fact that Jesus was on the way to Jerusalem with a pretty clear idea of what was going to happen to him there, it behooved Jesus to give his followers every opportunity to see how collective hostility against one person works, in the hope that they would learn to recognize the process when it happens in the Holy City, and that is what he has done here.

As with the Gerasene demoniac, Jesus performs an exorcism of the communal scapegoat, a quiet one this time, but just as effective. The result is that the homeostasis sustained by the scapegoating process is destabilized. There is some ambiguity as to whether or not Zacchaeus is actually converted by his encounter with Jesus or if he had repented earlier but nobody believed it. Bible scholars disagree as to whether the verbs used by Zacchaeus are in the present tense or the future. That is, Zacchaeus may be saying that he *will* give half of his possessions to the poor and pay back four times anybody he has defrauded, but he could be saying that he is *already* doing these things. If Zacchaeus is using the future tense, then he is announcing a change of heart. If Zacchaeus is speaking in the present tense, then he is claiming that he is better, or less terrible, than he has been made out to be. I think our best bet is to look at the implications of either interpretation of the verb tenses.

If Zacchaeus has been converted on the spot by Jesus, and we assume that Jesus did not zap people with a magic wand to override their free will, then we may ask ourselves how this conversion happened. The information in Luke suggests two possibilities. As the communal scapegoat, Zacchaeus had "the intelligence of the victim" and perhaps that intelligence led him to understand what it meant to other people to be the victim of his tax collecting. The other possibility is that an undeserved commendation from Jesus freed Zacchaeus from the necessity of acting in such a way as to justify his designation as communal scapegoat. It is more than likely that both factors played their part here. On the other hand, if Zacchaeus was speaking in the present tense, the implication is that the collective attitude of the townspeople was unjust, which would underline the arbitrary aspect of scapegoating. Generous actions on the part of a rich person who has drawn the collective resentment of the community often do not diminish resentment against him or her. It is also possible, of course, that Zacchaeus is trying to make himself look better than he really is. That is, he is boasting of his good deeds while overlooking the unjust means used for gaining the wealth that he uses for his acts of largesse. If I am right in taking this story as being primarily concerned with communal scapegoating, then the ambiguity enriches the story and there is no need to solve the grammatical problem once and for all.

The challenge of this story, however, is not limited to the possible conversion of one person. It extends to the possible conversion of the whole community. Whether or not Zacchaeus needed to be converted and, if so, whether or not he *did* change his life, is immaterial for the greater challenge. Either way, by singling out Zacchaeus and inviting himself to *that* man's house, Jesus has already robbed Jericho of its scapegoat. The unanimity has been irretrievably broken. That *everybody* turns to grumbling at Jesus for going to the house of a man who is a sinner suggests that Jesus is well on the way to becoming a unanimous object of hatred. Since Jesus is on the way to Jerusalem, where he would, once again, become the object of hatred, it is no surprise that it should happen in Jericho, while he was on the way to the Holy City. This development does not bode well for Jericho becoming a social climate of healing.

Meanwhile, Jesus' disciples have their own challenges with understanding Jesus. After a journey, Jesus asks the disciples: "What were you arguing about on the way?" (Mk. 9:33) The silence that follows is the most deafening silence I have encountered in print. One can feel the anger, shame, and humiliation on the part of the disciples when Mark says the reason for their silence is because "they had argued with one another who was the greatest." It should not be surprising, even if dismaying, that the disciples fell into mimetic rivalry like everybody else. This altercation follows the third time Jesus predicted his death at the hands of the religious authorities and, in Mark, each prediction was followed by scuffling among the disciples. Mark makes it clear that rivalry, betrayal, and persecution all go together.

In spite of their strife over who is the greatest, the disciples suddenly come to an agreement about a woman who enters the house of Simon the Leper in Bethany and pours an enormous amount of costly oil over Jesus to anoint him. (Mt. 26:6–13) A corporate condemnation of a marginal person has united the disciples. To their chagrin, Jesus defends the woman, saying that she has prepared him for burial, precisely the destiny Jesus is facing and the disciples are denying. It is quite possible, however, that for Judas Iscariot, Jesus' defense of the woman was the last straw. In both Mark and Matthew, Judas's fateful interview with the chief priests follows immediately.

Curiously, Luke has a version of the same story that is detached from the passion narrative. (Lk. 7:36–50) It involves a woman is called "The Woman Who Was a Sinner." Simon's attitude towards her suggests that she is a communal scapegoat. This woman makes Jesus' host uncomfortable when she shamelessly washes Jesus' feet with her tears. Simon's attitude mirrors that of the disciples in the other narratives. That is, the disciples who were normally on the other side of the fence from the Pharisee have joined him. This is another foreshadowing of the disciples' betrayal in Jerusalem.

John has a similar, but different account of the anointing of Jesus. (Jn. 12:1–8) The woman is Mary of Bethany and, far from being an intruder into somebody else's house, she is herself the hostess along with her sister Martha. As in Luke's similar story, Mary wipes Jesus' feet with her hair. This time the gesture is all the more suggestive of things to come as John places the incident just before the Last Supper, when Jesus washes the feet of his disciples. This time, Judas alone objects to the waste. John goes on to say that Judas was upset, not because he cared for the poor, but because he wanted to steal more money from the common treasury. The question is: If the disciples unanimously censured the woman as they unanimously opposed Jesus' predictions of his death, was Judas really the only betrayer? Chances are, Judas was saying out loud what the other disciples were thinking.

The little parable Jesus tells to Simon in Luke applies to all three stories, or variants of one story. (Lk. 7:41–43) Two debtors are forgiven by their creditor. Who would love the creditor more? Simon answers that it would be the one who had owed the greater amount. Likewise, The Woman Who Was a Sinner, the communal scapegoat, loved Jesus the most. She certainly loved him more than Simon did and, in the end, more than the disciples did as well. Like the paralytic who was healed, this woman's sins are pre-emptively forgiven.

Luke's story then ends with Jesus telling the woman that her sins are forgiven; her faith has saved her, and she can go in peace. Jesus' forgiveness is not as pre-emptory as it was for the paralytic in Mark in that the woman demonstrates much repentance as well as much love. Even so, Jesus' declaration is enough to scandalize the Pharisees who hear these words. In all of these stories, or possibly versions of one story, a person who is designated a communal scapegoat is upheld by Jesus in such a way as to challenge those who have been doing the scapegoating. When Jesus declares that the woman's sins are forgiven, he points to the blame others have laid upon her. This raises the question: How important is it for us to have someone upon whom we can lay blame? If this woman's sins are forgiven, what about ours?

So far, I have demonstrated how Jesus shows his deep understanding of mimetic rivalry and communal scapegoating. The enigmatic story of the Canaanite woman, (Mt. 15:21–28) however, shows Jesus inside the social matrix, needing to find his way out of it. Two things about the story are perplexing: 1) Jesus' harsh words to a person in need, and 2) Jesus losing a verbal exchange with another and apparently changing his point of view because of that exchange. We are troubled by these points because we usually assume that the divinity of Jesus requires that he was sinless and omniscient. I would argue that being *fully* human means that Jesus was *not* omniscient but had to learn life skills and develop his understanding of life just like any other human. The ludicrousness of the notion that Jesus knew everything about carpentry while an infant should convince us of that. Since sin is not essential to human nature, being sinless would not have compromised his full humanity. However, being fully human would mean that he was born participating in the mimetic matrix of his culture with both its salutary elements and its unsalutary ones. This story helps us explore how Jesus came to terms with a problematic aspect of his cultural inheritance.

Matthew's calling the woman a Canaanite was an anachronism that recalled Israel's historical relationship with this people, in much the same way that calling a contemporary Danish woman a Viking would invoke ten centuries of history for us. Jesus would have grown up absorbing his people's tradition that the Canaanites were the worst of enemies, enemies to be exterminated by the likes of Joshua, enemies who were periodic oppressors of Israel in the period of the Judges. Worst of all, Canaanites were dangerous because they tempted the Israelites to forsake their God in favor of their idols and sacrificial practices. Mark gave the woman the more up-to-date designation of a Syrophoenician. This meant she was a member of the oppressing class of the Roman Empire, which made victims of the Jews. Starting from early childhood, Jesus would have taken in this adversarial relationship before he knew what had possessed him. With this cultural inheritance, it is understandable, if not commendable, that Jesus would speak harshly to a Canaanite (Syrophoenician) woman who came to him for help. Many commentators try to get out of this difficulty by suggesting that Jesus was just testing the woman. That is possible but I would like to follow up the ramifications of accepting the plain sense of this story.

The Canaanite woman's retort is justly famous for its cleverness and humility, qualities that make her words subversive. Jesus seems as amazed by her faith as he is by the faith of the centurion who asked him to heal his servant. (Mt. 8:10) That the woman asked for the deliverance of a daughter possessed by a demon may have aroused Jesus' sympathy. The Gerasene Demoniac had shown Jesus how a dysfunctional culture can possess a person and need to be exorcized. That this woman wanted her daughter delivered of the demon possessing her own culture would alert Jesus of the need to eject the demon of hatred of the Canaanites that had possessed his own culture. This understanding of the story has Jesus modeling the ability and willingness to overcome an ancestral enmity by listening deeply to the reality of a person in need so that she ceases to be an enemy. We desperately need to learn to follow this kind of example offered by Jesus today.

I now wish to pause for a little thought experiment. Imagine being a child or a youth who is carrying five barley loaves and two fishes. A crowd has gathered to listen to a man speak. You've heard that he is causing a stir and might be interesting to listen to so you stop to hear what the fuss is about.

Maybe you are intrigued by what he says; maybe it goes over your head. After a while, you realize that many people are hungry. You are hungry too but you don't need all the food you are carrying. Maybe it occurs to you that you could make a lot of money by selling one of the fish and three or four of the barley loaves to the highest bidder. Before you have a chance to act on this idea, one of the men surrounding the speaker asks you to come meet the speaker. Maybe you are nervous about this, but you want to know why such a man should want to talk to you. To your shock and surprise, the speaker tells you that the people all around are hungry, and he asks if you would be willing to let him give the bread and fish to the crowd. Before you can reply, one of the men says: "But what is this among so many?" You are asking yourself the same thing, but the speaker shrugs off the question. What do you do? Maybe the challenge implied in that question inclines you to find out how many people really can be fed with those loaves and fishes.

As we know from John 6, the lad with the loaves and fishes gave them to Jesus, and Jesus fed the crowd with an exponential amount of food scraps left over. One fairly well-known theory is that the boy shamed everybody else into sharing their food when he handed over what he had. Maybe that is what happened. That would be a good example of a mimetic process creating abundance instead of scarcity. But I think there is more to this story. The references to God feeding the Israelites in the desert and the amazement in the narrative suggest that Jesus was re-enacting God's act of Creation in the wilderness. This mass feeding also recalls Isaiah's prophecy: "You that have no money, come, buy and eat! Come, buy wine and milk without money and without price. Why do you spend your money for that which is not bread, and your labor for that which does not satisfy?" (Isa. 55:1–2) The miracle takes on all the more power when we realize that Jesus did not create food out of nothing, which presumably he could have done, but he created it out of a human act of giving. This miracle, recorded six times in the four Gospels, shows us that God desires abundance in the sense of everybody having enough. (The manna in the desert spoiled if anybody tried to take too much.) But God provides through multiplying our human generosity to others, as the boy gave up the five loaves and two fishes to Jesus in the wilderness. Can we imitate this boy as this boy imitated Jesus?

Parables

Jesus' actions were teachings that we could say were parables in action. Many prophets acted out parables, such as Jeremiah walking about with a yoke over his shoulders to warn the people that they were about to fall under the yoke of Babylon. (Jer. 27:2) Such prophetic actions were like the guerrilla theater that was so popular in the Sixties. The spoken parables usually tell a story that has some action. The word "parable" literally means "something thrown or placed beside." We would expect, then, that just as Jesus' actions often had figurative meanings, that his parables would be stories with meanings below the surface. As Jesus' actions challenge to us to see the truth of how we relate with one another and with him, we would expect that his spoken parables would also deal with the same complexities of relationships, and that is indeed what we find.

One brief parable Jesus told is about two brothers asked by their father to work in the vineyard. One said he would go but he didn't, the other said he wouldn't go but then he did. Which did the will of the father? (Mt. 21:28–32) Jesus' listeners took the bait and took sides, but I don't think that is the way to respond. Short as this parable is, it suggests that the two brothers are embroiled in mimetic rivalry to the extent that they always say the opposite of what the other says and do the opposite as well. That is, they react to each other and not at all to the father. Both then, have failed to respond to the father and both are in need of forgiveness and mercy. When Jesus responds to his listeners by pointing out that tax collectors and prostitutes believed John the Baptist and they didn't, he is hinting that the victims of their mimetic rivalry are entering the Kingdom ahead (and maybe instead) of them.

The Parable of the Sower is given prominence in Mark's Gospel. (Mk. 4:1–20) I used to think the parable asked us what kind of soil we are, and that has some truth to it, but now I think that each type of soil represents not so much individuals as social environments. Thorns that choke the seed suggest social systems that aggressively engulf everybody and leave no room for anything but thorns begetting more thorns. A pathway is a social area where everything on it is trampled. Nothing can take root on a pathway that is only used to get from one place to another. The rocky soil suggests a hard-hearted environment. The more hard-hearted people there are in a social system, the more people will protect themselves through hard-heartedness. The good soil, of course, stands for a social climate receptive to the Word, where everybody nurtures everybody else so that fruit increases exponentially. Jesus' explication of the parable also has social themes. On the pathway, Satan snatches the Word away, an indication of mimetic rivalry taking over. The rocky soil represents a persecutory society. The thorns represent an overwhelming acquisitiveness that chokes compulsive getters and spenders.

It is discouraging enough that three of the four kinds of soil are so inhospitable to the seed (the Word). It is even more discouraging when Jesus says he speaks in parables so that "they may indeed look, but not perceive, and may indeed listen, but not understand; so that they may not turn again and be forgiven." (Mk. 4:12) These words echo Yahweh's words to Isaiah before sending the prophet out on his mission. (Isa. 6:10) It isn't that Jesus wants to be rejected, but the social system is so strong and hard that words alone aren't nearly enough. We all know from hard experience how difficult it is to convince a person who is going down the tubes through addiction or some other destructive behavior to try and turn things around. Mimetic rivalry itself acts as a kind of addiction that has a strong grasp on us. Telling rivals to stop fighting doesn't often end well, but it is important to try. The encouraging thing to note is that the sower doesn't just look for the promising soil and throw the seed there; the sower throws the seed *everywhere*, on the worst soil as well as the best. That is, God is planting the seeds of God's Word in each of us, not giving up on any of us because of our thorniness, rootlessness, or hardness. Jesus shows us this generosity by calling people like Matthew or visiting people like Zacchaeus, neither of whom looked like good soil. Jesus' Parable of the Lost Sheep also assures us that Jesus never considers anybody to be irrevocably lost.

Jesus' Parable of the Wheat and the Weeds (Mt. 13:24–30) throws out the challenge to deal with the discomfort that comes from having to put up with people we don't like. The end of the parable, however, and the explanation afterwards seem to give us the comfort of knowing that the people we don't like will get it in the end. Or does it?

The image of a field densely filled with intertwined plants is easily seen as an image of our entanglement with the desires of other people. Each person who wants something we want that we don't think can be shared is an enemy, a weed who should be pulled out and expelled from the garden. In such a situation, each of us is prone to consider ourselves one of the desirable plants and the others weeds. Of course, when we are preoccupied with how "weedy" everybody else is, we are totally wrapped up with them in our hostility. It is easy, then, to understand this parable as teaching us to mind our own business and not worry about everybody else. The trouble with this interpretation is that we are all in the thick of this garden, and we need to find a constructive way to live with everybody else in it. A deeper interpretation that is often offered, and one I have much sympathy with, is that we should commend everybody else to God and let God deal with them. To make this work, we have to commend ourselves to God as well. Otherwise, we are apt to think that we are commending those bad guys to God but we are good guys who can take care of ourselves.

If we give this parable a Christological interpretation, everything looks different. In being the stone rejected by the builders, Jesus was a weed. That's the way Caiaphas, Pontius Pilate, and Herod saw him. Jesus identified himself with a lot of "weeds" on the way to the cross, such as The Woman Who Was a Sinner who washed his feet at Simon's house. Every planter knows that it can be difficult to tell an intended plant from a weed. This is why well-intentioned but uninformed "helpers" are the bane of gardeners. If we try to weed out the garden based on our own judgment, we are likely to weed out Jesus himself.

The explanation of the parable seems to be at cross-purposes with the parable itself. Many scholars absolve Jesus of having ever given it, relegating the explanation to a later redactor of the text. Or, we can argue that Jesus was giving us a parody of what an obtuse listener who lacks ears to hear takes away from the parable, as Paul Nuechterlein suggests on his site *Girardian Reflections on the Lectionary*. The trouble is, self-righteousness takes us to such extremes that it is impossible to parody. Let's take a look at where the "explanation" takes us. First, we become preoccupied with weeding out the undesirable plants. Second, we identify with the angels who weed the garden. Third, we think we shine in righteousness, which blinds us to our self-righteousness. That is, we play the role of God. The end result is the weeping and wailing and gnashing of teeth for everybody and no harvest for anybody.

If we look forward to *harvesting*, as opposed to weeding, we get a totally different understanding that fits well with the parable itself. When it comes to harvesting, weeds just don't matter. The only thing that does matter is picking the fruits and bringing them in so they can give sustenance to others. When it's all about harvesting, things start to look a lot like the heavenly banquet that all of us can share without worrying about who is wheat and who is a weed.

There is a curious pair of parables, both of which have troublesome and troubling variants in a different Gospel. These are the Parable of the Wedding Feast and the Parable of the Talents. Luke's version of the Parable of the Banquet (Lk. 14:16–24) works well with its traditional and attractive interpretation that God is throwing a great party and everybody is welcome, even, perhaps especially, the outcasts. Matthew's version, which I will examine below, is so different that it could be considered a different parable that uses the image of a banquet. Here, the king acts much more like a tyrant than a gracious and generous host. In Matthew's version of the Parable of the Talents, (Mt. 25:14–30) the traditional interpretation that God gives us talents, some greater than others, that we are expected to do something with, works reasonably well. Even here, the Master is harsh, but there is plenty of room for Raymund Schwager's interpretation that the third servant is projecting a violent image on the Master that prevents him from seeing the generosity of the Gift-Giver. (Schwager 1999, 65) It won't do to attribute these differences to the different emphases of Matthew and Luke (with Luke being "nicer") because each has a violent variant and a kinder variant. Let us look at Matthew's version of the Parable of the Wedding Banquet first. (Mt. 22:1–14)

Here, the king's invitation is met with violence, which the king reciprocates with interest, and then he ejects a man who isn't dressed properly and has him thrown out into outer darkness. The severe dissonance of these details inclines me to consider alternate interpretations of this parable from taking it as an allegory of the "heavenly banquet." Marty Aiken has written a detailed paper arguing for just such an alternative understanding. He argues that Jesus' listeners would have immediately thought of King Herod when they heard the parable. The king in the parable certainly acts like Herod. These listeners would have remembered Herod bringing an army to Jerusalem and asking the people to accept him as king. If the offer was accepted, Herod would have consummated the deal by marrying the granddaughter of the high priest Hyrcanus. There's our wedding feast. The people of Jerusalem turned down the offer. Herod withdrew but then came back with his army and stormed the walls without stopping to negotiate. Antigonus, a descendent of the royal family, gave himself up to quell a violent situation. He was carried off in chains and beheaded by the Romans.

With this background in mind, we can see the guests who "made light of" the invitation as representing those who went home when Herod came calling and hoped everything would blow over. The other invited guests represent those who resisted Herod with violence. Both groups of guests are met with violent reprisals from the king in the parable. The rounding up of guests to replace the first lot is not, then, an act of charity for the poor but a forced gathering of whoever the king's slaves could find.

With this interpretation, the cryptic scene of the man without a proper wedding garment makes sense as being the second part of the same parable and not a separate parable tacked on to it. The king seems to be looking for a victim and he finds one handy, one who stands out by his attire. Like most kings, this one knows that the quickest way to unite a people is to focus on a victim. Moreover, this guest seems to be what we might call a nonviolent protestor, which is obviously threatening to the king. This guest's eerie silence suggests Jesus' silence before Pilate, which Matthew emphasizes. Aiken points out that grammatically, the king could have been the speechless one, which would refer to Isaiah 52:15, which says that kings will "shut their mouths" because of the Suffering Servant. The fate of this guest is the fate Jesus himself suffers and which had already been the fate of Antigonus. In this parable, the Kingdom of Heaven is not the banquet but the place of the victim who is cast out. Aiken recalls Jesus' words in Mt. 11:12, that up to this time, the Kingdom has "suffered violence." And so it does.

Along with Luke's version of this parable, the real image of the Messianic Banquet in the Gospels is the feeding of the five thousand and four thousand in the wilderness. Here is a generous feeding to all comers with no reprisals for anybody who happened to stay away. No political force is exerted in the invitation. Nobody gets thrown out for being badly dressed. The poor are not afterthoughts, invited only to replace ungrateful aristocrats. The poor as well as the rich are all invited right from the start. The banquet offered by Jesus in the wilderness, away from the centers of worldly power, shows the king's banquet in the parable for what it is. Instead of an offer we *cannot* refuse, Jesus gives us an offer that we do not *wish* to refuse.

Matthew's version of this parable suggests a deep concern with the principalities and powers, much as his exorcism of the Gerasene demoniac does. Luke's version of the Parable of the Talents (Lk. 19:11–26) suggests these same concerns. Here, "the Nobleman" is leaving to attempt to acquire a royal title, which suggests he could stand in for Herod (again) who made the same journey. The violent ending where the Nobleman orders that his enemies be cut in pieces sounds more like Herod than Jesus' heavenly Abba. Here, like the guest without the wedding garment, the servant who does nothing with the talent is more like a resistor against the oppressive social system than someone too lazy to use what talent he has.

I am not interested in trying to figure out which variants of the parables are authentic because I have no reason to deny the authenticity of any of them. It seems just as likely that Jesus would throw out a parable and then see another way it can go and throw it out again in a way that points it in a different direction. This would be especially likely if Jesus were to see more deeply into the oppressiveness of the imperial system as time went on. If parables sometimes change in Jesus' telling, it should not surprise us that they keep changing as we reflect on them.

This is an example of empire criticism that gives us a fresh look at many parables of Jesus. Empire criticism notes ways for how empire may have affected some parts of scripture. Given the power of the Roman Empire over the lives of Jews in Palestine, it should not be surprising if some of Jesus' teaching should reflect this reality. The cryptic Parable of the Corrupt Steward also benefits from this approach. (Lk. 16: 1–9) The steward was given notice that his employment was coming to an end, so he decided to feather his nest by giving favorable financial terms to those who owed his master money. In an oral presentation, Brian McLaren noted that this steward, like many characters in Jesus' parables, was a middle man in the power structure. In this respect, he was like Matthew and Zacchaeus, who had the job of extracting money from people below them and giving it to those above them. McLaren then suggested that those of us in such middle positions are being prompted to be generous to those poorer and weaker than themselves ourselves rather than strengthening the powerful. It takes this kind of clever trickster to sneak around the powers of empire.

Preaching the Kingdom

Jesus was repeatedly asked to explain things plainly. But judging by how he evaded explanations during his lifetime, having him on prime time TV today probably wouldn't help. Even when explaining things more "plainly" as in the Sermon on the Mount in Matthew, Jesus more or less spoke in parables. The meaning of the concluding words of the Sermon on the Mount (Mt. 7:24–27) seems obvious. To build a house wisely on rock rather than foolishly on sand is to build our own lives on solid foundations that protect us from the storms of life. The commentary on this image embodied in the famous story of the *Three Little Pigs* confirms this understanding. We must build our lives on discipline and hard work and, most important, strong materials that will resist attacks from the big bad wolf. This edifying insight confirms one of our basic prejudices: we must put ourselves into positions of strength from which we negotiate our way through life. The firmer our foundation, the less vulnerable we are. If we should go on to use this wise saying as the basis of a prayerful meditation, we can imagine ourselves pouring a slab of concrete and then building a fortress on this slab, equipping it with all the conveniences we want, arming it with ballistic weapons, and insulating ourselves from all those people who aren't bright enough to build in the same way.

But what kind of "rock" is this house really built on? The rock consists of being poor in spirit, meek, and persecuted for the sake of righteousness. (Mt. 5:1–11) I suggest that the opening and closing of the Sermon on the Mount forms an *inclusio.* This is a literary form often found in the Bible, where the first and final items (or stories) echo each other so as to make a sandwich out of that which comes in between. The resonance between the First and Tenth Commandments is another example. This is particularly fitting when we consider that many Bible critics suggest that the Sermon on the Mount is a New Torah, echoing the Ten Commandments and other decrees of the Torah issued on Mount Sinai. This means that the rock has been seriously re-defined by the first verses from what we normally consider a rock to be. If we look further at what is at the center of this "rock," everything gets worse. We shore up our foundation by turning the other cheek, walking the extra mile, and forgiving as our heavenly Abba forgives. Lest we think we have some security left from following all this good advice, we then find that we should stop worrying about what we will eat or wear, avoid judging other people, and ask God for those things that we need. We are now very far from the third pig that relied on his own strength and ingenuity. It is clear enough that the rock we are supposed to build a house on is a pretty strange rock. Indeed, following words such as these is more like building a house on quicksand. How will we ever get on in life if we build on this foundation?

We need to remember that Jesus was trying to build a movement that he called the Kingdom. This means that Jesus was not asking us to build a house in the sense of our contemporary Western notion of a house that is a place owned by an individual or a nuclear family and set apart from everybody else. In Jesus' time, a house was a network of an extended family, a household. As we have seen, a culture built on mimetic rivalry and reciprocal violence, where an eye for an eye and a tooth for a tooth is the law, is built on sand. Such a culture resolves its tension through collective violence. This resolution of societal tension is inherently unstable because there is a constant danger of another breakdown into mimetic rivalry that will necessitate yet another act of collective violence. The culture envisioned in the Sermon on the Mount is a culture where retaliatory violence and mimetic rivalry are renounced. This is the culture built on rock. Jesus, then, does not envision each of us building little houses based on the rock of his teachings. Rather, like Peter and Paul, he envisions a household with many members.

There is, however, a serious discord in the Gospels. In music, discords can be effective for at least some listeners, including me. But some discords simply ruin a piece. The discord I'm referring to here is the amount of vengeful texts attributed to Jesus, especially in Matthew. Jesus' teachings of non-retribution and forgiveness in the Sermon on the Mount and threats of eschatological retribution for those who fail to follow the way of forgiveness and non-retribution clash badly. To deal with these passages, it is more important than ever to use Jesus himself as the living interpretive principle. Forgiveness is a difficult part of Christian spirituality, and we will deal with it at length below. Since one of the difficulties of forgiveness involves interpreting scripture passages that seem unforgiving, we will deal with that difficulty now.

Raymund Schwager's dramatic theology is particularly helpful with this question. He divides the teaching ministry into two acts that give some explanation for this discord. (Schwager 1999) In the first act, Jesus proclaimed salvation as a free gift. This reversed the schema of the prophets who promised God's deliverance, if and when Israel repented. Jesus announced pre-emptory forgiveness as a means to elicit repentance and the fruits thereof. "Preceding, and at first independent of the human decision, it offers to oppressed humankind the pure mercy of God." (Schwager 1999, 56) Schwager goes on to say: "It does not presuppose conversion, but wants to awaken it." When "the offer of pure grace is rejected a person falls prey to all the consequences of his or her decision." (Schwager 1999, 56)

Schwager notes that Jesus pointed to the lilies of the field and the rain falling on everybody regardless of moral disposition to attest to God's ongoing care for us. That is, God gives us sustenance along with forgiveness as free gifts. The sower throws his seed everywhere, even on the seemingly worst of soil. Perhaps Matthew himself, who was called out of his tax collecting office while he was counting his money, understood better than most the significance of the sower's profligacy. So it is that Schwager says that "Even if the new community in the Kingdom of God contrasts completely with the old laws of the human world, it is however not something unrealistic. It only needs a new look to see signs of it everywhere in our everyday world." If we reject what is offered us, if we lock ourselves into our old world, we give ourselves up to "a process of judgment, which runs according to self-chosen and stubbornly defended norms." (Schwager 1999, 66)

As we have seen, Jesus did not just *talk* about a new society, he *did* many things to bring it about. Such a new society would create a social climate conducive to healing at all levels of the human being. In this, Jesus failed, and here we come to what Schwager calls the second act of the drama: the rejection of Jesus' teaching. The Gospels attest to the many people who gathered around Jesus for healing and to listen to his teachings. But except for the Twelve Apostles and the women who provided for him when he was in Galilee and followed him to the cross in Jerusalem, (Mk. 15:40–41) there is no indication of Jesus having a stable group of followers. Since many of them had to eke out a hard living on the land, probably most people gathered around Jesus when he was in town and that was about it.

The social teachings of non-retaliation and forgiveness in the Sermon on the Mount and in other parables were clearly on a higher plane than his listeners would have been used to. In fact, they pose such a severe challenge that many of the greatest Christian writers over the centuries have relegated these teachings to the margins and re-instituted retaliation both in moral theology and dogma. Maybe monks and nuns could turn the other cheek if a fellow monk or nun insulted them, but that was about it. (Actually, writing as a monk, I know that monks and nuns find this teaching difficult too.) Did the people who listened to Jesus and tagged along catch on to the preaching of the Kingdom based on peace and forgiveness in the midst of a world just as violent as our own? The indications I can see suggest that they did not.

The man who asked Jesus to make his brother share their inheritance equitably, only to be rebuked (along with his brother) for avarice, suggests that his listeners weren't giving up rivalry over possessions at the drop of Jesus' words. (Lk 12:13–15) The crowd's attempt to seize Jesus and make him their king right after he had fed them bread from Heaven seems to be John's retrospective image of what Jesus' listeners understood and hoped for. (Jn. 6:15)

Jesus' closest followers consistently failed to understand and absorb Jesus' teachings. The constant bickering among the disciples as to who was the greatest further exposes their incomprehension. When a Samaritan town refused to receive Jesus' disciples because they were on their way to Jerusalem, they asked if they should "command fire to come down from heaven and consume them." (Lk. 9:54) Again, this gives the impression that Jesus' teaching of radical non-retaliation was not sinking in. Moreover, when Jesus was arrested, he had to tell Peter to put his sword away "for all who take the sword will perish by the sword." (Mt. 26: 52) If Jesus' closest followers continuously showed themselves to be at such variance with what their master was teaching, it seems highly unlikely that other followers were doing any better.

The more Jesus is faced with refusal, the more threatening his teaching becomes, with the imagery of weeping and gnashing of teeth becoming prominent. We have seen this in the Parable of the Wheat and the Weeds, and we will see it in the Parable of the Evil Workers in the Vineyard as well. Given this refusal, Schwager suggests that Jesus is not threatening us with divine vengeance but is warning us of the built-in consequences of rejecting the free gift of forgiveness. Our rejection leaves us with the cycle of vengeance as old as humanity. This is the sandy soil of a persecutory society. This point is important because we easily let the threatening passages cancel out the teachings on non-retaliation and forgiveness. If Jesus is threatening us with Hell for not having our lamps lit, Jesus isn't as forgiving as many of his teachings and actions suggest he is.

The Parable of the Unforgiving Servant takes us to the heart of the paradox of forgiveness in Matthew's Gospel. (Mt. 18:23–35) This parable is set up by a dialogue between Jesus and Peter. When Peter asks if he should forgive someone who offends him seven times, he seems to think he is generously setting a high ceiling, an indication that he hasn't caught on to what his master was teaching him. Forgiving somebody seven times seems an awful lot, but Jesus breaks his bubble by saying that he has to forgive an offender seventy-seven times, or seventy times seven, in some manuscripts. Taking the higher number, one might think that counting up to 491 offenses legitimizes taking revenge after the magic number is passed, but that obviously misses the point. Jesus' reply is an allusion to Lamech's savage song in which he boasts that if Cain is avenged seven times, then *he* is avenged seventy-seven times. (Gen. 4:23–24) Quite an example of how revenge cycles escalate on to infinity. Jesus counters the infinite revenge cycle by making forgiveness just as infinite.

Then Jesus launches into the parable. After being forgiven outright a large sum of money owed to the master, the servant refuses to forgive a much smaller sum owed by a fellow servant. Having just been forgiven a large debt, the servant hardly has the excuse of being desperate for money. The point of the parable is clear enough: If you don't forgive, you won't be forgiven. But there is a small hitch here. The "forgiving" master suddenly becomes unforgiving, suggesting that the forgiving Abba in Heaven is not forgiving either, at least for this offense. Not forgiving is the unforgivable sin. Or so it seems.

The unforgiving servant is handed over to be tortured until he has paid his entire debt. The servant had been invited to a new way of living based on forgiveness but he rejected it. Living without forgiveness, which is tantamount to living by vengeance, is torture. It isn't God who is unforgiving; it is the servant. Clinging to vengeance in the face of God's forgiveness tortures us with our vengeance for as long as we are imprisoned by it. Ultimately, Jesus and the heavenly Abba forgive us our refusals to forgive in the hope that we will accept this free gift of forgiveness. Likewise, St. Paul says that Christ is at the right hand of God interceding for us. (Rom. 8:34) Just ahead of this parable, Jesus told the Parable of the Lost Sheep, for whose sake the shepherd left the ninety-nine to seek out the lost. Surely God searches out each one of us who is tortured by vengeance.

Immediately before this parable, Jesus instructed his disciples to seek reconciliation and treat delinquent members of the community like Gentiles and tax collectors. The juxtaposition of the two shows every sign of being intentional and instructive. We would do well to ask ourselves if Jesus' words about correcting fellow members of the community put us in the frame of mind of punishing people and casting them out or really seeking reconciliation (Mt. 18:15–20) Checking ourselves for such reactions is a good way of taking note as to how instinctive punishing and excluding are to us and how less instinctive are forgiving, including, and welcoming others. It is precisely this instinct to punish that makes it difficult to have ears to hear what Jesus is saying.

If we take a step back and ask ourselves what our instinctive reaction to being wronged is, we usually find that the first instinct is to seek revenge. If somebody hits me, I hit back. Simple. But Jesus tells us to go to the person and tell that person what they have done to us. This action puts a serious break on the revenge mechanism and moves in the opposite direction. After all, going to the person peacefully and honestly is the first step towards reconciliation, which is the last thing a person bent on revenge wants. If speaking to the offender does not resolve the matter, then the circle widens to two or three and then to the whole assembly. What is easily overlooked in this process as described here is that it presupposes that each of us is expected to take responsibility for the community and for one another. This is why we should warn a person who is acting destructively, but it is also why we should be open for others to approach each of *us* to correct us. Of course, anyone who has ever corrected another person knows that this can result in learning about our own shortcomings. One of our favorite slogans at St. Gregory's Abbey is: "You do it too."

Treating an unrepentant person like "a Gentile and a tax collector" sounds straightforward. We kick the person out and that's that. But that is *not* that. For one thing, this admonition is not about expulsion; it is an act of distancing. When used rightly, such an act shows that the reproved person has distanced him or herself from the community. It is realistic in that some people make themselves impossible and a peaceful parting is necessary. But that is far from the end of the matter. Matthew himself was a tax collector. How was he treated? Jesus called him to follow him and be a disciple. We need to keep in mind the context. We quickly forget that this list of instructions for dealing with a delinquent person comes just after the Parable of the Lost Sheep. This suggests that the way to treat a Gentile or a tax collector is to bring them into the Christian community in a spirit of forgiveness.

But wait a minute! Aren't we told that those we loose on earth are loosed in Heaven and those who are bound on earth are bound in Heaven? (Mt. 16:19; Jn. 20:23) Sounds like we have the power to bind other people for all eternity, and God's hands are tied for as long as we want them to be. How much power is that? Not so fast. Why is it that we so easily assume we are being allowed, even encouraged to bind on earth? Why are we slower to see that maybe we are being encouraged to *loose* on earth? Let's return to Peter's question about how many times he must forgive and Jesus' Parable of the Unforgiving Debtor. If we have to forgive others as God forgives us, and that without limit which is what seventy-seven times means, then we are indeed being encouraged to *loose* on earth. We are being *warned* that if we do not loose on earth, we are bound to our resentment for what others have done to us (or we *think* they have done to us.) If we remain bound to our resentments, we will be so bound even in Heaven since God's hands are indeed tied for as long as we refuse to let God untie us. Truly accepting this free gift of forgiveness entails passing this free gift on to others. We are all thrown into the same world together. The question is whether we will be tied up in vengeance or bound with others by forgiveness.

But Jesus seems to put a limit on forgiveness when he says that every sin and blasphemy can be forgiven with the exception of "blasphemy against the Holy Spirit." (Mt. 12:31) After our reflections above, it seems odd that God's hands should ever be tied in any circumstances. So are they? The suggestion that unforgiving people cannot be forgiven implies that withholding forgiveness would be the sin against the Holy Spirit. In Jesus' final discourse in John, he promises that when he leaves, he will send the Advocate to guide us in all truth. An advocate is a lawyer for the defense. So the Advocate Jesus sends is the defender of all who are accused—which is all of us. The Advocate "will prove the world wrong about sin and righteousness and judgment." (Jn. 16:8) The world runs on the fuel of accusation and revenge, and this is what the Advocate proves is wrong. If we bring Jesus' words about the Advocate to his words in Matthew, it appears that sinning against the Holy Spirit by not forgiving others cuts us off from our Advocate who would plead our case. If we boot out the only one who will take our part—what then?

We are still left with how all these teachings of Jesus squares with the numerous threats of burning in Gehenna. English translations along the lines of "hellfire" cause some readers to assume Jesus is talking about eternal damnation in the afterlife. Gehenna, however, was very much an image rooted in *this* world. It referred to the Valley of Hinnom just outside of Jerusalem. In Jesus' time, it was a garbage pit that was always smoldering. This is the "fire that never goes out." More importantly, this was believed to be the valley where the apostate Israelites sacrificed children to Moloch. (2 Chron. 28:3; Jer. 7:31) Gehenna, then, is a constant reminder of the old system of sacrificial violence that left no room for forgiveness. That the fire of Gehenna will never go out and the worm will never die is a highly apt way of imaging the insatiableness of mimetic rivalry. But Jeremiah, who denounced the Valley of Hinnom, held out hope even for this cursed valley, and thus also for cursed humanity. He promised that the whole city would be rebuilt after the exile "and all the terraces out to the Kidron Valley on the east as far as the corner of the Horse Gate, will be holy to the Lord. (Jer. 31:40) Jesus' warnings about Gehenna, then, turn out to be made in a redemptive context, and they fit well with Schwager's second act in Jesus' salvation drama. If we reject forgiveness, we will burn for as long as we reject it. I experience that on a daily basis.

The famous parable traditionally known as the Parable of the Prodigal Son (Lk. 15:11–32) is the quintessential illustration of pre-emptory forgiveness, one that closes the case on Jesus' teaching on vengeance and forgiveness. This parable is better called "The Parable of the Prodigal Father and His Two

Sons." The opening of the parable draws a triangle: "There was a man who had two sons." We expect tension out of a triangle, and we get it right off the bat when the younger son asks for his share of the property. The father accedes to his son's request (demand?) and the younger son goes off with the proceeds. The elder son stays at home with his share of the property, at least geographically. What kind of father would be so foolish? Why would a young man leave a father who would give him whatever he wanted? Was it to get away from his brother? The stories about paired brothers in Genesis predispose us to suspect that the two brothers are mirror images of each other.

The parable goes on to say that the younger son "squandered his property." Literally, he "scattered his substance." That is, the younger son, while trying to forge an individual selfhood separate from his father and brother, completely loses himself in dissolute living. Geographical distance has not freed him from continuing to be a mirror image of his older brother. Then comes a famine and the social crisis that comes with it. Chances are that the scarcity was magnified by created scarcity. In such a social crisis, there must be a victim. A foreigner is particularly vulnerable to being a victim in such a crisis. The younger son fit the bill perfectly. He was deserted by *everybody,* in spite of all the money he spent on his women and carousing friends. *Nobody* was willing to take him in. He ended up as a servant who feeds the pigs (an unclean animal for Jews) and "no one gave him anything." In this desperate situation, the younger son recalled how well-fed his father's servants were, and he "came to himself." Perhaps it was embarrassment that made him want to return as a servant, but perhaps he also didn't want to re-enter the triangle with his father and brother.

The father's ecstatic reception of the lost son and subsequent celebration blows apart the family triangle, leaving no room for mimetic strife. In contrast to the mimetic process that organizes society around a dispensable victim, the *in*dispensable victim who is no longer lost has been found. The elder son, however, wanted to preserve the old triangle. His sour attitude suggests that he still needs to have his younger brother live irresponsibly. The elder brother's universe would collapse if his younger brother began to play a responsible role in family affairs. No wonder the younger son ran away from a brother like that!

When the older brother keeps his distance, the father runs out to him with the same solicitude he showed the returning younger son. The elder son's disingenuous accusation of not being allowed to celebrate is shown up for what it is. Apparently, the elder son never thought to celebrate with his friends until his father threw a party for *that* son of his. What the elder son has done is put himself into competition with his younger brother, when there is no need for competition. This sort of mimetic rivalry creates a stumbling block in the way of forgiveness. It remains to be seen whether or not the younger brother will forgive the elder for his unforgiving attitude.

We are likely to judge the younger brother for his callous irresponsibility and the elder brother for his amazing insensitivity. But if we do that, we find ourselves ensnared in the mimetic struggle between the two brothers, comparing them and taking sides until our own capacity for love is obscured and our capacity for celebration fizzles. The Prodigal Father does neither. He does not upbraid the younger son for leaving; neither does he upbraid his elder son for being such an insufferable prig. He only invites both of them to the party. Most of us have a hard time even wanting to be a father like that!

The parable ends with this challenge of forgiveness and unconditional love: Do we rise to the challenge of the Prodigal Father and renounce our irresponsibility and self-righteousness?

Jesus' Face Set Towards Jerusalem

A mysterious event and a healing serve as a transition to Jesus' Passion and Resurrection. Just before Jesus is about to start the long trek to Jerusalem, where he meets his destiny, he takes Peter, James, and John up a mountain and is transfigured before them by a transcendent light. Moses and Elijah appear and speak of Jesus' "departure, which he was about to accomplish at Jerusalem." (Lk. 9:31) Jesus had just warned his disciples that he would undergo "great sufferings" and be killed and they too would have to bear their crosses. The transcendent light is often interpreted as a foretaste of the glory of Jesus' Resurrection to encourage them in the hard times ahead. But this light is also the glory that Jesus had from his Abba from the beginning, a sign of the goodness of Creation. As with almost everything else about Jesus, the disciples seem not to understand the event. One can sympathize with Peter when he thinks it is great to be there and he doesn't want to come down, but the dynamic of this event is to move all of them to Jerusalem. The fact that the disciples almost immediately begin fighting again about who is the greatest confirms their misunderstanding.

The appearance of Moses and Elijah indicates that Jesus is the fulfillment of the Law and the Prophets that preceded him. Both Moses and Elijah were victims of social violence and both barely survived these threats. Jesus was about to be a victim who would not survive the threat against his life. Moses and Elijah were also both compromised by violence. At times, Moses turned the accusations against him onto other people. In one such event, Moses ordered the stoning of a man who committed an act of blasphemy. (Lev. 24:10–23) Elijah slew the prophets of Baal. (1 Kings 18:40) Jesus, on the other hand, would eschew violence, accepting violence committed against him without returning it. The voice of Heaven: "This is my Son, my Chosen; listen to him!" recalls the heavenly affirmation of Jesus at the time of his baptism.

On the way to Jerusalem, Jesus heals the blind man Bartimaeus. (Mk. 10:46–52) This story is considered by many Bible scholars to be the closing bookend of an *inclusio*. The echoing story at the other bookend also involves the healing of a blind man. The middle of this sandwich is the journey to Jerusalem. The first healing (Mk. 8:22–26) takes place at Bethsaida. The second takes place as Jesus arrives at Jericho, the last stop before arriving in Jerusalem. The intervening journey is punctuated by Jesus' three predictions of his passion coupled with the incomprehension of his disciples. Each of these predictions is also accompanied by disputes among the disciples as to who is the greatest.

The blindness of the two men who need healing is often thought to represent the blindness of the disciples, who also need healing. With the man in Bethsaida, Jesus needs two tries to get the healing right, suggesting that the blindness of the disciples is difficult to heal. The much easier healing of the man in Jericho suggests hope that the disciples, though still blind, will also be healed.

I agree with this interpretation of the *inclusio*, but there is something else that has caught my attention. The crowd acts in a different way in these two stories. At Bethsaida, the people in the crowd ask Jesus to touch the blind man and give him back his sight. At Jericho, the people in the crowd rebuke Bartimaeus when he cries out and tell him to be quiet. Far from helping Bartimaeus be healed, they hinder him. In this, they act like the apostles, who just a short time ago had tried to keep the mothers from bringing their children to Jesus. Moreover, the crowd has shifted its focus from Jesus to Bartimaeus, and in an adversarial way at that. Again, this matches the disciples who focused on one another in their altercations rather than on Jesus. If the crowd at this point is an extension of the disciples, then they badly need healing. Yet, the more healing they need for their blindness, the more resistant they are to healing. Bartimaeus, in calling out to Jesus by his Messianic title, shows that he sees more than those who theoretically have eyes. Both the crowd and the disciples have failed yet again to create a climate of healing. If the healing of Bartimaeus is a sign of hope for the disciples' ultimate healing, it is a sign coming at a darkening moment.

Jesus' calling out to Bartimaeus makes it clear that it is his desire to heal the blind man. The crowd is thus convicted of being contrary to Jesus' desire. They might be surrounding Jesus, but they are not following him. We could say that the crowd at Bethsaida was a community in that they brought the blind man to Jesus. The crowd at Jericho acts in a persecutory way. The contrast between these two echoing stories in the *inclusio* presents us with the fundamental choice of joining a community of healing or falling back into a crowd that fights healing. Will we look at the blind person *and* at Jesus, or will we fail to see either of them?

The Passion and Cross

The long journey culminates in Jesus' triumphant entry into Jerusalem. That is, it was triumphant in the sense that throngs of people cheered him. But given the failure to create a movement renewing society through a peaceful way of living, Jesus could not have felt very victorious. Matthew says that the entry is a fulfillment of Zechariah 9:9: "Tell the daughter of Zion, Look, your king is coming to you, humble, and mounted on a donkey, and on a colt, the foal of a donkey." Zechariah's prophecy goes on to say that the king will "cut off the chariot from Ephraim and the war-horse from Jerusalem" and that "he shall command peace to the nations." This doesn't seem to be what the people are cheering about, something Matthew confirms when he says that Jerusalem was in turmoil with people asking "Who is this?" (Mt. 21:10)

The celebration of Palm Sunday includes the reading or chanting of one of the passion narratives where the congregation that has just sung praises of "Hosanna!" with palm branches in hand cry out for Jesus' crucifixion, a telescoping of the drama for liturgical purposes. Although I have seen articles insisting that the crowd cheering Jesus' entry is not the same crowd that demanded Jesus' crucifixion, the anthropological insight of the Church is that *we* both praise God and reject God. That is, we act out both sides of the word *doxa*: glory and disgrace. The Gospel writers had this anthropological insight before the liturgists did. There was one crowd in Jerusalem for the pilgrim feast and it was a big one. In Matthew, the chief priests wanted to arrest Jesus and kill him but wanted to avoid making a move during the festival because of the crowd. When Jesus' actions in the temple and Judas's betrayal changed the picture, they had to work on crowd control. Their crowd management might not have worked if Jesus had spoken before Pilate. I suspect that Jesus chose to be silent because any words at all, no matter what, could have been construed as an encouragement to the crowd to start an uprising. In the wake of Jesus' silence, the disappointed crowd who had wanted to make him king back in the wilderness were ready turn against him in furious disappointment.

The crowd had likely gotten a charge when Jesus knocked over the tables in the temple and drove out the animals. This incident shook up the authorities, as it should have. It can be seen as the climax of repeated protests of the Hebrew prophets against the sacrificial cult in the temple. Jeremiah mocked his listeners, who jabbered: "This is the temple of the Lord! The temple of the Lord! The temple of the Lord!" (Jer. 7:4) The Psalmist threw out God's mocking question: "Do you think I eat the meat of bulls and drink the blood of goats?" (Ps. 50:13) Amos railed about God's hatred of solemn festivals and insisted that God will not accept offerings of well-being. What God *does* want is to "let justice roll down like waters, and righteousness like an everflowing stream. (Am. 5:24) Most telling are the words of Hosea that Jesus quoted when criticized for choosing Matthew as a disciple: "I desire steadfast love and not sacrifice, the knowledge of God rather than burnt offerings." (Hosea 6:6) There is much debate as to whether the prophets wanted the abolition of the sacrificial cult or a reformation that would bring it in line with moral values. In driving out not only the money changers but also the animals about to be sacrificed, I think Jesus is doing a bit of guerrilla theater to prophecy the end of the temple cult, a prophecy fulfilled in 70 C.E. when the combined violence of militant Jews and the imperialistic Romans resulted in its destruction. When asked to explain his actions, Jesus said: "Destroy this temple and in three days I will raise it up" (John 2:19) A literal interpretation is promptly debunked by the evangelist when he says that Jesus was "speaking of the temple of his body." (John 2:21) So much for biblical literalism. The implication that Jesus is replacing the temple with his risen body is a strong indication that he intended to abolish the sacrificial cult. John's idiosyncratic placement of the cleansing of the temple at the beginning of his Gospel may well be his way of announcing this end of the cult. What was wrong with the sacrificial cult? The quote from Psalm 69: "Zeal for your house will consume me" shows us the problem if we note the context. Psalm 69 begins with "Save me O God for the waters have risen up to my neck." The Psalmist complains to God about suffering the same reproach people level against God: "The insults of those who insult you have fallen on me." This is one of the "passion psalms" that I commented on in Chapter 1.

The prophets consistently denounced the sacrifices made on the "high places," pagan sacrifices to deities like Moloch, including sacrifices the people made of their own children. The sacrifice in the temple was more humane in that it was restricted to animals, but the practice derived from the notion that "god" was angry and would be appeased only by sacrifices. The prophets' denunciations of the temple cult were consistently coupled with denunciations of social violence and injustice, where the poor were sold for a pair of sandals as Amos complained. (Am. 8:6) Although it is argued that the prophets thought the temple sacrifices were acceptable, maybe even laudable, if accompanied with righteous actions in the social sphere, they seem to have had a sneaking suspicion that the practice of sacrifice tends to *encourage* social injustice. The temple setup was, after all, a terrible financial burden on the poor. I think Jesus was outraged rather than edified over the widow who gave to the temple the last two coins she had to live on. (Mk. 12:41–44) The logic of sacrifice is that some living being is always dispensable, precisely as the victims of collective violence at the times of social crises are dispensable, and their deaths "necessary." Such was the logic of Caiaphas. These considerations suggest that the prophets were convinced that something was fundamentally wrong with sacrificial rites. Jesus, on the other hand, has a totally different, opposite logic to that of Caiaphas; a logic that Paul says is foolishness to the rest of the world. In John 6, Jesus says that everybody the Father gives him will come to him and nobody who comes to him will be driven away. (Jn. 6:37) The Parable of the Lost Sheep makes the same point that it is not the will of our Abba in Heaven that even one of his "little ones" should be lost.

Jesus believed this so strongly that he would accept death on the cross to make the point and, more importantly, return as the Forgiving Victim to gather all who will come to him, so that none of us should be lost. The pagan deities wanted sacrifices made to *them*. The prophets kept trying to impress the point that God pours out sacrificial love to all of us through Creation and redemption, and that God wants us to offer mercy in imitation of God, not sacrifices. Caiaphas was willing to sacrifice Jesus and anyone else who put a spoke in the wheel of the sacrificial logic. Jesus was willing to sacrifice himself rather than sacrifice any of us. That is why we do not slaughter bulls on the altars in church, but pass around the blood and wine through which Jesus gives His very self to each one of us.

Jesus warned the Jewish leaders of the violence they were in danger of committing against himself in The Parable of the Evil Workers in the Vineyard, the grimmest of all Jesus' parables. (Mt. 21:33–45) The workers covet the harvest of the vineyard for themselves and then covet the vineyard itself. They are willing to commit violence to that end and they do not shy away from violence when the opportunity comes. This parable is weighted down with much significance as the vineyard is a running image for Israel throughout the Hebrew Bible. It seems most particularly to be an allusion to Isaiah's Song of the Vineyard. (Isa. 5:1–7) Both stress the care with which the vineyard is set up to give it the best potential for a good yield. In Isaiah's song, the grapes grow wild in spite of everything. In the parable, the grapes grow well but the workers themselves are wild. Actually, Isaiah shows that the wild grapes in Isaiah refer to wild humans when he says that the vineyard stands for Israel and that God "expected justice, but saw bloodshed; righteousness, but heard a cry!" (Isa. 5:7)

After the workers have attacked the agents the owner has sent, the owner sends his own son, his own flesh and blood, believing that the workers will respect his son. But the workers realize that by sending his son, his substance, the workers have the opportunity to take the vineyard for themselves and take the owner's substance in the bargain. If one is not willing to affirm God's generosity, then one will take it from God by force. Not surprisingly, the chief priests and scribes were offended by this parable. These priests and scribes prove Jesus' point by wanting to arrest him. They only hold off from doing so because they have not yet drawn the crowds over to their side. Jesus is warning them that they are in danger of following in the footsteps of Jezebel, who plotted the death of Naboth so as to deliver Naboth's vineyard to her husband King Ahab. (1 Kings 21:1–16)

Jesus asks his listeners what they think will happen to the workers, and they reply that the owner "will put those wretches to a miserable death, and lease the vineyard to other tenants who will give him the produce at the harvest time." (Mt. 21:41) Jesus then quotes Psalm 118:22: "The stone that the builders rejected has become the chief cornerstone." I don't think it is too fanciful to suggest that Matthew may have had this verse in mind when he recorded Jesus' words about the house built on rock at the end of the Sermon on the Mount. It makes sense that the rock founded on the willingness to suffer for the sake of righteousness and forgiveness would be a rock rejected by most people. Yet Jesus was about to make that rock the cornerstone of the community he would gather after his Resurrection. This psalm verse confirms the parable's message that an act of collective violence seems imminent. Jesus goes on to call this stone a *skandalon*, a stumbling block: "The one who falls on this stone will be broken to pieces; and it will crush anyone on whom it falls." (Mt. 21:44) This refers to Isaiah's prophecy that the Lord of Hosts will became "a stone one strikes up against," that God will become "a rock one stumbles over." (Isa. 8:14) Jesus is saying then, that the weak stone is stumbled over when it is rejected by those who think they are strong.

Jesus then warned his listeners of the violence they were threatening to inflict against the Roman Empire. Rebellion was in the air, enough to make it likely that the cheering upon Jesus' entry into Jerusalem was in the hope that it was the beginning of a *coup d'état*. The social movement Jesus tried to create was quite the opposite of an armed rebellion. He had specifically rejected the option of a political takeover during his temptations. The memory of Judas Maccabeus was strong among the Jewish people and it stirred up hopes for a repeat performance. For Jesus, the memory was one of revulsion. He would have known that the result of the Maccabean Revolt was that the oppressive structures within Judaism were wrapped around by the imperial structures of Rome. Moreover, an armed rebellion would surely end in tragedy, which it did in 70 C.E.

The "apocalyptic" discourses in the synoptic Gospels are often taken as warnings of God's wrath to come, but all the wrath in these discourses is human. Robert Hamerton-Kelly argues that the "desolating sacrilege" refers to the desecrating violence on the part of the Romans and the competing zealot groups fighting over the temple as a focal point for rebellion. In these times of turmoil: "Those in Judea must flee to the mountains; the one on the housetop must not go down or enter the house to take anything away; the one in the field must not turn back to get a coat. Woe to those who are pregnant and to those who are nursing infants in those days! Pray that it may not be in winter." (Mk. 13:14–18) False Messiahs will come and vociferously call attention to themselves. There is no divine vengeance here; everything is human wrath and violence. "These are the sadly predictable human failings that cause human misery without any divine intervention." (Hamerton-Kelly

1994, p.40) The only thing God does is shorten the days for the sake of the elect and come to gather them.

So it is that by the time Jesus gathered with his disciples for what is called the Last Supper, not only had the social tensions in Jerusalem reached a point where all parties agreed that Jesus must be put to death, but the tensions among Jesus' disciples had increased as well. The disciples' fighting over who was the greatest, their incomprehension of Jesus' predictions of his imminent death, and their collective disapproval of the woman who anointed Jesus with oil all led to this point. I suggested above that Judas may have been a scapegoat in the sense that he did what everybody else had in mind, but they let Judas suffer the opprobrium for doing it. The famous collective question "Is it I?" in response to Jesus announcing that he was about to be betrayed reflects their uncertainty about their loyalty to Jesus. In their current collective frame of mind and heart, there was a real possibility that *all* of them would either join the crowd in crying for crucifixion, or would band together after his death as a tightknit rebellious group united by resentment over the death of their leader, thus thwarting the Kingdom of God that Jesus came to proclaim. Jesus had one last chance to do something that would keep his life and intentions alive for his disciples. He did two things.

The first thing Jesus did was wash the feet of his disciples. The act was so simple that anybody could do it. If the disciples follow his example, as he asks them to, they will not have time to harbor resentment over their master's death and plot vengeance for the deed. Instead, this simple act that embodies love and concern for others will cause that love and concern to grow within their hearts and drive out resentment and a desire for revenge. If more and more people imitate Jesus in this action, then the entire social order of the day will crumble around the communal life that emerges through this simple action.

The second thing Jesus did was tell them to eat bread that was his body and drink wine that was his blood in remembrance of him. Jesus was not just telling the disciples that he was about to die for them. That would be comprehensible, if unsettling. Rather, Jesus was telling them that he was giving them his very *life*. Jesus was not giving himself as a corpse in the hope that the world might become a better place if enough people felt bad about killing him. Jesus was giving himself *as a living being.* Gathering to break bread and pass the cup of wine in memory of Jesus would teach us the meaning of these gestures. As we meet to break bread and pass the cup in memory of him and recall the story of his death, we will begin to realize the extent to which the living Jesus was giving them not his death, but his *life.* In the Torah, it said: "But be sure you do not eat the blood, because the blood is the life, and you must not eat the life with the meat." (Deut. 12:23) So it is that Jesus poured out his *life* to his disciples at the *First Supper* and it is this *life* that Jesus pours out to us every time we eat and drink in memory of him. Eating and drinking the bread and wine would also will lead us to understand that just as God created a new people by bringing them out of Egypt, the event celebrated at Passover, God was now creating a new humanity based on washing one another's feet and eating and drinking his very life. This is why Jesus was not hosting the Last supper but the First Supper. This liturgical meal is a new beginning for us all.

Much could be said about the suffering of Jesus on the cross, but I will focus on Jesus' heartbreaking prayer at Gethsemane and its likely carryover to his dying moments. Twice, in Mark, Jesus prayed that the cup he knew he must drink be taken away from him. (Mk. 14: 36, 39) Jeffrey B. Gibson, in his analysis of the temptations of Jesus, suggests that Jesus was tempted to opt for the restoration of Israel by dominance. It was the same temptation he suffered when he called Peter "Satan" at Caesarea Phillippi. As he prayed in the garden, it appeared to Jesus that his whole ministry had come to nothing. "In Mark's Gospel Jesus prays to have pass by this 'hour' and to be relieved of his 'cup' because he doubts whether in the end the path of suffering will really be effective in achieving the task to which he has been commissioned. *Behind the petition in Mk. 14: 36 lies the question, 'How can I obey God, and trust in him, when he seems to be willing to jeopardize his own purposes?'* " (Gibson 1995, 252, italics in original) Like us, Jesus felt the pull of the mimetic spiral of violence. Worst of all, the full wrath of humanity's rejection of God from the beginning of time had fallen upon Jesus and there seemed to be no way for that human wrath to be quenched. That Jesus accepted the cup anyway shows a profound trust in his heavenly Abba at a time when his Abba's will was inscrutable to him. Jesus' piercing cry from the cross: "my God, my God, why have you forsaken me?" suggests that Jesus still didn't see how his death would fulfill his mission. (Mk. 15: 34) But then Jesus cried in words of trust in the face of his failure: "Father, into your hands I commend my spirit." (Lk. 23: 46)

Jesus' heavenly Abba did not want Jesus to start a violent revolt against Rome, but Jesus' Abba certainly could not have willed the violence inflicted on Jesus, either. That is, Jesus' Abba did not will any violence by anybody. It is a tragic irony that many Christian thinkers have suggested that God positively willed the sacrifice of Jesus for some cosmic purpose. Most commonly, many theologians have insisted that God was fiercely angry with wayward humans for sinning, and was somehow incapable of forgiving humans unless *somebody* took the punishment for human sin. What kind of god demands punishment and doesn't care who gets punished as long as *somebody* does? This idea, in various forms, has taken so great a hold in Christianity that we somehow have overlooked the fact that the Passion Story never says anything of the kind. This violent atonement theory fixates on the death of Jesus, proclaiming that we are washed in the Blood of the Lamb. Actually, we *are* washed in the Blood of the Lamb if we remember that the blood is not the death but the *life* of Jesus. Moreover, the pre-emptive forgiveness Jesus acted out many times and his teachings on non-retaliation make no sense if God *needed* to exact revenge for human sinfulness. Another fatal problem with the violent atonement is that it puts the Son, Jesus, in an adversarial relationship with his Abba whereas the Gospels say quite the opposite. In John, Jesus says repeatedly that anyone who sees the Son sees his Abba. We do not see in Jesus a Father who is a furious avenger of humanity's sinfulness. On the contrary, the pre-emptive forgiveness of Jesus *has* to be the pre-emptive forgiveness of his Abba. Perhaps it is our difficulty with forgiveness, with believing it is even possible, that makes it so hard for us to think God really *is* forgiveness.

The most thorough examination of the violent model of Atonement, one that leaves no biblical stone unturned, is *Atonement, Justice and Peace: the*

Message of the Cross and the Mission of the Church by Darrin W. Snyder Belousek. Although most of us who work extensively with Girard's thought see a non-violent Atonement theology as a logical outcome of his ideas, the push for a non-violent Atonement theology is much bigger than Girardian studies. Belousek himself, for example, is not a Girardian, and his arguments are built entirely out of scriptural exegesis.

If God did not will Jesus' violent death, what *did* God will? Jesus understood that his heavenly Abba's plan precluded defeating Caiaphas and Pontius Pilate with force, hard as that was to accept at the end. Using force would only keep the world forever embroiled in retaliatory violence. Hence his warnings in the Parable of the Evil Workers in the Vineyard and his apocalyptic discourse. But how was his death amid total failure going to bring on God's Kingdom that nobody seemed to have entered? Indeed, his death, by itself, would accomplish nothing. Something else was needed, and Jesus' heavenly Abba was about to provide that need.

Resurrection, Ascension, and Sending the Holy Spirit

But death, much as it was the plan of humans, was not God's plan, as a group of women found out early in the morning on the first day of the week.

Matthew introduces the Resurrection of Jesus with an earthquake. (Mt. 28:1–10) Just as an earthquake shakes up the earth, the Resurrection shakes us up. It fatally undermines the way we have lived our lives, and gives us a radical reorientation for the way we understand God and the created world. But did the Resurrection have to be an earthquake? Couldn't it possibly have been a smooth transition from a good quality of life to a better one?

According to seismology, an earthquake is caused by one or more faults under the surface of the earth. A fault can hold its position for some time but it is inherently unstable and it will slide sometime or other and cause the earth to shake. The Resurrection could not help but cause an earthquake because there were faults in human culture just waiting to shift when the event occurred. A look at the Old Testament readings during the Easter Vigil point out where the faults were and still are. The story of the Flood shows us a society overwhelmed with violence. They did not need God to send a flood to carry them away; their own violence had overwhelmed them like a flood. The near-sacrifice of Isaac by Abraham refers to the institutionalization of sacrifice to stave off the meltdown of the Flood. Like his culture as a whole, Abraham thought somebody must die, until an angel (messenger) of God told him otherwise. Pharaoh's Egypt was a society held together through institutionalized sacrifice that included the enslavement of the Hebrews. When plagues struck, Pharaoh blamed the Hebrews and drove them out. God transformed the event into a deliverance from slavery. Like the people in Noah's time, the Egyptians were overwhelmed by their own violence. These are the fault lines that could only slip and shake the earth when the angel of the Lord "descending from heaven, came and rolled back the stone and sat on it." The guards, representatives of the sacrificial culture, became "like dead men." Death is what sacrificial cultures lead to.

The angel's words "Do not be afraid" are at least as earthshaking as the earthquake. These words of peace turn us upside down and around in circles. What is the man we killed to stabilize society going to do to us now that he has risen? Why would the angel tell us not to be afraid? What is this world coming to? Two women named Mary, who lived on the margin of society, a society that would not let them testify in court as witnesses, were made witnesses by God to the news of this momentous presence of life. They run off with "fear and great joy." The two Marys don't get far before they meet up with Jesus, who greets them and repeats the angel's words: "Do not be afraid." Jesus de-centers us once again by taking us from the center of religious and political power and instructing the disciples to meet him back at that backwater Galilee, where he will start a new life for us. St. Paul says of the Hebrews who were delivered from Egypt that we all "passed through the sea and all were baptized into Moses in the cloud and the sea." (1 Cor. 10:2) When we renew our baptismal vows at the Easter Vigil, we renew our commitment to being overwhelmed by God's deliverance from a sacrificial culture that creates fault lines, and to entering a new culture based on the Forgiving Victim. These words are spoken not just to the two women but to the two guards and to each one of us. Can we spread the news to others and, most importantly, to ourselves that we have been delivered from the flood waters of our violence to a new land, a new way of living where we do not need to be afraid?

In contrast to Matthew, the ending of Mark's Gospel is abrupt and enigmatic. (Mk. 16:1–8) So much so that the early Christian community added a "completion" that doesn't connect well with what Mark wrote. There has also been speculation that an original ending broke off from the manuscript or that Mark was captured by the Romans and thrown to the lions just before he could finish it.

Mark's conclusion where the three women who came to the grave run away in fear is so strong that it is enough to make us forget that it is preceded by a ringing proclamation that Jesus has been raised. He has already arrived in Galilee, where he is waiting for them and the disciples. When we remember this proclamation and let it sink in, we realize that this enigmatic ending is not pessimistic or skeptical about the risen life of Jesus, but it is pessimistic and skeptical about the ability of human beings to come to grips with Jesus' risen life.

Mark is not unique in saying that the women at the tomb were afraid when they found the tomb empty. All of the Gospel accounts say as much. In fact, the risen Jesus has to tell *everyone* who sees him not to be afraid once they recognize him (which they usually don't at first.) What is unique to Mark is that he *only* says that the women were afraid as they ran off. Matthew, in contrast, says that the women left the tomb quickly with "fear *and* great joy." (Mt. 28:8) Moreover, in Matthew, they *did* tell the disciples. What were they afraid of? What are *we* afraid of? Usually fear is our response to a threat. If I think a big dog might bite me, I am afraid of it. If someone aims a machine gun at me, I am afraid for my life. But what about Jesus, who never bit anybody or fired a machine gun? Well, we can be afraid of having our understanding of the world turned upside down so that it feels like the earthquake in Matthew, and that is precisely what the Resurrection does. With Easter well-integrated into our yearly cycle of Christian worship, it can *seem* to be business as usual, but that is an illusion. The great value of Mark's blunt proclamation followed by women running off in fear is that it reminds us that the Resurrection is *not* business as usual; it is the bankruptcy of everything we thought kept us in the business of life.

But the Resurrection is a good thing, isn't it? What is there to be afraid of? If the Resurrection is just a happy ending to a story we celebrate and then move on to the business of living, then the Resurrection isn't much to worry about. But then it isn't much to celebrate, either. There are other excuses for having a party. The women ran away from the tomb, not to have a party, but to get away from what had just broken apart their lives as they understood them. Remember, in Mark's Gospel, *nobody* understood Jesus. And the misunderstandings of him only got worse the more Jesus healed people and taught them, until the story ended with Jesus hanging on a cross. So, how could the women or the disciples understand what was happening to them when they were told that Jesus had been raised from the dead? Maybe the disciples, maybe even the women who remained faithful to the end in tending to Jesus' body, were relieved that the man they did not understand was gone. At least they could understand grief and resentment over what had happened. But Jesus wasn't gone. They were going to have to go back to Galilee, where the whole story of Mark's Gospel started, and try again without the benefit of grief and resentment.

Being sent back to the beginning suggests that God was giving them, and us, a second chance. They and we have the advantage of knowing the end of the story, and we can use that as a key to understanding what led up to it. We have learned that the world was broken apart by a God who would choose to die on a cross rather than start a violent revolution. But that God remains alive in the face of such an appalling event, and thus is a God who remains alive in the appalling events we face today. Worse than that, Jesus has broken the cycle of resentment and rage that, though painful, was tight and cozy and predictable. This means we have to redefine the ways we relate to one another. Worse yet, we are threatened with the challenge of life that just isn't going to let up now that death is broken apart. Let us also go back to Galilee and see what else we can find.

A thought experiment can help us ponder the mystery of Jesus' risen life.

Imagine that everybody around you ganged up on you, leveled incredible accusations against you, and beat you up. Your friends either joined in the persecution or slunk away, too afraid to defend you. Your attackers pressed on until they had put you to a painful death. Imagine further that, miraculously, you found yourself alive three days later. Having already died, you could hardly die again. You have become invincible. What would you do to the people who had mistreated you? How would you approach your cowardly friends?

Perhaps this thought experiment can give us an inkling of how amazing it is that, when this very miracle happened to Jesus, he did not retaliate, but instead, invited everybody to a big whooping party that will never end. After rising from the dead, Jesus continued to do what he was doing before he was killed: gather God's people in peace by peaceful means only. That is, after his Resurrection, Jesus practiced what he preached in the Sermon on the Mount: return evil with good, hatred with love. The fullness of Jesus' forgiving love can be as earth-shattering as an earthquake or as gentle as stepping through a wall as if it weren't there.

If Jesus were dead and there was a body in the tomb for the women to anoint, chances are that Jesus' disciples would either have remained in hiding or they would have reacted to the violent act of the crucifixion with violence. But the young men in white asked the women: "Why do you look for the living among the dead? He is not here, but has risen." (Lk. 24:5) That is, God did not will the death of Jesus, God willed *life* for Jesus because that is what God wills for each one of us. As long as we stop at Jesus' death, we also stop at the grief and anger that leads to violence. If we move on to the *life* of Jesus, then there isn't room for grief and anger because Jesus is *alive* and wants us to be alive in Him. This is the forgiving aliveness we see in Peter when he preached to the crowd at Pentecost. His invitation to the people that they repent and be baptized was a far cry from the response we usually get from the followers of a slain leader. Peter had heard the cock crow, repented, and accepted Christ's forgiveness and love. (Mt. 26: 69–75) This is important because when we react to persecution with vengefulness, the only weakness we think about is that which made us vulnerable to persecution. We lose sight of the weaknesses we learn about when the cock crows. Peter had learned that he was a weak human being like the rest of us. If we face our own weaknesses, we can be like him.

The Ascension is perhaps the most puzzling event in Jesus' drama of salvation. The contradictory accounts in Luke, John, and Acts add to the puzzlement. One thing the accounts in Luke and John share is that they connect Jesus' departure with his sending the Holy Spirit. When Jesus said in John that the Holy Spirit would come to lead them into all truth, (Jn. 16:13) what truth did the disciples need that they hadn't learned already from their teacher? Why did Jesus think he *had* to leave before the disciples could learn from the Holy Spirit?

We recall that although Jesus warned his disciples three times that "he would be rejected by the elders, the chief priests, and the scribes, and be killed, and after three days rise again," (Mk. 8:31) the disciples seem to have thought (or hoped) that a Maccabean-like revolution against the Romans was just around the corner. (Gibson 1995, 212–238) After his Resurrection, Jesus tried *again* to get across to the disciples what his Kingdom was really all about. When Cleopas glumly said that he and his companion had hoped that Jesus "was the one who was to redeem Israel," (Lk. 24:21) Jesus, as yet unrecognized by them, rebuked them for their slowness of heart in believing what "the prophets have declared." Then he "interpreted to them all the things about himself in all the scriptures." (Lk. 24:27) Later, Jesus appeared to the twelve and explained that everything written about him in "the law of Moses, the prophets, and the psalms must be fulfilled." (Lk. 24:44) The special mention of the psalms is significant in that they include many laments over persecution from the standpoint of the victim. Jesus went on to say that when the scriptures say that the Messiah was "to suffer and to rise from the dead on the third day," it means that "repentance and forgiveness of sins is to be proclaimed" in Jesus' name to all nations, beginning from Jerusalem. (Lk. 24:47) Proclaiming repentance and forgiveness is a very different proposition from starting a revolt to restore the kingdom to Israel.

In spite of hearing this teaching for forty days, the disciples asked their Risen Lord: "Is this the time when you are going to restore the kingdom to

Israel?" (Acts 1:6) This was the last straw. The disciples were *never* going to stop asking him to restore the kingdom of Israel as long as he was walking on the earth with them. Jesus's Ascension scotched any notion that he would lead a second Maccabean-type revolution. The disciples were left with no choice but to receive the Holy Spirit. Of course, Jesus had already said that he had to leave the disciples before the Advocate, the Holy Spirit, could come to them. Even after having breathed the Holy Spirit on them in the upper room, Jesus had to leave before they could learn what the Spirit was teaching them about the forgiveness of sins.

So what is the Holy Spirit? Wrong question. The Holy Spirit is the third Person of the Trinity, not an "it." Our difficulty in thinking of the Holy Spirit as a person is a symptom of our cultural problem of really seeing other people as *persons.*

Many terms and images are given for the Holy Spirit: a roaring wind, tongues of fire, breath, gift, counselor, consoler, teacher, guide, and the bond of love, to list a few. Some of the terms are personal, some not. This only adds to the confusion unless we get beneath the impersonal images. Breath requires a breather. A person's temperament can be fiery. A bond of love can't really love without being a person who actually loves. Real teaching is given by real persons teaching with conviction, and a guide is a person who is leading another person from one place to another.

The Holy Spirit adds to our difficulty by being so shy. Jesus shows us his Abba, and the Holy Spirit shows us Jesus. Who shows us the Holy Spirit? Nobody. Look behind you and the Holy Spirit is still behind you. Look deeply into yourself and the Holy Spirit is deeper yet. If we want to know the Holy Spirit, we have to be as shy, as hidden as this Person. The more important self-assertion is to us, the less we will perceive the Holy Spirit.

Perhaps the Holy Spirit is hidden in much the same way as mimetic resonance is. As our resonance with other people's desires occurs below our conscious awareness, so does the work of the Holy Spirit within us. Perhaps there is a connection between the two. As our teacher and guide, the Holy Spirit conveys the desire of God. Better said, the Holy Spirit *is* the desire of God. What is this desire of God? The image of a fiery wind burning us without consuming us gives us a hint of God's fundamental desire: that we all may be one, just as the Abba and the Son are one.

Let us try thinking of the Holy Spirit as the Gatherer with fiery arms of Love. Mimetic resonance unites us with other people whether we like it or not, or even whether we think about it or not. Mimetic resonance deepens our lives when we share desires in mutually enriching ways. But when mimetic desire falls into conflict, it unites us to that person in the bad sense of being *stuck* together. The Holy Spirit weaves through the swirl of other peoples' desires with God's desire, teaching us and guiding us with fiery love how to fill all these desires between us with tongues of fire that deepen our communion with others beyond what words can say. In the following chapter, we will look at the ways the Holy Spirit gathers us in Christ.

Chapter 6

The Body of Christ

The Wedding at Cana of Galilee is a beautiful story of celebration. (Jn. 2:1–11) The only problem is the story makes no sense. That may be a way of saying that celebration is infinitely beyond sense.

Foremost among the oddities is the scarce presence of the groom and no mention of the bride. Jesus' central position in the story has the effect of putting *us* into the position of the bride of Jesus "as the bridegroom rejoices over the bride, so shall your God rejoice over you." (Isa. 62:5) The scarcity of wine, probably humanly created—Cana was a poor village—looks ahead to the scarcity of bread in the wilderness. Both times, Jesus counters scarcity with extravagant abundance.

Another puzzle is the dialogue between Jesus and his mother that is as strange as it is brief. Mary could be seen as acting as an intercessor when she tells Jesus that they have no wine for the wedding feast. Jesus' curt reply, however, seems to distance him from his mother. He says that they have nothing to do with each other and his hour has not yet come. Mary tells the attendants to do what Jesus tells them to do, suggesting she believes Jesus will change his mind and provide wine. Maybe Jesus thought turning water into wine was a bit frivolous when he could be healing the lame and the blind, and he needed some prodding to realize how important celebration is. Many pinch-faced Christians since have needed the same prodding.

Nearby are six stone jars that are supposed to hold water for purification.

That would be a lot of purity, but the jars are empty. Perhaps John would have us realize that purity laws and rituals are empty. They tend to divide humans arbitrarily into clean and unclean. That is, purity always creates a scarcity of purity and pure people. Quite the opposite of God's marriage with all God's people.

The water the attendants fill the jars with suggests baptism, as does the water at the well in Samaria, (Jn. 4) another story with nuptial overtones. The wine is a festive drink but it also becomes Jesus' life blood poured out for our redemption, just as the bread in the wilderness becomes Jesus' body broken on the cross to give us his life.

Dostoevsky makes powerful use of this story in *The Brothers Karamazov*. The great staretz (spiritual father) Zossima has just died. When his corpse follows the normal course of nature and creates a stink, many of the people are scandalized, including Zossima's youthful follower, Alyosha Karamazov. Late at night, the stricken Alyosha is praying in the hermitage where the body lies in state. Another monk is reading the story of the Marriage of Cana. The room expands to take in a vast celebration. Then Alyosha sees Zossima rejoicing. The elder says to him: "We are rejoicing . . . we are drinking new wine, the wine of great joy. See how many guests there are? He [Jesus] became like us out of love, and he is rejoicing with us, transforming water into wine, that the joy of the guests may not end. He is waiting for new guests, he is ceaselessly calling new guests." (Dostoevsky 1990, 361)

As a backwater, Cana was a place of no significance. The Temple in Jerusalem was the center of Jewish religion and culture. As with the outcasts at the manger, Jesus' party is in the backwater, not the center. In this new center, Jesus calls all of us to the party, the party that transforms the Body and Blood of Jesus into bread and wine of feasting and rejoicing, a party open to all of us. Jesus has indeed saved the best wine until last.

What does this story have to do with the Christian community or the Church? Where are the Gothic cathedrals and whitewashed steeples? Where are the vestments and bell towers? Where are the sober meeting houses and missionary schools? The Church isn't a bunch of country bumpkins drinking themselves silly, is it? The image is as absurd as saying that God is a rock and has a hand or two. If God is a mystery, the Church grounded in God is also a mystery, and we need cock-eyed images like corrupt stewards and women frantically cleaning house in search of a lost coin to throw us for enough loops to get the idea. What we have in this strange story is a party where everybody is invited, even Jesus and his mother, a party where everybody enhances the desires of one another to be intoxicated with joy in being the Bride of Christ our bridegroom. Of course the Church is serious business. That's why we need so zany an image to get us started.

The French modernist theologian Alfred Loisy famously quipped: "Jesus preached the kingdom of God and got the church." Many people before and since have expressed similar sentiments that pit the Jesus Movement against the Church that followed. There are indeed many grounds for cynicism as we note the abyss between the high ideals of Jesus' preaching and the way Christians often behave. But the parables about unjust stewards and farmers throwing seed all over the place should bring us back to earth with new eyes to see the Kingdom in unlikely places, such as a peasant wedding. Loisy's quip implies that the Jesus Movement was a utopia that disintegrated when Jesus died. In the last chapter, I demonstrated that this was not the case. The Person who gathered followers while he was still alive is the same Person who gathered followers after he was supposedly dead and continues to gather followers for all time. Given the many persecutions perpetrated by the Church, many against the Church's own people, it is understandable that some who are sympathetic to Jesus' teachings think it better to go it alone. Anyone who needs or wants excuses to shun Christian community will surely find them. On the other hand, persecutions on the part of fellow Christians have given some Christians no choice but to go it alone or band in very small groups. I have to admit that the Church often looks like a consolation prize in place of the Kingdom, but this just goes to show that Jesus called fallible humans during his life, and he continues to call fallible humans— like us. The cynicism based on Christian behavior tends to be based on the behavior of *other* people, *other* Christians. We aren't as quick to think about how *we* make the Church look bad. It's no wonder the Church is full of traps, especially since we set some of them ourselves through our disillusionment and cynicism about *other* Christians.

However, trying to be a Christian by ourselves doesn't solve the problems we have with Christian community. Since mimetic resonance with the desires of others runs through all of us all of the time, it is not possible to really go it alone. If we set ourselves over against everybody else in defiance, that very defiance makes us totally dependent on the people we are defying. After all, if we aren't defying *people*, we aren't doing much in the way of defying. The deeper problem is that when we make ourselves that dependent on other people, we are easily sucked into the power of persecutory mechanisms that we protest against. A lone individual cannot hold out against such a system. Our resentment against the Church tends to lead us to the same situation where we unite ourselves deeply to those Christians who have hurt us, or we think have hurt us, and thereby cut ourselves off from those who are deeply faithful to Christ.

Jesus announced the essence of the Church in his inaugural sermon in Luke that we have already examined when Jesus announced the Year of Jubilee, the Year of God's Favor. This year, which was no longer every seventh year, but every year, should bring good news to the poor, release to the captives, forgiveness of debts to debtors, recovery of sight to the blind, and freedom to the oppressed. Letting the oppressed go free refers to God's command to Pharaoh to let God's people go. This command applies to all of us insofar as we keep even one person in bondage in any way, including emotional blackmail. Years ago, at a workshop for Benedictine abbots, Demetrius Dumm, a seasoned monk of St. Vincent Archabbey, gave a series of conferences on biblical spirituality. At the climax of his addresses, he said, with deep solemnity, that he was afraid that at the final judgment, we would each be asked one question and one question only: "Did you let my people go?" Letting God's people go is one of the things the Church is about.

Although many, including many non-Christians, are inspired by Jesus' teachings, it was not the teaching but the *actions* on the part of Jesus that created the Church. That is, the risen Jesus forgave the Church into existence. In bringing the Church into being in this way, Jesus did not forgive us as individuals and leave us as individuals. Jesus forgave all of us as the *community* of humanity. Jesus stood alone against the persecutory crowd. We cannot do this as individuals. Only a community gathered on a radically new principle can counteract the old human community gathered the old way. This is what St. Paul was getting at when he said we have to become members of a new humanity in Christ. (Eph. 4:24; Col. 3:10)

How do we, as a Church, stand together in God's desire? It is through prayer. The inner essence of the Church is forgiveness, but it is prayer that quickens forgiveness. The forgiveness of the Forgiving Victim is proclaimed in public worship. It is the very act of worship that opens humanity to the Kingdom. Spending time praying and praising and repenting is totally wasteful unless God really has created and redeemed us. It is the worship that proclaims forgiveness and encourages us to live in the spirit of forgiveness.

There is actually a two-fold essence of the Church: worship and service in forgiveness. Of the two, service in forgiveness is the deeper essence, The Church may have spawned paraphernalia of cathedrals, miters, Geneva gowns, pointed steeples, smoking incense, choirs, organs and mega-buildings, and more, but you can take away all of that and still have the essence of Church, that without which we have no Church. This essence is forgiveness. Everybody everywhere and everywhen who gathers with others in forgiveness participates in the essence of Church regardless of what ecclesiastical cards, if any, one carries in one's wallet. This does not mean that eschewing prayer is desirable. For one thing, refraining from prayer makes participating in God's desire of forgiveness harder rather than easier. But the best preaching and most enthusiastic hymn-singing will be clanging noises without forgiveness. Of course, given the challenges of forgiveness, most of us gather through forgiveness only some of the time, struggling to live up to the challenges. I will probe these difficulties in Chapter 12. That means that most of us are partly in the Church and partly outside of it. Just like the Parable of the Wheat and the Weeds. This chapter will focus primarily on the deeper essence of forgiveness.

The New Testament word for Church, *ekklesia,* literally means "calling out of." Everybody, without exception, is being called out of human community based on persecution and called into human community based on forgiveness. Of course, some people respond to this call and some don't.

Actually, as noted above, most of us respond to the call some of the time but fail as often as not. Another way of putting it is to define the Church as the people who renounce mimetic rivalry and seek to share their desires with others in constructive ways, grounded in God's desire. As with forgiveness, we have our daily successes and failures with sharing desires constructively or not. Yet another simple image of the Church as grounded in Christ's forgiveness is Jesus' admonition to "give a cup of cold water to one of these little ones in the name of a disciple." (Mt. 10:42) It is instructive that these simple words follow after long instructions to the disciples to preach missions. Those missions led to some healing but ended in failure as far as gathering the Kingdom was concerned. The preaching mission had introduced the disciples to rejection and persecution, even from those closest to them. Giving a cup of cold water is, then, an act of forgiveness and grace in hard, violent times.

A distinction is commonly made between the visible Church and the invisible Church. The former is made up of people who wear clerical collars and vestments and those who sit or stand or kneel in pews and sing hymns or songs of praise. The latter is made up of those who actually have their hearts and minds conformed to Christ regardless of whether or not they place their bodies in buildings with a cross on it. When such a distinction is made, the invisible Church is the real Church, although people invested in the visible Church (sorry about the pun!) hope that at least some of them are in the real, invisible Church as well. Of course, this invisible Church isn't really invisible. It is perfectly visible to God and it is visible to all people who have eyes to see. Embodying the forgiving love of Christ and entering the place of the victim in opposition to the principalities and powers that feast on victims is just as visible as singing hymns and preaching in buildings that we call churches. Again, we hope there is at least some overlap between the two, preferably a lot of overlap, but we all know that the two diverge as much as they coincide. The Church, then, is visible in acts of worship and in charitable acts such as ministering to the poor. When these two visibilities do not connect, it is a cause of dismay if not downright confusion to some. Those who are devoted to both might find that the people they worship with and the people they work with in ministry are not necessarily the same. When worship and service are disconnected, both are diminished. We regret the divisions between various denominations and the more painful ones within denominations. The split between those who pray but do not serve and forgive and those who serve and forgive but do not pray is the deepest, most damaging split of all.

In 325 C.E., Christians celebrated the conversion of Constantine to Christianity and thus the conversion of the Roman Empire to Christianity. Since then, the event has often been seen as the conversion of Christianity to the Roman Empire. It would be good for Christianity to convert any empire since empires are among the principalities and powers. But history suggests that empires usually undermine the Church in ways we would expect. When empire defends Christian missionaries, their mission suffers. In the Spanish missions to the new world, many missionaries saw the problem and fought against the imperial Church as best they could. As anyone who has seen the movie "Mission" knows, the empire won as the empire always does. The Inquisition was a particularly notorious example of the Church collapsing into empire. In more recent history, the Nazi government of Germany ordered the Evangelical (Lutheran) Church to expel all members of Jewish descent from leadership positions. Complying with this demand was a betrayal of the Church's own members and of Christ. (The Nazi demands on the Church only got worse after that.) The Confessing Church that seceded in protest was a remnant of the Body of Christ until it, too, folded under pressure from the Nazi government. In all of this we can see that empire isn't about bad people getting together to do bad things for the sake of being bad. Social mimetic processes take on lives of their own as we have seen with collective violence. Social institutions like governments, business corporations, and—dare I say it?—the Church itself, take on lives of their own with a collective will for survival that transcends any of the individuals involved. That is what makes such entities principalities and powers. Even, and perhaps especially, CEO's can be imprisoned by such mimetic movements. It is tempting to be self-righteous in denouncing the Lutheran Church that compromised itself so badly with the Nazis. It is easier to affirm the Confessing Church in my time and place than it would have been for people who would expect to be persecuted for publically joining them.

Empire is a way of doing things through power brokering feeding on mimetic rivalry, whether it is a superpower nation or a small group in a country parish church intent on ruling their congregation as an oligarchy. Indulge in a little lighthearted gossip that has a bit of sting at somebody's expense, and next thing we know, we've fallen into empire. Actually, we usually don't know it because empire clouds our minds and hearts. Since forgiveness and giving a cup of cold water are threatening to empire, the forces against such things are very strong. When Jesus told the rich young man to give up all his possessions and follow him, he was giving that youth a chance to slip out of the imperial system. (Mt. 19:16–30) Being rich tends to greatly increase one's investment in the imperial system and make it hard to leave it, but an investment in empire doesn't need much in the way of resources to be imprisoning. Whether our bank accounts are small or large, if our hearts are strongly wed to an imperial structure of any kind, it will be easier for a camel to go through the eye of a needle than for such an invested person to enter the Kingdom that Jesus preached. Note that there was no resentment or envy in Jesus' words; just sorrow over a person's bondage. Perhaps this is also why Jesus told comical parables about corrupt stewards to lighten us up for the challenge.

Jesus shows this distancing from the system when confronted with the question of paying taxes to the Emperor, a question designed to entrap him. (Mt. 22:15–22) He asked his questioners to bring a coin, suggesting that he probably did not have one. That is, Jesus had distanced himself from the imperial structures to the extent he was able. By getting his questioners to produce a coin, he showed up the hypocrisy of their question. Since having Roman money showed that they were part of the system, they should act like it. In this respect, Jesus was acting out the part of the servant in the Parable of the Talents who hid his talent so that it would not feed the economic system. Perhaps this is the sort of thing Jesus had in mind when he counseled us to "be wise as serpents and innocent as doves." (Mt. 10:16)

Being the Church is not about dropping out of an imperial society. Jesus could not avoid living in the Roman Empire, and most of the time, neither can we. Far from dropping out, Jesus engaged the Empire directly in

Jerusalem, challenging the Empire to repent or show its violent reality for all to see. The fundamental thing to do is live and act grounded in the love and forgiveness of Jesus, the Forgiving Victim. No matter how much one might dislike the imperial aspects of the economic structure and governments, there is no way around using currency and credit cards to buy material goods. Besides, boycotts and economic sanctions are violence inflicted by other means than drone bombers that create much collateral damage in supposedly "good" causes. Separating by going off the grid is not usually helpful either, especially if it is done with resentment that keeps one glued to empire, while stewing in a remote cabin somewhere. Much more constructive is to engage in imaginative structures. The credit union is a good example of this. Vulnerable people in Europe and America, who were underserved by existing financial structures, were given valuable assistance by credit unions.

Most fundamentally, empire cannot be resisted in empire's terms, using violence of any kind. Least of all does one convert empire by acting out of resentment or envy of those who benefit from empire or seem to. Business tycoons and government officials and bureaucrats who abuse their power create many scapegoats. But if Girard is right that scapegoating is the problem, then making scapegoats out of Wall Street or the power brokers in our parish churches perpetuates empire. Being silent while standing in the place of the victim is perhaps the hardest thing to do, but this is what Jesus did before Pilate. If Jesus really is the wedding guest thrown out into the outer darkness and the penniless servant thrown out to the same place, then we can all join him in the outer darkness where the victims of empire are. If we do that, we will increase the light already shed there by the Light of the World.

On the world stage, empires fight about who is the greatest. When Christian denominations or differing religious traditions follow suit, they are acting in the same imperialistic fashion. Jesus' closest disciples emulated empire when they fought among themselves as to who was the greatest. When the disciples fought over who was the greatest or asked for the best seats in the Kingdom, Jesus showed infinite patience by not acting the way most of us in authority would. Usually, authority figures will quash any argument among people under them. But Jesus explains that it is the Gentiles who wish to exercise lordship over others and it should not be that way with his followers. There is an edge to Jesus' use of the word "benefactors" for those practicing lordship; such people used their benefactions more to assert their superiority and social control than to be charitable to others. Jesus goes on to say that he has come among the disciples as one who serves, not one who lords it over them.

In response to the disciples' wrangling, Jesus does something very simple. He places a child in their midst and tells them: "Whoever welcomes one such child in my name welcomes me, and whoever welcomes me welcomes not me but the one who sent me." (Mk. 9:37) Caring for a small child is the deepest manifestation of positive mimetic desire. Jesus subtly breaks up the closeness that the bond of enmity is creating among the disciples and instead tries to unite them in their desire to care for the small child. This story puts before all of us the choice of how we will connect with the desires of other people: Will it be in rivalry or in nurturing others? Saint Gregory the Great did not coin the phrase that "the Pope is the servant of the servants of God," but he was the first to make extensive use of it and make it such a quotable quote through the ages. The phrase certainly picks up the meaning of Jesus' words to the apostles as captured in Luke.

A deeper sign of Jesus' infinite patience with his disciples (and us) is his assurance that they will sit on twelves thrones to judge the Twelves Tribes of Israel. (Mt. 19:28) This assurance is startling since it seems to contradict what Jesus has just been talking about. But does it? If being a ruler means being a servant, as Jesus suggests and Gregory the Great averred, then maybe sitting on a throne to judge a tribe of Israel is not such a good deal for the judge. We tend to think that being a judge means being judgmental; that judging the Twelve Tribes of Israel means accusing them of their wrongdoings. But what if the judge is a servant? In his response to the disciples' infighting, Jesus is surprisingly nonjudgmental, although he makes it clear that they haven't gotten it right. Jesus continues to serve them through his example, such as washing their feet and leading them gently but firmly to a new way of seeing the world and, more importantly, living in it.

The thing is, Jesus didn't judge the disciples (and us) by browbeating them; Jesus judged them by serving them humbly. The Twelve Tribes of Israel is an expression for a renewed Israel for Gentiles and Jews alike. Judging them means serving them the way Jesus served them and the way Jesus serves us. It means offering a cup of cold water to the least of Jesus' people. It is our acts of loving service that will judge all people who exercise lordship by oppressing others. The Pope isn't the only one called to be a servant of the servants of God. In calling all of us to be the Church, all of us are called to be servants of Christ's servants. Although Jesus has "King of Kings and Lord of Lords" inscribed on his thigh, (Rev. 19:16) it is important that we not swell with pride over being part of Jesus' imperial court, but that we realize that Jesus exercises his kingship by being the Servant of Servants. In Philippians, Paul quoted what is believed to be an early Christian hymn by most Bible critics. (Phil. 2:6–11) This hymn sings about Jesus divesting himself of divine power to became a weak human, as a model for Jesus' followers.

Contrasting the Church with empire is a useful way to highlight what the Church should be and what it shouldn't. It is a helpful way to distinguish the two masters who cannot both be followed simultaneously. (Mt. 6:24) In not being able to serve both "God and wealth," it is not a matter of how many dollars, euros, or lakhs one has but how entangled one is with the imperialistic aspects of the world's financial system. The danger in this dualism is the temptation to think that *we* are in the Church and *other people* are invested in empire. The truth is that we are all involved with empire at least some of the time. Every time we engage in controlling behavior of others in a bullying way, we are being imperialistic. It is more important for us to judge ourselves rather than others. (Mt. 7:1–5)

In spite of Jesus' prayer that we all may be one, disunity among Christians and the history of violence among Christians has been a stumbling block for many since Jesus' Ascension. Paul scolded the Corinthians for their slogans: "I belong to Apollos!" "I belong to Paul!" (1 Cor. 3:4) This indicates that Church parties go back to the earliest days of the Church. Every time rivalry sets in, Christians slip into the role of accuser, because everybody's rival is always the one who started it. Some people solve the problem of division by leaving and starting a new congregation someplace else. Sometimes this sort of separation simply has to happen, sad as it is. It is important, however, for splitting groups to focus on what they stand for, not what they are against. Most churches were founded in protest against the ecclesiastical body they left, and so they were governed by what they stood against at least as much as for what they affirmed. Many splits are motivated by a desire to purify the Church. The problem is that when one starts expelling the impure, there is always going to be someone left who is impure who also needs to be expelled. In the end, everybody is expelled and there is nobody left as Jesus has also been expelled.

Denouncing the scandals and hypocrisy in the Church is just about everybody's favorite blood sport. Unfortunately, there really are serious scandals that have to be dealt with for the sake of those who are seriously injured by them. There is also the danger of getting so caught up in denunciations of scandals that we create a mental and spiritual fog that distorts everything around us. Jesus' teachings about seeking reconciliation while requiring accountability give us a way forward in dealing with these scandals. (Mt. 18:15–20) As an alternative, a look at some biblical images for the Church can be a powerful inspiration if we turn to them and strive to use them to bring our desires into harmonious relationships with the desire of other people and, most importantly, with God. These images can, of course, be discouraging because their high ideals seem out of reach, but if we never have anything to reach for, we'll never get a hold of anything above ourselves. Moreover, these images give us a sense of direction for how we might overcome the problems of empire and disunity in the Church. Each of these images has limitations, so if we take any of them too far, we end up in a place well outside of God's desire.

The analogy of the Church being the Body of Christ is the best-known image. (1 Cor. 12:12–28) The implication is that as the various parts of a body add up to a unity, the various members of the Church, different as they are, also make up a body. This analogy suggests each part must be well-coordinated with all the others. We can see this readily—and impressively— in the athletic maneuvers of acrobats, dancers, and musicians. In ensembles, such artists not only must have each part of their bodies well-coordinated, but each person must be well-coordinated with all the others. When they succeed, they act as one person although they are many. This image suggests a deep intuition on St. Paul's part about mimetic resonance. Just as each part of the human body must be sensitive and synchronized with one another other, so must each member of Christ's Body resonate with one another. As with the body, this resonance is a preconscious sensitivity to the other members. The most essential elements of this sensitivity are accepting the other members and not overstepping limits so as to take over any other part of the body. St. Paul affirms the interdependence of each part when he says that one part cannot say it doesn't need another part.

Paul's extension of the analogy to a list of various ministries in the Church makes it clear that if a foot wants to be a hand, the body won't walk very well. These destructive outcomes happen if the parts of the body fall into mimetic rivalry. The comic character Bottom in Shakespeare's *A Midsummer Night's Dream* is a perfect example of overstepping such boundaries. At the rehearsal of the play to be performed before the Duke's court, Bottom first accepts the part assigned to him but then wants every other part as it is doled out to the cast. The absurdity of Bottom's desire is clear enough if we try to imagine him doing all the parts in the play himself. It is the same absurdity we would have if the neck tried to do all the walking. Some parts of the body must look strange to other parts. The lung must look as strange to the hip as a solemn high mass with incense looks odd to a Pentecostal. But if the hip and the lung try to expel each other, the whole body will collapse. The breath of the Holy Spirit and the Body and Blood of Jesus all circulate through the Blood of the Body of Christ to all the other parts. Take out a part and the flow is hampered or stopped.

None of these considerations suggest that this analogy of the human body is intended to enshrine oppressive hierarchical structures. Unfortunately this has often happened. The image of the body as an image of the political body was often used in Greek and Roman thought with precisely this intention. So used, this image helped to institutionalize violence. This was one of the means of containing the violent potential of mimetic desire, but it did not solve the problem. Paul subverts this traditional intention by balancing the importance of all the parts in a deep mutual need. When this mutual need is perceived by all of the members, each part will have due reverence for all the other parts. Moreover, this body is *not* the political body but the Body of *Christ.* The political body is made up of parts, which puts its members in mimetic relationships with one another. Hence the importance of pulling rank. But the Body of Christ is grounded in *Christ.* That means that we are grounded in our relationship with Christ (or should be) rather than grounded in our horizontal relationships. All of this sets up the fundamental importance of servant leadership, which I discussed above.

Peter envisions the community of Christ as a "holy house" made out of "living stones." (1 Pet. 2:5) This image reminds us of St. Paul's admonition that individually and collectively we should each be a Temple of God. (1 Cor. 3:16) It is significant that Peter calls the building a house and not a temple, although this house is a place where priestly ministry takes place. I see here a hint that Christ's household is not a place set apart but a place for everyone, sort of like the City of God that doesn't have a temple because the whole place is one. As with the image of the Body of Christ, we have a sense of unity-in-diversity. There are many stones, and each has to be in its proper place, or the house collapses. The stones are not inert but living, vibrant. Again each living stone should resonate with all the other living stones, another powerful image of mimetic resonance working constructively.

If these living stones making up the "holy house" are truly vibrant, they are personal. One can't have mimetic resonance without humans and God. As "living stones," we should present our "bodies as a living sacrifice, holy and acceptable to God," which is our "spiritual worship." (Rom. 12:1) We are to be "transformed" by the renewing of our minds so that we "may discern what is the will of God—what is good and acceptable and perfect." (Rom. 12:2) This transformation should help us discern God's desire. Paul lists many signs of this transformation: That we "hate what is evil, hold fast to what is good; love one another with mutual affection; outdo one another in showing honor. Do not lag in zeal, be ardent in spirit, serve the Lord. Rejoice in hope, be patient in suffering, persevere in prayer. Contribute to the needs of the saints; extend hospitality to strangers." (Rom. 12:9–13) We should "bear one another's burdens, and in this way [we] will fulfill the law of Christ." (Gal. 6:2) Loving with mutual affection and bearing one another's burdens are ways we resonate deeply with the desires of others in supportive ways. We also participate in Christ who bears all of our burdens

Another possible biblical image that could be considered analogous to the Church is that of the vine and the branches. (Jn. 15: 1–9) Here, we are all connected with one another through the vine that is Christ. This image stresses our resonance with the desire of God but also our connectedness with others through God's desire. The images of the Body of Christ and living stones have contemplative dimensions that sink into us when we quietly pray with and through them, but this image of the vine and branches has the deepest contemplative dimension.

Another image of the Church is derived from the family. Even more than with other images there are strengths and weaknesses. The disparity between ideal and reality has the potential of being very great. Most importantly, it brings to remembrance our families of origin. If our family experiences are, on balance, good, then the biblical use of these images reinforce that. But if our family experiences are seriously bad, then the image becomes a stumbling block. If such was the case in our earliest years, then the people we encounter later in life tend to be repeat performances of the same stumbling. In such cases, we need to remember that healing was a major part of Jesus' ministry, and healing familial brokenness is a part of that.

The Fatherhood of God is an important familial image in Christian spirituality, as the Lord's Prayer reminds us every time we say it. This prayer is addressed to Jesus' heavenly Abba, and Jesus used the word before passing it on to us. In so doing, Jesus is attesting to the paternal care given all of us by God. More importantly, God's paternity comes to us through Jesus. At the Annunciation, the heavenly Abba, who had begotten the Son from all eternity, begets the human child in Mary's womb. As a conscious human, Jesus experienced the love of his heavenly Abba in a powerful way when he was baptized in the Jordan by John. The pre-emptive love of the child expressed by the Abba's words of affirmation is fatherhood at its best. It is like the happy parent who is overjoyed with the birth of a child simply because the child *is*. It is this pre-emptive love that is the foundation of the Church, the rock on which the Church is built. Also, in addition to his heavenly Abba, Jesus had Joseph as an earthly father, a flesh-and-blood presence to pick up the infant Jesus when he fell and to teach him how to make useful things out of wood. Failures in early nurturing create basic insecurities that are difficult to overcome. The Church as a whole is called to delight in every child and to nurture every child during maturation.

The image of mother, especially as embodied by Jesus' earthly mother, has often been used as an image for the Church. As a particular flesh-and-blood mother, Mary is Mother Church without being an abstraction. That she would nourish the baby Jesus from her own body makes her a perfect image of nurturing. When confronted with the mysteries surrounding Jesus' birth, she pondered them in her heart. Little else is told of her from scripture, but she stood by Jesus at the cross, making her the archetype of the many grieving mothers whose sons have been treated with the same sort of violence. The nurturing we receive from our mothers has a lot to do with our having a basic sense of security that helps us resist rivalrous mimetic desire as we grow up.

As important as these paternal and maternal relationships are, they belong to Jesus first and to the rest of us secondarily. That is to say, Jesus relates to us as our brother, and we are all Jesus' brothers and sisters. Considering the history of sibling rivalry in scripture, this is of immense significance. Jesus is the keeper of his brother that Abel never had, and he is Cain's keeper as well. Martha Reineke discusses the tension and fundamental choice a child is faced with when a sibling is born: whether to compete or to welcome the sibling as "more of me" rather than less. (Reineke 2014, 83) There is no competing with Jesus over Mama or Papa, so we might as well be civil brothers and sisters with him and with one another in the bargain.

It is also in passages of scripture about the family that empire intrudes with an iron fist. Slaves are admonished to obey their masters. (Eph. 6:5) The scattered verses that tolerate, if not support, slavery have had terrible consequences. In the United States, slave owners justified the "peculiar institution" with scripture. William Wilberforce, on the other hand, was convinced that the underlying teaching of scripture precluded slavery, and he led the movement to abolish slavery and the slave trade in the British Empire. Empire criticism comes in handy here as we take into account the very real possibility that Christianity could not have survived its first three centuries if it had overtly and unequivocally condemned slavery. In our time, it is troubling that the early Church tolerated slavery, or at least seemed to, as a compromise. It would be more troubling if the early Church was mostly indifferent to the indignities of slave labor. Paul's admonition to masters to stop threatening their slaves and to remember that they both have the same Father in Heaven can be seen as a time bomb set to blow up the institution of slavery sooner or later. (Eph. 6:9) Wilberforce obviously thought so. We know from recent history of totalitarian rule that subjects have to use veiled communications to get certain points across. This may have happened even with Holy Scripture.

In Mark, there are indications of tensions even in Jesus' family. While Jesus was speaking to followers crammed into a house, some of his family "went to take charge of him, for they said, 'He is out of his mind.'" (Mk. 3:21) Later, when Jesus is told that his mother and brothers and sisters are outside wanting to speak to him, Jesus points to the people who are listening to him and says that *they* are his mother and brothers and sisters. (Mk. 3:31–33) This indicates that even during his lifetime, Jesus is building a kinship network based on obedience to God's desire rather than bloodlines. Jesus promised that "There is no one who has left house or brothers or sisters or mother or father or children or fields, for my sake and for the sake of the good news, who will not receive a hundredfold now in this age—houses, brothers and sisters, mothers and children, and fields, with persecutions—and in the age to come eternal life." (Mk. 10:29–30) This promise demonstrates that Jesus is reconstructing the family and, through the family, society. These words come right after the rich young man went away disappointed, another indication that part, if not all, of his wealth was through family ties. Such ties are the camel that can't easily get through the "eye of a needle." (Mk. 10:25) There are people from broken families who find family through the Church. Building deep kinship ties through Jesus happens when we allow Jesus to bring us into the arms of his mother and the presence of the heavenly Abba, who is so well-pleased with us that our hearts melt and we really want to be pleasing to our brothers and sisters. That Jesus' mother stood by him at the cross and at least one of his brothers (James) became a leader of the Church in Jerusalem tells us that his worldly family, or at least part of it, was so reconstructed.

The importance of the family as an image of the Church is heightened when we recall Dumouchel's contention that loosening family bonds was one of the ways of containing violence, but it came at the cost of a "contract of indifference" that entailed what we might call a hidden or "quiet" violence. (Dumouchel 2015, 1–30) If the family is not strong, then family feuds and inter-family feuds are not going be strong either. That is the good news. The bad news is the loss of solidarity for helping in times of need. This neglect of others goes far beyond letting people quietly starve. Dumouchel also analyzes the chilling results in totalitarian societies where social indifference allows governments to persecute selected people, as the Nazis persecuted the Jews and communist governments took people away in the middle of the night. (Dumouchel 2015) These governments had to count on collective indifference to pursue their persecutory policies. I have already noted that a social mimetic movement can be as violent as a wildfire. It is also possible for a social mimetic movement to freeze into a collective ice box. What we have to do is strengthen the family in such a way as to weaken the violence that family ties can cause. This gives us an ascetical double whammy. We have to renounce the solidarity that leads to mimetic strife and collective violence, but then we must retain, strengthen, and extend these ties when it comes to providing for others. That is, the borders that made providing for family tenable have been exploded by Jesus.

Modern western notions of individualism that began to escalate in the seventeenth century are the results of this weakening of bonds that Dumouchel writes about. As we shall see later, an emerging sense of individual responsibility can be traced back to the Gospel as it seeks to wean us from the persecutory crowd. The conversion of Paul is a prime example of this. Unfortunately, the escalating individualism of modern times has largely lost its roots in the relationship with Christ, with each of us being parts of Christ's body. Paul Nuechterlein posted a brief note on his website about aspen trees. They look like a forest of individual trees, but it turns out that they all share one network of roots. This is quite a powerful image of what it means to be rooted in Christ. This escalated individualism skews many ethical issues, especially those of social dimensions. One of the reasons the Gospel's demand for social solidarity seems so onerous is that we tend to hear it through the filter of "the contract of indifference." That is, we think the entire burden falls on each of us individually. We forget that we are invited into a *family*, a family that is the Body of Christ. We do not each have to take responsibility for others on our own little lonesome. That would be rugged individualism all over again. Instead, we are encouraged to take responsibility for others as members of a Body. Jesus reaches out to everyone through each and every one of us. Our personal responsibilities are collective responsibilities.

Another biblical image of the Church is the Bride of Christ. Paul admonishes husbands to love their wives "just as Christ loved the church and gave himself up for her, in order to make her holy by cleansing her with the washing of water by the word, so as to present the church to himself in splendor, without a spot or wrinkle or anything of the kind—yes, so that she may be holy and without blemish" (Eph. 5:25–27) Here, Paul interweaves the image of spouse with that of the hierarchal family. Before taking too much umbrage at the apparent subordination of women to men in these verses, it is important to note the Christological dimensions of these admonitions. The husband is the head of the woman *as Christ is the head of the Church*. That is, the husband must *first* subordinate himself to Christ before he can properly function as the head of anybody else. By saying that Christ gave himself up for his bride, the Church, Paul makes it clear that subordinating oneself to Christ means subordinating oneself to the *self-giving* of Jesus, a self-giving that took him to the cross. This doesn't leave any room for dominating anybody in an overbearing way. Indeed, although parents have authority over children, Paul cautions against "provoking them to anger." (Eph. 6:4)

In Revelation, the seer sees a new Jerusalem "coming down out of heaven from God, prepared as a bride adorned for her husband." (Rev. 21:2) This deepens the Christological dimensions of the bridal imagery for the Church.

Throughout this book, the seer sees imperial violence for the destructive force that it is and foresees its inevitable collapse under its own violence. Meanwhile, although the Lion of Judah was announced to make an appearance, presumably to exact divine vengeance, which is what most people expect and hope for in the face of oppression, what actually appears is "a lamb appearing as if it had been slaughtered." (Rev. 5:5–6) That is, just as Jesus confounded his people's expectations of what kind of Messiah they would get, the risen Christ confounds these expectations yet again, which is precisely what the risen Christ did when he ascended to Heaven and sent the Holy Spirit.

There is a paradox in this bridal imagery because, although spouses are fundamental to families, they share an intimacy that other members of the family simply cannot share. In fact, the fecundity of the spousal relationship, that is most usually manifest in producing children but can take many other forms for nurturing other people, requires this private intimacy at its core. I have noticed acts of intimacy among spouses that go beyond physical acts of affection that show the depth of their union.

The Church as Bride of Christ is foreshadowed by Hosea, who married a prostitute and remained faithful to her throughout her infidelities. The prostitute, Gomer, stands for unfaithful Israel and for the unfaithful Church. More positively, the Church as bride is also foreshadowed in the Song of Songs, where the playful hide-and-seek games of the lovers celebrate the games we play with God and God plays with us. (Song 5:2–8)

The stronger paradox of the image of the Church as Bride of Christ is that every member of the Church shares a marital intimacy with God. This means we share a deep intimacy with one another in the Body of Christ. In this way, the image of the Church as "living stones" is personalized in a deep union through mimetic resonance with one another in Christ's Body. It is this image we see acted out at the Wedding at Cana, where Jesus is the bridegroom and we are, each one of us, the Bride. The deeper we move into brideship with Christ, the more subordination among humans melts away and we experience our fundamental equality and unity in Christ. Within this union, Christ is the head of each and every one of us in an intimacy beyond our imagining.

This is an intimacy we usually have to take on faith, but we may experience it in fleeting moments. Revelation tells us that this party is the occasion of rousing songs such as: "Worthy is the Lamb that was slaughtered to receive power and wealth and wisdom and might and honor and glory and blessing!" (Rev. 5:12) In Revelation's scheme of things, the empire is self-destructing, while the Church keeps on singing the praises of God. We will next look at the Church as a praying community.

Chapter 7

The Five Kinds of Prayer

Simply put, prayer is the meeting of our desires with God's desire. Although God meets us with an infinitely simple desire, we are not simple. That is why more than one approach to God is necessary for us. There are five fundamental kinds of prayer that Church tradition teaches, ways that immerse our desires ever more deeply into God's desire. We shall see that prayer also connects us deeply to the desires of other people. My seminary professor of ascetical theology, Donald Parsons, said that just as we need a balanced diet in our eating habits, we need a balanced diet of prayer. The five kinds of prayer give us a way to achieve this goal. In churches with a strong liturgical tradition, this balanced diet tends to be part of the package during times of worship, but we all need to be mindful of the types of prayer that keep us balanced.

Petition

Petitionary prayer is asking God to give us something for ourselves. This is often considered the lowest form of prayer because it seems selfish. Why should I want anything for me, myself, and I? Well, God wants to give gifts to those of us who knock so that the door can be opened. (Mt. 7:7) For that matter, God wants to give us gifts even when we don't knock, but God really desires that we knock.

We are filled with what James Alison calls our "smelly" desires. (Alison 2013, 412–420) This is because we are made by God to have desires both for what we need and for things beyond basic needs that will enhance our lives. Since we have these desires, we have to do something with them. One thing we can do is renounce them, but we can't do that unless we know what desires we are renouncing. So first, we have to be clear on what we desire.

In petitionary prayer, we bring our desires to God. In so doing, we increase our awareness of what these desires are: good, bad, and indifferent. We may not like having our stinkier desires but we all have them, and if we don't become aware of them, they will rule our lives without our knowing it. Of course, bringing our desires to God is tricky because we don't always know what we want. What we think we want does not always turn out to be what we really want. All of us have found this out many times when we got what we thought we wanted and ended up disappointed.

Knowing our desires is further complicated by mimetic desire. This is the problem of figuring where other peoples' desires end and ours begin, as we explored in Chapter 2. Sometimes we simply don't know which desires are our own. Presenting our desires, smelly and otherwise, to God can help us to see which is which, at least to some extent. Presenting these desires to God can also make us more aware of their rivalrous elements. For example, if I pray for my favorite baseball team to win the championship, I quickly realize that God is not going to play favorites, and the best and/or luckiest team is going to win no matter how hard I pray. That is, God's desire is not for one team or the other win but for everybody to enjoy the game no matter who wins and who loses. The same applies to more serious issues in life, such as personal relationships, especially those of a romantic nature. As we bring petitionary prayers of this sort to God, we find at the base of God's desire a will towards freedom. This includes the random bounces of the baseball and the freedom for people to react to us as they choose. It is often said that God answers a prayer with "No," and that can be the case, but not necessarily. Since God gives the rest of the world the same freedom God gives us, God is going to prefer that a person I am attracted to makes a free choice rather than chooses me out of compulsion. Because God gives this same freedom to everybody in the world, not everything is going to pan out the way God's desire might have it. The bombs dropping all over the world, in spite of all our prayers, make that very clear.

There are times when petitionary prayer will lead us into the depths of our own suffering as we become all the more acutely conscious of what we want and what we don't have. That is no big deal if I want a butterscotch sundae and can't get one because nobody has any butterscotch. But it is an overwhelming deal when I pray for peace and justice, and they don't happen. God probably doesn't care all that much about how many butterscotch sundaes I get. I've had enough in my life to feel fortunate. God surely cares very much that humans live in peace. But humans can use their free will to destroy peace or prevent it. Our prayer for peace will lead us into the heart of God's suffering over discord and war. Although we may not like suffering over these things very much, we find that God's desire strengthens us to live with whatever happens and to feed on God's desire so as to do as much as we each possibly can to make bad situations less bad and make good situations better.

Intercessory Prayer

Intercessory prayer is asking God to give something to another person rather than to me. In this respect, it seems much more generous than petitionary prayer and often it is. But not necessarily. Once again, our resonance with one another's desires creates confusion over what we want and what another person might really want. There is inevitably some overlap, and the same considerations we made for petitionary prayer hold for intercessory prayer as well. Actually, the problem can be more insidious when praying for others than with praying for ourselves.

The biggest pitfall in intercessory prayer is to ask God to meet *our* needs in our relationship with that person rather than to meet *that person's* needs. That is, we project our desires on the other and pray for that. More seriously, there is a chance that a hidden rivalry enters our intercessory prayer so that we pray *against* another in a self-serving manner. The most common way to clothe concern for others in this way is to pray judgmentally. This puts us in the "superior" position over the other. This is the prayer of the Pharisee who thanked God for being better than that publican. (Lk. 18: 9–14) Years ago, at a prayer meeting I attended, one man prayed to God to cure his brother of his "dirty, stinking habits." I'm sure that if the man's brother really had one or more destructive habits, God would want that person to be cured, but God is much more gracious in entering that person's deepest self and offering strength to that person rather than the person praying for him (or against him).

When we pray for others, we are entering into God's desire as we do with petitionary prayer, only now we have expanded the field to include other people in their needs. Praying for ourselves opens us to the deep love God has for each of us. Praying for others opens us up to the deep love God has for other people. There is no room for judgmentalism in prayer, since prayer is about humbling ourselves before God and before others.

Intercessory prayer is a good way, perhaps one of the best ways, of putting ourselves into the shoes of others. As we learn to really pray *for* others rather than against them, we enter into their desires with an empathy that helps us understand what they are going through. We come to feel their pain when they are suffering. This is certainly why Jesus admonished us to pray for our enemies. If we pray for those we hate and who hate us, we are led into a deeper sense of their humanity. We begin to understand them. We also begin to understand Jesus' saying that God lets the rain fall on the righteous and the unrighteous. (Mt. 5:45) What our Lord is telling us here is that God gives gifts and grace to all people pre-emptively before any of us do anything to deserve them, and God continues to give these gifts and provide for us regardless of what we do. We often take God's providence for granted when it comes to ourselves because we assume we deserve God's blessings and are entitled to them, but we aren't so sure about other people. What we learn from praying for our enemies is that they are frail humans like ourselves, and we are invited to join God in wishing that God give these people the same blessings that we wish God to give those we like much better.

Intercessory prayer also leads us into the mystery and anguish of unanswered prayer much more than does petitionary prayer. We often experience disappointment in petitionary prayers, but my experience is that the emotional investment is much stronger when it comes to praying for somebody else in need. Maybe this is one of the reasons we need to support each other in prayer. When the one we pray for does not recover from an illness, we are much more devastated than we are if we prayed for our own healing and didn't get it. This isn't the place to get into the ins and outs of a prayer that was answered with a No. The fundamental reason prayer for healing sometimes gets a negative answer is because we are all mortal, and the ultimate healing is on the other side of the grave. Another reason for the No is because God gives microbes and our body cells the same freedom God gives us. God doesn't usually forcibly stop humans from acting wrongly, although God did just that in the case of Pharaoh. Whatever the outcome, prayer for the healing of another moves us into the depths of God's healing power, which Jesus used to heal those who were brought to him. When we bring other people to God the way the friends of the paralytic brought him down through the roof to Jesus, healing does happen at one level or another.

At its best, intercessory prayer is a powerful participation in the desires of other people in a constructive way. Better still, it is a participation in God's desire for others. We share what is best in ourselves with the other for the good of the other and for the sake of the other. When we pray for others in this way, and they pray for us in like manner, we create an expanding web of prayer that reaches out to everybody. This is what our built-in mimetic resonance is for.

Penitential Prayer

Much of what is written about penitential prayer is centered on personal sin committed by ourselves. However, our tendency to desire according to the desires of others suggests that a more corporate model is needed in our approach to penance. To begin with, sin is never personal in an individual way. Our own participation in sinfulness is intertwined with the sinfulness of others. As with petitionary and intercessory prayer, penitential prayer is an important way of becoming aware of our own desires and their interactions. The old list of seven capital sins from traditional Catholic teaching is a handy structure for a brief look at how to confess these sins in the light of our participation in mimetic resonance.

Lust and gluttony are the sins most grounded in our physiology. We experience physical craving with these sins, but our physical urges are pulled and twisted by the advertising media and other cultural factors that spur us on to wanting a particular kind of sexual mate or this brand of cookies or this label of beer. Rivalry tends to surround what often passes for love in human relationships. Gluttony is not subject to rivalry in the same way but some people seem to make a point of consuming more than others as a way to feeling they are "winners" in the game of life.

Both lust and gluttony are subject to bodily addictions that are easily exacerbated by mimetic rivalry. The exasperation of people who live with addicts often amounts to a contest of wills. This is perhaps where the term "enabler" is most applicable. That is, the enabler adds to the tension caused by the addictive behavior so that the addict feels that he or she "loses" by giving up the addiction and being healed. In fact, many enablers fail to cope with healed addicts. Theories about family systems illustrate the elements of addictive behavior at a social level. Such theories reach for the jugular vein of the social system, not the capillary of the individual.

Envy and avarice are the most mimetic of the capital sins. Envy, of course, is pure mimetic desire, wanting what somebody else has and usually preferring to destroy what the other has if the envious one cannot get it. Avarice is envy in advance, or pre-emptory envy. An avaricious person wants what others want and tries to get it before anybody else can. Such a one often tries to anticipate what others will want, then deem that thing desirable, and then grab it before anybody else can.

Sloth is a sin that can be committed with little or no reference to anybody else except that the failure to perform deeds that others need or would appreciate affects those people. The Latin word is *acedia,* and it means a lot more than laziness, although it includes it. *Acedia* is primarily a lack of seeking the good; staying in the dumps rather than making an effort to do what is good. One way we are afflicted by sloth is by not noting how the desires of others are affecting us. When we fail to do that, we just float along on others' desires without taking any responsibility for our lives.

Anger is the opposite of sloth insofar as it is energetic while sloth is lethargic. While sloth is uncritically floating with the social mimetic process, whatever it is, anger is an equally uncritical participation in the contagion of the crowd's collective anger. Anger, of course, is the fuel for mimetic rivalry and most particularly for the desire for revenge. The more revenge is fueled by anger, the less examination there is as to the appropriateness of revenge. We tend to think of anger as personal because we feel it in our bodies but anger is always relational, even if it is in relationship with ourselves. That is, we get angry with whatever disturbs us about ourselves. This anger at self is easily projected onto others. Because of the involvement of body chemistry in anger, it poses the danger of falling into a substance addiction.

Pride and his cousin vainglory will be examined at length in the chapter on humility. In examining ourselves penitentially, we find that pride begins with the temptation to claim our anger, our possessiveness, or our lust as our own, something to fight for in opposition to the people we think want to take them away from us. In all mimetic rivalry, there is a strong dose of pride.

As we examine ourselves in these seven capital sins, we must remember above all, the Gospel's revelation of the truth of sacred violence. As the culture of lynching in the U. S. reminds us, collective violence can easily slip into a cultural phenomenon—"the way we have always done it"—so that the way we have always done it is taken for an eternal "truth," when the real truth is that the devil has been a liar and a murderer from the beginning. (Jn. 8:44)

The sacrament of confession is a well-known and oft-practiced therapeutic exercise that lifts heavy burdens from us. Even those who do not believe in penance as a sacrament find it important to confess their sins to another to get them off one's chest.

The mimetic dimension of our sinfulness also impresses upon us the necessity of turning to God, the One who is outside the system of the mimetic contagion that constitutes the principalities and powers. It is God as the Other who gives us an alternative to the principalities and powers. This is what we find at the heart of the penitential psalm par excellence. When the Psalmist prays: "Create in me a clean heart and put a right spirit within me," (Ps. 51:10–11) the Psalmist is praying for God to infuse God's desire into the penitent. Then, still noticing double-mindedness, the Psalmist goes on to pray that God sustain a "willing spirit." The story of Peter walking on water— or trying to—also illustrates this turning. (Mt. 14:28–33) The wind and the choppy waves represent our being overwhelmed by the mimetic movements that tend toward rage and persecution. When Peter looked at the waves instead of at Jesus, he started to sink. By himself, he would have sunk and drowned. By looking again at Jesus, Peter was pulled into the boat and the sea grew calm.

Thanksgiving

Thanksgiving differs from petition and intercession in that we focus on what we have and how grateful we are that we have it. Thanksgiving should accompany all of our petitionary and intercessory prayer because we should be thankful *in the act of asking.* Usually, we prefer to wait until a request has been granted before thanking the donor. Here, however, when we pray with thanksgiving, we thank the donor in advance. This does not mean asking God for something with confidence that the request will be granted in precisely the way we ask for it. Thanksgiving is gratitude for *whatever* is given us in whatever way it is given. In short, gratitude is an ongoing attitude that permeates our requests.

When Jesus tells us not to worry about what we are to wear or what we will eat, Jesus says that "it is the Gentiles who strive for all these things; and indeed your heavenly Father knows that you need all these things." (Mt. 6:32) The key word here is "strive." It is one thing to need certain things and quite another to *strive* for them. Striving, of course, implies mimetic rivalry; wanting things because other people want them or you think they want them.

Striving after goods is the quickest way to lose any sense of thanksgiving. If mimetic rivalry destroys gratitude, then gratitude quells mimetic rivalry.

Gratitude entails regarding what we receive as a free gift rather than something we have earned. In his speech before the Israelites entered the Promised Land, Moses warned them: "When you have eaten your fill and have built fine houses and live in them, and when your herds and flocks have multiplied, and your silver and gold is multiplied, and all that you have is multiplied, then do not exalt yourself, forgetting the LORD your God, who brought you out of the land of Egypt, out of the house of slavery." (Deut. 8:12–14) We exalt ourselves by thinking that: "My power and the might of my own hand have gotten me this wealth." (Deut. 8:17) When we think that we have *earned* what we have received, then we feel no gratitude for it. We don't write a thank-you note to our employer for paying us our salary. Likewise, if we feel that God *owes* us payment for our prayers or acts of service, then we don't thank God for what we are given. On the contrary, if "the wheat and barley, of vines and fig trees and pomegranates, olive trees and honey" (Deut. 8:8) fall short of our standards, we complain to God about them. It is important, then, to realize that a covenant between God and humanity is not a contract by which God gives us a pre-established "salary" for our good deeds. Rather, a covenant sets in motion a circle of giving. We give free gifts to God, and God gives free gifts to us.

Jesus' counsel that we not "worry about tomorrow, for tomorrow will bring worries of its own" (Mt. 6:34) is vital to an attitude of thanksgiving because of its focus on what we already have. When we strive for what we do not have, we are focused on what we lack and so we do not even think about what we have already, let alone give thanks for it. This attitude is also important in our human relationships as well. When we are thankful for what the people in our lives do for us and for what they mean to us, we are content with them as they are, even if there is room for them to grow in virtue and holiness. Striving to change another person easily becomes a contest against that person, where change for the better becomes a "victory." Being content with the other person *as that person is* can lead to complacency, but it is also a condition with great potential for encouraging a person to change.

Contentment with what we have does not deny the intrinsic value of those goods we lack. It only means that we can be patient about what we do not have because we appreciate the intrinsic value of what we have already. This is the key to letting our requests be known to God *with* thanksgiving. (Phil. 4:6) This does not mean that we pray with thankful hearts because we assume we are going to get what we want when we want it. Rather, this is a matter of praying out of contentment in the present where "today's trouble is enough for today."

Jesus gives us the true focus for gratitude when he goes on to admonish us to "strive first for the kingdom of God and his righteousness, and all these things will be given to you as well." (Mt. 6:33) Note that the word "strive" is used again here to show us that striving in itself is not necessarily a bad thing. What matters is the object of our striving. If we strive for God's Kingdom, then we do not strive for "all these things" like the "Gentiles." Striving for God's Kingdom, of course, entails striving to provide the needs and wants of other people, i.e., being "doers of the word" rather than hearers only (Jas. 1:22). When we strive for God's Kingdom, it becomes immediately apparent that our efforts cannot earn the good we are striving for. Our efforts fall far short, because we can *only* receive God's Kingdom as a gift. When we know that we cannot earn the Kingdom, then we don't require other people to earn it either. We become free of worry over whether or not the widows and orphans are worthy of the aid we give them. Likewise, we become free from the need to grumble like the workers in the vineyard who didn't like it when the master was generous with his money to *other* people (Mt. 20:15). This freedom from worry encourages us to become more open-handed and open-hearted towards other people in their needs. The more we open our hands and hearts to others, the more we receive to be thankful for.

Adoration

Adoration is the one form of prayer where we are not concerned with ourselves but with God alone. When we praise another person just for being that person, we are expressing an appreciation that transcends any tangible benefits we have received or ever will receive from the one we are praising. Likewise, the highest praise we can give to God is to praise God just for being God. Praise is an ecstatic liberation from all self-preoccupation.

Praise is an ecstatic rocketing into God's desire; mimetic resonance at its most glorious. Nothing could be further from mimetic rivalry than praise. Praise has nothing to do with wanting what other people want or even thinking of wanting anything for oneself. All that matters is wanting God for Godself. As thanksgiving moves towards praise, praise continues what thanksgiving started: it removes mimetic rivalry, all competition with everybody. Once thanksgiving is plunged into praise, gratitude and joy blend into one. Praise is the great unifier that brings all of us together

Since adoration is so totally centered on God, there is very little we can do on our own to praise God. Praise is not a commodity we can pull out of our inner selves at will. We can only open ourselves up to a flow of praise that comes from outside of us, but penetrates deeply within us and flows back out of us to God. Praise is a gift from God; it is the water welling up within us unto Eternal Life.

Praise may be as exciting as blaring trumpets or as quiet as the still small voice that Elijah heard. (1 Kings. 19:12) In fact, we praise God most deeply in silence. When we are silently directing our attention to God, we can gently lay our preoccupations to one side and simply enjoy God's presence. In silence, we come to appreciate more deeply the three Persons that God is. Since praise transcends words and dissolves them, praise takes us far beyond rational thought. Praise, then, moves into contemplation where we rest in God for the sake of resting in God with no thought about what God will get out of it, let alone what we will get out of it.

Just as the praise of lovers for each other turns into babbling, so does praise of God, as we is shout it out in Psalm 148:

> Praise the LORD!
> Praise the LORD from the heavens;
> Praise him in the heights!

Praise him, all his angels;
Praise him, all his host! (Ps. 148:1–2)

Next thing we know, all of Creation gets into the act of praising the Creator:

Praise him, sun and moon;
praise him, all you shining stars!
Praise him, you highest heavens,
and you waters above the heavens! (Ps. 148:3–4)

The mountains and hills and stormy winds and sea monsters all join in. When all of Creation, including earthly rulers, are praising God, covetous desires vanish.

In Heaven, God is praised continuously, so when we offer praise, we are anticipating life in Heaven. Praise is not an escape from earthly life but an enrichment of it. Praise gives us the strength to face life with the conviction that God will bring all Creation into God's eternal glory. No matter how much we fear the ways we can destroy God's world, the praise we allow to flow through our hearts and our bodies remains a light that no darkness can overcome.

Chapter 8

Liturgical Creatures

The reality of mimetic resonance guarantees that we will engage in liturgical activity. Being mimetic animals means being liturgical animals. What kind of liturgical activity and for what end has many possibilities. Much liturgy takes place in churches and temples, but liturgy can be done anywhere at any time.

Girard suggests that the origins of ritual and liturgy are found in the spontaneous mob violence against a victim that "solves" a massive social crisis. At first thought, one would think there is nothing liturgical about collective violence; it just happens. But collective violence is a very predictable phenomenon that consistently works in a certain way once it gets started. We all know that once the persecutory ball gets rolling, it is almost impossible to stop it until blood has been spilled. The relatively few instances where a persecutory wave is stopped short of bloodshed also follow a predictable pattern. In such a case, the mimetic contagion of a mob is redirected into another, less destructive direction. This is what Jesus did when the Jewish elders were gathered around the woman caught in adultery when he stopped the show and asked the first person without fault to throw the first stone. (Jn. 8:7) This is what Christians do to this day when celebrating the Holy Eucharist.

Although I think Girard is right about the origin of sacrificial rituals in collective violence, I think that ritual itself is rooted more deeply in human nature. As imitative creatures, we instinctively coordinate our bodily movements with those of others. This sort of mirroring is instinctive to mothers, especially in their interactions with their babies. This coordination of movement unified a family, a clan, and a tribe. These coordinated movements naturally turned into communal dancing and singing. Such coordinated action also naturally moved into re-enactments of primal collective violence.

There are practical reasons for this trait, among them coordinating movements during hunting expeditions, the way soldiers do military drills to facilitate coordination in battle, and the way football teams synchronize their actions. Then there are the rituals performed by football fans. Singing together over common work such as gathering fruits and preparing meals might not have been as necessary for success as the coordinated movements of hunting parties, but perhaps were as necessary at another level. Maybe nobody dies of boredom, but we often feel that we can, and maybe we do in the sense that lack of interest in life isn't conducive to living a long life. Singing and dancing together and moving together in other ways are among the activities that spark our interest in life today, and most likely have had the same effect since the dawn of humanity.

Many people today are dismissive of liturgy because they associate it with stuffy church services. But the ways we greet people, especially when introducing ourselves to strangers, are little rituals that we take so much for granted that we don't think of them as rituals. Plays and classical concerts often have a quasi-liturgical atmosphere with dimmed houselights and norms for audience decorum similar to what is usually expected in church. The more raucous and extroverted actions at rock concerts are also liturgical in their own way. When I was young, many people who never set foot in church, linked arms in the streets and sang "We Shall Overcome." Gathering with others always has some liturgical overtones, in the sense of repeating actions we are used to doing together. Drinking parties tend to follow the same patterns.

In my book *Tools for Peace*, I discuss liturgy and human synchronized movement at some length with the help of William McNeill's book *Keeping Together in Time*. McNeill draws a comparison between medieval monks and nuns doing the Divine Office and Prussian soldiers drilling. Both activities feature what McNeill calls "muscular bonding." (McNeill 1993, 3) This comparison confirms the anthropological basis of liturgy that I have been discussing. It is important to note, however, that although the "muscular bonding" of monks and soldiers might be the same, the end of this bonding is very different. Monks and nuns pray together to praise God. Soldiers drill to be more efficient at killing people in battle.

This contrast between monks and Prussian soldiers makes it clear that we have to use our brains sufficiently to know where the mimetic process of liturgical action is taking us. McNeill knows this very well, and he coins the term "literary inspiration" to point to the reasons for which muscular bonding is done. The power of muscular bonding to carry us away makes it all the more important that we have some idea of what the muscular bonding is for. The movie "Brother Where art Thou?" which I analyze in *Tools for Peace*, shows muscular bonding in two very different ways: a baptism in the river by members of a black church and a rally of the Ku Klux Klan gathered to lynch a young black man. (Marr 2007, 119–121) We will examine the relationship between "muscular bonding" and "literary inspiration" from several angles below.

Given this human trait to gather through ritual, it was inevitable that any who wished to gather with others in memory of Jesus would gather liturgically. Once the Risen Jesus had re-gathered his followers, they would continue to gather to sing and tell stories. It is this gathering and remembering that helped them to strengthen one another in the forgiveness with which Jesus had gathered them. While both myths and rituals obscure the sacrificial stories on which they are based, the Eucharist *clearly* tells the story on which it is based: the betrayal of Jesus, his subsequent crucifixion, and rising from the dead. This earliest account of the Eucharist in First Corinthians, predating all of the Gospels, enshrines the Words of Institution that are repeated in celebrations of the Eucharist two thousand years later. (1 Cor. 11: 23–26) The Eucharist teaches us through its story, but it also teaches us at a deeper, more substantial level by tangibly feeding us with the Word of God. Celebrating the Eucharist places our desires into Jesus' desire for us to gather with him and the other Persons of the Trinity.

The meal is possibly the oldest liturgical ritual. Eating is the first activity that immerses us into the mimetic resonance of the community we are born in. By the time we are old enough to be conscious of what we are eating and to desire certain foods, the desires around us have exerted a strong effect. However, as much as meals provide necessary bodily nourishment, they are always more than that. An intrinsic part of learning to eat is learning how to eat in the company of others. It may be culturally arbitrary whether we use eating utensils and plates or large leaves and fingers, but in every culture I have ever heard of, there is always a *way of eating* that is learned. By rooting liturgy in a meal, the Eucharist roots worship in the sensuous act of eating; of tasting food and drink on our tongues.

In First Corinthians, Paul brings up the matter of table manners in regards to the Eucharist. He berates the richer members of the congregation for their insensitive treatment of those who are more economically challenged. To flaunt their richer food in front of those who cannot afford it, without offering them anything, is a serious violation of everything the Eucharist stands for. This desire shared by one group in the congregation to demonstrate their superiority over others, to put them in their places, breaks the unity the feast is supposed to create and strengthen. Paul makes it clear that there is much more to worship than saying or singing words together while celebrating Jesus' last meal. (1 Cor. 11:17–22) James also rails against the favoritism based on the material wealth of a visitor, or the lack of it. "Have you not made distinctions among yourselves, and become judges with evil thoughts?" he asks. (Jas. 2:4) If people are not treated well, worship is diminished if not rendered nonexistent.

In John's version of the feeding in the wilderness, all of these themes come together. While Matthew and Mark recount two feedings in the wilderness, one for the Jews and one for the Gentiles, John has one story of feeding for all people. Jesus' blessing of the bread and fishes has ritual elements, although the feeding is taking place away from synagogues and the Temple. The social unity that Paul enjoins is embodied in John's vision, in which the various people eat together on an equal basis. Unfortunately, right after the people are fed, the people unite in trying to make Jesus king. This undermined the social vision of the feeding just as much as the misbehavior of the Corinthians did. The Eucharist teaches us that we don't outgrow our earliest lessons: table manners. Without them, we don't grow up.

We also receive early lessons from listening to stories. Young children show a ritual instinct by wanting to hear their favorite bedtime stories night after night. We resonate with stories and with the actions of the characters at a very deep level. Aristotle famously called it "catharsis," a purification of our emotions that occurs when we identify with the emotions of a character on stage. Mimetic realism gives us increased awareness of this phenomenon. I discussed in Chapter 3 how Girard noted that the best novelists and playwrights had discovered this resonance in audiences. Sophocles is a prominent example as he is the one who had inspired Aristotle's concept of catharsis.

Mirror neurons add further scientific understanding to the way we resonate with stories. Realizing that our mirror neurons are activated by the intentions of others, we now know that whatever actors on stage or on the screen do also activate our mirror neurons. This is why we are so affected by what they do and most particularly what they desire. By identifying with a thief who is the protagonist of a story, we easily find ourselves desiring the thief's success, although in real life most of us would normally not desire that at all. But then again, perhaps the story has revealed a hidden desire in ourselves to get away with theft. Or, perhaps a desire that wasn't there has been created by the thieving action. Or a combination of all of the above.

Theater, movies, and novels are often considered ways to escape our daily lives. Tolkien points out, however, that the escape offered by the best literature is like an escape from prison rather than an escape from reality. (Tolkien 1984, 148) On the contrary, great literature confronts us with the truth of ourselves and, in its greatest moments, the truth of God, as Girard has amply demonstrated. In our theatrical escapes, we try on different characters with whom we identify to see how they fit. In real life, we may experience the characters we try on to be highly variable, ranging from totally fantastic to very close to the bone. To varying degrees, we take in theatrical events (and all other forms of storytelling) in the company of others. This is especially the case with actual theaters where we are part of a live audience and the mimetic process is quite strong. We laugh when others laugh, and we cry when others cry. Even with the overflow of modern conveniences that allow isolated theatrical and musical pleasures, we are still connected to others. Other people's attitudes have a lot to do with why we are watching a specific movie, reading this particular book, or listening to this mp3 track. The Internet, of course, has us interacting with fellow members of audiences all the time.

This is where the debate rages about whether or not violence or any other reprehensible actions should be allowed by law in movies, on the stage, or even in books. Does the violence observed or read about make one more violent, or does it cause a catharsis that acts as a safety valve to prevent violence in real life? As far as I can tell, the answer goes both ways. After the Columbine school shooting, a certain video game was blamed for causing the killers to go on a shooting spree, but this accusation overlooks the huge number of adolescents who played that game and committed no violence at all. What we are left with, I think, is the need to take some responsibility for what we watch and read, and more importantly, for how we react to them. For some, watching cops-and-robbers programs are mild entertainment. For others, it is more a thrill of surrogate righteous violence. If it is the latter, does this surrogate thrill suffice, or does it lead to inflicting violence against the "bad" guys in real life and feeling righteous about it? Or, do we act out these feelings of righteous indignation without knowing what we are doing? This would put us in the position of those who crucified Jesus. In his book *Dangerous Games,* Joseph Laycock examines at length the effects of role-playing games and the social panics that ensued. He builds a strong case that these games were scapegoated by society as a shortcut to easy and simple answers to complex social problems.

Some solemn words from Jesus may help us. He pleaded for understanding when he said: "There is nothing outside a person that by going in can defile, but the things that come out are what defile." (Mk 7:15) When Jesus elaborated on this, he said that the food we take in does not defile us or make us unclean, but noxious actions and attitudes that come *out* of the human heart *do* defile us. Mark adds that with these words, Jesus had declared all foods clean. (Mk. 7:19) Jesus is suggesting that certain foods were being scapegoated when they were declared unclean. That is, the food was being blamed for uncleanness, when the problem was the human heart. Perhaps rejecting some foods as unclean is no big deal, but in his list of vices that can come out of a person's heart, Jesus is calling attention to our tendency to consider other *people* unclean.

Through mimetic resonance, we ingest the desires of others just as we ingest food. If we experience desires that make us uncomfortable, including those that should, we blame other people for arousing the desires in us and we protect ourselves by expelling them from ourselves. Or trying to. These desires don't go away so easily. On the contrary, the more we try to expel them, the more they well up within us. Jesus is telling us that just as foods do not make us unclean, other people do not make us unclean either. It is what *we* do with the desires of other people that make us clean or unclean. We can indeed be corrupted by bad company, but if we spew back at them the envy and slander and pride we ingested from others, or, spew these desires at others who have fewer defenses, then *we* ourselves are bad company that threaten to corrupt others. This gives us another angle on Jesus' famous warning that if we judge, we will be judged. In judging others, we see the speck in the eye of the other but don't see the log in our own. (Mt. 7:1–5) We may think that any envy, deceit, or licentiousness we experience in ourselves comes from the other, and maybe we do catch these traits from another, like catching a virus. But a virus caught from another only hurts us if our own bodies react in destructive ways to make us sick. Likewise, the envy, deceit, and licentiousness of another only make us sick if we allow them to flare up inside of us. If we then expel them in the direction of others, they become the victims of what has come out of us. Even when defiling desires really are coming out of other people, our own defiling desires in response to them magnify the impurity in the social atmosphere. That is, the uncleanness is neither in ourselves nor in the other. Defilement occurs only in relationships built upon projecting and expelling the perceived defilement of others. These considerations may seem to have taken us away from theater, but they show that the dynamics of how we take in plays and movies are fundamentally the same as they are with our interactions with real people.

Should we pull the logs out of our own eyes rather than judge others, a strange alchemy can take place: what we take in from others can become pure, or at least a lot less impure, and the social atmosphere improves. Then we can all breathe in the Holy Spirit.

We need to be alert, then, to how we are affected by the books we read, the plays and movies we see, and the music we listen to. Jesus makes it clear, though, that we are not polluted by what we take in but by what we cast out of ourselves. More important, reading edifying books is not enough. They do not do us any good unless we allow them to bring virtues such as compassion and human sympathy out of us. A play or movie depicting violent actions can move us to sympathy for the victims and also for the perpetrators. Some of us find some books and plays like that hard to take or fear they will draw bad things out of us. This is a judgment call we all have to make. If we avoid some books and movies out of this fear, we shouldn't assume the same is true of other people. It goes without saying that the exposure to media that we allow for young people needs to be age-appropriate. By paying attention to what comes *out* of us when we take in movies and read books, we take responsibility for how we handle what comes into us and avoid scapegoating movies and books just as Jesus would not have us scapegoat the food we eat.

On the whole, we don't usually think of worship as theatrical, although everything I have said about the theatrical applies to liturgy in some way. One reason we don't usually make the connection is because we are constantly advised that we don't go to church for entertainment; we go to worship God. That is true, but if the liturgy is boring and the sermon more boring still, then it is hard to feel motivated to go back. This fundamental reason for going to worship does not invalidate the theatrical elements of worship, although the overwrought style of delivering sermons by some preachers can be dramatic overkill. A stronger reason we usually don't associate worship with the theatrical is because we don't have to be Puritans to buy into the puritanical notion that theater is frivolous and worship is serious. On the other hand,

Jesus compared himself to a burglar breaking into our houses, (Mt. 24:43) so maybe worship centered on him shouldn't be too solemn all of the time.

The main reason worship is theatrical is because it is centered on stories. Recall that Greek plays were performed at religious festivals. This means that the expulsion of Oedipus was a liturgical event. In Christian worship, the liturgical action is bound up with stories about Israel and the story of Jesus. Listening to the Word activates the mirror neurons, hopefully making us identify with the heroes and heroines of faith and most particularly with Jesus. In the reading of scripture, preaching on what is read, and acting out the Eucharist, we are immersed in the central story of Jesus' death and Resurrection. We also absorb the many side stories that help us understand and celebrate in worship this central mystery of our faith.

Søren Kierkegaard wrote a meditation on the story about the "Woman Who Was a Sinner" (Lk. 7:36–50) as a preparation for the Eucharist. Carl Hughes insightfully analyzed its theatricality in *Kierkegaard and the Staging of Desire*. Kierkegaard was deeply drawn to this story about the woman who crashed Simon's dinner party, and he seems to have thought it a particularly important story to reflect on before receiving Communion. Those of us who are proper and polite probably act like Simon more often than we act like the weeping woman who dried Jesus' feet with her hair. However, Kierkegaard would have us realize that if we don't identify with the Woman Who Was a Sinner, we completely fail to identify with Jesus. It is when we come to Jesus as a penitent that we are in a position to receive the forgiveness Jesus gives us so freely. Kierkegaard dramatizes the Eucharist through this drama centered on a woman who was, to say the least, theatrical. One could take this as dramatized *Lectio Divina*, where the author's speaking the text out loud would resonate in the listener much more deeply than reading it by oneself in silence. So it is that this story brings us to the story celebrated at the altar. If we approach the altar to receive the bread and wine in this same spirit of penitence, we receive the forgiveness that Jesus granted the Woman Who Was a Sinner.

The Christian story is dramatized in the Divine Office and in the Eucharist. Both include what is called the Liturgy of the Word during which the Word of God is spoken and listened to. In my monastic tradition, the Divine Office is a major part of our worship. However, this is not merely a monastic devotion. *The Book of Common Prayer* features the offices of Morning and Evening Prayer with the intention that they would be done every day. Although use of the Divine Office outside of religious orders became mostly dormant for many centuries, they have had a strong revival in the past several decades, and many people from several denominations are using an office in one form or another.

Along with scripture readings that tell the fundamental stories we celebrate in worship, the Divine Office features use of the Psalms, which have been staples since monks began to go out to the deserts of Egypt and Palestine. We have already noted how the apostles found the story of Jesus already expressed in the psalms. Most importantly, as I have already pointed out, the psalms often give voice to victims of collective violence. Frequent use of the psalms can help us to remain mindful of the human tendency to bond through scapegoating behavior and to be alert for any movement of worship in that direction. The psalms present us with a full spectrum of the ways we experience God and our fellow humans. They range from ecstatic praise to existential despair and everything in between. Often extremes of emotion are expressed in the same psalm. One of the greatest treatises on the spirituality of the Psalms is "The Letter to Marcellinus" by Athanasius of Alexandria (298–373). Athanasius says that the Book of Psalms teaches us "not only not to disregard passion, but also how one must heal passion through speaking and acting." (Athanasius 1980, 108) Further on, Athanasius says, "these words become like a mirror to the person singing them, so that he might perceive himself and the emotions of his soul and thus affected, he might recite them." (Athanasius 1980, 111) In this way, saying or chanting the psalms is a powerful way to understand ourselves in relation to God.

Through this comprehensibility, the Divine Office pulls us out of our current states of affairs. If we pray only out of our own subjectivity, we pray with a limited range. If we feel rotten, we want to pray psalms of lamentation. If we feel good, we want to praise God. But when we read the psalms comprehensively, we are reminded of what everybody in the Body of Christ is going through. We follow the words of St. Paul: "Rejoice with those who rejoice, weep with those who weep." (Rom. 12:15) Most importantly, we are brought in touch most especially with the unjust suffering many people endure. If it seems we're suffering unjustly, we're reminded that we are not the only ones. If we are free of persecution or other hardships at the time, we are yet mindful of those who are suffering for Christ. Most importantly, we are saying the psalms in community. When it is possible to do the Divine Office with others, we strengthen one another as we journey through the mirrors that the psalms are to each of us and also for the whole Church. Even if we have to pray the Divine Office alone, we aren't really alone. We are with God, of course, but we are also praying with other people in a way that transcends time and place. This means that we are praying the Divine Office with C. S. Lewis, Evelyn Underhill, and countless others. The communion of saints is an immense cloud of witnesses.

The Divine Office and the Eucharist are both highly repetitive. In general, plays and concerts are not repetitious like Christian worship that tells the same old story time after time to make it sink more deeply into us each time. It should be noted, though, that many people like to hear the same symphonies time after time, and some people have favorite movies they see more times than they can count. In the Paschal Mystery, there is disclosure of the deepest truths about the way we humans live but also how we ought to live and could live by absorbing the character of Jesus. This is a story that never ends. This repetition comes up in Christian worship for those who do daily offices and attend Eucharist regularly as the same readings come up time after time. I have heard many of Jesus' parables read time after time after time, just as children hear the same stories every night at bed time.

When the psalms are sung, the music is usually repetitive. This is very much the case with plainchant and Anglican chant. The "muscular bonding," that takes place with such singing is what, at least at times, can be experienced as a quiet ecstasy. Chanting the psalms on plainchant is not dramatically emotional, but they seep deeply into the bones of any who sing them in this way. There are many other styles of singing in Christian worship besides plainchant, although plainchant has had a resurgence. Lively hymns top the list with most worshipers. The mimetic resonance of hymn-singing is obvious to everybody who has ever been to church. However, the music and dance at the banquet at Herod's court warns us of the danger of music binding people in a sacrificial direction. (Mk. 6:14–29) With the "muscular bonding" that takes place in liturgy, the strength of collective mimetic desire is expanded in a geometrical progression. This mimetic bonding carries the often meager efforts of each of us so as to keep all of us afloat. Other people support us in prayer so that we can support them in prayer. In a group, we feel our need for others keenly. Not only does the Spirit help us individually by praying in us when we do not know how to pray, the Holy Spirit also guides the prayer of the group at worship. The important thing is for the group to want to be guided by the Holy Spirit, the Paraclete who is the Advocate for *everybody.*

While taking in some movies, plays, and books can be questionable, at least for some people, we assume that taking in Christian worship and listening to the Christian Story is unequivocally a good thing. It should be, but there is much evidence that we can't count on it. Taking in the story of the Woman Who Was a Sinner is good, but how does this story come *out* of us? That is, do we kneel before Jesus in penitence and weep for forgiveness? As true and false prophets are known by their fruits, (Mt. 7:15–16) true and false worshipers are also known by their fruits. We must not forget that lynching came *out* of Christian worshipers. For centuries, Jews had to keep their distance from Christians during Holy Week, if they valued their safety. If worship and the reading of scripture elicit rage and violence, as it has done with many Christians, that which has come out of us has defiled us. Bringing good things out of us makes us good and holy. Giving a cup of cold water to one of Jesus' "little ones"—and much more—should come out of us after taking in an act of worship. When we pay this kind of attention to what comes out of us as a result of worship, then the theatrical aspect of worship has been far from frivolous entertainment, just as plays and books are far from frivolous when good things come out of us after we have taken them in.

Christian liturgy is not, however, about "muscular bonding" for the sake of "muscular bonding." Christian worship is deeply embedded in the story of Israel culminating in Christ. Through telling the story and immersing us in it time and time again, the liturgy teaches us the story not only in our minds but in our hearts, in our bones, and in our mirror neurons. We experience the transforming power of the Word of God as a community, resonating with God and with one another. However, the celebrations of Baptism and Eucharist take our collective embodiment in the Christian story to a much deeper level, where God works directly to transform our hearts. It is to these two celebrations that we now turn.

Chapter 9

Clothed with Christ and Eating Christ

Baptism

Since baptism is our initiation into Christ and his Paschal Mystery, this sacrament is the underlying dynamic of our lives in Christ. Dying and rising with Christ is something we need to do every day. The Greek word *baptizo* means to be dipped, but also to be overwhelmed, inundated. In baptism we are overwhelmed by and inundated with the Paschal Mystery. I will explore this mystery by looking at a few key scripture passages that give us variations on this one theme.

Jesus himself was baptized in the River Jordan by John the Baptist. For John, it was a baptism of repentance from the violent society of his time, to prepare for God's winnowing fork in "the wrath to come." (Mt. 3:7) But when Jesus came, he did not bring a winnowing fork; he only brought himself and asked to be baptized. As he was baptized, the heavens opened, the Spirit descended, and a voice from heaven said: "This is my beloved Son with whom I am well pleased."

This proclamation refers to two key verses in the Hebrew Bible that tell us what baptism is all about. In Psalm 2, the king, the Messiah is singled out from the raging nations that are rising up against the Lord and his anointed. The inundation of baptism draws Jesus *out* of the inundation of the nations raging against one another. In Jesus, we too are drawn out of this inundation and so freed from raging against everybody else. But we are not freed from being the target of raging nations when they unite against the one who has been freed from their wrath. These baptismal words spoken to Jesus also refer to Isaiah 42:1, the first line of the first song of the Servant of Yahweh. Throughout these songs, the Servant has been called out of a violent society to become instead the victim of that society's violence. Unlike the Psalmist who threatens the raging nations with a rod of iron, (Ps. 2:9) the Servant does not retaliate in any way against the violence inflicted on him. In baptism, we too are overwhelmed by the Servant's suffering, but then we are also overwhelmed by God's vindication of the Servant.

John's Gospel does not narrate the baptism of Jesus, but, as in so many other instances, John tells the underlying story in a different key. Right after Jesus has turned over the tables of the money changers in the temple and driven out the sacrificial animals, Nicodemus, a member of the Sanhedrin, approaches Jesus by night. In the strange dialog that follows, Jesus reaches out to a member of the establishment that he has just challenged, while Nicodemus fails to understand Jesus.

Nicodemus is confounded when Jesus tells him that he cannot see the Kingdom of God without being "born anew," born "from above" by water and the Spirit. (Jn. 3:3) The water and the Spirit both suggest baptism. Jesus wishes Nicodemus to be overwhelmed by the Holy Spirit just as he himself was overwhelmed at the River Jordan. Nicodemus, however, is overwhelmed with puzzlement and perhaps, so are we. Jesus compounds Nicodemus's puzzlement (and ours!) by suddenly shifting to a mysterious event recorded in Numbers where Moses raises a bronze serpent in the wilderness during a plague-induced social crisis. (Both the disease and the violence against Moses were contagious.) (Num. 21:9) The phrase "lifted up" is the same phrase used when Jesus was raised on the cross and then again when he was raised from the dead. The bronze serpent, then, becomes an image of Jesus being raised on the cross to draw all people out of the old, violent society into a new society as free of violence as Jesus is himself. It seems that being born "from above" entails being born from the raised-up cross, which is the entry into a new way of living, what John calls "eternal life." (Jn. 3:14) St. Paul said: "We were buried therefore with him [Jesus] by baptism into death, so that as Christ was raised from the dead by the glory of the Father, we too might walk in newness of life." (Rom. 6:4)

This is the context of the famous words that follow in John's Gospel: "For God so loved the world that he gave his only Son, that whoever believes in him should not perish but have eternal life." (Jn. 3:16) These words echo, in a different key, the acclamation of the voice Jesus heard from heaven when he was baptized. John goes on to assure us that God did not send his Son into the world "to condemn the world, but that in order that the world might be saved through him" (Jn. 3:18) These two verses should be strong enough to prevent us from thinking that the solemn verses that follow concerning condemnation take back even a smidgen of the proclamation of God's love. The judgment is *not* God's judgment but the self-judgment of those who "loved darkness rather than light." If God's very Being is light and we don't like it, what else can God do but keep on being the light until, hopefully, we learn to like it and then love it and so turn away from the darkness in our hearts and turn to the cross that gives us a new birth from above?

Two dramatic events from the Hebrew Bible are interpreted in the New Testament as prefiguring baptism: the Flood and the deliverance at the Red Sea. Both are deliverances from highly dysfunctional societies into opportunities for new societies grounded in God's desire.

Genesis 6 portrays humanity as consumed with violence. This is no wonder if everybody was like Lamech who boasted about inflicting seventy-seven-fold vengeance on anybody who wronged him. (Gen 4:24) In his first epistle, believed by many scholars to be a baptismal homily, Peter says that the deliverance of Noah and his family corresponds to baptism that saves us now through the Resurrection of Jesus Christ. (1 Pet. 3:21) Girard has suggested that a flood is an apt image for a society overwhelmed with retaliatory violence. In such a scenario, anyone who tried to *not* be a part of this violence would be an obvious choice to victimize, thereby uniting the fragmented society. The Christological interpretation in Peter's epistle suggests that by being baptized into Christ's death, we are brought out of a society consumed by violence and given the chance to begin life anew, the chance that Noah and his family had after the flood waters receded. It is worth noting that when referring to Jesus' descent into hell (Sheol), Peter does not say that Jesus only brought out righteous people like Abraham but that he preached to the very people who had brought humankind to the boiling point while Noah was building his ark. (1 Pet. 3:19–20)

Of the deliverance at the Red Sea, St. Paul said that we all "passed through the sea and all were baptized into Moses in the cloud and the sea." (1 Cor. 10:2) Once again we have an overwhelming flood and a story of a people delivered from a violent and oppressive society. Given the kind of society Egypt was, we can suspect that the narrative of the Jews' escape from Egypt is very different from what we can guess was Pharaoh's point of view. Given what we know about social scapegoating behavior, it is likely that the Jews were blamed for the plagues striking the country. This is what happened to Jews in medieval Europe, as we have seen. But if the Jews were expelled from Egypt, why did the Egyptians run after them to bring them back? Perhaps they realized they would implode without the victims who were deemed responsible for their turmoil. This is what seems to have happened with the Gerasenes when their demoniac was cured by Jesus. Being overwhelmed by the waters is, again, an apt image of a society succumbing to its own violence once the scapegoats are gone. The flood at the Red Sea can be seen as the same kind of flooding that happened in Noah's time, only on a much smaller scale.

Unfortunately, neither chance at a new life went well. Noah's drunkenness and the rivalry among his sons that made Ham a scapegoat set humanity on a course where the curse laid on Ham was used to justify slavery and lynching. (Gen. 9:18–27) The people delivered at the Red Sea suffered from chronic social unrest to the point that Moses had to raise the bronze serpent in the desert to stop the plague of violence. Likewise, the Church continues to fall back into the same rivalry and persecution in spite of the great opportunity opened up by Jesus' Resurrection. A tendency to see baptism as a personal deliverance reinforces such backsliding. Baptism is not a magical deliverance from individual sin but is a constant invitation to be reborn into the new social life of God's Kingdom centered on the Forgiving Victim who, like the bronze serpent, was raised up to draw all people to himself. In the Paschal

Mystery, we die to one way of relating (or misrelating) with people in order to live to a new way of relating to others.

The traditional triad of renunciations of the world, the flesh, and the devil confirms this social element of baptism. The three are nearly synonymous, but their varying shades of meaning are illuminating.

The New Testament word *kosmos* (world) has mainly negative connotations, especially in John's Gospel where it means, not the material world as created by God, but the social world organized in opposition to God. In baptism, then, we renounce organizing ourselves socially around scapegoating and persecution. It is important to remember, though, that it was this very *kosmos* that God loved so much that God gave God's only son to save it. As Jesus was overwhelmed by the *kosmos* during his death, we, too, may be overwhelmed by it if we renounce it.

Flesh does not refer to the material aspect of our existence, but rather to our tendency to live embodied lives without reference to God. When we live in the flesh, our social lives are dominated by mimetic rivalry that consumes us. The contentions that Paul denounced in his first letter to the Corinthians were cited as examples of living by the flesh. If we renounce the flesh, we renounce this contentious way of relating, and we allow our embodied lives to be guided by the Holy Spirit in whom there is no rivalry or resentment.

Renouncing the devil does not mean renouncing a wicked supernatural creature with horns and a pitchfork. The New Testament word *skandalon* refers to no such thing. Rather, this word means a stumbling block, an obstacle. This is the word Jesus used when he warned us not to "put a stumbling block before one of these little ones who believe in me." (Mk. 9:42) When we live according to the flesh, we allow other people to be stumbling blocks to our desires and we are the same to them. That is, our rivals become the organizing principles of our life rather than God. In scripture, Satan is also the accuser, which is what rivals do. They accuse each other endlessly, as opposed to praising God endlessly. So, renouncing the devil means renouncing rivalrous activity that causes others to stumble.

The renunciations in the rite of baptism as formulated in the 1979 *Book of Common Prayer* amount to much the same thing. Renouncing "Satan and all the spiritual forces of wickedness that rebel against God" may seem to imply supernatural forces. I do not rule out such supernatural beings who, according to the story enshrined in Milton, put themselves into mimetic rivalry with God. But it is the anthropological level that is most important when it comes to turning away from *skandalons* in this life. The power of stumbling blocks in our relationships can be so strong that they seem transcendent, but they are really an accumulation of human desires spun out of control. Renouncing "the evil powers of this world which corrupt and destroy the creatures of God" acknowledges the systemic evil of the *kosmos*. "The sinful desires that draw [us] from the love of God" point to our own responsibility to do what the fourth question asks of us: to "turn to Jesus Christ and accept him as [our] savior" and "put [our] whole trust in his grace and love."

Baptism is an initiation, a beginning. It is not the middle and certainly not the end. Baptism must be sustained day by day, hour by hour. St. Paul reminds his readers: "You have stripped off the old self with its practices and have clothed yourselves with the new self, which is being renewed in knowledge according to the image of its creator." (Col. 3:9–10) When Paul goes on to say that there is "no longer Greek and Jew, circumcised and uncircumcised, barbarian, Scythian, slave and free," he is making it clear that baptism is indeed the entry into a new culture that overcomes the traditional divisions of humanity. Living by the Spirit in baptism, then, is allowing ourselves to be clothed by Christ rather than the rivals who usually define us. Being renewed in Christ leads us into a quality of life that we can't easily imagine. These new clothes seem much too big for us, and we get lost in them. Can we allow Christ to stretch us to fit into the new clothes of the resurrected life? How do we build on this new beginning so as to grow into our new clothing?

Eucharist

The Eucharist feeds us on the way that began with baptism. Just before the distribution of communion, we say: "Christ our Passover is sacrificed for us." (1 Cor. 5:7) This line says everything about the sacrament and more.

Intriguingly, Robert Daly says that, in Paul's epistle, it's a throwaway line, said in passing while writing about church discipline. (Daly 2009) That indicates how fundamental a presupposition it was in the early Church.

For the Jews, Passover is the rite in which they re-live their deliverance from Egypt. This ties the Eucharist closely with baptism. The origins of Passover are obscure, but it may have been a spring time rite shepherds did to ward off evil that included smearing lambs' blood on the door. The Jews may have been performing this rite at the time they were expelled from Egypt for ostensibly causing the plague that killed many more Egyptian children than Hebrews. Nowadays, there is the simple scientific explanation that the Hebrew slaves were rigidly segregated from the Egyptians, so that it is reasonable that one social group could escape a plague that struck the other. Jesus made it quite clear that God is not a child-killer when he welcomed the children whom his disciples tried to keep away. (Mt. 19:14)

The Passover quickly moved away from its sacrificial origins and became a domestic feast that is to be repeated every year as outlined in Exodus 12. In Jesus' time, the Temple priests slaughtered the Passover lambs for those who came to the Holy City for the feast. In the chronology in John's Gospel, Jesus was crucified precisely at the time that the Passover lambs were being slaughtered. The Passover was an annual practice of remembrance of God's deliverance, but it was a lot more than storytelling to bring to mind what had happened. Passover was more of a re-enactment, one that made Yahweh's actions at the Red Sea present once more. Several psalms retell this story in the context of a national lament. That is, in times of crisis, they bring the past deeds of Yahweh to the present time, when they need a similar act of deliverance. Psalm 77 is a particularly clear example of this use of memory to make the past present. This psalm asks the questions: "Will the Lord spurn forever, and never again be favorable? Has his steadfast love ceased forever? Are his promises at an end for all time?" (Ps. 77:7–8) Then the Psalmist calls to mind the deeds of the Lord and retells the story of the Red Sea.

The Eucharist is a repeated renewal of our baptism. Its frequency varies from church to church, ranging from weekly to quarterly. As the Red Sea deliverance was made present at Passover and in many psalms, the death and

Resurrection of Jesus are made present at the Eucharist. The story of Jesus that is spread out in the readings at the Divine Office and the Liturgy of the Word is compressed into the piece of bread and cup of wine. When Jesus told his disciples to do this in memory of him, he was using the word "memory" in the Jewish sense of making his death and Resurrection present on the altar and present to the people who gather around it to eat and drink the bread and wine. For those who enjoy science fiction and fantasy literature, we could note that this sacrament constitutes time travel of a sort. This is not time travel with the intent to change the past, but time travel to change the present and the future. The fundamental change is to bring ourselves and our communities out of sacrificial, persecuting societies into forgiving societies grounded in the Forgiving Victim.

In Exodus 12, there is a sense of urgency to the Passover. It must be eaten "hastily" with loins girded, sandals on feet, and staff in hand. (Ex. 12:11) That is, the Passover re-enacts the urgency of the night the Jews escaped from Egypt. We don't usually feel this same sense of urgency while celebrating the Eucharist, but maybe we should. Insofar as we are governed by Pharaoh's way of living, we shouldn't waste any time moving away from that and entering more deeply into the way of the Forgiving Victim. The bread and wine are gifts to give us what we need to finish what we started at baptism. When we eat "Christ our Passover," we need to ask ourselves: How ready and willing are we to pass over from one way of living to another? How willing are we to serve one another as demonstrated by Jesus' washing the disciples' feet?

Jesus' feedings of the multitudes in the wilderness are worth revisiting for their Eucharistic vision. These stories make present, if only for a time, the new life that baptism initiates and the Eucharist sustains. The multiplication of food through both divine and human generosity is quite the opposite of the accusatory, slave-driving society of Egypt and the chaotic violence before the Flood. In continuity with the Passover motif, the bread given by Jesus recalls the manna that the escaped slaves received in the desert. Raymond Brown pointed out that rabbinic teaching interpreted the manna as symbolizing the Torah, thus uniting food and teaching, something the Eucharist also does. (Brown 1966, 273–274) Just as the manna needed to be renewed each day, we need to be renewed by the Eucharist on a regular basis. John's Gospel warns us of how easily we fall away from living the Eucharistic life by drifting back into contention and rivalry in our attempts to seize Jesus and make him king. (Jn. 6:15) Making Jesus a political ruler could only drag us back into the violently competitive life that baptism delivers us from. We murmur against Jesus when he tells us that he himself is the bread come down from Heaven, and then even more when Jesus says that we must eat his body and drink his blood. Murmuring is the very same word used of the Jews who contended with Moses and God in the desert.

The term could just as well refer to the bitter arguments that have ensued among Christians as to how exactly Christ can be present in the bread and wine. It seems to me that we should take Jesus at his word and accept at face value that he feeds us with his death and resurrected life. That's the hard point; not the metaphysics of what is called the "real presence" by many theologians. We balk at the idea that Jesus' *death* and his ongoing resurrected life can feed us. In a sense, Jesus' Body and Blood are poison to the kind of life we're accustomed to living.

It is typical of John's slantwise means of conveying the Gospel that he puts Jesus' discourses about eating his body and drinking his blood in a context outside of the meal in the upper room and connects it instead to the Feeding in the Wilderness. This has the advantage of stressing the ongoing nutrition Jesus offers in the Eucharist. Curiously, this separation also seems to spiritualize the Eucharist by speaking of it in terms of Jesus dwelling in us to give us life, but this comes with a shocker that English translations cannot convey. The Greek word used here for "eat" is *trogein*, a very strong verb that doesn't mean to dine nicely with good manners. It means to chew, gnash, and grind. Jesus pushes right in our faces the fact that our eating is a *sacrificial* act. We are to be painfully mindful of the sacrificial way of life we left back in Egypt, even as we carry it with us through the desert. The sixth chapter of John ends with most of Jesus' followers leaving him because of these hard words. (Jn. 6:66) By being both the food that nourishes us and a reminder of how sacrificial we tend to be, Jesus is indeed refusing to be the king who fixes everybody *else's* wagons. The conclusion of this chapter shows us how quickly we can wander far from the community of sharing portrayed at the beginning of this chapter, the place where Jesus wants us to be.

It is the claim that Christ in some mysterious way imparts his very substance to us in the Eucharist that has led to charges of cannibalism from early Christian times up to the present day. Interestingly, Girard accepts the accusation. In a snippet from an unpublished interview, he suggests that the Eucharist recapitulates the entire history of sacrifice and its violence, including cannibalism. When I took a college course on African and Oceanic religions, one of the essay questions on the final exam was to discuss some eyewitness accounts by anthropologists of cannibalistic practice. This was the first time I had encountered anything like it and the question was jolting. What struck me about the accounts was how these people were intentionally absorbing, through ingestion, the *being* of the person, sometimes in mockery but more often in respect. (My take on these documents was affirmed by my professor with a top grade.) This is also Girard's take. He ties this data into his analysis of the dynamics of mimetic rivalry where a rival moves beyond envying the possessions of another to envying the very *being* of the other. Interestingly, Jesus himself seems to agree with Girard and the anthropologists on this matter. We have noted the strong language Jesus uses in John 6 when he tells us that we must eat his body and drink his blood. The words suggest cannibalism and seem to have been interpreted as such by his disgusted listeners who, for the most part, went away so as not to hear anything more about it.

Cannibalistic language is often used figuratively in human speech and that is true of Holy Scripture as well. The Psalmist affirms God's deliverance from people who assail and devour his flesh. (Psalm 27:2) St. Paul warns the Galatians that if they "bite and devour one another," they should take care that they "are not consumed by one another." (Gal. 5:15) These examples refer to situations of serious mimetic rivalry, and even if the Psalmist's enemies and the people of Galatia are "civilized" enough to refrain from literal cannibalism, they are indulging in the essence of that practice.

Jesus reverses the cannibalism where humans devour one another by freely offering himself, Body and Blood, in the bread and wine so that we may receive the *being* of Jesus as a free gift rather than as the spoils of a violent victory. In John, Jesus speaks of his self-giving as indwelling in each person who takes him in: "Those who eat my flesh and drink my blood abide in me, and I in them." (Jn. 6:56) What we eat and drink is God's desire so that God's desire can penetrate into the depths of the human self. This implies that his death on the cross is a gift to humanity and is not loot taken away from him against his will. Quite a reversal of what the Roman Empire thought was happening.

What are we receiving when we receive the being of Jesus? In ancient times, people absorbed the bravery and fighting skills of worthy enemies when they devoured them. With Jesus, what we get is something very different. This is demonstrated in Jesus' act of washing the feet of his disciples as a sign that we should serve one another in all ways. The personal being we receive in the Eucharist is one who, far from wishing to devour another person figuratively, would wish to build up another person in actuality. When we receive the being of Jesus, we receive personal courage beyond imagining. It is not the courage of one who fights and wins battles against violent foes, but rather the courage of one brave enough to serve others, even if it means death on the cross.

St. Paul solemnizes his narrative of Jesus' breaking bread and passing the cup of wine by saying that he is passing on to the Corinthians what he has received from the Lord. (1 Cor. 11:25) The words Paul uses here are specialized terms for receiving and passing on a sacred tradition. The only other time Paul uses them is to testify to Jesus' appearances after his Resurrection. Eating and drinking to "proclaim the Lord's death until he comes" go together with Resurrection. After all, the risen Lord comes every time we eat the bread and drink the wine in his memory.

These solemn words in the epistle are an island of peace and tranquility in the middle of a storm of human passions. Preceding them is Paul's denunciation of the bad table manners that I commented on in the last chapter. The generous sharing of food by Jesus in the wilderness has deteriorated. Paul warns his readers that they are eating and drinking judgment by "not discerning the body." In his fit of temper, Paul seems to suggest that the Body and Blood of Christ make people sick and even cause some to die. (1 Cor. 11:29–32) Paul is concerned about the Corinthians' failure to recognize the presence of Christ, not only the sacrament, but in the worshipping body. But considering how strongly Paul insists on God's free gift of grace, Christ's Body and Blood can only be more free grace and forgiveness. However, when we fail to see the Body and Blood of Christ in others, sickness, hunger and many more social ills will abound.

With a church in shambles, is the miracle of the Feeding in the Wilderness a distant memory? It can't be if the Eucharist celebrated in memory of Jesus is making all of Jesus' life present in the here and now. When we eat the death of Jesus, we enter into our own discord that tears the Body apart with cries such as "I am of Cephas!" and "I am of Apollos!" When we eat the Resurrection of Jesus, we eat the forgiveness with which Jesus greeted his disciples to gather them back together.

Chapter 10

The Human Self, God, and Grace

The Human Self

With this chapter I shift from corporate spirituality to personal spirituality. I say this advisedly because our deep connections with the desires of other people and, most importantly, to God's desire, remain as important as ever. I hope I have shown that the autonomous self is an illusion. Girard and Oughourlian have coined the term "interdividual" to point to and stress the importance of relationships to a sense of self. If a person succeeded in being totally autonomous (a highly dubious possibility), that person would end up with no sense of self. At the same time, the desires of others do not usually obliterate a sense of self except in extreme cases. The Body of Christ is made of many members. Although no member is self-sufficient, each member has some distinctiveness. If that were not so, there would be no connectedness between "living stones" or parts of the Body of Christ.

Each of us instinctively has some sense of self, some sense of who we are. Much of the time we take having a self for granted. It's as obvious as the air we breathe. Or is it? If we're asked to stop and think and explain what the self is, we draw a blank. The self isn't a thing we can grab hold of like a coin or a pearl. Most of us know better than to stop and ask either ourselves or others who we are. If we do, other people think we are having a crisis of self-identity, and maybe we are! Many of us go through a period of trying to "find ourselves." It happened to me. But when I found myself in the sense of gaining a sense of direction in my life, I had found God first. The solicitude for every lost person that Jesus expressed in the Parable of the Lost Sheep (Lk. 15:1–7) is also shown in the Parable of the Lost Coin. (Lk. 15:8–10) When the lost coin was found the woman who found it spent it on a party that's still going on. We find ourselves when we give ourselves away. It is like the merchant who sells everything in order to buy the pearl of great price. (Mt. 13:45–46)

A self should be inside us and in a certain sense, should *be* us. If my self is not within me, where could it be? But if I try to grasp my self in any way, I come up empty. And yet I can't imagine getting up in the morning and doing anything at all if it isn't *I* who is doing it. If it isn't *I* who sits down at a computer to write this book and put my name to it, then who is writing it? If I say, as some do, that God is dictating every word and I'm just God's secretary, who am I to be such a secretary? Am I anybody at all? All this is to say that the more I discuss the self, the more paradoxes will abound. Many of the most profound paradoxes come from the literature of the mystics who have deeply reflected on these matters. I have been hinting at the contemplative dimension of Christian spirituality throughout this book, as contemplative prayer is the strongest practice for living with mimetic resonance. Starting with a brief examination of the self, which can only be done obliquely, this book will take a more contemplative direction from now on. The notion of the self is so problematic that some mystics, many Hindus and Buddhists for example, conclude that there is no self at all. Christianity tends to hold fast to a notion of the self but turns and twists it through paradoxes that make it unrecognizable to people who think the self is the entity that has breakfast in the morning and drives to work.

In everyday life, we experience the self as the motor that drives us through life. We assume we are in the driver's seat, but in our more introspective moments, we notice that much of the time we seem to be in the passenger seat and we have no idea where we are going. If we come to this realization, it's easier to enjoy the ride and wear a crash helmet. It's also easier to plunge into distractions that help us forget that we aren't as sure about who we are as we want to be. Other people help us by distracting us, and we help them in the same way until everybody is distracted from their selves. In the end, we have a social conspiracy of interlocking distractions that keep us from realizing that we are being driven willy-nilly and either whooping it up or crawling in under the seat, waiting for the crash.

What puts us in the passenger seat of the car we think we're driving is mimetic resonance. We get carried away by our social ambience before we know it, and often we *don't* know it. Everything I've said about mimetic resonance should make it clear that whatever the self is, if the self is anything at all, is far from clear. Although we instinctively think the self is the center that creates desires for what is out there, it is often the desires of other people that drive us, just as our desires drive them. This is why we have the problem I mentioned earlier of not knowing where our desires end and those of others begin. Is it ever possible to say that *I* like Mozart piano concertos and the masses of Victoria, or am I totally carried off by streams of other people who like Mozart and Victoria? Is there more to the human self than the mimetic desires in each person's horizon? Or, is it possible to reach a point where my personal sense of liking a symphony, a poem is *shared* with others as they share their desires with me?

If there is no such thing as an autonomous human self, does this mean there is no self after all and I can move on to the next topic? No. What mimetic realism denies is the notion of a self as some sort of walled off center of personal agency that is independent of the external world. As I have shown, we are dependent on the external world not only for sustenance but for our desires. In spite of all the evidence against such an autonomous human self, this destructive myth is hard to kill. The paradox here is that the further we are from the driver's seat, the more convinced we are that we are at the steering wheel. How does this happen?

In *Sickness Unto Death*, Søren Kierkegaard analyzes two fundamental forms of despair in typical paradoxical fashion. We are in despair over not willing to be a self or we are in despair over *willing* to be a self. The first he calls weakness, which is feminine; the second he calls defiance, which is masculine. If we can't avoid either weakness or defiance, how can we *not* be in despair? If there is a way out, it has to be right on the sharp point of the dilemma, and we aren't going to get there without some help. Mimetic realism gives us insight into these two forms of despair. One who despairs in weakness by not willing to be a self gives in to the mimetic field and eschews all responsibility. Such a one melts in with the crowd, into the values of one's group (company, country, family, whatever) with little or no remainder. This abdication of self paradoxically entails grasping at the self (that is, trying to and grabbing nothing but air). If the values of the crowd are indistinguishable from our selves, they constitute our identity, and we defend this fused identity to the death. One who wills to be a self through defiance tries to grasp the self aggressively, in rivalry that is ultimately rivalry with God. Even when our shared desires are benign, we can be anxious if we fear they are not really *our* desires. When we fear that other people are driving our desires or snatching our desires from us, we fight back, insisting that *I* am the one who wants whatever it is and others are copying *me*. The more rivalrous the mimetic desire, the harder we fight for a false autonomy. Where or what is the self in all this? When mimetic rivalry causes us to struggle all the harder against the myth of autonomy, the more we tear ourselves apart until there really is nothing left.

By either not willing to be a self or *willing* to be a self, we try to perpetuate the myth of the autonomous self. Either attempt leads to the point where there is no self at all. Unfortunately, when we tear ourselves apart in these ways, we tear other people and things apart as well. If all of human society takes this route, there will, in the end, be nothing and nobody at all. Mimetic rivalry is directly related to the deterioration of the autonomous self that occurs when we aggressively cling to it. In *New Seeds of Contemplation* Thomas Merton warns us that "Every one of us is shadowed by an illusory person: a false self. This is the man I want myself to be who cannot exist, who cannot exist because God cannot know anything about him." (Merton 1961, 34) Merton also says that a sign of the disorder of our desires is that we look "for a greater reality in the object of our desire than is actually there." (Merton 1961, 26) This is Merton's way of saying that mimetic desire gives an illusory weight to the desired object, even while it whittles the object away to nothing.

Here is just one example of how deeply Merton understood mimetic issues. The false self is constantly in rivalry with other equally false selves. In a battle such as this, each falls into the abyss that is all that such illusory selves have become.

Ernest Becker's thesis outlined in *The Denial of Death* is helpful for getting some understanding of this "false self." In his book *Slavery of Death*, Richard Beck outlines Becker's demonstration that the existential fear of death and the subsequent denial of death leads one to strive for "heroism." For Becker, heroism is a compulsive drive to succeed, to prove that one matters, and to gain recognition for one's efforts. One might think that there is nothing wrong with that, but a neurotic striving for "heroism" comes at the expense of other things in life, such as family and friends. Moreover, the social settings for such striving tend to magnify aggressive behavior, so that those motivated by fear of death meld into social groups that persecute others to validate themselves. We can see themes of mimetic desire in the need for validation from others and a need to outdo others. The aggressiveness spurred on by the denial of death leads to scapegoating. Much scientific testing has verified Becker's theory where people who score higher on death anxiety also score higher on intolerance, fear of others, and a tendency to blame others for anything that goes wrong. (Pyszczynski et al. 2003; Beck 2014) When we consider how tenuous our fields of mimetic resonance make the sense of self and how this tenuous sense of self shrinks to the vanishing point through intensified mimetic rivalry, we can see well enough how an increased fear and denial of death will bring people, social groups, and perhaps the whole world to a boiling point.

Impressive as Becker's insights are, they are very bleak and they don't offer humanity any constructive way out of the denial of death except, perhaps, a heavy dose of Stoicism. Most humans find this cold comfort at best and an impossible prescription at worst. Thomas Merton, after having warned us of being deluded by a "false self," leads us to a more comforting, if challenging, position. The nothingness underlying both the abdication of the self to our mimetic fields or the aggressive attempt to build a self on our own terms is the way to arrive at a "true self." In his correspondence with John Wu concerning his translation of Chuang Tzu's Taoist writings, Thomas Merton suggested that "it is the void that is our personality, and not our individuality that seems to be concrete and defined by present and past, etc." This "not-I" is seen by Chuang Tzu and Thomas Merton as a source of freedom, a freedom that can save us from being "completely enslaved by the illusory." (Merton 2013, 264) The irony of willing to be a self in defiance is that, although it is the way of strength rather than weakness, it pushes us out of the driver's seat just as much as does the weakness of *not* willing to be a self. Another way to pose this fundamental dilemma is to suggest that defiance may seem strong because it is self-assertive, but in this self-assertiveness, the self dissolves in mimetic rivalry. If we lose our selves both by abdicating and by grasping, how do we ever have a self at all?

The only alternative to the horns of this dilemma is to *receive* our selves. In many ways, we receive our selves by taking in ambient desires as we grow up. But to keep from being determined by these ambient desires, we have to let go of this matrix of desires to reach a deeper level of desire, where we find ourselves called *by name*. This is a call we all receive by virtue of having been created by God. Isaiah says: "But now thus says the Lord, he who created you, O Jacob, he who formed you, O Israel: Do not fear, for I have redeemed you; I have called you by name, you are mine." (Isa. 43:1)

This is what happened to Saul of Tarsus. He thought he knew very well who he was because he was "circumcised on the eighth day, a member of the people of Israel, of the tribe of Benjamin, a Hebrew born of Hebrews; as to the law, a Pharisee; as to zeal, a persecutor of the church; as to righteousness under the law, blameless." (Phil. 3:5–7) Everything in this list is potentially good except for being a persecutor of the Church. But his being a persecutor confirms that he had a bad case of heroism as understood by Ernest Becker. He melded with the mob that stoned Stephen, tending their clothes and approving their action. But when he was knocked to the ground and heard a voice from Heaven crying to him: "Saul, Saul, why do you persecute me?" (Acts 9:4) everything changed. Perhaps everything had started to change while he was attending the clothes of those who stoned Stephen. Sometimes the reality of collective violence breaks through to somebody who is watching it happen. Maybe some instinct caused Saul to hold back and not throw any stones himself. Saul knew the scriptures. Maybe the songs of the Suffering Servant from Isaiah came to his mind at some point. In any case, the bottom fell out of Saul's life during his journey to Damascus. It must have been a frightful moment that felt like free fall save for the voice that was calling out to him. From that moment on, he was a strong individual known as Paul, a person completely grounded in Jesus, who had given him his real self.

In a remarkable paper, "Ego Credo," Michel Serres probes the emergence of personal identity in St. Paul as a new thing brought into being by God. Serres argues that up to the time of Christ, most human identity was submerged within group identity. This is what one would expect in cultures grounded in sacrificial violence, where the emergence of a differing voice out of the crowd could not be tolerated. In Paul, identity becomes distinct from belonging. Paul had belonged to Pharisaic Judaism, Roman Law, and Hellenistic rational wisdom. His identity was formed by these elements until the voice called out to Saul. Then, "the good news [Paul] proclaims is incarnated and grafted in him and through him; in him, the branch of a new creature springs forth." (Serres, 1) Right after his assertion of identity in Philippians 3 quoted above, Paul said he had come to "consider these gains as loss because of Christ." (Phil. 3:7) That is why Paul said: "there is neither Jew nor Greek." (Gal. 3:28) Serres explains that "for Paul, the only thing left is this 'new creature': *I*, the adoptive Son of God, through faith in Jesus Christ; *I* full of faith and without works, without pride; I, empty, poor, and nothing: universal." (Serres, 2)

From much earlier times, God had been calling people out of the crowd, just as he called Paul. Abraham was called out of Ur to go to a land God would show him. (Gen 12:1) Understandably, Abraham was a model for Paul. Moses was called away from his flock to lead a group of slaves out of Egypt. The prophets were called to step out of Israel to call the people back to God. In the Gospels, Simon and Andrew, and James and John were immersed in the culture of fishing, until Jesus called them out of it. There is nothing wrong with catching fish. How else would we ever get a fish dinner? But there was something deeper for these men to fish for. Matthew, like the rich young man, was called out of a sacrificial economic structure. The woman with the hemorrhage was part of the crowd that treated her as an unclean victim until she stepped out of it to reach for the hem of Jesus' garment. (Mk. 5:25–34) Zacchaeus slipped out of the crowd to climb a tree to get a better look at Jesus, and Jesus called out to him. (Lk. 19:4–6) Bartimaeus was blind until he called out of the crowd as Jesus was passing by. (Mk. 10:46) These examples prove that we don't have to be St. Paul to be called by Jesus. It can happen to anybody. Which is to say, the call happens to everybody.

In Revelation, Jesus promises that: "To everyone who conquers I will give some of the hidden manna, and I will give a white stone, and on the white stone is written a new name that no one knows except the one who receives it." (Rev. 2:17) In one of his *Unspoken Sermons*, George MacDonald suggests that this new name is not based on "popular judgment or prejudice or humor" or anything else derived from the "eyes of the people," but it is what God sees in us. This name is given to those who have "overcome." This overcoming begins in penance, our turning from a rivalrous culture, and blossoms into the person we were always meant to be through climbing "the stair of [our] God-born efforts and God-given victories," until we see our faces in the face of the one who gave us the white stone. (MacDonald 1976, 236–238) This white stone, then, is not something we can lock in an iron chest and sit on. This is a living stone that helps build up the Church. (1 Pet. 2:5) A living stone helps us breathe the Holy Spirit and keep moving in the way of Christ. The living stone given to each of us, then, is the gift of self we receive when we cease *not* willing to be a self in weakness or *willing* to be a self in defiance.

The Forgiving Victim gives each of us a name, a personal identity that is grounded in the Trinity, a name that is a mystery to ourselves and yet one that anchors us in ways we do not fully understand. In all this, it is most important to realize that the Trinity is a story much more than it is a doctrine. That is, when the Persons of the Trinity invite us into their lives, they invite us into their *story* in the same way they enter into our personal stories. As a story, the Trinity is no more graspable than the wind, as Nicodemus found out. (Jn. 3:8) It is the nature of stories to be ungraspable. Try to grasp anything in a story and you lose everything but the fragment you grasp. You might as well grasp at the note of a song. The story of the Trinity is the story of the Paschal Mystery, told succinctly in the famous verse: "For God did not send his Son into the world to condemn the world, but to save the world through him." (Jn. 3:16) In the sending, the Spirit acted as the bond of love between the Father and the Son. The Trinity also enters into the stories of each and every one of us, making us adopted sons and daughters, joint heirs with Christ. In Christ and the Spirit, we participate in Christ's suffering and glory so that our own sufferings are shared by Christ, and Christ's glory becomes ours. After the threefold cry of "Holy! Holy! Holy!" in the temple, (Isa. 6:3) the Spirit sends the prophet Isaiah to preach to the people. Like Isaiah, we also are sent by the Spirit to each other.

The Trinity shows us that a person is not a rugged individualist. Rather, a person *is* relationship. No relationship, no person. Our analogies with stories and music help us again here. The words of a story or a poem have very little meaning individually, but words take on much meaning in relationship to one another. The same is true with individual notes in music. An isolated note makes little sense, until it is joined to other notes and then becomes a song or a symphony. A triad is made up of three notes, but it is one chord. The Persons of the Trinity hold nothing back from one another, and ideally neither should we with one another. Trying to grasp our non-existent individuality is like trying to grasp a story or a song or the wind. If we are to be ourselves, we must let go as the Persons of the Trinity are always letting go. When we let go, we are free to go where we are sent, whether it is halfway around the world or—as is most often the case—to the person next to us. Receiving our identity in Christ opens up a whole new dimension for taking responsibility for our lives as it did for Paul. Once we have received an identity in Christ, we can belong with other people without being submerged in the group. In Christ, we have the grace to see when the group becomes persecutory and can call the group out on it. This is good because we can't get on without living with the desires of others. We still have to belong with our families, political parties, countries, and churches. But more fundamentally, we belong to Christ and Christ's desire, and that makes all the difference.

Who is God?

Who is this God from whom we receive a human self that dissolves into the mystery of God? Many theologians, especially those inclined to mysticism, say that God is unknowable. Any terms we use to speak of God fail because God is infinite and we humans are finite. Isaiah seems to corroborate this notion when he quotes Yahweh as saying: "For my thoughts are not your thoughts, nor are your ways my ways, says the Lord. For as the heavens are higher than the earth, so are my ways higher than your ways and my thoughts than your thoughts." (Isa. 55:8–9) But Isaiah was not a philosophical theologian, so he was not writing a treatise on the unknowability of God. The preceding verse does seem to tell us something about God: "Let the wicked forsake their way, and the unrighteous their thoughts; let them return to the Lord, that he may have mercy on them, and to our God, for he will abundantly pardon." If God is merciful and will abundantly pardon, then we *do* know something about God. Moreover, this oracle includes the invitation to what scholars call the Messianic Banquet: "Ho, everyone who thirsts, come to the waters; and you that have no money, come, buy and eat! Come, buy wine and milk without money and without price." Here we are told that God is generous. It is the same generosity that Jesus would act out six times in the wilderness during his earthly ministry. We need only recall the human rivalry and rage recounted in scripture to see that God's way of abundantly pardoning is radically different from the way we humans tend to operate.

The more I reflect on the twists and turns of both affirming and denying qualities to God, the more I think that affirming and denying are actually two sides of the same coin. We don't get anywhere if we can't say *anything* about God, and yet everything we say about God has to be wrong. God isn't a rock on somebody's front lawn any more than God is Pure Being. The dark cloud on Mount Sinai, the Cloud of Unknowing, and the Dark Night all indicate negation, and yet dark clouds and dark nights are still images that have to be denied. The basic problem in speaking about God is that one way or another, any human word used about God is going to be corrupted by human projections. John said that "God is love." (1 Jn. 4:8) That is undoubtedly true, but we have trouble imagining God's love as uncontaminated by mimetic rivalry. We know from experience that human love relationships are invariably tainted by mimetic rivalry at least a little. Usually they are so tainted a lot. John also says that "God is light and in him there is no darkness at all." (1 Jn.1:5) Again, this is very hard for us to imagine, much harder to imagine than a "dark cloud." Many mystics have explained the experience of darkness as our being blinded by God's light because our inner eyes are too weak for such light, just as the sun blinds us if we try to look straight at it. Let us look at some biblical images that are easily overlaid with human projections and see how they are corrected by prophets like Isaiah in his best moments and, most importantly, by what the Gospels and other New Testament writings tell us about the Forgiving Victim.

In many places, scripture proclaims God's greatness by extolling God's overpowering presence: "The Lord is great in Zion; he is exalted over all the peoples" (Ps. 99:2) and "The Lord is king, he is robed in majesty; the Lord is robed, he is girded with strength. He has established the world; it shall never be moved" (Psalm 93:2). We use the glamor of worldly power as a springboard to try and imagine God's absolute total power. Earthly rulers boss everybody around and make their nations serve them. Therefore, God bosses everybody around and rules from Heaven as an autocratic ruler. After all, we dream of being omnipotent and invulnerable, so we assume that the Master of the Universe is like that. Such images of power spill over into nature's more spectacular, if destructive, moments. "The voice of the Lord causes the oaks to whirl, and strips the forest bare; and in his temple all say, 'Glory!'" (Ps. 29:9) Our human tendency to wish to be as powerful as kings and nature in her more cantankerous moments should suggest that if God is not like us, that means God is not an autocratic ruler as earthly rulers often are, or try to be. If God is the greatest being, God is great in a different way.

In a similar fashion, Isaiah saw Yahweh in the invading armies from Assyria: "Ah, Assyria, the rod of my anger—the club in their hands is my fury! Against a godless nation I send him, and against the people of my wrath I command him, to take spoil and seize plunder, and to tread them down like the mire of the streets." (Isa. 10:5–6) Yahweh isn't mindlessly destructive like a storm; there is method in Yahweh's madness. Yahweh is punishing Israel for turning the needy aside from justice and robbing the poor of their right. (Isa.10:2) However, from what we know about Assyria, they sent themselves to Israel the way they sent themselves to a lot of other places to build their empire. The huge winged bulls they carved are still on display as images of their imperial disposition. Israel, like Assyria, fell into acting like an empire, although a relatively small one, and empires tend to collapse and fall. After Israel, Assyria was next in line for a fall.

If the wrath of the Assyrians is not God's wrath, and if storms are the work of nature and not manifestations of God's wrath, is God wrathful? Many preachers have certainly claimed so with great drama. Hell and brimstone sermons notwithstanding, there is too much in scripture about God's mercy for it to be ignored altogether. We tend to the notion that we can just add up everything said in scripture about God without questioning any of the components, and somehow get "God" as a final result. But does this get us a "god" whose ways are not our ways? I think not. What we get is a Janus-faced "god" who, in the end, we really cannot trust to be Emmanuel, which means "God with us." The bigger problem yet with this approach is that we don't really end up with a paradoxical deity made up of paradoxical parts of violence and peace. Instead, we get a deity who is just plain wrathful, violent, and vindictive. How so?

Our experience of mimetic resonance shows us how violence breeds violence until its contagion becomes an epidemic. In my experience, when a person blows up into irrational anger a few times, those outbursts tend to set the tone for how I see that person. That is, those few outbursts have cancelled the many more peaceful and good moments. If God is considered even a little vindictive and violent, then these traits take over and set the tone for how we understand God. Our relationship with a "god" who is even a little wrathful is not grounded in reverence and awe but in terror of being squashed like a bug for not toeing the line in picayune detail. A deity who is even a little bit violent and vindictive fails to be a credible voice that can break from outside our systems of principalities and powers and draw us into a whole new way of relating with one another and with God.

The biblical analogy of the punishing parent is a case in point. (cf. Heb. 12:7–11) Delinquent behavior poses challenges few of us handle well. No matter how loving we are, we can succumb to feelings of revenge if children's behavior becomes exasperating. When we have the power, as parents have the power over small children, we can be tempted to exact that revenge. Punishment that mixes revenge with genuine caring to teach a child accountability gives the parental relationship a rivalrous aspect. Approaches to child-rearing based on notions of "breaking the will of the child" make mimetic rivalry inevitable. Maintaining salutary and necessary discipline over/against vengeful punitive action is difficult but is an important goal to strive for. We need to be mindful that because children are vulnerable, they can easily be the victims of the rivalry between adults. That is, a child could receive the punishment we wish we could have inflicted on a stronger person who has power over us. The growing tendency to ask a child to take a "time out" makes good sense as we become conscious of mimetic resonance. It creates a space where the child has the opportunity to let go of anger and rivalry as well as learn accountability. Vengeance is, however, considered God's prerogative, as Deuteronomy quotes God as saying: "Vengeance is mine." (Deut. 32:35) These words are quoted by both St. Paul and the author of Hebrews, so they have had a strong grip on Christians from the start. The problem of leaving vengeance to God on the assumption (or hope!) that God will punish people who have offended us is that it creates a double-standard: We humans must be forgiving, but God may be vindictive whenever God chooses to be so. If we sincerely wish for God to avenge the wrongs done to us, we are as caught up in these wrongs as we are when we try to gain revenge ourselves. It looks like being asked to do what God tells us and not as God does. If God does act vindictively, even some of the time, then Jesus' accepting death on the cross ceases to be the ultimate revelation of God that Christianity claims it to be. If violent retribution on the part of God is the last word, then the hard practice of non-retribution doesn't seem to be worth it.

I hasten to say that vengeance is solely a divine prerogative, just as scripture says. God is indeed the only being in the universe with a *right* to vengeance. Whether God ever exerts that right or ever believes in doing so is another question that I will get to shortly. Vengeance is solely a divine prerogative because only God can justly and evenly exact vengeance. The mimetic contagion of violence among humans guarantees that it will escalate, even though everybody thinks they are giving tit for tat. In World War II, Pearl Harbor and the London Blitz were answered by the bombing of Dresden and Hiroshima. Jeremiah's anguished prayer that his persecutors be destroyed with "double destruction" (Jer. 17:18) powerfully expresses the tendency for vengeance to escalate. I have read numerous times about experiments where the participants were instructed to take turns squeezing the finger of the other. Each person was instructed to match the pressure the other had just exerted. Sensitive instruments measuring the amount of pressure actually exerted consistently indicated an increase of pressure with each squeeze. That is, what felt like the amount of pressure received by the one squeezing the finger of the other was almost always more pressure than was actually received. With humans, mimetic resonance constantly expands exponentially, with the inflated results beyond mathematical calculation. Every time we react to another mimetically, we are reacting with all the intensity that has invaded us along with the intensity we add to it. It's no wonder that feuds between families or within families and wars escalate the way they do. Only God could return the same amount of violence but no more. But does God actually do that? The actions of the risen Forgiving Victim suggest that the answer is No.

We have already noted that Jesus practiced what he preached about nonresistance. Peter expressed it succinctly: "When he [Jesus] was abused, he did not return abuse; when he suffered, he did not threaten; but he entrusted himself to the one who judges justly. He himself bore our sins in his body on the cross, so that, free from sins, we might live for righteousness." (1 Pet. 2: 23–24) This doesn't look like exacting vengeance to me. The context of these words is both troubling and challenging. It follows on verses admonishing slaves to be obedient and not to retaliate if unjustly treated. It's easy to see these verses tolerating slavery, especially with the *méconnaissance*, misrecognition, that mimetic rivalry can cause. However, it is the unjustly beaten slave with whom Christ identifies, not the punishing master. The writings of the New Testament make it clear that torturing and killing Jesus was *not* acceptable, and therefore, treating others like Christ in the sense of doling out abusive behavior is also not acceptable. By extension, Christ identifies with all vulnerable people and *not* those who take advantage of that vulnerability or who purposely imprison (and so enslave) others into vulnerability. This passage also supports the view that overthrowing unjust systems through violence is not Jesus' way. God chooses to be a vulnerable victim rather than a being who corrects injustice through violent force.

Although storms and vast armies provoke awe at what appears to be divine, Elijah, who had called down fire on the prophets of Baal, found, while hiding in a cave from Jezebel, that God was not in the earthquake or the fire, but rather was found in "a sound of sheer silence." (1 Kings 19:12) This "sheer silence" is not heard as long as we try to "imitate" God by sending the military on shock and awe campaigns. Isaiah warns us with this oracle: "But all of you are kindlers of fire, lighters of firebrands. Walk in the flame of your fire, and among the brands that you have kindled!" This is what we shall receive from God's hand, and it will cause us to "lie down in torment." (Isa. 50:11) Clearly this is a torment of our own making. Just as torchlight in our eyes prevents us from seeing what is in front of us, violent fire within us prevents us from seeing God's presence even deeper in our hearts.

As was Elijah's experience, it is in nature's calmer moments that we more easily see God. Even unbelievers tend to feel some reverence when they see mountains and trees with squirrels scurrying about in them. The stars in the sky and stones and lakes and growing things all resonate with God's desire. God has a profound respect for even the smallest pebble and hazel nut because God willed them to be. The more we participate in God's desire, the more we also will respect what is in nature. Although we must use nature, we will use it in a sharing way rather than by dominating it. Nature does not grasp at anything. It just is. This is why nature can teach us to desire in a non-rivalrous way.

It is also in our calmer experiences with people that we see God in human relationships. We see Christ in other people even though they do not always (or often) act like him. While the lilies of the field do not strive for the things of tomorrow, people do. In marriage, at least when it works reasonably well, one's spouse is the primary image of God to the other. There is nothing romantic here, as each partner knows the foibles and vices of the other very well. In community life, such as in a monastery, there is not, of course, the focused spousal relationship (except with God), but we have daily opportunities to see Christ through the struggles and kindnesses of others in the community. The image of Christ in the Gospels helps us straighten out the distortions that other people create, even as Christ plunges us deeply into his presence within them. Learning to resonate constructively with the desires of other people is part and parcel of learning to resonate with God's desire.

The clearest biblical witness for how God exercises power (and doesn't) is in the great hymn that Paul quotes in Philippians, where Jesus "though he was in the form of God, did not regard equality with God as something to be exploited, but emptied himself, taking the form of a slave, being born in human likeness. And being found in human form, he humbled himself and became obedient to the point of death—even death on a cross." (Phil. 2:6–11) Some religious thinkers, particularly process theologians, have suggested that God's power is limited. This idea gets God off the hook in the sense that we can't blame God for not blasting our enemies out of the water at our convenience. But if God can't exercise such power (and process thinkers usually have problems with Creation and sometimes even with the Resurrection), then God is not modeling the renunciation of power as a moral and spiritual virtue. One might as well give me a medal for not beating up a body builder. The vulnerability of God, then, is an amazing divine virtue only if God chooses to be vulnerable to Creation, even to death on a cross. In this vulnerability, there is no longer any room for projecting the violent power of worldly potentates onto God.

If God is not a whirlwind of overwhelming power or a cosmic tinderbox of wrath, neither is God a mild-mannered Benedictine monk like me. God's love as expressed in Hosea is so passionate that it's like being embraced by a whirlwind. Like the prophet Hosea who had married an unfaithful harlot, God suffers deeply the pain of a spurned lover. God loved Israel and called her out of Egypt. Of the Ephraimites, God said: "I led them with cords of human kindness, with bands of love. I was to them like those who lift infants to their cheeks. I bent down to them and fed them." (Hos. 11:4) And yet, Israel and Ephraim forsook God. As a result, "the sword rages in their cities, it consumes their oracle-priests, and devours because of their schemes." (Hos. 11:6) This violence is not from God; it is from and among the people who forsake God. But God still cannot give up Israel or Ephraim. God will roar like a lion and "his children will come trembling from the west." (Hos. 11:10) So passionate and wild is God's love that it is understandable that at times it feels like wrath. The passionate love God has for each of us is overwhelming. The passionate love God has for *other* people is just as overwhelming. When we wrong others, God's passionate love for *them* burns through us. It isn't wrath, but it feels like it. This is the kind of love that can turn us upside down and twist us in knots. It is a love that never stops, not for all eternity. This passionate love is not vindictive, because God will not stop forgiving no matter how often God is forsaken.

Grace

What happens when the mysterious, unknown human self meets up with the even more mysterious, unknown Self of God? When our desires interact with the desires of other people, there is give and take or a push and shove. Sometimes, unfortunately, there is a complete takeover of one by the other. With God, there may be pushing and shoving on our part, but God simply gives. The less we take and push and shove, the more we get. This is grace.

Over the centuries, there has been as much debate about the relationship between grace and human effort as there has been about free will. The Reformation was a period when the debate was most intense. Much ink and blood was spilled over the issue as mimetic rivalries engulfed all of Europe. In calmer times, there is a tendency to see a mysterious connection between the two, where the lines between the two are there but blurred. The growing consensus today is supported by Paul's words to the Philippians: "Work out your own salvation with fear and trembling; for it is God who is at work in you, enabling you both to will and to work for his good pleasure." (Phil. 2:12–

13) Nothing could be clearer in stating the necessity of both human effort and God's grace for our salvation.

Usually God inspires us to live in the Trinity's bond of Love by letting us experience the emptiness at the center of our lives. This emptiness is an inner voice placed within us by our creator so that we may yearn to know God deeply. We compound this emptiness when we try to claim our desires, since we do not generate desires by ourselves. Rather, part of our inner poverty is the need for our desires to be stimulated through mimetic resonance with others. No amount of riches in money, love, virtue, or human experience can fill this void. The more we strive to have more of any of these riches than other people, the more empty we are, because mimetic rivalry makes our desires insatiable. Usually, we do not channel our need for God in God's direction until we have tried filling our emptiness with cheaper pursuits and intense rivalry. This void impresses upon us the poverty of our humanity. We must accept this poverty before we can receive the riches God desires to give us. When we allow ourselves to be poor, then the beauties of this life and the friendships we cherish and joys in our accomplishments can be filled with God's desire. Usually we wait until the emptiness really hurts before we consider doing anything about it. Even then, we may reach for any pain-killer we can find, preferably rage at a rival, rather than deal with our emptiness. God, however, wants much more for us than the alleviation of pain. God desires to share with us eternal joy that is without rivalry.

When God reaches into the depths of our being to draw us to God, we find that God has already given us the power to respond. Meanwhile, our inner being echoes God's yearning for us. This is the mimetic resonance at the core of our being. We do not turn to God on our own, God turns us to God. Is there no escape? Yes and no. We cannot escape the reality of our God-given nature any more than we can escape mimetic desire. We cannot escape the natural yearning we have for God, but we also have a mysterious gift of freedom that allows us to contradict our nature and the end God desires for us. The only escape route offered us leads us away from God and into the thick of the mimetic ambience around us.

If God calls us and effects the movements of the spiritual life within us, it seems to follow that we can and should do nothing. Many theologians and mystics have said as much. An extreme example is a school of thought of the seventeenth century known as Quietism that made an absolute out of this notion. The Quietists said we should do nothing except wait for God to act in us. They were right except for one thing: we must constantly call on God while we are waiting. If we don't, we have not made the fundamental choice toward God, and unconscious desires, unbridled emotions, and the social mimetic swirl take over. We have abdicated our responsibility to use our free will. When we give up trying to exercise the will at all, we end up assuming that every whim of ours is God's desire, and we do so with ruinous results. The current desires in our mimetic ambience take over and eclipse God's desire.

We might fear that the grace of the Holy Spirit will eclipse our humanity. But far from being a nullification of our humanity, spirituality is a fulfillment of it. If the Holy Spirit fulfills our humanity as well as transcends it, then we can hardly have spirituality without the lumps of humanity that we are. That would be like trying to make a cherry pie without the cherries. We each have a mind, a will, feelings, and a body, all of which we can direct toward God or away from God as we choose. But our spirit is not an immaterial thing floating in us or through us. The spirit is not a human faculty at all. Rather, our spirit is an emptiness that only God can fill. It is like the emptiness of a bowl that has the potentiality of being filled to overflowing, but cannot fill itself. We must empty ourselves as much as we can of the desires swirling within us so that we can receive God's desire. This is something we do through deep prayer, as I will explain below. Both the Hebrew word *ruach* and the Greek work *pneuma*, often translated as "spirit," literally mean "breath" and "wind." We have both the potential and the need to breathe air, but the air comes from outside ourselves. We don't have any air within us unless we breathe it in. The spirit is not a passive emptiness waiting to be filled any more than our lungs are. The human spirit is a dynamic movement within us that yearns for the quickening that only God's Spirit can give.

It is the breath of God's desire that gives us the gift of freedom to choose between rivalrous desires and God's desire. This breath is God calling us each by name. When God's call has gripped us, we find space for the greatest freedom of all. We can say "yes" to God's desire. When we have said "yes," we remain free to follow God ever more deeply into the love flowing within the Trinity. We also remain free to turn back to ourselves and our rivalries at the drop of a hat. When we say "yes" to God, we make ourselves available to God. We accomplish this task by making a specific act of will that we renew time and time again. In his book *Will and Spirit*, Gerald May suggests that we have the fundamental choice between being willful, where we try to run our own lives, and being *willing*. When we are willing for God to act on us and in us, we have given God the opening God asks for.

Our relationship with God is not unlike our human experience of romance. When two people fall in love, it is not something that either person caused; it just happens. But a romance cannot go anywhere unless both people actively make themselves available to the other. If we make no response to the overtures of the other, the other has no way of knowing we are interested in a personal relationship. How else can God safeguard our freedom than by waiting for us to respond to God? We must make it clear to God that we *do* want God to enfold us with God's Love, cost what it may.

If our greatest desire is to share God's desire, why do we choose anything different from God's desire? In the end, there is no answer to this question. That is the *aporia* of freedom, that abysmal glitch that gives us the choice of not willing to be a self, willing to be a self in defiance, or accepting our self as a gift from God. We are tempted to choose destruction in order to escape receiving our selves from God even as we yearn for God to deliver us from self-destructing. The contradiction between the two conflicting desires makes no sense; it is totally irrational. But there it is, right at the center of our human experience. We might as well face the fact that sin is irrational, but it is real. Even when we think we have made a choice between one "will" or the other, the conflict continues. We can't escape from God, but neither can we escape from mimetic contagion and the futile attempts to rebel against one or the other or both. No matter how intense the inner conflict, we can make the movement of prayer, even when it does not feel like prayer, even when the rebellious "will" and the social flood continues to pull us away. Sometimes all we can do is want to want God.

That is how we find ourselves back in the driver's seat. When we receive our selves from God, we accept that God has made the vehicle and that God fuels the vehicle with the breath of the Holy Spirit. We are free to be a self every time we receive it. This is why the biblical heroes and heroines and the saints show such individual personalities in contrast to the often faceless functionaries of empire. In our daily struggles, we find ourselves pushed and pulled from pillar to post between sitting in the driver's seat and getting knocked up against the passenger seat. Learning to be a self takes more than a lifetime; it takes an eternity. Fortunately, God has all the time in the world and God shares that time with us.

Chapter 11

Essential Habits of the Heart: Respect and Humility

Respect and humility are the two fundamental attitudes that are most conducive to living constructively with mimetic resonance and avoiding its destructive potential. Both attitudes need to become habitual dispositions to be effective. Such habitual dispositions are not automatic the way many habits (especially bad habits) tend to be. They need to be renewed every day, every hour, or they will fall away.

Although St. Benedict attaches great importance to outward action, both in manual work and what he calls "the Work of God," i.e., the Divine Office, Benedict also attaches much importance to the inner disposition. In his short Chapter 20, "Reverence in Prayer," Benedict says: "Whenever we want to ask some favor of a powerful man, we do it humbly and respectfully, for fear of presumption. How much more important, then, to lay our petitions before the Lord God of all things with the utmost humility and sincere devotion." (RB 20:1–2) When the Gospel is read at the end of Sunday Matins, the worshipers should "stand with respect and awe." (RB 11:9) After each psalm, we should stand in honor of the Trinity. (RB 9:7)

Respect and humility are so intertwined that it is hard to separate them. One cannot have one without the other. However, there is some distinction between them in that respect is directed towards the other, whether God or our neighbor, whereas humility rests in the self as an attitude supporting the outreach of respect. I want to deal with respect first and then move on to humility.

Respect

The first question that might come to mind is: Why respect instead of love? Isn't love the primary Christian virtue? Yes, love in the sense of *agape,* is the primary Christian virtue, and I will discuss it below, but we need to start with respect. Just as we need to be served milk before solid food until we are ready for it, we need to be trained by respect in order to love rightly and "to distinguish good from evil." (Heb. 5:14) If we try to leapfrog this prerequisite, there is a real possibility of mistaking lust and other noxious attitudes for love. Don Giovanni claimed that he loved all the women he wooed, making conquests by the hundreds, if Leporello is to be believed. But did Don Giovanni show respect for Donna Anna, Donna Elvira, or Zerlina? Not on your life. What erroneously passes for love sidesteps respect entirely and sidesteps love as well.

In seeking honor, we may be tempted to win respect from another by conquest, but any attempt along those lines is bound to fail. In any case, we can't control whether another will hold us in respect, and aggressive attempts to gain it look pitiable. What we *do* have control over is our own attitude. We can offer other people respect. That is no guarantee that we will receive respect in return, but chances are better if we maintain respect for the other in a gentle way, even if it is not reciprocated. Far from attempting any kind of conquest, reaching out with respect necessarily renounces mimetic rivalry. Whereas love without respect tries to woo another person into conformity to one's own feelings, respect does no such thing. My respect does not require that another person feel the way I do about anything. Respect is about relating to another, not winning anything. Respect is an important accomplishment because it involves overcoming our mimetic rivalry with others. Conquering ourselves in this sense saves us from the need to conquer others.

Relating respectfully with another involves, in fact requires, courtesy. Courtesy is so mundane that those of us who like to think we are sophisticated tend to look down on it. But there is something profound about courtesy in its simplicity. Courtesy is not focused on the inner disposition the way respect is; it is more geared to external action. However, the outer action of courtesy is grounded in respect and, more importantly, it deepens respect. There is a ritualistic aspect to courtesy that we learn as children to help us act politely before we reach the point of actually *feeling* polite and respectful. Here we have a connection with worship that is also an external action that fosters and deepens the inner attitude of respect and reverence for God.

Routine encounters with others, such as the person at the checkout counter, are so trivial as to seem not worth noticing, but that is partly because we take respect so much for granted that we don't notice it. We all know how much we appreciate doing business with people who are respectful and how much we avoid doing business with those who aren't. In such cases, respect isn't so much a feeling as it is a set of actions and a way of speaking. Although receiving respectful treatment gives us a low-grade sense of well-being, disrespectful treatment makes us instantly angry. When that happens, all sense of respect for the person who insulted us flies out the window. Disrespect makes the smallest exchanges seem big and highly significant, while we don't think much of respectful encounters. This is an indication of how much we take courteous exchanges for granted. Both respect and disrespect are highly contagious, but the latter is especially so. We don't get caught up in a polite response, but an impolite response grabs us by the neck and we have the other person by the neck before we know it. Respect and courtesy need to become deep habits that keep us from reacting instantly to discourtesy.

We tend to think we are owed respect just because we are who we are, and we feel violated if we do not receive it. Yet we are apt to think *other* people should *earn* our respect. This looks like a double standard, but I can sympathize. The problem is that when we take courtesy for granted, we assume we are being courteous and respectful even if we are being abusive. We hear much of the rage on the part of people who feel they have been treated disrespectfully by others. Perhaps they have been treated in a reprehensible way, but the people who complain the most about being disrespected are often not the people who win any prizes in etiquette contests. When we become preoccupied with the respect we think people owe *us*, we are caught up in ourselves to the point of becoming oblivious to the other.

God's unconditional love for us is the model for human relationships, and since respect is the basis for genuine love, God also gives us unconditional respect. It follows, then, that we should give others unconditional respect, which can be harder than unconditional love. This is what I mean by suggesting that "love" can be a smokescreen for our lack of respect, and therefore our lack of *agape*. It is commonly said that we should hate the sin but love the sinner. This sounds good and even loving, but somehow, in real life, this almost always ends up as conveying serious disrespect for the sinner whom we "love" in theory. This is the problem with loving in theory. It gets us off the hook of respecting people in reality when they haven't earned our respect. If we start to think in terms of hating the sin but *respecting* the sinner, maybe we can get somewhere. I think this is at least partly why James Alison prefers to speak of God's *liking* us rather than "loving" us because of the ways the word "love" gets misused and misunderstood. (See Alison 2004.)

On a mostly (but not always) lighter side, an important example of positive mimetic resonance is laughter. The way we use laughter is a sure index of the amount of respect that we have. Laughter is one of the first things a baby learns in imitation of a mother, father, or other caregiver. So it is that laughter comprises the first bonds a newborn child makes. At its best, laughter is spontaneous and infectious. How many times do we laugh without knowing why, just because other people are laughing? When children are laughing helplessly while playing, happiness spreads to everyone around them. We laugh with others because we don't want to be left out of the joke, even if we don't know what the joke is. Just think of some of our best times when we laughed with family and friends with no other reason than we were together and we got caught up in laughter.

There is a darker side to laughter, however. Actually it is a darker side of us and our mimetic resonance, rather than a darker side of laughter. Often laughter is used to wound others, to score points against them, or to put others down to lift ourselves up. Almost as soon as they learn how to speak, small children use laughter in this way. School playgrounds are filled with cruel mockery. Children learn cruel laughter from one another. Unfortunately, children also learn much about cruel laughter through being shamed by adults who think ridicule is a good way to prepare children for the hard knocks of life. Such laughter continues to be a bond between people, but it is a bonding at the expense of someone, a butt of jokes, a victim.

When he discourages laughter as a sign of pride, St. Benedict surely had this darker side of laughter in mind, although it is possible that he had a blind spot for the value of spontaneous, bonding laughter. (RB 7:56–61) Certainly, when laughter is a put-on act to gain attention, it is the opposite of spontaneity and is a prideful act, an act seeking to dominate by drawing attention to oneself at the expense of others.

We get so habituated to using laughter as a weapon instead of a bond of love that we hardly know what the latter is. One way back to healthy laughter is to learn to laugh at ourselves and help others laugh at themselves. At its best, comedy does just that. In Mozart's *The Marriage of Figaro*, laughter is used as a means to overcome mimetic triangles and tensions and bring reconciliation. Shakespeare does this sort of thing in a masterly way in comedies such as *Twelfth Night* and *As You like It*. In *The Merchant of Venice*, Shakespeare sets a trap for the unwary, leading us join the persecution of Shylock before unmasking this derisive laughter for what it is. I experienced the same sort of conviction while watching a performance of *Twelfth Night*. The famous scene where Malvolio is tricked into presenting himself before the countess in yellow cross-gartering had me and the audience in stitches, but at the end of the play, the production stressed the extent that Malvolio, although an unpleasant fellow himself, was a victim of insensitive behavior. Learning to laugh at ourselves without laughing *at* other people is a delicate business.

The chapter on the cellarer of the monastery in the Rule of St. Benedict is the most concise and articulate portrayal of respect and courtesy that I know. The cellarer is the monk responsible for providing for the community and guests. To do his duties well, he needs to respect the tools and all other material goods to the extent of treating them as if they were "sacred vessels of the altar." (RB 31:10) Here is an indication of the continuum from respect for material reality in one's work to respect for God in prayer. The cellarer should provide "the allotted amount of food without any pride or delay lest they be led astray." (RB 31:16) That is, the cellarer ought to be respectful of the needs of others and should not take advantage of his position to play petty power games the way some bureaucrats do with their tiny turfs. The Latin for "leading them astray" is *scandalizaverit,* which means to scandalize or to place a stumbling block before the other. We have noted that this is the word Girard uses to describe mimetic rivalry, where two or more people become stumbling blocks or scandals to each other. It is the word Jesus used when he warned against causing his "little ones" to stumble, a verse Benedict quotes. Jesus and Benedict are alerting us to a human tendency to make oneself a stumbling block for another by making a simple encounter a contest of wills. This is precisely what Benedict wants the cellarer to avoid.

If the cellarer does not have a requested item, he should "offer a kind word in reply." (RB 31:13) When I was guest master for the monastery, there were times when I did not have room to accept any more guests when somebody called. I kept Benedict's admonition in mind and tried to speak kindly and give encouragement to the caller's chances for coming at another time. If the cellarer should be the one who suffers discourtesy, he should "reasonably and humbly deny the improper request." (RB 31:7) The onus is on the cellarer to stem any escalation of disrespect by treating even a disrespectful person with respect.

The situation of the cellarer of the monastery providing for people who depend on his solicitude is quite the opposite of the person who approaches God in prayer "humbly and respectfully." (RB 20:1) The cellarer himself would be on the other end of the stick on this one. Here, we have the danger of projecting worldly power on to God and approaching God in that spirit. If we picture God as a whimsical potentate who grants favors or withholds them in power plays, then we slip into playing these power games with people who depend on us. Benedict forbids the cellarer to act in this way because it goes against the Gospel.

Benedict gives us another vision of respect and courtesy in one of the more remarkable and attractive chapters in his Rule: "Summoning the Brothers [and Sisters] for Counsel." Although Benedict was not so democratic as to have matters put up for a majority vote (as most modern monastic constitutions do), Benedict considered it essential that the abbot listen to *all* members of the community before making a decision. (RB 3:1) As abbot of my community, I am profoundly grateful for the suggestions and cautions I have received from my fellow monks on numerous occasions. Most writings on the Rule remind us that the opening word in the Rule is "Listen." Much is made of the need to listen to others as a means of listening to God. Here, Benedict reminds the abbot to listen to the community. Given the toxic atmosphere of much debate in political and religious matters, I cannot stress enough to importance of listening as a first principle to healing the exchange of thoughts and opinions.

We can make it easier for others to listen to us by expressing ourselves in a way that makes it easier for them to listen. Benedict says that we will do this if we "express [our] opinions with all humility, and not presume to defend [our] own views obstinately." (RB 3:4) If we take a moment to think about how hard it is to listen to a person who does the opposite, we will see the importance of this admonition. When views are expressed humbly and without obstinacy, it is easier to be focused on the issue rather than our relationships with other people, which, in the course of debate, tend to become more competitive than constructive. Benedict would have us discern the right thing to do, not strive to gain the most debating points.

There is a qualitative difference between honest disagreement and rivalry, but there is also a fine line between them. We can easily start with honest disagreement and fall into rivalry if we allow ourselves to become more obsessed with the person we disagree with than with trying to see what is true and what should be done. This matter calls for constant self-examination, continually asking ourselves: What side of this line am I on? We also have to be alert to whether we are actually listening to what the other is saying or only thinking about what *we* want to say. If we neglect this self-examination, we are pretty certain to fall over into the wrong side of the divide and become lost in mimetic entanglements.

Even more startling, Benedict says that the reason the *whole* community should be called together is because "The Lord often reveals what is better to the younger." (RB 3:3) This is not an over-idealization of young people. Elsewhere Benedict notes how exasperating young people can be. But it is a salutary reminder that the points of view of marginal people, which includes the young, may prove to be vital to a right discernment. If respect becomes habitual, we will not draw hasty conclusions about marginal people.

St. Benedict famously insists that "all guests who present themselves are to be welcomed as Christ." (RB 53:1) Benedict goes on to quote Matthew 25 to emphasize the point. Likewise, the cellarer, when attending to fellow monastics and guests should do the same. Benedict also says that "care of the sick must rank above and before all else, so that they may truly be served as Christ." (RB 36:1) Once again, Benedict quotes Matthew 25. Benedict may refer to God as "The Lord God of all things," (RB 20:2) who is greater than "a powerful man" from whom we might ask a favor, but Benedict is clear that this Lordly God identifies with all humans in need. That means that anyone entrusted with care of others should share the same solicitude.

We all have a hard time respecting people in positions subordinate to us, especially if they are needy. We instinctively look down on them because we think we are the ones with something to give or withhold. In other words, we are in the winning position and we like it that way. However, if Christ assumes the "losing" position, and Christ is the king whom we should obey, then we should be respectfully obedient to the needs of others. We might say that Christ makes other people respectable even if they have no respectability within themselves. The implication of this, of course, is that we also lack respectability within ourselves and it is Christ who gives *us* respectability.

The theological principle for saying that a person is entitled to respect just for being a human being is that we are each made in the image of God. That is true, but Christ intensified his identification with each person in need by dying for us. Since Christ died for *everybody*, Christ identifies with everybody. By identifying with each of us, Christ takes the rivalry out of our relationships.

The way we relate to one another has nothing to do with winning or having the upper hand in some way. Christ has leveled the playing field. Christ is focused on the needs of each one of us. That means Christ is focused on our own needs and also the needs of the people we encounter. This means doing what we can for another's needs and having a kind word when we can't. In all this, we participate in Christ's respect for us, which makes us more respectable than we were.

Respect is a humble virtue, so humble that it moves below the radar screen in much the same way as do the currents of electricity running through our houses. But if the current stops and the lights go out, it's a big deal. Respect may be a humble virtue but it is a virtue that keeps the world going the way the movement of electrical currents keep our houses powered. Respect is a virtue for little things, a humble way of small renunciations such as pushing the wheelchair of a crabby person who complains about every bump on the way. The person pushing the wheelchair is not the one who is noticed, but that person is keeping the wheelchair in motion.

Humility

Humility tends to evoke images of groveling before potentates, such as when Anna was ordered to bow before the King of Siam in *The King and I*. Such popular images project human images on God. Those images have nothing to do with Jesus, who was more interested in finding the lost sheep of Israel than having anybody bow down to him.

In Chapter 7 of his *Rule*, Benedict outlines twelve steps of humility, likening the steps to a ladder. (RB 7:5–9) This image leads us to expect a more systematic chapter then we get. The first and final steps form an *inclusio* with the first step dealing with the fundamental inward disposition of humility, and the final step describing the outward deportment of this virtue. In the middle is a cluster of verses dealing with suffering with references to Jesus' suffering and another cluster on the hazards of insensitive laughter, which I discussed above. I discuss this chapter in the *Rule* in greater detail in *Tools for*

Peace. (Marr 2007, 87–108)

The first and most fundamental step of humility for St. Benedict is that we keep "the fear of God always before [our] eyes and never forget it." (RB 7:10) That is, before humility is anything else, it is living in the presence of God. This is indeed something very different than groveling in the dust. This step reminds us of our constant need for God and also of God's sustained presence in our lives. It is precisely in our desires that our need for others shows itself. We often think we need others to fulfill our desires, but it is really more a case of needing others to desire. We often claim these desires for ourselves, which is an act of serious pride. Humility, then, involves accepting the interaction of our desires with the desires of others and accepting our mutual need of one another's desires. But as this first step of humility teaches us, we most need to be in tune with our need for God's desire.

We tend to forget not only God's presence but, even more seriously, God's desire when we are immersed in the desires of other people. We have noted many times how our involvement with the desires of other people tends to become rivalrous, which draws us further from God's desire. The more we are grounded in God's desire, the more constructive we are apt to be in the way we act in terms of the desires of others. We are freer to treat others with respect and courtesy when we don't need to "win" our human encounters, because we are grounded in God's desire, which has nothing to do with winning but has everything to do with providing for others.

The inner attitude of living in the memory of God's presence is balanced by Benedict's twelfth and final step of humility where external deportment at all times and places helps to remind us of God's presence to us. Once again, we have outer action and inner attitude reinforcing each other just as they should during worship. The last thing Benedict would want is for us to put on an act. When they flow out from right inner attitudes, our actions are natural with no sense of putting on airs. The more we are mindful of living in God's presence, the more natural the deportment of humility will be. Paying attention to this outward deportment tends to have a humbling effect that strengthens the right inner attitude.

The middle steps of humility in Benedict's Rule, the heart of his chapter, take us to the depths of the Paschal Mystery. They involve obedience "under difficult, unfavorable, or even unjust conditions" (RB 7:35), where we "quietly embrace suffering," being "content with the lowest and most menial treatment" (RB 7:49) and admitting in our hearts that we are "inferior to all and of less value." (RB 7:51)

This looks a lot more like groveling before the King of Siam than it does holding fast to the memory of God's presence. But obeying under unjust conditions is what Jesus did during his earthly life, most of all during his last days. This step isn't about bowing before imperious rulers; it's about bowing to everybody, including those we consider the most despicable of human beings. Jesus did it. What about us? When we are being ill-treated, we console ourselves with the thought that at least we are better than those who mistreat us. But that is not what Jesus did. Jesus treated even Pontius Pilate and Caiaphas with respect, although the guards of the high priest didn't see it that way. (Jn. 18:22)

This consideration adds a deeper perspective to the first step of humility that posits being ever-mindful of being in God's presence. From our point of view, there is a bit of a Big-Brother-is-watching-us oppressiveness about God's perpetual mindfulness of everything we do and think. However, God is shown by Jesus' actions to be quite the opposite of "Big Brother." "Big Brother" watches over us in search of blameworthy behavior or thoughts. God watches over us as the Forgiving Victim, always hoping to welcome us back when our actions and thoughts stray from God.

We are not easily content with "the lowest and most menial treatment." On the contrary, we tend to think that the world owes us the good things in life. If and when we don't get them, we become highly resentful of everybody we hold responsible for what we don't have. If and when we do get some good things in life, we think we only got what was coming to us. Of course, most of us find ourselves having to take the bad along with the good, and we are resentful only most of the time. This is the case even if we get good things more often than not. Bad things always make a stronger impression on us. In short, *we* are the ones who act like the King of Siam, not God. When we stop expecting the world to give us nothing but the best and become more concerned with those who don't have good things because of our inordinate greed, then we become more grateful for what we actually have. Gratitude is an essential part of humility. If we are not thankful, we are not humble.

In these middle steps of humility, hard as they are to embrace, we come to grips with the incomprehensible love God has for us. Christ didn't take time to dwell on how much more righteous he was than those who taunted him and nailed him on the cross. Jesus was too busy thinking about bringing even these people into his Kingdom to have room in his heart for anything else.

So it is at the bottom of humility that we find divine love. Benedict hints at the experience we can have of God's love when we let go of our pride when he says that, by following these steps, we "arrive at that perfect love of God which casts out fear." (RB 7:67; cf. 1 Jn. 4:18) At this level of humility, there is no dread of God because we have dropped our projections on God and have become free within the depths of God's desire.

Although pride is usually posited as the opposite of humility, the early eastern monastics distinguished vainglory from pride. It is not easy to see the distinction between the two. Vainglory, sometimes called "boasting" or "conceit," is understood as trying to gain glory and acclaim from humans, while pride is more directly related to our relationship with God, such as thinking or acting as if we don't need God. In terms of mimetic theory, vainglory is seeking to stir up the desire of other people for our own actions or, better yet, for our very being. In short, vainglory is an addiction to being admired, whether we deserve it or not. (And most of us know how easily we are turned off by *other* people who assiduously seek our admiration.) Vainglory is acting like the hypocrites who make such a public display of almsgiving "that they may be praised by others" (Mt. 6:2) or of their fasting for the same reason. Jesus says they have "received their reward," which presumably is to be praised by other people. Unfortunately, this addiction to praise distances us from God's desire. The great fourth-century monastic writer John Cassian says that vainglory "has many styles, forms, and variations" as it can strike at everything we do since every action or even every inaction can be motivated by vainglory. (Cassian 2000, 163)

It is difficult not to want to be admired. Moreover, although it is vainglorious to want people to acclaim our books and other accomplishments, there is no sense and no edification in writing badly or doing bad work. When Benedict says that readers in church or at table should read well enough to edify the hearers, (RB 38:12) or that the guest quarters should be well prepared for visitors, (RB 53:21) he makes it clear that we should try to do every task assigned to us well, whether it is writing a book or vacuuming the hallway.

Some of the desert monastics were ruthless with themselves in their attempts to stifle vainglory. This was difficult because they were admired by many people who heard about their lifestyle. In one famous anecdote, a group of admirers came to see Abba Moses. They asked a monk they came across where Abba Moses could be found. The monk told them to go away because Abba Moses was a fool and not worth seeing. The visitors turned away, only to find out from some other monks that it was Abba Moses himself who had driven them away. Some people take this reverse strategy to the extreme by assuming that if people revile us and persecute us and utter all kinds of evil against us falsely, then we are blessed. (Mt. 5:11) Maybe, but in a talk I heard Gil Bailie give, he said: "We aren't blessed if people revile us for being a clod." The problem is that when we are still clods, we are preoccupied with the opinions of others, even if we revel in opprobrium. As long as we are clods, we are not reviled on Jesus' account.

Jesus gives us a clue about how to avoid vainglory when he follows his admonition not to trumpet our almsgiving and other good deeds by adding: "Do not let your left hand know what your right hand is doing, so that your alms may be in secret." (Mt. 6:3–4) In his commentary on the Sermon on the Mount in *The Cost of Discipleship,* Dietrich Bonhoeffer notes the tension between these words and the admonition: "Let your light shine before others, so that they may see your good works and give glory to your Father in heaven." (Mt. 5:16) Bonhoeffer suggests that the trick is to hide our good works from ourselves. To do this, we must hide from ourselves any admiration we get from others as well. (Bonhoeffer 1959, 158)

As John Cassian pointed out, we can be haunted by vainglory when we write a book or vacuum the hallway or do anything else. The best we can do is concentrate on the work itself rather than what others think of our efforts or what we want others to think about them. As an act of charity, we should try to write a good book that is helpful to others and vacuum the hallway to make the house nicer for those who live there. When the table reader begins the job for the week, Benedict asks that "all pray for him so that God may shield him from the spirit of vanity." Then he has the table reader pray the verse "Lord open my lips" (Ps. 51:15) with the rest of the community repeating it three times. (RB 38:2–3) Perhaps the best advice Benedict has to offer is: "Do not aspire to be called holy before you really are, but first be holy that you may more truly be called so." (RB 4:62)

Chapter 12

Forgiveness: an Ongoing Process

While respect and humility are attitudes that need to be cultivated so as to be habitual, forgiveness is more of a process, especially when one has suffered severe injuries at the hands of another. In such cases, it can take much time before we even scratch the surface of habituating ourselves to forgiveness. We can hope for forgiveness, too, to eventually become a habit, but even then, it is a habit that takes time, often lots of time, perhaps even a lifetime to cultivate. Forgiveness is a process that gives no guarantee of a conclusion. Sometimes it cannot be fulfilled in this life. Even when we have done much forgiving, we often find there is still more forgiving to do.

It is my pastoral experience and of that of those with more experience and expertise, that abused people do not move forward in life successfully without some measure of forgiveness of the crimes committed against them. On the other hand, it is also my pastoral experience, and that of others, that pressuring a person to forgive almost always does more harm than good. Forgiving is not something a person can decide to do at the drop of a hat. Paradoxically, assuring a victim that he or she need not forgive the perpetrator usually helps the victim let go of the hurt enough to lower a need for revenge. In any case, a victim of severe abuse carries much guilt for being a victim, since perpetrators are good at blaming the victim and society tends to follow suit. These victims do not need to have the added guilt that comes of being asked to forgive before they are ready.

That forgiving is the "Christian" thing to do is ultimately the greatest glory of Christianity, but in the midst of severe trauma at the hands of humans who abuse power, forgiveness can be the greatest stumbling block to living the Christian life. I have discussed the radical forgiveness of God, but now it is time to discuss the actual doing of forgiveness on the part of humans. Even if we hold tightly the faith that "for God all things are possible," (Mt. 19:26) we can have trouble believing that, even with God's help, forgiveness can be possible.

Forgiving the Unforgivable

Forgiving the unforgivable sounds like an oxymoron. Does God forgive the unforgivable? Is anything unforgivable to God? Killing God Incarnate might be judged the worst of all crimes, yet Jesus said, while dying on the cross: "Father, forgive them; for they do not know what they are doing." (Lk. 23:34) This verse, among the most profound and edifying in all scripture, is missing in many ancient authorities. In several translations, it is bracketed as doubtful. Could this verse have been added later by an insightful scribe? Or was this verse too challenging for some scribes, so they dropped it? Given the difficulties with forgiveness that we have noted, the latter possibility seems more likely. The general rule in evaluating manuscript sources is to accept the "harder" reading, as it is more likely to have been dropped than added. In any case, as discussed at length above, the Risen Christ returned with forgiveness and a total lack of vengeance. Although deicide is a great crime, nobody knew at the time that this was what they were doing. However, everybody knew they were killing a human being. The Jewish leaders were (wrongly) convinced of Jesus' guilt. Pilate announced that he could "find no case against him," (Jn. 19:4) yet he turned Jesus over to be crucified anyway. The *méconnaissance* uncovered by Girard would indicate that the collective violence they were committing was something they could not see.

The pain of Jesus' Passion, from the scourging, the mockery, to being nailed to the cross is narrated in the four Gospels. There is no detail, let alone any emotional outpourings in the text. The first hearers and readers of the

Passion narratives would have known all too well what crucifixion does to the body, and they would have responded with appropriate emotional anguish and sympathy. Starting with the Medieval Period, there are many devotional writings that depict the agony of the Crucifixion with profound sympathy. The visions of Julian of Norwich begin with several visions of Jesus' sufferings. While meditating on Jesus' words "I am thirsty," (Jn. 19:28) Julian "understood that the body was wholly dried up, for his blessed flesh and bones were left without blood or moisture." (Julian of Norwich 1978, 207) Julian goes on to describe in some detail the deleterious effects of dehydration that Jesus suffered in his cruciform position. The nails driven into Jesus' body and the thorns pressed onto Jesus' head catch our attention—as they should—but dehydration is an agony that doesn't come to mind so easily, and it is among the most cruel tortures of crucifixion.

And yet, in the midst of such agony, Julian hears Jesus ask her: "Are you well satisfied that I suffered for you?" Julian, of course, is more than satisfied. Jesus then says: "It is a joy, a bliss, an endless delight to me that ever I suffered my Passion for you; and if I could suffer more, I would suffer more." (Julian of Norwich 1978, 216) Jesus is not forgiving his tormenters through gritted teeth; Jesus is forgiving his tormenters with joy, because his love is so great. Actually, this joy and love is so great that forgiveness for the pain that afflicted him has melted away in this love. This vision of Julian's is both wrenching and awe-inspiring. However, we need to look to human pain to see where forgiveness is deeply challenged.

Amnon was one of King David's sons. Tamar was one of King David's daughters and a half-sister to Amnon. Overcome with desire to possess Tamar, Amnon follows the counsel of a crafty friend to trap Tamar. Feigning an illness, he maneuvers Tamar into serving him alone and grabs hold of her. Helpless, Tamar cries out: "No, my brother, do not force me; for such a thing is not done in Israel; do not do anything so vile! As for me, where could I carry my shame? And as for you, you would be as one of the scoundrels in Israel. Now therefore, I beg you, speak to the king; for he will not withhold me from you." (2 Sam. 13:12–13) But Amnon refuses to listen to her and he forces himself upon her. Afterwards, filled with loathing for the young woman he has just abused, Amon has a servant put Tamar out and bolts the door after her. Tamar puts ashes on her head as she goes away, crying. Absalom, Tamar's full brother, tells her: "Be quiet for now, my sister; he is your brother; do not take this to heart." (2 Sam. 13:20) Hardly comforting words for a woman who must spend the rest of her life in Absalom's house as "a desolate woman." Absalom goes on to murder his brother out of revenge, while Tamar disappears from the story.

I feel that there is an abyss between Jesus' comforting words to Julian of Norwich and the desolation of Tamar. Can it ever be bridged?

Difficulties with Forgiveness

The most immediate difficulty with forgiveness is the pain we suffer from the injuries inflicted on us. The Psalms of lament give voice to the helpless victim:

> I am the scorn of all my adversaries,
> a horror to my neighbors,
> an object of dread to my acquaintances;
> those who see me in the street flee from me.
> I have passed out of mind like one who is dead;
> I have become like a broken vessel.
> For I hear the whispering of many—
> terror all around!—
> as they scheme together against me,
> as they plot to take my life. (Ps. 31:11–13)

And again:

> I am like an owl of the wilderness,
> like a little owl of the waste places.
> I lie awake;
> I am like a lonely bird on the housetop. (Ps. 102: 6–7)

I can imagine Tamar using these words to express her desolation. But can words such as these plumb the depths of her pain? Words fail me when I try to answer this question.

At the opposite end of an individual's pain from a devastating injury are the structures of society. One of the biggest problems with forgiveness is the social matrix we live in. Although the legal system in the U. S. presumes the accused innocent until proven guilty, in social media, it is usually the opposite. It seems that every time a public figure does something that somebody disapproves of, online petitions circulate condemning the person. Condemning everybody we don't like doesn't help build a forgiving society. The U. S. is hardly unique in being governed by this systemic vengefulness. We see it all over the world today, and we see it throughout history. Vengefulness is one of the characteristics of societies governed by the principalities and powers, and Paul and Revelation suggest that all nations are so governed. The penal system is just one glaring example among many of how vengeance has taken over other considerations such as rehabilitation. It's like Absalom's vengefulness runs a whole society. But it's worse than that. When the principalities and powers are fueled by vengeance, they lose a caring heart to tend to the excruciating pain of victims such as Tamar. Absalom illustrates this trait to a chilling degree. We see embedded in oppressive social structures social attitudes that perpetuate abuse suffered by society's victims. If society is ever going to turn away from a network of vengeance, society must open up to the care of victims.

The story of Amnon's rape of Tamar comes immediately after the sad tale of David and Bathsheba. (2 Sam. 11–12) This puts the story into the context of the royal family system. Denounced by the prophet Nathan, David repents, and the penitential Psalm 51 is attributed to him. David marries Bathsheba, so she is not thrown away as Tamar was, but considering the power differential between David and Bathsheba, it is highly doubtful that she could have given a free consent to anything that happened to her. Years later, however, Bathsheba succeeded in manipulating the aging King David into granting succession to her son Solomon instead of to David's older surviving son, Adonijah. (1 Kings 1:11–21) The flow of the narrative strongly suggests that Amnon imitated his father's assault on a woman, compounding this crime with incest, but did not imitate his father's repentance. This story is framed by a broader context of violence: "In the spring of the year, the time when kings go out to battle, David sent Joab with his officers and all Israel with him; they ravaged the Ammonites, and besieged Rabbah. But David remained at Jerusalem." (2 Sam. 11:1) Bathsheba's husband was killed by being purposely exposed in battle. (2 Sam. 11:11–14) After David's repentance and the death of Bathsheba's child, David finally joins Joab in battle to finish crushing the Ammonities. (2 Sam. 12: 26–31) As has been noted many times, military violence and sexual violence accomplish their destruction together. One mimetic process of violence leads to another mimetic process of violence. As Amnon and Absalom show us, repentance and forgiveness are in short supply in such situations.

Militarism and persecution are shown to have contributed to an unforgiving society in the final chapter of Joshua. Anyone committed to giving every verse of scripture equal weight will have a problem sorting out what is said there with what Jesus says in the Sermon on the Mount and with many assurances of Yahweh's forgiveness proclaimed by the prophets. Before the assembly of the people, Joshua recounts the journey through the desert and the conquest of Canaan. Then he says: "You cannot serve the Lord, for he is a holy God. He is a jealous God; he will not forgive your transgressions or your sins. If you forsake the Lord and serve foreign gods, then he will turn and do you harm, and consume you, after having done you good." (Josh. 24:19–20) In the context of the pre-emptory forgiveness we have seen on Jesus' part, this stark denial of Yahweh's forgiveness is quite startling. What happened? For one thing, there was a lot of strife in the community throughout the time in the desert. Then the people achieved unity by driving out the Canaanites before them. The stoning of Achan at Joshua's command (which he attributed to God) indicated a persecutory society. This sort of behavior does not seem to have been what God was challenging Israel to do with their deliverance from Egypt. I do not think it is a coincidence that Joshua's insistence that Yahweh is *not* forgiving sets up the circular vengeance that unfolds in the Book of Judges. This is enough to make us wonder what "god" the people were promising to serve. In any case, in Judges violence accelerates throughout Israeli society until it becomes indistinguishable from its Canaanite neighbors, who were to be driven out to "purify" the land. Judges ends with unspeakable atrocities and more unspeakable revenge with another woman being a victim of collective violence. (Judg. 19–21) Here, the difficulty with forgiveness is not only because of the pain of being treated ruthlessly but the blunting of sensitivity that comes from being an oppressor. It has always puzzled me that the angel Gabriel insisted that the Child announced to Mary be named Jesus, the same name as this violent military leader. (In Hebrew, both Joshua and Jesus are styled "Yeshua," which means "Yahweh Saves.") My best guess is that Jesus came to redefine the name and show what it means that Yahweh, Jesus' heavenly Abba, is a God who saves.

The story of Jacob and Esau is a telling illustration of the difficulty of believing in forgiveness, let alone accepting it. Jacob has patently wronged his brother Esau in stealing Esau's blessing. Esau's rage at the time is murderous, and he vows to kill Jacob when the days of mourning for his father have come and gone. (Gen. 27:41) Jacob prudently flees for his life. Years later, after much more intense wrangling with Laban, Jacob returns with his wives, his children, and his flocks, which had all grown too plentiful for Laban's taste. Jacob has every reason to fear what will happen when he meets up again with Esau. Hearing that Esau is coming to meet him with four hundred men is not reassuring. The nighttime struggle with a dark figure seems to embody Jacob's combative personality. Being the shifty coward he's always been, Jacob puts the maidservants and children he cares least about in the most vulnerable positions in the front so that he can escape with his favored sons and wives if need be.

What follows is an amazing surprise. Esau embraces Jacob with no reservations and shows not the slightest sign of resentment. No matter how many times one reads or hears the story, it is hard to believe. Jacob doesn't believe it. Repentance and forgiveness aren't Jacob's things, and he hasn't given them any practice. The constant mimetic rivalry experienced with his brother earlier in life, and the protracted mimetic rivalry with his father-in-law, Laban, have combined to make forgiveness unintelligible to Jacob.

Jacob's words: "Truly to see your face is like seeing the face of God," (Gen. 33:10) are among the most profound words in the Bible as the ultimate revelation that divine mercy is a human face. But Jacob doesn't believe his own words in response to Esau's warm greeting. He turns down the invitation to travel with Esau, using the excuse that he can't drive his flocks too hard in one day. They separate almost as soon as they have met. Jacob, still shifty and cowardly, manages to avoid ever meeting up again with his brother for the rest of his life. Think of the years of friendship and companionship they missed out on!

The story of Jacob's return to Esau illustrates the difficulty of believing in, let alone accepting, forgiveness. The story of Joseph and his brothers takes us through the difficulties of forgiving and further develops the difficulties of accepting forgiveness. Consider Joseph's serene words that it was God, not his brothers, who had sent him to Egypt, and that, although they had meant him harm, God had used it for good. (Gen. 50:20) Taken by themselves, these words suggest an easy forgiveness on the part of Joseph, but the story is—well—another story.

To put the Joseph story in deeper perspective, and to note some of the added difficulties hindering forgiveness, I will start with Dinah. She was a daughter of Jacob by Leah. While out visiting some women, Shechem, "prince of the region, saw her, he seized her and lay with her by force." (Gen. 34:2) Afterwards, Shechem fell in love with Dinah. Hamor, Shechem's father, approached Jacob to negotiate a marriage. "The sons of Jacob answered Shechem and his father Hamor deceitfully, because he had defiled their sister Dinah." (Gen. 34:13) The deal was that Shechem could marry Dinah, if all of Hamor's family be circumcised. They accepted the deal, but while the men were recovering from the operation, Simeon and Levi, two of Dinah's full brothers, attacked their city and killed all the men. As with Absalom's act of revenge, there is no hint that Dinah's brothers care about *her*. They are only concerned with what they consider an affront to family honor. After the attack by Simeon and Levi, "the other sons of Jacob came upon the slain, and plundered the city, because their sister had been defiled." (Gen. 34:27) This attack, then, was an act of collective violence. Jacob berated his sons for what they had done, but not out of concern for Dinah, but out of concern that other neighboring tribes might attack them. (Gen. 34:30) Looking back to the negotiations with Hamor, we can see that Hamor had economic reasons for the proposal, and Jacob's sons, in turn, also had economic reasons for the attack. Did Joseph participate in the attack? We don't know. The violence committed here leads into the violence committed against Joseph. Like Tamar after her, Dinah disappears from the story, leaving a chilling silence.

Joseph's brothers so hated him that they "could not speak peaceably to him." (Gen 37:4) Meanwhile, his father "loved Joseph more than any other of his children." (Gen. 37:3) Being singled out both for adulation and opprobrium is a perfect recipe for an act of collective violence. Joseph's egotistical dreams of grandeur don't help the situation, and even his doting father is angered by them. (Gen. 37:1–11) In contrast to the origin of collective violence as envisioned by Girard, there are a couple of cracks in the unanimity to kill the victim. Both Reuben and Judah differ and manage to have Joseph thrown into a pit rather than killed. (Gen. 37:21–22; 37:26–27) As a result, Joseph is sold into slavery, but at least has escaped with his life.

Curiously, the story of Joseph and his brothers takes a lengthy detour that seems unrelated to the main narrative, one that also seems to be out of sequence. Tamar (not to be confused with David's daughter) was Judah's daughter-in-law. When Judah's son, Er, died, and his next son suffered the same fate, Judah withheld his youngest son from her, apparently out of fear that marrying Tamar was fatal. (This is a case of the "Levirate marriage" where, if a widow is left childless, the oldest eligible brother must marry her to bear children on behalf of his brother.) Tamar resorts to an act of trickery. While Judah attends a sheep-shearing, Tamar dresses like a prostitute and lures Judah into begetting a child by her. He leaves behind a pair of identifiable tokens to be held until Judah can pay for her "services." Later, when Judah sees that Tamar is pregnant, he orders that she be burnt. Tamar presents the tokens that prove that Jacob is the father of the child. Judah has no choice but to repent of withholding his youngest son from Tamar. Since Tamar takes the initiative, she is not a victim in the way Dinah is, but she had to use trickery to work around the masculine power in her society. Judah's penance likely made him more sensitive towards his brother Joseph, and led to the leading role he would take in the family reconciliation.

We return now to the story of Joseph and his brothers. While Esau welcomed Jacob back with open arms, in spite of the harm Jacob had done him, Joseph does no such thing when his brothers come to Egypt in search of relief from the famine. Like Esau, Joseph has done very well, his brothers' intent to hurt him notwithstanding. In fact, he benefitted in the end from what they had done to him. But Joseph holds back when his brothers appear before him without knowing who he is. Joseph remembers his youthful dream where his brothers bowed to him when he sees that dream come true right before his eyes. Joseph goes on to play an elaborate series of mind games that amount to torture. It is possible that Joseph's harsh way of speaking to his brothers is an act to start an educative process, but I can't help but feel that the anger was very real and at least a little raw. As a test to see if they can treat the youngest, Benjamin, better than they treated him, it was hardly necessary to lock Simeon in prison for a year and threaten his own family with starvation if they didn't obey all of his demands that could make little sense to them. One could say that Joseph was being kind, or at least economical in only imprisoning one brother, when he could have imprisoned all but one and sent just one brother back home. That would have made the journey more dangerous and possibly fatal. With choosing one brother, apparently at random, Joseph re-enacts the sacrificial mechanism where one person is sacrificed in place of the whole group. Joseph's father Jacob also suffers because of the loss of another son and fear that he might lose Benjamin as well. While Jacob never shows any repentance for the way he treated Esau, Joseph's brothers have such a guilty conscience that they think their suffering at the hands of Egypt's steward is a just punishment for what they did to Joseph. (Gen. 42: 21–22) For his part, Jacob renews his earlier sin of favoritism by preferring that Simeon remain in prison rather than risk Benjamin making the Journey to Egypt with his brothers.

When the brothers return with Benjamin, Joseph frames his youngest brother by having his divination cup placed in Benjamin's bag as the brothers are leaving. We don't know if Joseph was just testing his brothers further, or if he was plotting to keep Benjamin for himself. As things turn out, Judah triggers Joseph's forgiveness by offering himself as a slave to spare Benjamin that fate. This offer redirects the mimetic process among the brothers away from persecution to reconciliation. More fundamentally, Judah has entered the place of the victim by offering himself in place of Benjamin, who appeared to be the new designated victim at the time. (Judah had not reached this point during the earlier visit and did not offer to take the place of Simeon in prison.) Joseph is won over and he forgives his brothers, but not until he has worked through a great deal of anger on his own part. Maybe it was his intention to put his brothers to the test as a means of reconciliation. Maybe Joseph was only, or mostly, exacting revenge. As it turned out, Joseph himself was put to the test by Judah. Fortunately, Joseph had the grace to give up his control of the situation, which had finally slipped out of his fingers, and cry on the necks of his brothers.

Like Jacob, Joseph's bothers have difficulty believing their brother's forgiveness. When their father dies, they concoct a story about their father making a deathbed plea that Joseph forgive his brothers. This seems almost certainly a ruse as nothing in the narrative suggests that this happened. On the contrary, in his deathbed hymns about his sons, Jacob has good words for some of his sons, but he shows that he never forgave Reuben, Simeon, and Levi for their transgressions. Even his ostensible second favorite, Benjamin, is dismissed as a "ravenous wolf." (Gen. 49) Jacob died, having never fully appreciated the grace of forgiveness either for himself or others; although his blessing of both Joseph's sons did show some emerging good sense in his declining years.

Following carefully in our own hearts Joseph's steps to forgiveness—his anger, his pride, his manipulations, but also his crucial willingness to accept Judah's intervention—can be a way for us to track our own difficulties of forgiving the hurts we have received in life and move through them to an awareness that although certain people intended us harm, God has used these harmful actions for good. We also see that forgiveness needed to be worked out by all of the brothers as a group. Forgiveness is a matter for community, not just isolated individuals.

But if we think the story is all wrapped-up, we have forgotten a couple of people. Presumably both Dinah and Tamar moved to Egypt with the rest of the family, but they were not at the table with Joseph and his brothers. What about Leah, Jacob's remaining and despised wife, for that matter? Joseph forgave his brothers, but what about Dinah? Did she have a chance to forgive her brothers? Did her brothers ever ask her forgiveness? Although the road to repentance and forgiveness was difficult for Joseph and his brothers, they all had freedom of agency to engage one another. This is what Dinah lacked. That women were systematically denied personal agency increased their vulnerability to attack, such as what she suffered at the hands of Shechem, and this same lack of agency gave her no route for conceiving of forgiveness and reconciliation. That is how I read the silence concerning her. The familial bonds that inspired her brothers to act in vengeance also led to their making her as invisible as possible. Denying women and any other people agency and a voice to express what has happened to them stops the channels for forgiveness. All slaves are in the same position. Zilpah and Bilhah, maidservants of Leah and Rachel, each bore two of Jacob's sons, but they were not consulted in the matter. Social silence is just as destructive a mimetic process as social violence.

"The Woman Who Was a Sinner" is another woman who took an initiative that was considered scandalous by everybody except Jesus. (Lk. 7:36–50) I have already noted her role as a social scapegoat. It is usually assumed that her "sinfulness" was tied to her sexuality. This assumption does not necessarily imply an inordinate preoccupation with sexual sins on the part of some moralists; it is a realistic awareness of the severely limited career opportunities open to women at the time and for many years since. Maybe she differs from Dinah and Tamar, David's daughter, by not being the victim of a sexual assault, but then there is a very real possibility she was so victimized, and maybe that is even the reason she was considered a sinner. In any case, she is victimized by society. Jesus says her sins were many, but they have been forgiven her. Compared to the likes of Amnon, and considering what some men had most likely done to this woman, one could think that others, Simon among them, had a much greater need of forgiveness.

Nonetheless, the forgiveness Jesus grants this woman is important because it affirms the initiative she has taken and strengthens her as a personal agent. Instead of being possessed by the scorn of everybody in town, she has become possessed by Jesus. What Jesus is doing is giving this woman and Tamar, David's daughter, and Dinah a place at the table where forgiveness is asked for and granted. His disciples didn't accept it at the time, but Jesus opened the way for *all* people to build up the Kingdom.

Forgiving others and accepting forgiveness from others may be challenges, but *being* forgiven raises serious challenges of its own as the story of Jacob shows us. To look further at this challenge, we will turn to a novel that has been made into a musical and a movie.

Although far from the most subtle of novels, and maybe because of its bluntness, Victor Hugo's *Les Misérables* is among the most powerful portrayals of the challenges and difficulties of forgiveness that I know. The movie of the musical, with its simplification of the novel's meandering plot, is even more finely honed to this theme

Jean Valjean, rejected by all as an ex-con, is invited to eat and sleep in the bishop's house. Still embittered, desperate, and untrusting, he runs off with a silver plate. When brought back by the police, the bishop says that the plate was a gift and orders the police to release him. The bishop gives Valjean his candlesticks on top of the plate and presents this act of mercy as a challenge to make the most of his second chance at life. The self-sacrifices required of Valjean to live up to this challenge make it clear that the forgiven life is far from easy or soft. Among other acts of self-sacrifice, Valjean would not allow another man, mistaken for Valjean, to be unjustly imprisoned. He admitted his identity and fled, leaving behind a lucrative business he had built up. Meanwhile, the police officer Javert, deeply scandalized by the bishop's forgiveness, makes a career of tracking down Valjean in the name of justice. Javert is a perfect illustration of how mimetic rivalry impedes forgiveness. Through the years, he forces Valjean to stay on the run, seriously disrupting Jean's life.

During the 1832 uprising in Paris, Valjean joins the rebels, mainly to protect his daughter's lover Marius. Meanwhile, Javert infiltrates the rebels but is exposed, sentenced to be killed, and then handed over to Valjean for execution. With the chance to exact his revenge, Valjean frees Javert, doing for the self-righteous officer what the bishop had done for him so many years ago. After a tragic street battle, Valjean drags the wounded Marius through the sewers of Paris (a Christ-like descent into Hell, if there ever was one). Javert ambushes him but can't bring himself to arrest the convict. Totally disoriented by the prodigal forgiveness offered him, the legalist representative of the law throws himself into the Seine. Javert had so wrapped up his identity in his mimetic rivalry with Jean Valjean and his stern sense of justice that he could not cope with the bestowal of a free gift of forgiveness. His universe did not allow for free gifts, and so he could not live when a free gift was bestowed upon him.

Although Paul considers forgiveness a free gift, this free gift is both an empowerment to act in certain ways and a challenge to do so. It is because we have been called by God and given the Spirit that we should bear the fruit of the Spirt that "is love, joy, peace, patience, kindness, generosity, faithfulness, gentleness, and self-control. There is no law against such things. And those who belong to Christ Jesus have crucified the flesh with its passions and desires. If we live by the Spirit, let us also be guided by the Spirit. Let us not become conceited, competing against one another, envying one another." (Gal. 5:22–26)

Our strongest resistance to forgiveness is that it just isn't fair. It blows apart everything we think we know and believe about the economics of life. We think everything has a price, or should. We instinctively keep a tally of what we owe and what is owed us. Usually the latter is much higher than the former. This tally makes up a huge amount of our identity, an identity that forgiveness shows to be totally false. The tally is a desperate attempt to separate ourselves from others by letting the figures on our running tally come between us and them. This keeps mimetic rivalry alive and well. (And keeps us not so well.) The Parable of the Vineyard Workers (Mt. 20:1–16) speaks to this resistance. The workers who worked all day grumble when they get only the day's wage they agreed on after the workers called in at the last hour of the day got the same day's wage. I think all of us identify with the grumbling workers. The master sees the problem and seems to shrug his shoulders and say with a divine smile: "This is how I operate. Get used to it." God's economy takes a lot of getting used to. We are wise to start practicing now.

Even as we probe these difficulties with forgiveness, the pain of severe injury pulls us back to this, the most immediate and intense difficulty. When we have been traumatized by others, we often remain imprisoned by the people who have injured us. Mimetic realism helps us understand this dynamic. The connections mimetic resonance create with the people who surround us as soon as we are born and before we are capable of conscious thought simply cannot be broken off. We are as closely interrelated with those who do us good as we are with those who do us harm. If anything, we are more closely interrelated with those who hurt us because the pain and the anger glues us to them with more intensity than the goodness received from others. Trying to pull away only adds to the tension. It is like stretching a rubber band. The difference is that the rubber band of mimetic resonance is unbreakable, and it will stretch forever no matter how long and hard we pull on it.

Retaliatory violence, however justified, is a huge problem. It has the potential to escalate and engulf a society. Vengeful anger easily gets displaced against someone *else* who happens to be more vulnerable than the victim who has been injured. So it is that vengeful violence continues to escalate in a society and becomes harder and harder to resist. This circular quality of mimetic vengeance radically distorts our conscience. When we feel entitled to exact revenge, we quickly slip into thinking that we are entitled to do—well just about anything. Bombing another country into nonexistence is *quid pro quo*. However, we need to distinguish the retaliatory violence we saw in the attack of Jacob's sons on Shechem's family and how Dinah might have felt about revenge. We have no way of knowing, but it is certainly possible that she might have had more hurt feelings against her brothers than against Shechem. Men fighting out of a sense of "honor" are fired by mimetic resonance that fuels increasing levels of anger and violence that have little or nothing to do with the kind of injury suffered by a woman like Dinah. Jesus' teachings on non-violence are, at times, applicable to injuries suffered from superior force, but many of his teachings are aimed more at the tit-for-tat reciprocal violence that Simeon and Levi represent. Reducing such mimetic violence would go a long way towards increasing the safety of women and children and would move towards a social climate conducive to healing.

There is a deep, joyful mystery here. When Jesus told the paralytic that his sins were forgiven, the Pharisees were upset because only God can forgive sins. (Mk. 2:5) (Not that the Pharisees seemed interested in having the paralytic's sins forgiven.) In the upper room, Jesus breathed on the disciples and gave them a ministry of forgiveness. Being admonished to forgive often seems oppressive because we feel commanded as individuals to bear the burden of forgiveness. But when forgiveness is a gift from God that we should share, we are not left alone with this burden. It is a community, the Church, that is given this ministry. Each of us is a living stone among others building a web of forgiveness in the face of the web of unforgiving empire. With Christ, forgiveness becomes an easy yoke that Christ bears before us, along with us, and for all eternity.

The Steps of Forgiveness

Now that we have taken stock of how difficult forgiveness is, we will examine the process of forgiveness itself. As a process, one expects that there are several steps to forgiveness that we take one at a time. It isn't as simple as that. There are steps that can be articulated to give us a sense of direction for the process, but they are all so closely interrelated that it is more like disentangling a tangle of yarn than like climbing steps on a staircase. The image of the tangled yarn, something that often feels more like a rope around our necks, suggests that the process has a lot to do with loosening something that is tight. This is precisely what the Greek word often translated as forgiveness, *aphesis*, is about. Letting go of that which has tied us up takes time.

Desmond and Mpho Tutu have written a valuable book called *The Book of Forgiving* that helps us understand the process of forgiveness. In my own reflections, I don't come up with precisely the same list of steps, but it comes close, and the four-step process in Tutus' book gives us something with which to work.

The first two steps listed by the Tutus are: 1) Telling the Story and 2) Naming the Hurt. These two steps are so closely related that they feel like one step to me, although a complex one. I am inclined to call this first step: own the hurt. This step seems simple, but it can be difficult emotionally because it means facing the pain and that is—well, very painful. It is, however, pain that is necessary for healing, just as an infection has to be opened before it can be healed. Because of the pain of the hurt, it can, for some people, take much time, even years, before it is possible to take even this first step. A mysterious inner process of pre-healing has to happen before one can tell the story. When the time comes, one will know. Community support is important as one almost always needs at least one sympathetic listener and often many more than that. The importance of telling the story is that when another has invaded us by injuring us, we are *suffering on the terms of the perpetrator*. The first step of suffering on our *own* terms is to tell the story, to face the truth of what has happened to us. With this step, we take ownership away from the perpetrator, and take ownership of the hurt ourselves. We cannot forgive what we have not seen and faced. As long as the truth of injury is repressed, it holds us in its grip. Over the years I have listened to people tell their stories about childhood sexual abuse. Listening to them makes it clear that the very act of telling the story changes the story from what it was before. Something moves within us when we tell our stories.

South Africa's Truth and Reconciliation Commission, chaired by Bishop Tutu, is to date, the most powerful communal telling of stories. Everybody who wished was allowed to tell the truth of the injuries they had received during Apartheid. Perpetrators were also invited to tell their stories and were granted amnesty for doing so. Telling the story also makes it clear that much more is at stake than forgiveness by the victim. Those in South Africa who listened to the testimonials, from the bishop to those watching on TV, were challenged both to face the truth of what had been done and to forgive the reprehensible actions that had occurred. It is important to note, however, that the Truth and Reconciliation Commission operated *after* the end of Apartheid. It could not have happened *during* Apartheid. Creating social structures conducive to repentance and forgiveness is crucial.

The reason I name this first step "own the hurt" is because it isn't enough to tell the story; it is necessary to tell the story in a listening way. That is, we must listen to *ourselves* when we tell the story. The importance of at least one more person listening is that a good listener can help the teller listen more deeply to him or herself. The mimetic resonance that occurs when two or more people *hear* the story increases the listening that occurs. Since the abuse one has experienced is inscribed in the body, we need this deep listening to reach a deep gut level so that the muscles that have been tightened over what has happened can loosen. The act of loosening happens in our bodies before it happens in our heads. We can't put our hearts into forgiving another until our guts have done it. I have listened to enough people to have learned that there is a strong and clear distinction between those who listen to what they are saying and those who don't. Those who listen well to themselves move towards healing. Those who do not listen to themselves remain stuck in their pain, trapped with no exit until they learn to listen. Deep listening so as to own the hurt does not make it hurt less, but it is the first step toward healing and forgiveness. Owning the hurt is the beginning of letting go, which is the second step. This shows us how closely related the steps are.

For some people, some of the time, letting go and forgiving happen simultaneously so as to seem like one movement. But for most of us, most of the time, the two are distinct, though closely related. This is most clearly the case when the reverse psychology that allows an act of letting go leads to forgiveness. Absolving the victim of forgiving the hurt makes it possible for that person to let go of it. Letting go removes the hurt from the center of our lives where it has been a major, often *the* central, organizing principle of our lives and gives us the freedom to move on. Letting go does not mean that the hurt doesn't hurt any more than owning the hurt does, but letting go loosens the hold the hurt has on us.

The most important element in letting go is non-retaliation. Here is where the famous admonitions in the Sermon on the Mount come into play: turning the other cheek, walking a second mile, giving up a shirt after the cloak is taken. Non-retaliation is not, in itself, forgiveness. Withholding a counter punch while turning the other cheek does not necessarily mean that one has forgiven the injury to the battered cheek. What non-retaliation does is push the pause button on violence to keep it from escalating out of control, a scenario that makes forgiveness harder for everybody.

Letting go, especially in the form of non-retaliation, is a renunciation of trying to "win" a situation and instead assumes the position of the "loser." Renunciation of retaliation is a renunciation of mimetic rivalry. Seeking revenge is fundamentally an attempt to "win" a struggle against the other, and thus it perpetuates mimetic rivalry. In the heat of battle, winning is everything. When the battle is over and we are scarred more than ever, winning turns out to be nothing but the burden of holding on to the hurt that keeps us in its relentless grip.

This is where humility comes in. Humility is the willingness to be a "loser," in the hope of a deliverance from the one who injured us. Occasionally, we can even hope to win over the oppressor. Humility is particularly important here because when we do not retaliate, we are tempted to think we have taken the higher moral ground. The tricky thing is that we *have* taken the higher moral ground, but if we pat ourselves on the back for that, we become obsessed with ourselves. This turns the situation back into a contest of wills, which is mimetic rivalry. At which point, we tumble from the moral heights we thought we had attained. This is a case in which it is important that the right hand not know what the left hand is doing. The humility I am talking about here is about reclaiming personal agency. Non-retaliation is an important way to do that. Such humility is practiced in the presence of God and is a participation in the non-retaliation Jesus not only preached, but also practiced.

The importance of non-retaliation is that it gives us a tangible means of knowing when we really have let go of the hurt. If we slug the person back or sincerely wish we had, we have not let go. If we refrain from slugging the person back and don't wish we'd thrown the punch, we have let go.

The most important thing to realize about letting go is that we are not cutting the connection between us and those who injure us. Trying to do that is futile. Our mirror neurons see to that. What letting go does is loosen what had been a tight, strangling connection to the other. This loosening gives us room to maneuver and changes the situation. We can't, of course, take responsibility for what the other person does with the space opened up by this loosening. We can only take responsibility for ourselves. That is all we can handle anyway. More importantly, non-retaliation provides room for God to enter into the broken relationship and fix it.

After letting go of the hurt, we have to make sure we don't grab it back. Sustaining the act of letting go opens us to the mystery of forgiveness itself. This can be a challenge, especially when being a victim is a prime ingredient of our identity. Letting go can cause an identity crisis where we have to stumble towards a new understanding of ourselves. Fortunately, the Forgiving Victim is always there to offer us a new self, clothed with God's forgiveness. Even then, this new self will seem too big for us and we'll have to grow in it.

This final step of forgiving is to forgive. Simple as that. Or is it? Well, yes and no. Forgiveness is a simple act, although in some cases it can take years to actually unfold when the hurt is very deep. The thing about forgiveness is that I don't think any of us really forgives another; God forgives the person through us. That is to say, forgiveness is an act of grace from God. The first two steps of owning the hurt and letting go can be done by us and need to be done by us, although, even here, God strengthens us to do it. Although letting go is not forgiveness in itself, it opens the way for forgiveness to happen. We open the door for the Paraclete, the Divine Advocate for the defense, to come in. This is all the more reason not to pressure traumatized people into forgiving their perpetrators. One cannot rush grace that runs on God's time.

What has happened when we forgive someone? If we take Jesus as our model, then we have found ourselves loving our enemies. (Mt. 5:44) We shouldn't let the many preachers who have made this verse a platitude keep us from trembling at the thought. If this has really happened, then it is Christ within us who has done it. If it is God who loves within us our most vicious enemies, then we should not grit our teeth and force ourselves to do it. As it is ultimately God who forgives, it is ultimately God who loves our enemies.

I find forgiveness to be particularly difficult when it involves the wrongs done to other people, whether they are people I know or people I have never seen but who I know are being hurt and killed through economic injustice and war. It occurs to me that a sense of helplessness adds to this difficulty. If a wrong is done to another, it is hard to forgive on behalf of that person. Not only that, but it seems presumptuous. What we need to remember is that God forgives the wrongs done to other people all the time. At the same time, though, God suffers with all who are suffering grievous wrongs, and God is also suffering along with the ruin of the perpetrators themselves. When we open ourselves to forgiving such people, we also suffer the hurts suffered by both victims and perpetrators. The more we share this hurt of others, the more we feel that the hurt inflicted on others has been done to *us* as well. This is another way God models forgiveness for us because God considers *all* injuries inflicted on anybody as done unto Godself. To forgive all injuries ever committed is costly to God. Insofar as we participate in God's forgiveness of people who harm others, we begin to experience some of that cost in ourselves.

As difficult as is forgiveness for trauma, it is forgiveness for the small things on a day-to-basis that I find most difficult. When an emergency comes along, we respond quickly and generously, even when our response takes much time and resources. But giving up small bits of time for the benefit of other people is difficult, sometimes excruciatingly so. It's the same thing with forgiveness. When we get nickel-and-dimed by petty offenses day in and day out, we get fed up with people and lash out at them. When we suffer these little stabs, they are so immediate, compared to the long-term sufferings we endure, that they seem a lot bigger than they are. Bishop Tutu relates the story of a small event that enraged him so much that forgiveness was difficult. On a long drive on a hot day, he wanted to stop for some ice cream, but the vendor would not serve a black family. This seems like a small matter compared to fighting Apartheid, but then this is one small case of fighting Apartheid. People who have to stand in long lines at hostile checkpoints to get anywhere experience ongoing injury on a daily basis. Here is where we need a habit of letting go that is rooted in humility. St. Paul said that he died daily. (1 Cor. 15:31) Dying daily is "losing" daily, which is what letting go amounts to when these petty offenses come. It's when we receive a barbed comment that we want to come back on the spot with a retort that gives us the satisfaction of revenge. Swallowing our words in these situations is difficult. And yet, learning to forgive in these small situations strengthens us to forgive the longstanding hurts that we suffer. Letting go is letting go, whether the matter is big or small. If we are going to be forgiving people, we have to keep working at it.

A memorable speech by M. Shawn Copeland, a professor of Black Studies at Boston College, provides a good example of a group cultivating forgiveness over time. The killings at the AME Church in Charleston were fresh in all of our minds and hearts at the time of the conference at which she spoke. She had much to say about the event and spoke strongly about the forgiveness all of those bereft of loved ones expressed at the time, although the personal cost to them was evident. Copeland said that the members of a church which emerged out of slavery have had centuries to practice forgiveness, and it is this long practice that made the forgiveness expressed on this occasion possible. The forgiveness expressed in the wake of the tragic event had not come out of the blue; it had come from practicing hearts.

Since granting forgiveness and receiving forgiveness go hand in hand, it is receiving forgiveness that completes the forgiveness cycle and breaks the cycle of revenge. In looking at the Parable of the Unforgiving Servant, we stressed the need to grant forgiveness in order to receive forgiveness. The circle works in the other direction just the same. We have to receive forgiveness in order to grant it and that can be just as difficult as forgiving.

Receiving forgiveness as a free gift sounds like a good deal until we remember that receiving forgiveness necessarily entails accepting our need to be forgiven. If we are convinced we have done nothing wrong, then we do not receive forgiveness no matter how often and ardently forgiveness is offered us. Forgiveness only makes sense when we are penitent. This does not negate the pre-emptory forgiveness given by God, neither does it negate the pre-emptory forgiveness on the part of those who try to imitate God in this way. God's pre-emptory forgiveness reveals the truth of the wrongs we have done and God's forgiveness strengthens us to live up to the challenge to amend our lives. Just as forgiving requires the renunciation of mimetic rivalry, so does accepting forgiveness. Just as one becomes a "loser" in granting forgiveness, one becomes a "loser" in receiving it. This is the tragic difficulty of Javert in *Les Misérables*. The mimetic rivalry on his part, which was never reciprocated by Valjean, made Javert relentlessly unforgiving and it made him just as relentlessly incapable of receiving forgiveness. He could not renounce his irrational quest to "win." And so he lost everything.

Another reason receiving forgiveness is essential for true forgiveness is that, as with non-retaliation, the one granting forgiveness is prone to claiming the higher moral ground over the one forgiven. If we think we have no need for forgiveness ourselves when we forgive others, we put ourselves above those we forgive, which is pride and, more importantly, a short-circuiting of forgiveness. It is a sobering thought to realize that it is much easier to see what wrongs of others we need to forgive than it is to see the wrongs we need others to forgive us.

These considerations help us understand the puzzling verse in Romans 12:20. Paul tells us to feed our enemies who are hungry and give water when they are thirsty, for by doing this we will heap "burning coals on their heads." Paul is quoting Proverbs 25:22 here, which only pushes the puzzle back to the sage who wrote it. For someone who badly needs to repent and be forgiven, a free act of forgiveness can be very painful. For Javert, the free act of forgiveness he received from Jean Valjean felt like the heaping of burning coals on the head. Paul, and the sage before him, realized that forgiveness will burn the person who does not accept it.

The principalities and powers are fueled by the cycle of revenge. God's Kingdom is fueled by the cycle of forgiveness. Both cycles are just as infinite, but the cycle of forgiveness is infinitely larger than the other. Giving and receiving forgiveness connect us deeply to others, they to us and all of us to God.

The final step in the Tutus' path to forgiveness is restitution. Even if and when one has let go, forgiven, and renounced revenge, it is a major lift to receive restitution from the offender. Often, an apology is all that can be done, but it means a lot to a victim to hear those words. Needless to say, they have to be said sincerely and from the heart. When it comes to apologies, one's ears are sharper and deeper than normal, and hollowness rings out when that is all that is behind the words. Apology is often all that can be offered as restitution simply because there is nothing that can pay for the damage done. For that matter, it is not possible for humanity to pay for the damage done to God's Creation. This is why God's pre-emptory forgiveness is ultimately the only answer.

Of course there are times when restitution can be made. If one has stolen from another, one should pay back what was stolen, although this, too, can be an unpayable debt. However, even if only a token payment can be made, it is healing for both parties to pay that token. Perhaps one can do something or give something that gives the victim an experience that is memorable in a happy way. This doesn't make up for what happened, but it is the sort of thing that can swell many times its size. This is the sort of gift that God matches ten-fold.

There are, of course, many times when restitution simply can't be made. This is painfully the case when perpetrators are unrepentant, unwilling, or unable to face the fact of the hurt they inflicted. Many times, the perpetrator has died. In such cases, we can gain much healing by writing a letter to that person, stating clearly and accurately what happened, and how we felt about it then and how we feel about it now. If we have been given the gift of forgiveness, then saying words of forgiveness in this letter will be healing. It is my experience that relationships can and do evolve, even, maybe even especially, with someone who has died. We can, of course, do this same exercise with someone we have wronged but have no means of saying so in this life.

Nineveh Redeemed

The Book of Jonah comes across to me as a direct refutation of the book of the prophet Nahum. Nahum's mercifully short book is one gushing gloat over the bloody downfall of Nineveh. Jonah is a counterfactual fantasy of Nineveh being converted by a preaching mission. When Jonah resists God's call to preach to the Ninevites, we are apt to think that he just doesn't want to take on so onerous a task. We find out later, after his famous sojourn inside a big fish, that Jonah fled because he was afraid that God would undercut his prophecy of doom by being merciful. (Jon. 4:2) That is indeed what happened. Jonah did not want God to forgive Nineveh.

Jonah's readers, having experienced Assyria as "the rod of God's anger," (Isa. 10:5) would not likely be in a sweet enough mood to imagine God forgiving these ruthless invaders. Like Jonah, they were likely inclined to sulk at the idea and go back to relishing Nahum's prophecy. Jonah's story ends quietly with a bit of comedy. A bush grows to give him shade, but then the bush withers the next day. Jonah grows angry about the bush that had given him comfort only to die and leave him unsheltered in the sweltering heat. God then asks Jonah: "Should I not be concerned about Nineveh, that great city, in which there are more than a hundred and twenty thousand persons who do not know their right hand from their left, and also many animals?" (Jon. 4:11) This book gives us a chance to laugh at ourselves over our desires for vengeance. If ever we should manage to laugh, we will have begun to let go of our vengeful desires, at least a little. This book is a challenge thrown out to a whole nation with fresh memories of a severe trauma. They, and we, are asked to choose between Nahum and Jonah. The message of love of enemies in this tale surely inspired Jesus as he read the scriptures. When asked by the Pharisees and Sadducees for "a sign from heaven," he told them the only sign they will get is "the sign of Jonah." (Mt. 16:4) This sign is God's call to *all* people to accept God's merciful love. The Pharisees and Sadducees didn't seem to like that. What about us?

We can get so wrapped up in the theme of forgiveness here that we forget that Nineveh *changed*. God was merciful towards Nineveh, but Nineveh had repented of being a violent city and had switched to being a merciful city. It became a city like "the holy city, the new Jerusalem, coming down out of heaven from God, prepared as a bride adorned for her husband." (Rev. 21:2) Jerusalem, a city filled with violence that the prophets constantly denounced, has also been transformed. The heavenly banquet could easily take place in such a city. But will everybody be at the party?

My series of short answers is: I don't know. Maybe. God hopes so. I should hope so, too, but I struggle with that. Everybody is definitely invited, but anyone who races for a "seat of honor" will have to learn to be content with a lower place—and learn better table manners. In order to be a heavenly party, it has to be safe. Tamar and all others who suffered a similar fate have to be safe, or it's not a heavenly party. Too many earthly parties have turned out be *un*safe for some people. One of the paradoxes of forgiveness is that it is given freely, but, just as Nineveh had to change, so do Amnon and all other predators. Jesus and all sensitive readers and listeners to the story of Amnon feel the anguish of Tamar. Can Amnon, in the mystery of forgiveness that transcends time, feel Tamar's pain?

In one of her later visions, Julian of Norwich "understood Christ's Passion for the greatest and surpassing pain. And yet this was shown to me in an instant, and it quickly turned into consolation." (Julian of Norwich 1978, 225) The love emanating from this consolation leads to the ringing words: "All will be well, and every kind of thing will be well." (Julian of Norwich 1978, 225) Having experienced famine, plague, and civil violence among many other trials, Julian had a hard time understanding how this could be so, and yet, in the face of her doubt, Jesus assured her "any good result could ever come" of "any deeds which in our eyes are so evilly done," and Jesus reaffirmed his promise "that all will be well." (Julian of Norwich 1978, 231–232) The making of all things well will be done by God who "is that goodness which cannot be angry, for God is nothing but goodness." (Julian of Norwich 1978, 259) If God is so wholly without wrath as Julian claims, then forgiveness is open to all. If there will be no divine wrath at the heavenly banquet, then there can be no human wrath, either.

Chapter 13

Faith, Hope, and Love

Faith, hope, and love are called the theological virtues, not because they belong in dusty tomes of systematic theology, but because they are gifts of God that we receive apart from—or, better said—beyond our human efforts. Given the mysterious mix of divine gifts with human response that we have examined, we would expect some deep interaction between God's desire and our human desires when it comes to faith, hope, and love. Mimetic realism would have us believe that faith, hope, and love bring our desires close into the heart of God's desire.

Faith

Faith is often presented as conformity to a set of doctrines, such as those laid out in the Nicene Creed. I believe what the Nicene Creed says, but that isn't faith. Since St. Paul famously teaches that we are saved by faith in Jesus Christ, let's look there. We immediately run into a problem. The Greek phrase Paul uses, *pistis Christou,* is ambiguous. It can be translated as "faith in Christ," but it can also be translated as "the faith *of* Christ." Since scholars are still debating this, I have to make an informed decision as best I can. Douglas Campbell (2009) is a staunch defender of the translation of "the faith of Christ." What he actually means is that we are saved by the faithfulness of Christ. That is, the word refers to Jesus' faithfulness to his heavenly Abba by enduring the mockery of humans and the pain of the cross. It is these faithful acts of Christ that save us. We are not saved by an act of faith of our own; we are saved by Jesus' faithfulness. This unequivocally makes salvation a free gift from God as Paul proclaims. Understanding faith as faithfulness chimes well with mimetic realism which consistently stresses the *participation* of humans in God's desire. We are saved by faith when we participate in the faithfulness of Jesus.

John M. G. Barclay is among the scholars who take the other position. However, far from distancing us from participating in Jesus' acts, Barclay insists that faith *in* Christ plunges us *into* the acts of Christ. For Barclay, faith *in* Christ is "the mark of those whose lives have been reconstituted and reordered by the death and life of Christ." (Barclay 2015, 379) All of this presupposes the faithfulness of Christ discussed above. We can hardly participate more deeply in Christ's acts than this. Fortunately, we do not have to choose one grammatical interpretation over the other for faith to immerse us into God's desire.

For Paul, Abraham is the father of faith because of his faithfulness, what he *did* when God called him by name. Abraham was told to leave the only life he had known and move to a land God would show him. (Gen. 12:1) This is precisely what we are called to do in baptism. We are to leave the life we have known, the life that has formed us and clothed us in what Paul calls "the old self" and move to a life we have never known, a life that will form us and clothe us in "the new self." (Col. 3:9–10) This may seem laughable to those of us who were baptized as infants, but the baptismal vows of renouncing the world, the flesh, and the devil, even if made on our behalf, are still our responsibility as we come of age. As we grow up (or down), we are formed by the social matrix around us that Girard argues is run primarily by mimetic rivalry and sacrificial mechanisms and what Paul called the principalities and powers. In baptism, we are called out of these social matrixes into a way of life grounded in the Forgiving Victim.

What makes Abraham's journey so remarkable is that he was traveling into uncharted territory. He moved out of a culture based on sacrificial violence without a New Testament in his hip pocket to tell him what kind of story he was entering. Like Jesus, Abraham was a pioneer of faith. Both put their lives on the line, though in different ways. Abraham only had a promise that his descendants would be as numerous as the stars in the sky, although he had begotten no children up to that time. Jesus hoped to receive from his heavenly Abba descendants just as numerous (Jn. 17:10), although it looked hopeless when even his disciples deserted him. Abraham's wife Sarai went with Abraham on this journey, making her also a great pioneer of faith. I doubt that either of them could have done it alone. It is because this pioneering move is so fundamental to Abraham's faithfulness that Paul denies that circumcision constitutes the faith that was reckoned as righteousness. (Rom. 4:9–12) That is, Abraham was circumcised *after* he had set out for a new land. This is why Abraham is the ancestor of both Jews (the circumcised) and Gentiles (the uncircumcised.)

Abraham's geographical move was not enough, of course. Indeed, if faith has to do with migrating from a sacrificial culture to a culture based on forgiveness, it is the spiritual geography that matters. After all, Canaan was in the thrall of sacrificial culture as much as Ur of the Chaldeans. Indeed, the act of faithfulness for which Abraham is praised fit right in with the sacrificial culture of the country he left as well as the country he had gone to.

The near-sacrifice of Isaac by his father Abraham, the father of faith, is the most troubling of stories. It should be. Jeremiah says Yahweh denounced the sacrifice of children, saying "that such a thing had never entered my mind." (Jer. 19:5) Perhaps we are right to be troubled by any notion that Abraham was right to even let the idea enter his mind and even more troubled by any thought it ever entered into God's mind. But even if sacrificing children never entered Yahweh's mind, the idea had entered the minds of most of the people among whom Abraham was living.

Bob Dylan makes a bitter burlesque of the story in his song "Highway 61." The "god" who requires the sacrifice is a bully, warning Abraham that if he doesn't "kill me a son," "next time you see me, you'd better run." When Abraham asks: "Where do you want to see this killing done? God says out on Highway 61." Highway 61 is also the place where Georgia Sam, who "had a bloody nose" and to whom "the welfare department they wouldn't give him no clothes," was told to go. This is also where Louis the King says Mack the Finger can place "forty red, white and blue shoestrings and a thousand telephones that don't ring." Worse, when the rovin' gambler "who is very bored" wants to know where to stage the next world war, he is told to "put some bleachers out in the sun and have it on Highway 61." As with so many Dylan songs, the imagery reveals a society filled with mimetic rivalry, victimization, and violence where sacrifice and war become spectator sports.

The great World War I poet Wilfred Owen saw the emerging sacrificial culture of the twentieth century. In a sonnet that retells the story of the Sacrifice of Isaac, Abraham builds parapets and trenches around the wood, suggesting that the sons sent off to the war were religious sacrifices. (Owen was severely disillusioned by the Church's enthusiastic support of the war.) But when the angel of the Lord admonished Abraham to "slay the ram of Pride instead of him . . . the old man would not so, but slew his son, / and half the seed of Europe one by one." Owen and Dylan have traced for us the trajectory from primitive sacrificial violence to modern violence in world wars.

Søren Kierkegaard's searing *Fear and Trembling* is arguably the most profound meditation on this story, troubling as his reflections are. One of the complications is that the "author," Johannes de Silentio, is himself a character in the book who does not necessarily represent Kierkegaard's own thinking. Is the category of the "teleological suspension of the ethical" intended to mean that Abraham was right to sacrifice his son out of belief that God had commanded it? Does Kierkegaard accept a sacrificial reading of the story? Given Kierkegaard's profound insights into social mimetic processes and its scapegoating activity, this seems unlikely. When this troublesome category is coupled with what Johannes de Silentio calls "infinite resignation," we wonder if this praises Abraham's willingness to kill his son by God's command. I think not. Johannes is clear that infinite resignation falls far short of *faith,* and faith is what the biblical story and Kierkegaard's book are all about. Faith is receiving back what is given with infinite resignation "by virtue of the absurd." So what is the value, if any, of infinite resignation? And how absurd is faith in Kierkegaard's thinking?

"Infinite resignation" may not be faith, but it is the prerequisite of faith. I find mimetic realism helpful in understanding this concept. "Infinite resignation" is a total giving up to God of everything, most especially that which is most loved. This is *not* a sacrifice of another but a *self*-sacrifice. This act of commending everything to God is a renunciation of all mimetic rivalry. The vignettes in *Fear and Trembling* about weaning and other developmental issues connect infinite resignation to the renunciations any parent or caregiver must make for the sake of the child. It is the renunciation of the rivalrous elements in parent-child relations. It is also, of course, renunciation of mimetic rivalry on a much broader scale. This means renouncing the mimetic rivalry that Dylan and Owen write about in their poetry. The Abraham bossed around by "god" and the Abraham who "slays his son and half the seed of Europe one by one" do *not* reach infinite resignation. On the contrary, they destroy it by their immersion in sacrificial violence fueled by mimetic rivalry. "Infinite resignation" may not be faith, but it is a movement that opens one up to the gift of faith, at which point Abraham receives back what he has renounced.

Traditionally, Abraham's near-sacrifice is understood as prefiguring God the Father's willingness to sacrifice His only begotten Son. This also is also troubling if understood in terms of the violent Atonement theology that I criticized above. However, Jesus did not go to the cross with infinite resignation. Rather, he believed that his Abba, being the God of Abraham, Isaac, and Jacob, was "God, not of the dead, but of the living." (Mt. 22:32) And so Jesus received the resurrected life by "virtue of the absurd." This analysis coincides with Paul's contention that we are saved by the faithfulness *of* Christ, the faith that, on the cross, embraced not death, but the life of his heavenly Abba. The "virtue of the absurd," then, is the ecstatic embrace of God's love so filled with life that there is no room for death for anybody.

And so it is that Abraham's real act of faithfulness was not stretching out a knife to kill his son, but bringing Isaac *back* from Moriah. In a culture that demanded sacrifice so powerfully that even Abraham thought he had to participate in it, he listened to the voice from outside the system that told him not to lay a hand on the boy. On his way to Calvary, Jesus in being a pioneer of faith, (Heb. 12:2) had to believe that he had been sent from outside the sacrificial system and would return to a place outside that system after having cracked its structure for all time. This is the way we, too, are called to follow Abraham and Jesus in faithfulness. There is some mimetic resonance in believing certain things that other people believe. There is a *lot* of mimetic resonance in *doing* what other people are doing. If we follow Abraham and Jesus in renouncing sacrificial violence, then faith, as faithfulness, penetrates deeply into our hearts.

Hope

Abraham's faith was grounded in hope, but it was not hope in the subjective sense of hoping things will turn out okay if we smile nicely. In the Gospels, things don't turn out so well in the sense that Jesus dies on the cross. Jesus wasn't just hoping against hope that his story would have a happy ending. The words of his heavenly Abba at his baptism must have convinced Jesus that he would never, under any circumstances, cease to be the Son pleasing to his Abba. This is why Jesus was faithful even unto death. His hope was not grounded on wishful thinking, but on a conviction of the *truth* of what his heavenly Abba was like. Like Abraham, Jesus trusted that his heavenly Abba gave life, not death.

In a provocative paper, James Alison helps us redefine hope, which is to say that he shows us how Jesus redefines hope. Redefined hope is grounded in the death of Jesus that seemed to blot out all hope. Jesus' Resurrection from the dead might be enough to revive hope in the subjective, "hopeful" sense, but it does not redefine hope. What *does* redefine hope is that the risen Jesus adopted all of us as brothers and sisters so as to make all of us adopted daughters and sons of Jesus' Abba. Alison picks up on the dynamics of inheritance proclaimed in Paul's epistles and runs with it. When Alison's mother died, the family inheritance entered the process of coming to him and his two siblings. They had not actually inherited the estate right away, but they were already placed in a new status because the transition of transferring the estate was in process, and one day it would be completed. They weren't "hoping" they would get the estate; the estate was already theirs once the will was put into effect.

If we return to Abraham and Sarah, we see that their faith was strengthened by hope when they understood that the promise of many heirs meant that they had already been made the progenitors of countless descendants. Perhaps it was his prearranged status as a forebear that alerted Abraham to any sign that confirmed this status. When he saw the ram in the thicket, he took it for a sign that we would indeed be a forbear through Isaac. Perhaps this even was the dawning of understanding that the new culture he was being led to was about *sparing* the sacrificial victim. Even when it looked like he would have no heirs after all, Abraham acted like the progenitor God has already made him to be, and so he spared Isaac.

With us, the pre-established status is the opposite. We are not progenitors but heirs. This is why "faith is the assurance of things hoped for, the conviction of things not seen." (Heb. 11:1) The assurance is the testament of our inheritance in Jesus. Alison says that this assurance is a *demonstration* of what is not seen. The change of status as an heir has *already* changed us: "At the testator's death, the promised inheritance is substantially mine even when it is not yet in my possession, and because of that, I already now find myself starting to become a publicly visible demonstration, a reliable sign of what is on its way. Who I am is objectively being altered as someone else's promise, their desire, moves towards its fulfilment in my reception of it." (Alison 2015)

Let us follow this anthology further. Imagine a ten-year-old son who is the future heir of a vast estate. Although he is not yet the owner of the estate, because of his status as heir, his father takes him around to begin teaching him how to run the estate: How to handle the workers, make sure the foremen order supplies at the right time, etc. This boy spends time learning these things *because* he is the heir.

Now let us change the story the way God changed it. Imagine being one of the workers in the vineyard of this vast estate, who is sweating profusely while a well-dressed boy coolly walks by with his father on his tour of the place. Imagine further being caught up in the rebellious fervor that spreads among the workers so that you go on strike and allow the grapes to grow wild. When the son, grown into a young man, comes to collect the produce, you join in the attack and kill the heir. Then comes the reckoning. You and your fellow workers are brought to the magistrates, and you expect to suffer a grim fate for what you have done. To your shock, the owner of the vineyard shows up in court with the son you killed. The young man is very much alive, although the wounds inflicted on him are still bleeding. This really has you shaking in your boots. But to your further shock, the father gets out his will and announces that the vineyard was bequeathed, not only to the son but to *all of the workers*. More shocking still, the father and his son welcome all of you back to work in the vineyard as joint owners. As fellow heirs, you are ready to act like heirs who will work to keep the grapes from growing wild so as to produce so much wine for the wedding feast that it will never run out. So it is that hope is, in Alison's words, "a realignment of our whole way of being towards what really is, as what really is begins to manifest itself in us." (Alison 2015) This is not a realignment that occurs by human deviousness or ingenuity. It is a realignment brought about by God.

Love

We saw that faith and hope are based on God's actions. The substance of faith is the Paschal Mystery of Jesus' fidelity to the heavenly Abba in dying on the cross and rising from the dead. The substance of hope moves further back to the beginning of time, as hope is grounded in God's adopting all people as adopted sons and daughters to inherit the vineyard God laid out at the dawn of Creation. Love goes past the beginning of time to Eternity when God's love was poured out into the Creation of the world. In God's eyes, the "vast expanse of interstellar space," as Eucharist Canon C in the *Book of Common Prayer* has it, is small in God's eyes, "something small, the size of a hazel nut" as Julian of Norwich imagines it. But God loves "that something small," and therefore, "everything has being through the love of God." (Julian of Norwich 1973, 183) Julian goes on to explain, based on her visions, that God loves "that something small" so much that when that little thing in the form of a servant goes on a mission and falls into a ditch, God sends a second servant to get the fallen one back out of the ditch, an act that causes all of the dirt and grime of the pit to stain the clothes of the saving servant. So it is that Julian is convinced that it was love and pity that motivated the Father to send the servant to suffer for the fallen one, and that there was no trace of wrath whatever in the process. (Julian of Norwich 1973, 267–278)

Rebecca Adams, a feminist colleague of Girard, offers us a compelling articulation of what God's love is all about. In an act of authorial generosity (more love in action), Vern Redekop created space in his fine book *From Violence to Blessing* for Adams to articulate her understanding of love at some length. It was Adams who, noting how Girard tends to stress the negative side of mimetic desire, prodded him in an interview to admit that there was such a thing as "positive mimesis," where mimetic desire works among humans for constructive and humane purposes. (Girard 1996, 65)

Adams gained her inspiration from a Star Trek episode where the pivotal character is a metamorph from another planet. A metamorph is all mimetic desire to the extent that such a person is incapable of any personal subjectivity. A metamorph can only be a perfect mirror of another person's desires. Metamorph culture, then, is mimetic resonance gone mad. We can see that however mimetic resonance works, it is not intended by God to be the destruction of the core of another's personhood. This metamorph, a woman, is a pawn in an interplanetary marriage arrangement where she will be married to a callous, corrupt official. Captain Picard of the Star Trek crew wants to save her from this fate, but the metamorph can't even imagine wanting any other alternative, let alone fighting for it. Picard solves the problem by desiring that the metamorph *have* a subjectivity of her own. Because of her susceptibility, she is so engulfed in Picard's desire that she begins to desire a subjectivity for herself and so begins to gain her independence. This is sort of like being the "tiny little thing" becoming a hazel nut with the potential to grow into something large, like the mustard seed becoming a large tree. (Mt. 13:31–32) Picard proves to be a fine model of willing the subjectivity of another person, something he must have been doing habitually with the people in his life all along.

Adams sees this Star Trek episode as providing a third alternative to attempting to be either autonomous or deriving one's subjectivity completely from another. This relational willingness of the subjectivity between persons gives each "the capacity to participate fully in a loving dynamic of giving and receiving in relation to others." (Adams in Redekop 2002, 263) This willing the subjectivity of another is something that will spread, so that if two people "start desiring not only their own and each other's subjectivity," they will also "desire the subjectivity of others as well." (Adams in Redekop 2002, 267) As opposed to the closed system of mimetic rivalry, we have an "open system of intersubjectivity with its own creative, generative dynamic which potentially could expand to include everyone and everything." God, of course, already and always wills the subjectivity of all. This helps to explain why respect is the essential prerequisite to love. Adams's vision is a model of love as ultimate respect for the other, a respect that gives the other a self as a gift, while we in turn receive a self from God as a gift. When respect reaches this level, we can say that it has become love grounded in God's desire. It is also what Paul admonishes us to in Romans 12:12: "Love one another with mutual affection; outdo one another in showing honor."

There is a thought that gives me pause, however. What about the subjectivity of the callous, corrupt official and the subjectivity of those who are arranging the marriage? What about the subjectivity of one who commits violent abuse? Adams can't possibly mean to embrace such a subjectivity. For one thing, there is no mutuality, because an abuser tries to destroy the subjectivity of another rather than will it to flourish. Moreover, Adams says that she has suffered such abuse, so clearly she does not affirm this kind of subjectivity. On the contrary, this experience has taught her the importance of respecting the other's subjectivity as a mutual process. However, the question that poses itself is: Does an abusive person have a subjectivity, or much of one? If all of us can truly be a self only when that self is received as a gift, then trying to take away the self of another would entail rejecting the gift of a self from God.

All signs point to God's desire that everyone have a sense of self as a gift from God. It is not difficult to imagine willing that the metamorph woman have a subjectivity so as to be free to will something other than that forced upon her by society. This is a matter of giving one a sense of self to flourish where there hasn't been one. This is what we would try to do for any deeply battered person whose sense of self has been destroyed by violence and needs to be strengthened for a rebuilding process. On one level, we could say that the corrupt official has also been robbed of a true subjectivity by his society. That is true, but this non-self takes an aggressive and violent form. One cannot willingly walk into this kind of lions' den, expecting to defeat the lions on human strength alone. After all, it was God, not humans, who closed the mouths of lions when Daniel was thrown in among them. (Dan. 6:16–13)

The best we can do is let God's love do the work. When God offers the likes of the corrupt official a self, we can tiptoe into God's offer and share in that offer in our own small way. This is not something we should do just as individuals but as members of Christ's Body, the Church. When love as ultimate respect is given to one such as the corrupt official, then this love is also forgiveness, another gift of God and grounded in God's love. Let us not speculate on whether or not the corrupt official ever consents to receive a self from God. Let us ask ourselves if we are willing to receive this ultimate respect ourselves from God and offer it to others.

Paul's famous Hymn to Love zeroes in on what love, as *agape*, is all about: "Love is patient; love is kind; love is not envious or boastful or arrogant or rude. It does not insist on its own way; it is not irritable or resentful; it does not rejoice in wrongdoing, but rejoices in the truth." (1 Cor. 13:4–6) In these qualities, we can see love as a deep renunciation of mimetic rivalry. Insisting on our own way, being resentful, rejoicing in the shortcomings of others, are all ways of putting ourselves on top of other people. Surely this short list is meant to stand for any attempt to put ourselves above other people. As long as we try to "win," we lose at love. When we are willing to "lose," we win at love.

In *Works of Love*, Kierkegaard plumbs the depths of what it means for love to "believe all things" and "hope all things." (1 Cor. 13:7) Kierkegaard's first axiom is: "Love believes all things—and yet is never deceived." (Kierkegaard

1962, 213) Believing all things is a tall order when we know, with the Psalmist, that "Everyone is a liar!" (Ps. 116:11) Kierkegaard examines the lengths we go to avoid being deceived by another. Such a one practices much cleverness in this task. For Kierkegaard, cleverness is not a good thing; cleverness is the trait that cuts us off from other people and, most particularly, from God. If we think we love while we calculate possible deceptions of the other, we are deceiving ourselves. If we abandon ourselves to love to the extent of believing the other person, and that person deceives us, it is the *other* person who has deceived him or herself. (Kierkegaard 1962, 225) A second axiom is: "Love hopes all things—and yet is never put to shame." (Kierkegaard 1962, 233) As with believing all things, hope is hoping all things for oneself *and* other people. As with believing all things, Kierkegaard explores the cleverness with which we lower our standards in relationship with God, and so are put to shame because we did not love enough to hope all things. If ever the prodigal son should, in the end, be lost, the father who remains steadfast in love has not been put to shame. It is only the lost son who is put to shame. In hoping for the salvation of other people, we are renouncing all mimetic rivalry that might tempt us to loosen this hope even a little bit. With these two axioms, Kierkegaard has shown us how love fulfills the other two theological virtues of faith and hope, so that "the greatest of these is love." (1 Cor. 13:13)

In his treatise *On Loving God*, St. Bernard of Clairvaux outlines four stages in loving God that give us a brief, but profound capsule of the spiritual journey. In the first stage, we love ourselves for own sake. That is not very noble, but it is where we start. In the second stage, we love God for *our* own sake. This is still self-centered, but God has been brought into the picture. As I pointed out when discussing petitionary prayer, we have to bring our smelly desires to God in order to see them for what they are and for what they can become in God's sight. In the third stage, our lives are flipped so that we love God for *God's* sake. We have shifted from trying to bend God to our desires to allowing God to shape our desires according to God's desire. This is the stage of giving ourselves up to God, a stage that entails giving of ourselves to other people. This stage has our hearts overflowing so much that we assume that this is the ultimate stage, but Bernard explodes the universe with the fourth stage (brace yourself): We love *ourselves* for *God's* sake. I've always had a hard time wrapping my mind around this one, but mimetic realism has gradually helped me get a fleeting sense of what this stage means. All along, God has been loving us with God's desire. In loving ourselves for God's sake, we are turned back to ourselves, consumed with God's loving desire for us.

Chapter 14

Contemplative Indwelling in God's Desire

The First Epistle of John overflows with declarations of God's pre-emptive love: "Not that we loved God but that God loved us and sent his Son to be the atoning sacrifice for our sins." (1 Jn. 4:10) This pre-emptive love of God is not just a vague benevolence, but a sacrificial act. God has and always will act on our behalf. John goes on to describe God's love as an abiding presence within us, what amounts to being possessed by God: "By this we know that we abide in him and he in us, because he has given us of his Spirit." (1 Jn.4:13) Is this just an added treat in life? Surely being possessed by God is much greater than that. Being possessed by God is totally contrary to the many cases of possession that Jesus dealt with in the synoptic Gospels. I suggested above that the people Jesus healed had been possessed by other people. We only need to reflect on how we become possessed by people we are seriously at odds with. If we put John's teaching of God's indwelling love together with demonic possession, we are confronted with the conclusion that we are going to be possessed by somebody. It is not possible to remain aloof from the intentions and desires of other people. They will possess us whether we like it or not. The question is: By whom are we possessed? Jesus told a little parable about the evil spirit that was cast out, but then returned to the house with seven spirits "more evil than itself." (Mt. 12:44-45) This parable teaches us that casting out the spirit that has possessed someone is not enough. One must become possessed by the Spirit of Christ, who is full of love, one who is not in rivalry with us or with anybody else.

Jesus' image of the vine and the branches in John 15 gives us another take on the importance of being possessed by God's love. Once again, we have the language of mutual abiding. The branches depend on the vine for both their lives and the vitality that gives them the power to grow and bear fruit. If we stick to the vine, God prunes our competitive spirit so that we can bear more fruit. (Jn. 15:2) While pruning us, God sustains us in God's love. This possession protects us from possession by the persecutory crowd and frees us to bear good fruit. This freedom opens our hearts and minds to discern what we can do to help others in need with what resources we have. This freedom is dangerous. It could strengthen us enough to follow Jesus into the depths of the collective evil spirit that had possessed the workers in the vineyard, leading them to put the owner's son to death. (Mt. 21:33–46) Yet it is in that dark place that Jesus pulled off the greatest exorcism of all time, on the cross. The more possessed we are by God's love, the more we can trust God enough to make such a journey that takes us through Jesus' death to his Resurrection.

We can experience this indwelling of God at any time, any place, but most habitually through the practice of contemplative prayer. The disciplines discussed so far for living consciously with mimetic desire all have a contemplative element to some degree or another. Liturgical prayer is enriched by contemplative prayer, and liturgy feeds contemplative prayer. Prayerful reading of scripture leads to contemplative prayer, if we let the words in scripture and other spiritual writings sink deeply into us. Contemplative prayer is the strongest practice for connecting us to God's desire in a deep way. Unfortunately, although we are experiencing a resurgence of this practice, it still remains a closed book to many. In this chapter, I will provide practical guidelines to help readers learn how to move more deeply into God's desire.

Techniques in Prayer

There are numerous techniques for prayer that help make us available to God. None of these techniques cause prayer, but they open us to the Holy Spirit to come and pray within us. These techniques also help us direct our attention to God and wait on God. They are concrete acts of will that demonstrate our willingness to let God enter us and enfold us in love. When and how God enters us is up to God. God is God's own cause for what God does.

Since the journey of prayer takes us into the darkness and mystery within ourselves, it is important that we focus on Jesus as our guide. Interior prayer is not concerned with achieving an altered state of consciousness for its own sake, or discovering a god-like substance within us which we have by right. Our human spirit is a potential for something we lack, not something we have. Rather, the purpose of interior prayer is to become conscious of God's presence already within us. It is God we are seeking, not ourselves. If we try to find ourselves instead of God, or if we seek a mind-altering experience for its own sake, we probably will wander, lost in the depths of our psyche. If we pursue this journey in and through Christ, our minds and hearts will be altered and enlarged by the Holy Spirit, leading us to an ever-deeper vision and love for God and Creation.

There are two fundamental methods of focusing our prayer. One is called discursive meditation. This method makes use of either images or thoughts about God. The other method focuses our attention through use of a short, repetitive prayer. In recent years, it has been given the useful term of centering prayer. Here, we eschew the use of images and thoughts from the start. Both discursive meditation and centering prayer have been used extensively in the Christian tradition, and history suggests that either can work. Each individual is usually better suited for one method or the other. Therefore it is best not to push one method to the exclusion of the other. Let us not be side-tracked by those who insist that only one way or the other is legitimate. Both have worked for great saints in the past. Both have validity today.

Since Christianity is based on the Incarnation, God made flesh, there is much to gain from meditating on images. But God is mystery, and all images and ideas fall short of God. If we are going to have contemplation worth its salt, we must enter into a "dark night" where we experience God without really knowing who God is. Even in this night, prayer is still Christ-centered, but in some mysterious way, we are taken inside Jesus where we come to the Abba's ineffable presence at the center of our Lord.

No matter whether we pray by affirming images or denying them, we must be ready to experience the opposite pole. If we don't, our prayer will be unbalanced. Since the image of the human Jesus is the perfect image of God, we are not left in unrelieved darkness as to what God is like. Moreover, when God took on human flesh, God showed us that the material Creation is fundamentally good. It follows that our experience in the flesh should be an integral part of our spirituality. Even if we do not make use of images in our prayer, we must still be nourished by the images of the Gospel. Contemplative prayer must be supported by liturgical worship and regular prayerful reading of scripture. The Eastern Orthodox Church stresses the interior spirituality of imageless contemplation, based on a short prayer such as the Jesus Prayer. But this practice is balanced with a strong devotion to icons and a very rich liturgy. Images resonate deeply with our mirror neurons to enliven our sharing in God's desire. But since God is mystery, we only hold ourselves back from experiencing God's presence in a deep way if we think we know who God is. If we meditate with the use of images, we must not cling to them. We should be open to the possibility of being carried inside the images where we enter the darkness of God's naked presence. It is not a simple case of graduating from the human nature of Jesus to the Divine Nature. Rather, we follow the one Person of the Trinity who took on human flesh. The humanity of Jesus assures us that we don't get beyond our humanity, but Jesus' divinity stretches our humanity. Just as Jesus poured himself out of his Divinity to take on human nature, so we pour ourselves out of our human experience to receive a taste of God's divinity. Yet, far from losing ourselves, we have, just as Jesus promised we would, found ourselves in God.

Any means we use in prayer are just that, means. These techniques, whether with or without images, are means to the end of simply being with God. We do not sit down to pray in order to finish a pre-planned meditation or say so many thousand Jesus Prayers. We pray in order to be with God. When God gives us the experience of God's simplicity, we experience God through unknowing. When God centers our prayer, we have no need to center it ourselves. We must avoid turning prayer into a conjuring act. If we call on the Holy Name of Jesus, Jesus will come of his own free will. But if we think our calling on Jesus *causes*

Jesus to come, all we get is fantasy. If we think God owes us gifts of grace because of all the time we spend on our knees, we will get the reward we have really earned: Nothing except our empty selves.

Discerning which method is best for each person does not follow a hard and fast rule. Perhaps an intellectually inclined person will be attracted to something like the Jesus Prayer because its simplicity is an antidote to a heavy diet of mental activity. One of the more reliable criteria is that if we tend to experience some fervor and longing for God spontaneously when we sit down to pray, we are more likely to find of a form of centering prayer helpful. Others may need to focus on an image to stir up some sense of devotion. Each of us must do a little experimenting to find out which is most effective for each of us. Chances are, we will have an instinct or hunch as to which to try. We should follow up that hunch at first. It shouldn't take long to find out if we are on the right track or not. A word of caution, however: The muddling that most of us have to go through should not degenerate into a perpetual restlessness. We should not expect instant contemplation. Some difficulty along the way should not immediately be construed as meaning that a change is in order. A common dictum among early spiritual teachers is that a tree transplanted too often will never take root.

The bodily position we adopt for prayer is important, but there is room for several options. The essential thing is to place ourselves in a disciplined posture with the back straight. Since we are seeking to make ourselves alert for God's coming to us in prayer, our positioning should reinforce this alertness. We can sit cross-legged in the oriental lotus position, kneel, or sit up in a straight-backed chair. Making ourselves uncomfortable does not usually help us pray better, but making ourselves too comfortable is more conducive to daydreaming than to prayer.

Half an hour is a good length of time for contemplative prayer. This allows us to move deeply into prayer but is also long enough for us to experience the tedium of it—a purifying experience. We may be led by the Spirit to pray longer in some instances. If it is not normally possible to spend as much time as half an hour because of other God-given commitments, try to spend at least fifteen minutes at this prayer.

Meditation on Images

The technique of meditating on images achieved its most elaborate articulation during the Counter-Reformation period, particularly in the *Spiritual Exercises* of St. Ignatius Loyola and the works of St. Francis de Sales. These two writers developed, to a high degree of complexity, a technique which had been used throughout the Middle Ages. Its basic principle is to involve our rational, imaginative, and feeling faculties in prayer. St. Ignatius systematically involved all five of the senses in each meditation. When using this technique of prayer, it is important not to let the imagination just float in any direction. In the end, we must give up all our ideas and imaginings. We make a modest beginning in this renunciation by focusing on the images offered for a particular meditation.

Some may find it helpful to follow St. Ignatius to the letter, but I recommend recapturing the simplicity of this technique from earlier sources of the tradition. In choosing to use Gospel stories as the subject of our meditations, we imagine the scene in some detail so that we see and smell and feel everything. Such a meditation is not like watching a movie. Meditation is not a spectator sport. We must put ourselves into the scene. In the story of the miraculous catch of fish, (Lk. 5:1–11) for example, we place ourselves in the boat where we cast out the nets but catch nothing. Jesus comes along and says: "Try again." So we do. We experience the shock and surprise of getting a full net, and we know we are not worth as much as a finger of this man. After imagining the story, we sit with it. We let the shock and the joy of the event sink in. We do not necessarily have to think about what the story means at this time. We can do that later. We just rest in the Gospel scenes or parables and let them roll around in our minds, allowing them to burrow deeper into our hearts.

A favorite traditional image for meditation is the crucifixion of Jesus. The famous Gospel song "Were you there when they crucified my Lord?" captures the point of meditating on this image perfectly. We are at the foot of the cross, where we sit with Jesus during his last moments. This is the center of our redemption. There are no haloes. The scene is not pretty. But there is a dignity that causes a glow in our hearts, because we cannot forget who this crucified one is. Blood and water flow from his side, when the soldier thrusts a lance into him. This blood and water is Jesus' life flowing into us.

On the other hand, we could meditate on something a little more abstract, such as St. Paul's image of taking off the Old Self and being clothed with the New Self. (Col. 3:9–10) Here the mind must do a little more thinking, but it is important not to let our prayer time become a mere exercise in thought. We should relax and play with the idea prayerfully. First, we reflect on how we might takeoff the Old Self and then how we might put on the New Self. What habits and attitudes might we need to put off? What habits and attitudes might we need to put on? Then we rest in God and open ourselves to the newness Paul promises when we allow God to clothe us with God's glory instead of our own. Then, we should attend to this promise and use it as our anchor of attention.

The Lord's Prayer is another great source for meditation. We could easily spend half an hour or more with the short prayer that Jesus himself taught us. What do we mean when we say "hallowed be thy name?" Are we really giving God (instead of ourselves) the glory when something goes well in our lives? What are our trespasses? How forgiving are we of others? This prayer can take us through the whole Christian life each day.

Centering Prayer

The other basic method of prayer is the way of simplicity. Here we do not meditate with images or thoughts. Instead, we use a brief repetitive prayer to anchor our attention. This method has a long history in many world religions with the Buddhist chant "Om Mane Padme Hum" being a well-known example. The universal use of this technique suggests that it makes use of a deep reality in the human psyche God has given us. The earliest monastics of the fourth century would take a Psalm verse and repeat it over and over again. A favorite one was Ps. 70:1: "O God make speed to save me, O Lord make haste to help me." Use of this verse evolved into being the opening of the

Divine Office. The translation used here comes from the opening of Evening Prayer in the *Book of Common Prayer*. Sometime during the fourth or fifth century, if not earlier, these monastics began using an invocation of the Divine Name of Jesus as an anchoring prayer that became known as the Jesus Prayer. Various formulas of the Jesus Prayer have been used over the years. The longest version is: "Lord Jesus Christ, Son of the living God, have mercy on me a miserable sinner." One may prefer a shortened version such as: "Lord Jesus Christ, have mercy on me." "Jesus — Mercy" is shorter yet, and one can reduce the prayer to just the Holy Name itself: "Jesus." Each person must discern which version is most helpful for one's own use. The author of *The Cloud of Unknowing* suggests using as short a prayer word as possible, preferably just one syllable, such as "God" or "Love." This prayer word should be used as a dart of Love directed at "the cloud of unknowing." John Main in his fine book *Word into Silence* prefers to use a more abstract prayer word as a safeguard against bringing images into prayer unnecessarily. I am not as worried about images as he is, as long as they are centered on God, but since the prayer word does not primarily use images, an abstract word has some value. John Main's favorite is *maranatha* which means: "Come Lord!" Another good one is *metanoia*, the Greek word for repentance used in the New Testament.

When using a repetitive prayer or prayer word, say it mentally in a slow, rhythmic way without allowing the rhythm to become an end in itself. Being relaxed with our prayer word helps us avoid becoming overwrought. From the start, our use of the prayer must be detached from our feelings. The shorter the prayer or prayer word, the more important it is to be relaxed, as a short word has a greater chance of making the prayer too intense. When we use a short prayer word, it is easy to cling to it, and if we do cling to it, we could end up in a state of self-hypnosis. Rather, we should treat the Jesus Prayer, or any prayer word, as a walking stick as we move into the interior non-place of the Spirit. To shift to another metaphor, the prayer word is an anchor that holds down our prayer, while the mind, like a boat, drifts about in circles on the water's surface.

A number of breathing exercises have been tried with the Jesus Prayer.

With expert guidance they can be of some help, but without that they can be dangerous. In any case, they are not of prime importance. On the other hand, the role of breathing should not be overlooked altogether. We can help our prayer by taking good, relaxed, deep breaths and exhaling slowly in a relaxed rhythm. If the breathing becomes so heavy as to make the prayer too intense, we do well to break the rhythm, relax, and gently begin using the prayer again. We do not have to strain to do the work God intends to do within us.

That's all there is to it. The use of centering prayer is so simple, it seems like an insult to our intelligence. Surely we aren't doing anywhere near enough work to earn any rewards from God?! How hard it is for us to stop being over-achievers! None of our human faculties can bring us to God in prayer. All we can do is give them up, and this renunciation is precisely what the prayer word accomplishes for us. We give up our own thoughts and our own ideas. We give up our own imaginings and our own feelings. We pour all of ourselves into the prayer, until we are dispossessed of all we thought we were.

Distractions

Our biggest difficulty is distractions. It seems that when Jesus told us we would always have the poor with us, (Mt. 26:11) he could have told us we would always have distractions in prayer as well. We should not be too surprised that this is so. Our minds and imaginations have a lifelong habit of working nonstop, and they are not about to quit all of a sudden when we ask them to. In fact, it is the nature of our minds and imaginations to work the way they do. Their activity, in itself, is not a sign of sinfulness or rebellion against God. Our journey in prayer will also show us that these human faculties have the potential for being seized by the Inconceivable. It is easy to use prayer as an escape from the reality of our humanity, but true prayer brings us face to face with reality. Our distractions in prayer are salutary reminders that we are human. They remind us of what our humanity is really like, both the good and the not so good.

Even so, distractions hamper our prayer. No question about it. But we have to handle distractions in the right way. Usually we try ruthlessly ripping out our thoughts as if they were weeds. This approach is counterproductive. The story of the sorcerer's apprentice in Goethe's famous poem can help us here. The apprentice had used a magic spell to activate a broom to bring water into the castle, but then he couldn't stop the broom after it had brought in more than enough water. In his desperation, he chopped the broom in half, with the result that he had two brooms bringing in twice as much water. Approaching our distractions with a hatchet tends to give us the same result. We get so involved in our distractions by trying to stifle them that we have no room left for prayer. Since many of our distractions are rooted in our involvement with mimetic rivalry, fighting them so aggressively keeps us firmly entrenched in the rivalry they represent. Less combative methods are called for. It is best to renew our focus on our image or prayer word. Perhaps the parable of the Wheat and the Weeds can teach us the humbling lesson of being patient with our distractions.

Since our distractions represent aspects of our humanity that most need to be handed over to God in prayer, it is important to be gentle with them. Put away the hatchet and pursue peace. There will be times when the distractions are nothing more than idle chatter in the mind. When that is the case, it is not hard to ignore them. Let the chatter continue, but don't pay any attention to it. We simply return our attention back to God. Some distractions at this level are so pleasant and innocent that we hate to move them aside. We can integrate them into our prayer. For example, if I keep thinking of the new frisky kitten that came our way, I can think of the kitten as an image of God playing with Creation, and my prayer is redirected to God.

Some distractions are so strong that it is not possible to lay them aside and make them to go away. These distractions are caused by aspects in our lives that have taken deep root in us. Others have to do with our sinfulness. We have to accept the fact that, in the interior journey of prayer, we are going to discover deep-seated emotions such as lust and anger. At times there will seem to be no end to the fantasies arising from these feelings. We would like to ignore them because we like to think we are not as subject to these temptations as we really are. At the same time, we are fascinated by our less salutary impulses and are reluctant to see them go. The only way to deal with these distractions is to make them a part of our prayer. We are offering ourselves, remember, and if what we have to offer are these fantasies, then that is what we offer. We must pour these distractions and our helplessness into the Holy Name of Jesus and let God take them. We must give up both these impulses that weigh so heavily on us and the pride that makes us assume we can fix them ourselves. Jesus was not disturbed by stormy waters, not even when his disciples thought they were in mortal danger. (Mk. 6:48–50) So perhaps we need not always be as disturbed by inner storms as we assume we should be. This is precisely the moment when we should simply come to Jesus, who is waiting for us. The author of *The Cloud of Unknowing* helpfully suggests that when distractions are intense, we should avoid fighting them and "try to look over their shoulders." (*Cloud* 1981, 181)

Other distractions have to do with more positive sides of our character. We may be inspired by a bright idea we have been waiting for. It is difficult to give up a thought like this but we must. Again, it is not a case of trying to ignore the thought or root it out, but rather than clinging to it, we must pour this thought, too, into our prayer. Our thoughts are not to be our own thoughts. If we give up the best of our thoughts, we can trust God to give them back to us at the right time. What a wonderful way to test these bright ideas; to see what they are like after we have rested with them in the Heart of Jesus!

Our most intense distractions are caused by worry and anxiety. It is easy to say that we shouldn't fret about our problems while we are at prayer, but sometimes we simply can't help it. Moreover, when the cause of our anxiety involves serious illness or injury to someone we love, it is uncharitable to try to ignore their problems for the sake of an egocentric serenity in prayer. At these times, we should bring those we care about deep into our prayer with God, so that two or three are gathered together with God, instead of just oneself and God. When we are upset about ourselves or about other people, it usually doesn't work to try and calm ourselves; it is better to let God do that. When we pour our pain into the Holy Name of Jesus, we cease to be wrapped up in our worries.

Sometimes a severe emotion, caused either by recent events or distant memories, may feel like a huge lump stuck in the middle of the body. This lump refuses to move and it blocks everything else we wish to accomplish in prayer. There is no sense in trying to move the unmovable. Often such lumps are caused by trauma that we have trouble forgiving. Painful as it is, there is nothing for it but to pray with this lump, holding it up to God. After all, it is our faith, not our own efforts, that moves mountains. (Mt. 17:20) If the inner pain is approachable, it may be helpful to imagine the pain as a hurt child within us who needs to be comforted. We bring the "hurt child" within ourselves into our prayer the same way we bring in another harmed person so that God can give the comfort we cannot give ourselves. If the pain is so great that we feel we cannot touch it or come near it, then we should keep it at a distance until we are ready to deal with it. In that case, we do better to pray with our anxiety and our reluctance to deal with the pain. We should pray through the steps of forgiveness, beginning with telling the story, to letting go, to gradually receiving the gift of forgiveness from God deep within ourselves.

On the other hand, sometimes it is joyful feelings that distract us, such as the ecstasy of falling in love. We may think that such joys are not worthy of prayer where we are seeking a greater good than any earthly love, but let us not reject this human experience too quickly. Earthly love, when we are seeking the other's good as much as our own, is an image of our love relationship with God. Let us share our human joys and loves with God and find out what God will do with them in prayer.

We should avoid becoming so absorbed in ourselves and our problems that we stew in our own juices. We also should avoid taking off on flights of admiration for our great inspirations. We are hardly praying if we are devising sermons for the benefit of other people. Even so, our prayer should be closely connected with ourselves. If we let our prayer move back and forth between ourselves and our concerns at one pole and then to God at the other, and if we keep bringing ourselves to God, we will gain clarity about what we and our loved-ones are like in God's eyes. Sometimes, that is the best way to see that some things are not as important as we thought, while seemingly insignificant matters are large in the eyes of God.

There is one more type of distraction that is so insidious we may fail to recognize it as a distraction. It strikes right at the time when we think our prayer is going well. There is nothing wrong with prayer going well, but the hazard is we might take the credit for it. I start to think that *I* am praying so well. Boy! Have *I* come a long way since I started! Once again, the ego has intruded, but with such cunning that I hardly think anything of it. When we catch ourselves thinking in this way, we have reached the point where we must throw ourselves onto the mercy of God. More than at any other time, we should be wary of taking ourselves too seriously. Rather, remember our Lord said that when we have done everything asked of us, we are still "unworthy servants." (Lk. 17:10)

All types of distractions reflect our desires and the complex interactions of our desires with the desires of others. We have noted many times how bewildering this nexus can be. Contemplative prayer gives us a great opportunity to let go of all of that and rest in the Lord. From petty grumbling and idle chatter to fierce passions and deep trauma, these desires swirl about within us, sometimes gently, sometimes intensely. As we sit quietly with our mimetic resonances, they slowly sink into God's desire. Even in the midst of these distractions, we can feel God's desire seeping into our hearts.

Since the more unsavory fantasies may seem to come from the deepest parts of our subconscious, it is important to remember that the inner chaos there is not the deepest part of ourselves. The Image of God within us is deeper yet. We must not be misled into thinking that we are as bad as some of our wilder distractions suggest. When we offer the broken pieces of our lives to God, asking God's help and giving thanks to God for what is good in us, we will find that God will lead us through Christ's death into Christ's risen life, where God will put our pieces together in ways we could never have imagined. If we should experience inner horror, we can trust God to take us deeper yet, to where our twisted desires and fantasies are transformed into the straightness and radiance of God's Love.

Dryness and Patience

Sooner or later, we will encounter dryness in our prayer. Sometimes, dryness is caused, in part, by our sinfulness that makes us shy about turning to God. If that is so, there is nothing for it but to wait patiently for God to move gently through this block, so that we can feel comfortable with God again. In the meantime, we must practice what discipline we can against our sinfulness. But more often dryness indicates something other and deeper than our sinfulness. There will be times when our experience cannot be considered a feeling at all; it may be a sense of suspended animation. We can't do anything in the way of prayer, but God doesn't seem to be doing anything either. Again, the only thing for it is to wait. God often works in hiding. Ruth Burrows, a contemporary Carmelite, uses the phrases "light on" and "light off." Usually God works within us with the light off, where we cannot sense what God is doing. This gives us the opportunity to grow in trusting God.

We like to think that the dryness resulting from a deepening of our journey is more "high class" than dryness caused by lassitude or sinfulness, but it is not wise to jump to conclusions. Dryness can easily be a combination of the two. Regardless of the cause, dryness teaches us the crucial distinction between will and feeling. When we feel cold or numb, we are still *willing* to direct ourselves to God. It may be that our feelings are active, but they are drawn to our distractions rather than to God. Even then, we can direct the will towards God. In times such as these, there is no need to try to force our feelings to conform to our wills. The Holy Spirit will work on that in God's own time. The experience of dryness teaches us is patience.

Lack of patience can be a real stumbling block. We can't help but wish to be in deep union with God as soon as possible. We are used to achieving other goals in life quickly. We can turn lights on and off with the flick of the switch. Why doesn't prayer work like that? I don't have the answer to that question. We must trust that God has chosen the best way to bring us to the greatest good. The hardest thing to realize is that it is precisely when our prayer seems most jumbled, either through distractions, emotional upset, or dryness, that God is accomplishing the most work in us with the lights off. As time goes on, we should have moments when, even in a swirl of distractions, we become dimly aware that God is supporting us by praying within us through these distractions. The two may seem incompatible, and they are, yet there are times when they co-exist in the depths of our being. We go away from such a prayer time both humbled with our emptiness and filled with God's gifts.

But then, unexpectedly, there may come a moment, maybe so brief as to go almost unnoticed, when God *takes* our attention. Then, we are so caught up in God that it is almost a non-experience. I say a non-experience because we are not self-conscious enough to reflect on what is happening. Such an occurrence is like becoming so engrossed in a book that we forget ourselves. This is what God does with us in prayer from time to time. The prayer continues on its own because the Holy Spirit is praying within us. When this happens, we may become frightened and think we are losing ourselves, and we are! We are on the threshold of gaining life by losing it. This is the experience of being filled with the fire of divine fire. Some may find this experience more frightening than attractive. We are so used to being in control and getting things done on our own terms that it is not easy to give up our self-assertiveness. If we aren't *doing* something, we assume that nothing is getting done. But in prayer, something *is* being accomplished. It's just that we can't articulate what is happening because God is the one doing it. So, when God takes our attention, we should stop trying to pay attention by our own efforts. If God has really taken our attention, then we won't be dwelling on anything short of God. If God invites us to rest in God, then we should rest.

There can be times when we experience desolation, times that we might call, with St. John of the Cross, "the dark night of the soul." I hesitate to use this phrase glibly because many people use it when they experience minor setbacks. This is not what John of the Cross wrote about. However, desolation can come, and when it does, we have to endure it in faith and hope and love, and we must wait on God. It is possible that we are experiencing our own inner desolation. After all, giving up self-constructed mimetic relations, many of them rivalrous, will open up a gaping emptiness as we wait for God to fill it. Sometimes, we experience the pain other people are going through as we get close to God's abiding love for them. It is costly even for God to embrace the horrifying emptiness of the most severely malicious perpetrators of atrocities. The more deeply we sink in God's desire for even the worst of villains, the more we experience the cost of this sacrificial love in ourselves. Raïssa Maritain, wife of the great Catholic philosopher Jacques Maritain, was one of the great contemplatives of the twentieth century. Being a Russian Jew, she suffered in the core of her being the horror of the Shoah inflicted on her people. Being safe in New York and Chicago with her husband did not spare her suffering with God's suffering.

Stages in Prayer

Many writers on spirituality have delineated various stages of development in contemplative prayer. In these schemes, our own efforts predominate in the earlier stages and God's work takes over in the higher stages. Some of these classifications are rather complex, others are simple. Though they offer clarification of the experience of prayer, these stages should not be taken too seriously, especially in regard to oneself. Trying to decide whether or not we are at Level One, Level Two, or Level Three can be a distraction from prayer itself. Still, some awareness of the various levels of prayer alerts us to the different experiences we are likely to have. There will be times when we seem to be doing most of the work, but God is drawing us along, using our thoughts and emotions to bring us closer to God. Then there will be times when we seem to be an equal partner with God. We are still directing the will towards God, but God is also praying within us. This paradoxical state has been called "acquired contemplation" by some writers, while others have argued that this category is a contradiction in terms. How can God's work of prayer within us be acquired? In terms of logic, we have a real problem, but the experience itself is just as paradoxical as the term. Somehow, the efforts we make and God's work meet. Then there are times beyond this paradoxical stage when God takes over completely and our prayer is a total gift from God.

Timothy (Kallistos) Ware, an Orthodox monk and a leading writer on the

Jesus Prayer, offers an attractive set of simple categories as a map of prayer levels: 1) the prayer of the lips, 2) the prayer of the mind, and 3) the prayer of the heart. (Ware 1966) We can readily see that each stage represents an ever-deepening level of prayer. At first we are saying the words, or thinking them. As the prayer moves inwards, the intellect becomes conformed to the prayer. Then, the prayer penetrates to the heart. The heart does not refer just to the physical organ; it refers to the depths of the whole person. Even so, at this stage of the Jesus Prayer, we may feel the prayer's presence in the region of the heart. When prayer has reached the heart, it takes on a life of its own.

When stages of prayer are numbered, we get the impression that the only way we will go is up. Our concrete experience, however, is that prayer has its ups and downs. It is important not to assume that the way things went yesterday is what we should expect today or tomorrow. We must remain open to what God wants to do at any given time. God might take over completely one day to encourage us, and then leave us with our own feeble efforts the next. It may be that there are parts of our personality that still need to be integrated into our prayer. This integration will happen at what God deems to be the right time. We must to be patient with ourselves. God is still waiting. When we seem to have sunk to a low point, we should not assume that we are moving backwards. Prayer has a rhythm with its ups and downs. Both periods will be used by God for our good.

Prayer in Daily Life

Our journey of prayer is incomplete unless we bring prayer into the rest of our lives. God makes an impression on us as a seal makes its impression on wax during our times of prayer. We will carry the gifts God has given us even when we don't know it. Just as we must continually renew our acts of will to choose God during our time of prayer, we must renew our choice at all other times. One method, arising out of the Ignatian style of meditation, is to take one basic thought from a meditation, what St. Francis de Sales calls a "spiritual nosegay," and let that thought accompany us throughout the day.

We can also take an image or line of text from our spiritual reading or the Divine Office and carry that throughout the day. The phrase "the fullness of time" in Galatians (Gal. 4:4) suggests that time can be empty as well as full. We can take such a thought—empty time/full time—and keep asking ourselves if we are allowing God to fill our time, or if we are emptying our time of the content God has given it. Also, we can use our prayer word, or some other short prayer, whenever we have spare room in our minds as we do our work. Perhaps we can give the radios in our cars and our homes a rest once in a while just so that we can do a little extra praying.

We do not make our journey in prayer alone with God. We need spiritual companionship in several different ways. Liturgical worship is an important balance and support for contemplative prayer. It is worth reflecting that St. Benedict seems to have known that devotion to the Divine Office as the heart of the monastic routine, along with study and work, would inspire and teach contemplative prayer.

When it is at all possible, we should make prayer a shared experience for the whole family. There may be times when this will not be possible, since the journey of prayer requires, above all things, willingness. But if spouses can pray together, there will be a bond of unity that will be a support when serious differences arise. When children are included in a brief time of silent prayer, they have the chance to build up an intimate love of God from an early age. These times of prayer are not foolproof ways of solving family problems. In fact, prayer is not a solution to anything at all. Sometimes we are left with the mystery of brokenness. But in prayer, the brokenness is not the same as it would be if we were on our own, for God is sharing our pain. If nothing else, prayer will leave us with a healing touch that gives us a greater freedom for dealing with our brokenness.

Praying with another person when opportunity allows can be enriching. At the abbey where I live, we pray in silence for half an hour after Vespers, and the presence of others is strengthening. Quakers, of course, experience this in their silent meetings. It is important not to trust in ourselves. We grow in humility by attending to what others see in us. Sharing modestly what we experience in prayer and listening to others can strengthen bonds with them.

We should, however, avoid being compulsive about talking about our "experiences" so as put them on a pedestal for all to see. The people we live with, even if they are not well-versed in prayer, are often the first to give us signals as to whether or not our prayers are flowing into our actions. The point is, if our prayer is doing the work of the Spirit, other people should find us more, rather than less, generous in the way we live in relation to them.

Our prayer should strengthen, rather than weaken, our concern for other people. In fact, prayer leads us to embrace the whole world in God. This does not mean we can solve all the world's social problems, but prayer can strengthen our discernment of what specific actions are realistic and helpful. In the arena of social witness, depth of contemplative prayer is most important, as it is so easy for us to put a Christian facade over opportunistic political positions. We need to search our hearts constantly as to whether we are acting out of the compassion of God, who identifies with the sick, the imprisoned, and the poor. The more our lives are based on prayer, the more our human impulses of love toward others will be transformed by God's impulse of love toward all whom God has created. Most importantly, God uses our prayer to help other people without our ever knowing anything about it.

In contemplative prayer, we empty ourselves of our thoughts and wishes and desires so as to be filled with God, even when God's fullness feels empty. In a small way, we are acting out the kenotic action of Christ, who emptied himself of his divinity so as to become a human being. (Phil. 2:6–11) This kenotic aspect of prayer should extend to life as a whole so that, in our actions with other people, we empty ourselves for their sake in the way we empty ourselves in prayer. Paul's exhortations, especially in 2 Corinthians, about the collection for Jerusalem he had initiated, gives us a powerful model of the self-giving that should flow from our prayer. Many times, Paul speaks about the joy of giving, not only with money (which Paul had in short supply) but in time and energy and concern for others. It is Paul who passed on Jesus' words: "It is more blessed to give than to receive." (Acts 20:35) It amuses me that the joy Paul would have us take in giving generously and joyfully is *hilarotes*. That is, we should give with hilarity. (2 Cor. 9:7 I realize the Greek word doesn't have the boisterous connotations of our English word, but I still like the joy expressed by "hilarity."

This appeal is much more than a plea to help the needy in Jerusalem. Paul points to the Christological depth of giving when he makes it clear that contributing with enthusiastic hilarity is modeled on Jesus. Though he was rich, for our sakes he became poor that we through his poverty could become rich. (2 Cor. 8: 9) This verse is used in the 1979 *Book of Common Prayer* in one of the collects for saints who followed the religious life. Once again, we have an echo of the hymn in Philippians, where Christ humbled himself to enter the human condition and suffer the same vulnerabilities, including death, which humans suffer from. We can't compete with Christ in generosity, but we can at least empty ourselves of what we do have for the sake of others.

In both deep prayer and in action, our self-emptying is modeled on Christ. Faith is receiving what we renounce with infinite resignation. When Jesus poured out his divinity to become human, Jesus received back his divinity. (Actually, Jesus could not ever have lost his divinity.) We pour out our humanity as a gift to God and in return receive Christ's divinity as a gift. Many early Church Fathers, among them Irenaeus, said that God became human so that humans could become God. Eastern Orthodox writers call this deification. (2 Pet. 1:4) This does not mean we become God; it means that we are filled with the non-rivalrous love of God so as to become more fully human than ever. It is a powerfully sober thought to reflect that Jesus chose to enter our humanity because walking on this earth as a human is a good thing.

Another term from Eastern Orthodox spirituality is *hesychia,* a Greek word that means resting. It is used for resting in God during our time of contemplative prayer. We are called to rest in God's desire, and we are also called to move in God's desire so that moving and resting in God fills all that we do.

Chapter 15

Where We End Up

The word "end" can mean stop, to cease. But this word can also mean the goal, fulfillment. Jesus' teaching is not about endings in the first sense, but it is about the second. The goal is the Kingdom, a goal that does not end in the sense of stopping or ceasing. This goal draws us to it in the here-and-now, and it will never stop drawing us. We experience the Kingdom of God every time we overcome mimetic rivalry with the help and sustenance of God's desire. The Greek word used in the New Testament for the end as the goal is *telos*. It is a form of this word that Jesus used on the cross when he said: "It is finished." (Jn. 19:30) Many translations used the word "fulfilled." Jesus' death was not the end, but the beginning. John symbolizes this new beginning with the "blood and water" that came out of him when the soldier pierced his side with a spear. Jesus' gift of life *is* the Kingdom. (Jn. 19:34)

Throughout most of human history, rituals of the dead have not been about memorializing and remembering the dead, but about separating the dead from the living. Blurring distinctions between the living and the dead raises horrifying issues. To begin with, it calls into question what life and death really are. Zombies and vampires, creatures that blur this distinction, are very popular today. The idea of being "undead" is a haunting and unattractive possibility. Rites of the dead are more *against* them than for them. Informants of anthropologists express fear that the dead envy the living. If the dead get a chance to break into the land of the living, they will destroy the life we cherish. That is, the dead are perceived as rivals for life that has been made scarce. These anxieties project the rivalry we experience with people who are alive on the dead, who have (hopefully) departed this life.

The execution of Jesus followed by his Resurrection opened up a whole different paradigm of death when Jesus appeared, not as a vengeful ghost, but as the Forgiving Victim. Christian martyrs who gave up their precious lives to witness to Christ were believed by the early Church to be, not vengeful ghosts, but saints in Heaven who actively work for our good with their prayers. In Christ, the dead have ceased to be rivals. They have become part of *one* Church that bridges the gulf between the living and the dead. Medieval Christianity developed a powerful vision of those living on Earth and those living in Heaven supporting each other in prayer without resentment or rivalry.

The most solemn and moving chapter in Kierkegaard's remarkable book *Works of Love* is "The Work of Love in Remembering One Dead." Throughout this book, Kierkegaard models love on God's *agape*, love that is not transactional and therefore requires nothing in return, as modeled by Christ. After exploring such self-giving love in live human relationships, Kierkegaard avers that remembering one who is dead is a work of the most unselfish love. This is the purest love because it is nonreciprocal; the dead "make no repayment." (Kierkegaard 1962, 321)

However, the dead are not as dead as Kierkegaard seems to think. The dead continue to live in us in a dynamic way that can be enriching. Caring for the dead, as with caring for any live person, tends to lower resentment if there is any to start with. We say we should not speak ill of the dead. The instinct behind this adage is that sympathy for the dead person, warts and all, tends to kick in automatically at the time of death, making the release of resentment and forgiveness free gifts from God that we can pass on to the dead. There is something about death that helps us see that person as God sees him or her, indeed everybody, without exception, with forgiveness and freely given love. Resentment makes any relationship destructively static and God is completely boxed out. This is how one creates an idol out of the one who is resented by making that person central to one's life rather than God.

The lessening of resentment allows a relationship to change. This is just as true of a relationship with a dead person as it is with that of a person who is still alive. This dynamic of letting go allows us to understand aspects of the person we had never understood before. Giving this dynamic free reign with a dead person frees the dead person to reciprocate, in a sense, because the dynamic of increased sympathy and understanding is so rewarding. And so it is that the dead, living with God, can give us much more in return for our care than we can give them. This is the Kingdom of God.

When the Pharisees challenged Jesus to tell them when the Kingdom was coming, Jesus said that the Kingdom was "not coming with things that can be observed." It will not be found by scrambling all over the place crying: 'Look, here it is!' or 'There it is!" For the Kingdom of God is among us. (Lk. 17:21) It is not impossible to believe that the Kingdom is among us when we are in the presence of caring people who help us build the Body of Christ. It becomes humanly impossible to believe that the Kingdom is among us when we focus on the swirling violence in the world today.

I have already discussed how sacred violence has lost its ability to hold humanity together since the death and Resurrection of Jesus. This failure puts all of us in peril of an uncontrollable meltdown. Jesus describes such a possibility in the verses that follow the presence of the Kingdom among us with reference to the Flood and the destruction of Sodom. (Lk. 17:25–30) In *Battling to the End*, Girard discusses Clausewitz's analysis of war as a duel that becomes an "escalation to extremes." (Girard 2010, 1–25) The attacks on 9/11 and, even more, the violent aftermath of counter-attacks, make this escalation crystal clear to all of us. As I write, some politicians are being granted the headlines for engaging in inflammatory rhetoric, causing many others to react with furious denunciations of certain ethnic and religious groups. This gives us the mirroring effect where we mirror the inflammatory rhetoric some are giving out. When we do that, the violent speakers mirror our violent rhetoric back to us. So we end up with an escalation to extremes, two extremes that look exactly alike. In all this, we can feel, with St. Paul, that "the whole creation has been groaning in labor pains until now." (Rom. 8:22) Creation continues to groan and we with it. Unfortunately, some preachers seem to revel in such destruction, hailing it as ushering in God's "kingdom," but their frantic pointing all over the place is precisely what Jesus said is *not* the Kingdom. God is not in the fire of an empire's implosion. God is not in the burning of the earth and fouling of the waters as described in Revelation. (Rev. 8:7–11) It is not possible for me to conceive of God wishing in any way for the unmaking of Creation. God was not in the fire or the earthquake when Elijah sat in the cave. God was instead heard as "a sound of sheer silence." (1 Kings 19: 12) It is in this sound of sheer silence that the Kingdom of God is among us, even in the tumult of a world going crazy with mimetic rivalry. What brings this space of sheer silence into the Kingdom? Simple acts of giving a cup of cold water to the least of God's people, so that these acts can mirror each other in an escalation of giving. The Kingdom is present when we share desires constructively with one another and with God's desire. In this respect, the Kingdom of God is a present reality, so far as we reach out to each other in solidarity rather than rivalry.

The Sadducees posed a different challenge to Jesus. Not believing in the Resurrection as did the Pharisees, and so not interested in where the Kingdom might be, they pose a scenario that makes a mockery of life after death. Citing the law in Deuteronomy 25:5 that states that if a man dies childless, his brother, if unmarried, must marry his brother's widow, the Sadducees present a scenario where seven brothers all marry the same woman in succession and then die without issue. Then the seven-times married woman also dies. They ask Jesus: "In the resurrection, then, whose wife of the seven will she be? For all of them had married her." (Mt. 22:28) Jesus responds by saying that there is no marrying in Heaven so that is not an issue. Then he challenges their disbelief with this stunner: "And as for the resurrection of the dead, have you not read what was said to you by God, 'I am the God of Abraham, the God of Isaac, and the God of Jacob?' He is God not of the dead, but of the living." (Mt. 22:32) The crowd was amazed, and we should be just as amazed.

In debating with the Sadducees, Jesus had to quote from the Pentateuch, the Five Books of Moses, because they only accepted those books as authoritative. This didn't give him much to work with for questions about life after death. For that matter, there wasn't much of anything elsewhere in the Hebrew Bible on the subject. The Psalmist laments: "For in death there is no remembrance of you; in Sheol who can give you praise?" (Ps. 6:5) When Isaiah tells King Hezekiah that he is about to die, the king cries out to God: "Sheol cannot thank you, death cannot praise you; those who go down to the Pit cannot hope for your faithfulness. The living, the living, they thank you, as I do this day; fathers make known to children your faithfulness." (Isa. 38:18–19) Sheol was a shadowy place in the underworld where the dead subsisted. It was generally believed to be beyond the reach and concern of Yahweh. Jesus, however, spoke from the deep conviction that his heavenly Abba could and would continue to care about him and all other people at and beyond the time of death. It is with this conviction that Jesus told the Sadducees that when the voice from the burning bush claimed to be the God of Abraham, Isaac, and Jacob, the three patriarchs had to be alive, because it was not possible for Yahweh to be the God of anyone who was not alive. Therefore these patriarchs could not be dead, not even in the present time. They must still be alive.

An important thing to notice about Jesus' response is that he declares Heaven to be a place (or state of being) that has no mimetic rivalry. The Sadducees had posited a scenario rife with rivalry, where seven brothers would all be fighting over the same woman. Marriage, an institution with the (relatively minor) function to stifle mimetic rivalry, has become the *occasion* of mimetic rivalry. But Jesus is telling us that when there is no mimetic rivalry, there is no marriage. All of the social structures that in any way support mimetic rivalry are blown away in the Resurrection. In *Raising Abel*, Alison brilliantly points out that marriage is a reality only "to a world of death." A world filled with mimetic rivalry is, as we have seen all along, a world filled with death. "Having children is a necessity only for those who have been dominated by death." (Alison 1996, 38)

But there is more. Jesus went on to tell the Sadducees that they did not understand the power of God. Alison says that this power, "this quality that God always is, is that of being completely and entirely alive, living without any reference to death." (Alison 1996, 39) Common sense would have us believe that Abraham, Isaac, and Jacob are dead. After all, they aren't still walking around on earth. But Jesus imagines God as being so utterly Other in relation to death that life in God is *not* the opposite of death. Death just isn't anything. Jesus imagines "God as radically alive, as a-mortal, as in no way shaded by death." Alison goes on to say that while the Sadducees are greatly mistaken, they haven't just made a mistake, as a student might make a mistake on a test. Rather, "their whole perception is radically wrong, distorted, and it is so because it is stuck in a vision which flows from death to death, a vision which has not acceded to God, the entirely death-less." (Alison 1996, 39)

We fear death. We fear our own individual deaths, and we fear the possible death of all humanity that could very well happen if our violence becomes too explosive. After all, we have the explosives to go along with our human explosiveness. We cannot imagine living beyond death; we cannot imagine Heaven. But it is even more impossible to imagine living day-by-day, in this life, with no reference to death. What this really means is that we can't imagine living day-by-day without mimetic rivalry. The reason God has nothing to do with death is because God has nothing to do with mimetic rivalry. For God, mimetic resonance is all about giving, without rivalry of any sort.

Dante, a poet who had learned more about mimetic rivalry than he ever wanted to know by the time he was exiled from his beloved Florence, knew how important it was that banishing Satan from Heaven entailed banning mimetic rivalry. When Dante, early in his journey through Paradise, asked Piccarda if she had any resentment over being placed in the lowest sphere of Heaven, she made the famous reply: "His will is our peace." (Paradise III: 85) Beatrice then explains the equality in diversity in Heaven: "All share one sweet life, diversified as each feels more or less the eternal breath." (Paradise IV: 34) In the sphere of the sun, where dwell the philosophers and theologians, a breed much given to mimetic rivalry, all discord is melted in the flames of the sun. When Gregory the Great learned that he had gotten the angelic hierarchy wrong and Dionysius had gotten it right, he burst into laughter, and he hasn't stopped laughing since.

Does this mean we don't really die, even though we have cemeteries all over the world to prove otherwise? The question really is: What is death when God has nothing to do with death? St. Paul also seems convinced that, with God, there is no death when he says: "Neither death, nor life, nor angels, nor rulers, nor things present, nor things to come, nor powers, nor height, nor depth, nor anything else in all creation, will be able to separate us from the love of God in Christ Jesus our Lord." (Rom. 8:38–39) If God is the God of Abraham and Isaac and Jacob, then God is also the God of all of our ancestors who have gone before us and the God of all who are living now and the God of all who ever will live. The living God has united us with all of the living on either side of what we see as the Divide. We get glimpses of God as the God of the living in those who are dying, but are dying in God's life. The glimpses are strongest when the person has let go, thus achieving that important step in forgiveness and renunciation of mimetic rivalry. I have seen it myself several times, most powerfully in Fr. Anthony, my novice master in the Benedictine life. As he was dying of ALS, all of us around him could sense that the life of the God of the living was living through him and this life would never end.

Glossary of Terms

abba. An Aramaic word meaning father. It appears occasionally in the New Testament and is believed to be the word Jesus used to address his heavenly Abba. (Mk. 14:36)

acquisitive mimesis. Imitating the desire of another person for the same object to the extent of entering into conflict with that person to acquire that object for oneself.

agape. Love that is totally altruistic, offered with no strings attached, with total regard for the well-being of all people who receive it. Most commonly attributed to God. Humans may participate in *agape* as a gift of **grace.**

anthropological. Pertaining to fundamental human characteristics. Does not preclude humanity's relationship with God. Girard presupposes this relationship in his understanding of humanity.

apocalypse. From the Greek word *apokalypsis,* which means "unveiling" or "disclosing." Commonly thought to refer to unveiling the future, but many apocalypses unveil the deeper truths of the present situation, i.e., what God is doing underneath the human activity. Apocalyptic writings can be future-oriented and project where present trends are likely to end up. The "apocalyptic discourse" of Jesus in Mark 13 is a warning of the violence to come if his hearers continue on the course they have set.

Atonement. In Christianity, the reconciliation of God and humanity through the death and resurrection of Jesus Christ. Several theories of the Atonement have been constructed by various theologians. Girard rejects all theories that suggest that sacrifice was *necessary* on God's part. For Girard, the necessity for sacrifice is all on the part of humanity.

baptism. From the Greek word *baptizo*, meaning "to inundate, overwhelm, immerse." In the water baptism of John the Baptist, people were immersed in water. St. Paul interpreted the immersion of water baptism as also overwhelming the subject with the death and Resurrection of Jesus. (Rom. 6)

Body of Christ. Image for the **Church** used by St. Paul. (1Cor. 12:12–31) Suggests unity-in-diversity among the members. Also suggests a collective participation in Christ.

cellarer. The monastic who is put in charge of managing and distributing the material goods of a monastery.

Christology. Theological reflections on Christ, most especially the relationship between Christ's divinity and humanity.

Church. The community of the followers of Jesus Christ, manifested primarily in acts of worship and acts of charity. More deeply, the Church is called to be a community of **Forgiveness**, which participates in the forgiveness of the **Forgiving Victim**. I generally use it to refer to all Christian groups as a whole, while acknowledging that the Church is divided into many separate communities, some still in conflict with others.

climate of health. Promotion of and sustaining health at a societal level, where people care for one another.

collective violence. Violence committed against an individual or group of people by a crowd of people, usually a mob of some sort. Often done outside legal processes, but legal procedures can be rigged to the same purpose as happened with the **Passion** of Jesus. Lynching is a tragic example of collective violence from American history.

conflictual mimesis. Imitating another person with whom one is in conflict over a mutually desired object.

Contagion. In medicine, the spreading of diseases through human contact or from germs travelling in the air. For Girard, an apt description of the workings of mimetic desire, particularly in its violent forms. Violence can easily spread through a society exactly the way a plague does. Contagion can work the other way. In an oral presentation, I heard Gil Bailie refer to Christianity as a "virus" that can spread in a society, like leaven leavening a batch of bread. (Mt. 13:33)

contemplative prayer. An approach to prayer that seeks to empty the mind so as to direct one's attention to God without images or trains of thought. The point of this emptying is to open oneself so that God can come and dwell within.

Creation. Theologically, refers to God bringing the universe into being. It can refer to God's continuing nurturing of the world.

death. In ordinary usage, the cessation of bodily life. In a deeper sense, alienation from God and all other people. If Alison is right, there is no death in God, regardless of what eventually happens with the body. Hope, the promise of being heirs of Christ, suggests an inheritance beyond our earthly life. Certainly the death caused by **mimetic rivalry** and worse will cease. Beyond that, we don't know what to expect or hope for as we put our trust in God.

demon. See **possession**.

desire. Dictionary synonyms, such as "wanting" or "craving," don't seem to plumb the depths of this word. In **mimetic realism**, it refers to a deep-seated complex of wants, needs, and wishes. Some of these needs are biological, but most of them have social dimensions. Many desires arise through the desires of other people we are in relationship with. This is **mimetic desire**. God's desire is simple: a deep-seated cosmic wish for unity with all creatures.

Divine Office. A liturgical event featuring the use of hymns, psalms, and canticles.

dramatic theology. As far as I know, first formulated by Hans Urs von Balthasar; used with a different thrust by Raymund Schwager. Stresses the narration of the Christian story as a basis for developing theology.

empire. In the New Testament, refers to the Roman Empire. I use it to refer to every social structure **institutionalizing sacrificial violence**. In this respect, it refers to any country or government in the world today insofar as it exerts coercive violence on its own people or those of other countries. The dynamics of empire can easily occur in a small social group, such as a parish.

empire criticism. An approach to interpreting biblical texts that takes careful note of the impact of **empire** on what is said in the text.

enemy. Often, somebody who helps us define who we are by being what we are not (or think we are not). Such an enemy may be the subject of many projections and fantasies that are half-truths or complete lies. Sometimes, tragically, an enemy is someone who has committed a devastating injury, requiring much healing. It is very important not to confuse these two senses of enemy.

Eucharist. A **liturgical** celebration of the Last Supper that re-enacts Jesus' distribution of bread and wine on that occasion. Usually preceded by "the liturgy of the Word" comprised of scripture readings and, sometimes, a sermon. Also known as Holy Communion or the Lord's Supper.

exorcism. The act of casting out one or more demons that have possessed a person. In mimetic realism, it refers to delivering a person from **possession** by other people through therapeutic means.

external mediation. Girard's term for a **model** for another person, or group of people, who, by level of competence, social status, or distance in time, is mostly beyond competition from others. External mediation was the norm in hierarchical societies. It is the opposite of **internal mediation**.

faith. Participating in the faithfulness of Jesus who died on the cross. This includes participating in the trust Jesus had in his Heavenly **Abba**.

Flood. A cataclysmic event in the Bible where all but eight people and selected animals were drowned. Girard sees the Flood as an apt image for a society reaching the boiling point of a **mimetic crisis**.

forgiveness. In its fullness, a full-hearted benevolence toward those who have wronged us. In the cases of abusive injury, this level of forgiveness is a **grace** from God. Steps in the direction of forgiveness include letting go and renouncing retaliation.

Forgiving Victim. Term coined by James Alison to refer to the Risen Christ who, though a victim of **collective violence**, returned to life with forgiveness towards all those who wronged him.

freedom. The state of having some sense of personal agency in desiring and willing. **Mimetic desire** and especially **mimetic rivalry** compromise personal freedom but, in most cases, they do not rule it out. Acts of **grace** from **God** restore this sense of agency.

gift economy. A social network where goods and service are freely offered to everybody within the society. Theologically, a gift economy is grounded in God's free gifts of creation and grace.

God. The Supreme Being of the Universe. In many religious traditions, including Christianity, God is believed to be the **Creator** of the **World.** God is an ineffable mystery to humans, but in many religious traditions is believed to have revealed some truths about God's character, disposition, and purpose in various ways. In Christianity, the life and teachings of Jesus Christ are believed to be the ultimate revelation of what God is like.

grace. The usual English translation of *charis*, meaning gift. It refers to all gifts God gives to us, most particularly the gift of God's presence within us. Other gifts include strengthening us to love beyond our human capacity and endure trials when they come.

grumbling. See **murmuring.**

healing. Curing bodily and/or emotional and moral ailments to restore health to a person. See **climate of health.**

Heaven. A social realm that is free of all **mimetic rivalry** and conforms completely to **God's desire.** Insofar as people relate without mimetic rivalry in earthly life, Heaven is present. Given the reality of earthly life, Heaven will be mostly experienced beyond this present life. This futuristic **hope** does not diminish our responsibility to do what we can to pursue the dynamics of Heaven while on earth.

Hell. Traditionally a place of eternal torment for those believed to deserve it. The tendency for theologians who are using **mimetic realism** to see Jesus as revealing God as non-violent, not wrathful, and loving, leads to doubts about Hell's existence. In an oral presentation, Robert Daly called Hell the "ultimate violence." The notion of Universalism, the doctrine that, in the End, all people will be saved, goes back to early Christianity. St. Gregory of Nazianzus was one of the more prominent proponents of this hope. Insofar as Hell might exist, mimetic realism would envision it as a realm, or state of being, completely filled with **mimetic rivalry**. Dante's *Inferno* can be understood as illustrating this state. God's allowance of human **freedom** would seem to permit individuals to choose such an eternal destiny. Given the ways mimetic rivalry severely compromises freedom, there is a question of whether or not anyone can *freely* choose Hell eternally, in which case Universalism is true. In the end, we don't know in this life.

Holy Spirit. The Third Person of the **Trinity**, also the Advocate, the one who defends accused persons. The Holy Spirit is the **Person** who bestows **grace** on humans, including inspiring acts of **love** and **forgiveness**.

hope. Trusting in God's assurance that our inheritance as sons and daughters of God will be received in its fullness at a future time determined by God.

humility. Popular belief that humility means self-abasement obscures the richness of this virtue. The first step of humility in Benedict's Rule, that one should be constantly aware of living in the presence of God, makes a much firmer starting point for understanding this virtue.

identified patient. Phrase coined by Edwin Friedman. The identified patient is the person in a family system or community who absorbs its communal dysfunction more than anybody else, suffering physical, mental, and emotional symptoms. Focus on the identified patient's symptoms helps the community avoid facing the deeper, underlying issues causing its dysfunction.

Idol. Anyone or anything, other than **God**, who becomes the primary organizing principle of one's life. In **mimetic rivalry**, a rival can become an idol.

Incarnation. The doctrine that the Second **Person** of the **Trinity**, known as the Son, and called "the Word" in John 1, took on human nature via the Blessed Virgin Mary and became a particular human being, namely Jesus of Nazareth.

individualism. The illusion that a **person** is an autonomous individual, not connected with other people. Asserting individualism is bound to fail, with bad results for the person and all others affected by that person.

institutionalized sacrificial violence. Social structures, such as **empires**, in which some people, or groups of people, are **sacrificed** through economic oppression or other forms of social injustice. Slavery is a notorious example of this.

intelligence of the victim. Phrase coined by James Alison. The privileged viewpoint of the victim who understands the dynamics of persecution that persecutors are unable to see when they kill or expel victims. Andrew McKenna coined a more technical phrase, "the epistemological privilege of the victim," to say the same thing.

Interdividual. Term used by Oughourlian and Girard to stress the importance of relationships in the constitution of the human self.

internal mediation. Girard's term for a **model** who is close in social rank, competence, and time to another. The opposite of **external mediation**. In such a relationship, **mimetic rivalry** becomes a very real possibility. In modern democratic societies where a large number of people have fairly equal opportunities, mimetic rivalry tends to be prevalent.

Jubilee. The fiftieth year when, according to legislation in Leviticus, Chapter 25, all debts were to be forgiven and slaves were set free. Isaiah 61:1–2, read in the synagogue by Jesus in Luke 4:18–19, refers to this Jubilee.

kenotic. From the Greek *kenosis*, meaning "emptying." In theology, it refers to the self-emptying of Christ through entering human nature and dying on the cross as expressed in Philippians 2:6–11.

Kingdom of God. The social vision of Jesus in which people live without **mimetic rivalry** and forgive and support one another. Ultimately, it is a vision of **Heaven**, but it is presented as the ideal for Jesus' followers to strive to establish on earth.

lectio divina. Latin for "holy reading." Reading for the purpose of fostering spiritual growth. Scripture is the primary text for *lectio,* but other reading material of spiritual value may also be used.

liking. Term used by Alison in preference to **love** to avoid erotic and self-centered uses of the term in popular culture.

literary inspiration. A phrase used by William McNeil to describe liturgical texts and religious teachings informing liturgy or any other instance of **muscular bonding.**

liturgy. A **ritual** performed by a religious community. In Christianity, it most particularly applies to the **Eucharist**, but also applies to the **Divine Office.**

Love. Ultimate respect for other people, sincerely wishing for the well-being of others. At its best, it is *agape,* a gift from God.

méconnaissance. A French word, used by Girard and Dumouchel, that does not translate well into English. "Misrecognition" is the closest equivalent, but the French word includes an element of, usually **preconscious**, willfulness in the misrecognition.

Meditation. In Christian spirituality, refers to a systematic reflection on a Bible story or a spiritual theme, such as **forgiveness.** Not to be confused with meditation as understood in Eastern traditions such as Hinduism and Buddhism, which stress the emptying of the mind in various ways, akin to **contemplative prayer.**

Memory. In Jewish and Christian worship, indicates more than the common meaning of the word. When it is a case of remembering the acts of **God**, these acts are *made present* to the assembly. In the **Eucharist**, Christ and his acts are believed to be present during the celebration.

messiah. Royalty in the Jewish tradition. At the time of Jesus, there were various prophecies of a coming messiah, many of them envisioning a violent conqueror of Israel's oppressors. Girard argues that kingship is a **sacrificial** institution. The behavior of Jesus in light of messianic prophecies suggests that Jesus radically redefined kingship to the extent of repudiating its traditional meaning.

mimesis. Normally this word means "imitation" or "representation." In the works of Girard, it takes on the more specialized meaning of "imitating the desire of another person."

mimetic crisis. A situation where **mimetic rivalry** has become so rampant in a society that there is a real possibility that the society will destroy itself. If the society survives this crisis, it is usually through the **scapegoat mechanism**.

mimetic desire. A desire that is caused and/or intensified by the desire of another person for the same thing.

mimetic doubles. When two people enter into conflict because each is imitating the desires of the other, they become indistinguishable mirror images of each other.

mimetic process. Refers to the movement of mimetic resonance in a social group that takes on a life of its own beyond what any one individual wills.

Mimetic realism. Term coined by Robert Hamerton-Kelly to refer to **mimetic theory**. It grounds Girard's insights in **mimetic desire** in the body and lived experience rather than just an idea in the mind.

mimetic resonance. Term coined by the author to suggest that our desires resonate with the desires of others without necessarily copying particular desires of other people or desiring exactly what other people want. This does not preclude humans copying particular desires of others, but it avoids the determinism that **mimetic desire** can imply.

mimetic rivalry. Rivalry where two or more people imitate each other in their desires and attempt to attain the desired objects for themselves.

mimetic theory. Girard's theory that a human's desires are derived from the desires of others. That is, not only do people copy the external behavior of other people, but more fundamentally, people copy the *desires* of others.

mimetic triangle. A triangle formed by two persons desiring the same object and whatever they both desire. Two men pursuing the same woman in conflict with each other form a mimetic triangle.

mirror neurons. A recent neurological discovery (1980's) of neurons in the brains of primates and humans firing when the intentions of another are discovered. That is, the same neurons that fire when a person picks up a banana fire when a person sees somebody *else* pick up a banana. Research to date suggests very strongly that mirror neurons are a physical and neurological basis for **mimetic resonance.**

model. Girard's term for a person who acts as an example for one or more people. Girard's interest in models is strongest in the matter of modeling desires. This elicits **mimetic desire** where one tends to desire what the model desires. In early life, care-givers are particularly strong models for **desire.** Such modeling can be nurturing and non-rivalrous, but it can easily lead to conflict if what the model desires cannot be shared, or it is *believed* that it cannot be shared. One can relate to a model either through **external mediation** or **internal mediation.** If one's relationship with a model becomes one of **mimetic rivalry,** the model becomes a **skandalon,** a stumbling block. It is quite possible for two people to be models to each other, in which case they become **mimetic doubles**.

murmuring. Complaining about a situation in such a way that nothing is likely to be done about it. The Israelites murmured against God in the desert. (Ex. 16:2; 1 Cor. 10:10) NRSV translates the word as "complain." Benedict considers murmuring to be one of the most destructive vices in a community.

muscular bonding. A phrase coined by William McNeill. The unity that humans experience when they engage in synchronized bodily actions.

myth. Usually a story that explains the origins of cultural institutions. Girard believes that these narrations often disguise spontaneous acts of collective violence that became institutionalized in **sacrificial** rites. Not *every* myth functions in this way, but most, particularly cosmic and creation myths, do.

original sin. Also known as **the Fall**. A Christian doctrine that accounts for the entry of **sin** into the world. **Mimetic realism** tends to stress the collective dimension of the Fall, seeing it as a **mimetic process**. Paul's discussion of Adam as the one who brought **sin** into the world points to the responsibility of individuals in participating in the mimetic process. (Rom. 5) Most Christian thought believes that the Fall has compromised human **freedom**, though to varying degrees.

parable. From the Greek *parabole*, meaning "to place side by side." Refers to a story built on a comparison of some sort. The term used for many stories and brief comparisons told by Jesus.

Paschal Mystery. From the Greek *paschein*, "to suffer," in reference to the suffering of Christ during his Passion and death, and *mysterion*, meaning "a divine secret." In the Gospels, this becomes an open secret, but one whose meaning cannot be totally understood by humans.

Passion. Refers to the suffering endured by Jesus, beginning with his entrance into Jerusalem, up to his dying on the cross.

peace. An absence of conflict to begin with, but, in its fullness, an active cooperation of people with one another to create a society of mutual nurturing.

person. A being capable of awareness and **desiring**. Refers to human beings but can also refer to supernatural beings and to God. It is also used for the knowing and desiring centers within the **Trinity**. The Persons of the Trinity are primarily differentiated by their relations to one another. In much theology, including that developing **mimetic realism**, the Persons of the Trinity are considered a model for human personhood. I.e., to be a person is to be in relationship with others.

positive mimesis. Although **mimetic desire** often causes conflict, it is very possible for shared desire to work in constructive ways where people imitate one another in building one another up.

possession. A state of invasion by another personal being that inhibits or destroys personal agency of the person. In Jesus' time, this phenomenon was attributed to supernatural beings called demons. Without ruling out the possibility of these beings, Oughourlian and Girard have suggested that mimetic resonance can lead to people being "possessed" by other humans. In either case, an **exorcism** is needed.

prayer. A dialogue with **God**. It includes requests for self and others, confession of **sins**, thanksgiving, and praise. Can also be a silent colloquy with God.

preconscious. Awareness of something that affects one without one's quite knowing it. Girard sees **mimetic desire** as acting primarily at a preconscious level. It is, of course, possible to become conscious of that which had been preconscious.

primitive sacred. The religions of early humanity that Girard believes are founded on **sacred violence**. By extension, it can refer to any religious system that continues to perpetuate **sacrificial** structures.

principalities and powers. Used by Paul to refer to the transcendental dimension of coercive power that attacks the well-being of people. In **mimetic realism**, this term is useful for referring to the **mimetic process** in a society that ensnares people in oppressive structures, especially political and economic. It is a near synonym of **empire**, but stresses power of these structures beyond what the humans involved consciously will.

prohibition. Term used by Girard for the tendency of early cultures to quell **mimetic crises** by structuring society hierarchically to reduce **internal mediation** and to create laws for the same purpose.

prophet. In the Hebrew Bible, a prophet is not primarily one who foretells the future, although this happens occasionally. A prophet is a person who expresses a special insight from God as to what God is doing in the present time. Sometimes there are future ramifications to what God is doing in the present. Girard uses this word loosely for many figures in the Hebrew Bible who can be construed in any way as prefiguring Christ. Without prejudice to the broad biblical meaning of this word, Girard pays particular heed to Jesus' definition of a prophet as one who witnesses to God's truth as a victim of collective violence (Mt. 23:34–36).

real presence. The theological doctrine that, in a mysterious and undefined way, Jesus is present *in* the bread and wine consecrated during the **Eucharist** and distributed to the assembly. The biblical understanding of **memory** is usually invoked to support this notion. Some churches, such as the Roman Catholic and Lutheran churches, define the presence more narrowly. Many denominations do not accept it. Almost all churches affirm the Eucharist as an occasion for **God's grace** being given to all worshipers.

religion. Comes from the Latin *religio*, meaning "to bind." In Girard's **mimetic theory,** it has a negative connotation as referring to the binding of people in the **primitive sacred.** The word also refers to what are considered the great world religions, all of which, in various ways, reject the **primitive sacred.**

resentment. A continuous, seething anger directed at a person, group, or at society as a whole. Usually filled with envy of others without necessarily **desiring** what other people have. A deeply stuck disposition that clings to hatred with an iron grip. Dostoevsky's "underground man" is a profound depiction of this trait.

respect. Affirming the dignity of other people. It presupposes courtesy and is open to liking and even loving others.

Resurrection. Jesus' being raised from the dead on the third day after dying on the cross. His risen body was different enough from his former earthly body that he was often not recognized, even by those who knew him well. It was ethereal enough that he could walk through walls, but solid enough that Thomas could touch the wound in his side. (Jn. 20:27–28)

ritual. Can be used loosely to refer to any synchronized set of actions done by a group of people. **Muscular bonding** is an example of this. In more narrow usage, it refers to acts of worship that use coordinated activity of some sort.

sacred violence. Violence that is sanctioned by religious tradition. See **sacrificial.**

sacrifice. Refers primarily to ritual acts where something or someone is destroyed as an offering to a deity. In **mimetic theory,** sacrifice has a negative connotation as it arises from the **primitive sacred.** Many of these rituals presuppose that humans have to sacrifice something to **God.** One reason for the negative connotation is because in these rituals, something or, much more seriously, someone *else,* is sacrificed. Jesus reveals himself as God who, rather than asking sacrifices from humans, sacrifices himself *to* humans. As a model of self-sacrifice, Jesus re-defines sacrifice as a positive act, one made on behalf of other people.

sacrificial. In addition to the usual meaning of rituals involving sacrifice, Girard uses this word to refer to an underlying attitude that assumes that harmony between humans and with God requires either the death or the exile of a living being. It is also used in its more positive meaning as referring to a voluntary giving of oneself for the sake of others.

Satan. Without prejudice to the existence of a supernaturally evil being associated with this word, Girard uses this word primarily in its biblical meaning of a stumbling block, an adversary. In this usage, any person can be a "Satan" to another, as Peter was to Jesus (Mt. 16:23). In scripture, Satan is called "The Accuser." (Rev. 12:10) This is also apt, as people in **mimetic rivalry** with each other accuse each other of being responsible for the violence. In cases of **collective violence**, the victim is accused of crimes disrupting society that make the murder "necessary."

Scarcity. Dumouchel refers specifically to scarcity that is humanly created. Although material goods in the world are finite, they can become more scarce than they really are through **mimetic desire** and especially **mimetic rivalry.** In an example commonly used by Girard, if a child reaches for a toy in a room filled with toys, and then all, or most, of the other children want that toy, toys have suddenly become scarce. In the dynamics of economics, scarcity can be created in various ways, particularly when people with the most economic power compete with one another, leaving little for other people.

scandal. Derived from the Greek *skandalon.* Girard uses this word in its biblical meaning of a "stumbling block" or "obstacle." He suggests that when two or more people enter into conflict fueled by **mimetic desire**, they become stumbling blocks or obstacles to one another.

scapegoat. A goat that bears the **sins** of the Jewish people and is cast out into the desert according to Leviticus 16:7–26. Girard makes use of this traditional meaning but usually uses this word to refer to the selective blaming of one person or group for the misfortunes of the whole community.

scapegoat mechanism. An unconscious communal process that happens in times of **mimetic crisis,** during which a victim is selected and either killed or expelled.

self. In normal usage, the essential core of an individual's identity distinct from all others. Christian literature accepts this meaning but denies that the self of any created being is autonomous. The human self may be distinct from all other selves, but it is not self-sufficient; it is grounded in the selfhood of God. **Mimetic theory** says that the human self is not autonomous to other human selves either. The self is formed through interactions with the desires of other persons. Each human self functions best when it is aligned foremost with the desires of God and secondarily with the desires of other people.

Sin. Often used loosely to refer to any act of wrongdoing. Theologically, the word refers to acts, thoughts, and even **desires** that are contrary to God's desire.

Suffering Servant. An anonymous "servant" who is the subject of five songs within chapters 39–55 of the Book of Isaiah. Isaiah 52:13–53:12 is particularly devoted to the persecutions that this Servant suffered at the hands of the people. Much Jewish tradition has interpreted the Servant as standing for the whole of Israel in its persecution by other nations. Much Christian tradition has interpreted this Servant as a prophecy or forerunner of Christ. Girard believes that this Servant was a victim of the same sort of collective violence as Jesus.

Theater. Usually refers to acted out performances of stories on stage. In this book, I extended the meaning as a shorthand way of referring to several artistic media that involve narrative content, including novels and movies. I extended the meaning even further to include the **Eucharist** insofar as it has dramatic, narrative elements.

Trinity. Refers to both the complete unity of God *and* the distinction of three Persons: Father, Son, and Holy Spirit. It is a highly paradoxical teaching that arose to account for God's unity and ministry of Jesus (the Son **incarnate**) and the **Holy Spirit** as bringer of gifts through **grace**.

unconscious. Memories and other aspects of the human **self** that are hidden in various ways from conscious awareness. Repressed memories of trauma and **desires** one wishes not to acknowledge can cause harm and may need therapeutic intervention. This level of the self, however, has positive aspects that are rarely acknowledged in our time. Deep insights into the unconscious can be found in the works of many of the great spiritual writers in Christianity, among them St. Augustine, St. Bernard of Clairvaux, the author of *The Cloud of Unknowing*, St. Ignatius of Loyola, St. John of the Cross, and Thomas Merton. These writers discern the presence of **God** in the unconscious, a presence of **grace**, to help ground us in God's **desire**.

world. Usually a term referring to the whole universe and everything in it in a morally neutral way. In some New Testament writings, especially in John's Gospel, it carries a negative connotation of referring to a collective of human attitudes opposed to God's **desire**.

Bibliography

Aiken, Marty. "The Kingdom of Heaven Suffers Violence: Discerning the Suffering Servant in the Parable of the Wedding Banquet." Online article. Link available at http://indestructiblelife.blogspot.com/2006/04/parable-of-wedding-banquet.html, 2006.

Alberg, Jeremiah. *Beneath the Veil of the Strange Verses: Reading Scandalous Texts*. East Lansing: Michigan State University Press, 2013.

Alison, James. *Knowing Jesus*. Springfield: Templegate, 1993.

————. *Raising Abel: The Recovery of the Eschatological Imagination*. New York: Crossroad, 1996.

————. *The Joy of Being Wrong: Original Sin Through Easter Eyes*. New York: Crossroad, 1998.

————. *Faith beyond Resentment: Fragments Catholic and Gay*. London: Darton, Longman & Todd, 2001.

————. *On Being Liked*. London: Darton, Longman & Todd, 2004.

————. *Undergoing God: Dispatches from the Scene of a Break-in*. New York: Continuum, 2006.

————. *Broken Hearts and New Creations: Intimations of a Great Reversal*. New York: Continuum, 2010.

————. *The Forgiving Victim*. Glenview: Doers, 2013.

———— "Taking Cinderella to the Ball: How a mimetic anthropology restores the theological virtue of hope."

http://www.jamesalison.co.uk/texts/eng76.html, 2015.

Antonello, Pierpaolo, and Paul Gifford, eds. *Can We Survive our Origins?: Readings in René Girard's Theory of Violence and the Sacred*. East Lansing: Michigan State University Press, 2015.

_____. *How We Became Human: Mimetic Theory and the Science of Evolutionary Origins*. East Lansing: Michigan State University Press, 2015.

Antonello, Pierpaolo, and Heather Webb, eds. *Mimesis, Desire, and the Novel: René Girard and Literary Criticism*. East Lansing: Michigan State University Press, 2015.

Astell, Ann W., and Sandor Goodhart, eds. *Sacrifice, Scripture, & Substitution: Readings in Ancient Judaism and Christianity*. South Bend: University of Notre Dame Press, 2011.

Athanasius, Saint. "The Letter to Marcellinus" in *The Life of Antony and The Letter To Marcellinus*, translated by Robert C. Gregg. New York: Paulist Press, 1980.

Attali, Jacques. *Noise: The Political Economy of Music*, translated by Brian Massumi. Minneapolis: University of Minnesota Press, 1985.

Augustine, Saint. *Expositions of the Psalms, 33-50*. Hyde Park: New City Press, 2000.

Bailie, Gil. *Violence Unveiled: Humanity at the Crossroads*. New York: Crossroad, 1995.

Baker, Sharon L. *Razing Hell: Rethinking Everything You've Been Taught about God's Wrath and Judgment*. Louisville: Westminster John Knox Press, 2010.

_____. *Executing God: Rethinking Everything You've Been Taught about Salvation and the Cross*. Louisville: Westminster John Knox Press, 2014.

Bandera, Cesáreo. *The Sacred Game: The Role of the Sacred in the Genesis of Modern Literary Fiction*. University Park: Pennsylvania State University Press, 1994.

_____. *The Humble Story of Don Quixote: Reflections on the Birth of the Modern Novel*. Washington, D.C.: Catholic University of America Press, 2006.

_____*A Refuge of Lies: Reflection on Faith and Fiction.* East Lansing: Michigan State University Press, 2013.

Barclay, John M. G. *Paul and the Gift.* Grand Rapids, MI: Eerdmans, 2015.

Bartlett, Anthony W. *Cross Purposes: The Violent Grammar of Christian Atonement.* Harrisburg: Trinity Press International, 2001.

_____*Virtually Christian: How Christ Changes Human Meaning and Makes Creation New.* Lanham: O-Books, 2011.

Beck, Richard. *Unclean: Meditations on Purity, Hospitality, and Mortality.* Cambridge, U.K.: Lutterworth Press, 2012.

_____. *The Slavery of Death.* Eugene: Cascade Books, 2014.

Becker, Ernest. *The Denial of Death.* New York: Free Press, 1973.

Bellinger, Charles K. *The Trinitarian Self: The Key to the Puzzle of Violence.* Eugene: Pickwick Publications, 2008.

_____. *The Joker is Satan, and So Are We: And other Essays on Violence and Christian Faith.* Fort Worth: Churchyard Books, 2010.

Belousek, Darrin W. Snyder. *Atonement, Justice, and Peace: The Message of the Cross and the Mission of the Church.* Grand Rapids: Eerdmans, 2011.

Bernard, of Clairvaux, Saint. "On Loving God" in *Treatises II*, translated by Robert Walton. Washington, D.C.: Cistercian Publications, 1974.

The Book of Common Prayer and Administration of the Sacraments and Other Rites and Ceremonies of the Church According to the use of The Episcopal Church. New York: Church Hymnal Corporation, 1979.

Bonhoeffer, Dietrich. *The Cost of Discipleship.* New York: SCM Press, 1959.

Brown, Raymond: *The Gospel According to John.* Garden City: Doubleday, 1966.

Burrows, Ruth. *Guidelines for Mystical Prayer.* London: Sheed and Ward, 1976.

Campbell, Douglas. *The Deliverance of God: An Apocalyptic Reading of Justification in Paul.* Grand Rapids: Eerdmans, 2009.

Cavanaugh, William T. *Theopolitical Imagination: Discovering the Liturgy as a Political Act in an Age of Global Consumerism.* New York: T & T Clark, 2002.

Canetti, Elias. *Crowds and Power*. London: Phoenix, 2000.

Carroll, James. *Jerusalem, Jerusalem: How the Ancient City Ignited our Modern World*. Boston: Houghton Mifflin Harcourt, 2011.

Cassian, John. *The Institutes*, translated and annotated by Boniface Ramsey. New York: Paulist Press, 2000.

The Cloud of Unknowing, edited by James Walsh, S.J. New York: Paulist Press, 1981.

Collins, Brian. *The Head Beneath the Altar: Hindu Mythology and the Critique of Sacrifice*. East Lansing: Michigan State University Press, 2014.

Cone, James H. *The Cross and the Lynching Tree*. Maryknoll: Orbis, 2013.

Conway, Daniel, ed. *Kierkegaard's Fear and Trembling: a Critical Guide*. Cambridge, MA: Cambridge University Press, 2015.

Cowdell, Scott. *René Girard and Secular Modernity: Christ, Culture, and Crisis*. Notre Dame: University of Notre Dame Press, 2013.

Cowdell, Scott, Chris Fleming, and Joel Hodge, eds. *Violence, Desire, and the Sacred: Girard's Mimetic Theory across the Disciplines*. New York: Continuum, 2012.

Daly, Robert J. *Sacrifice Unveiled: The True Meaning of Christian Sacrifice*. London: T & T Clark, 2009.

Dante Alighieri. *The Divine Comedy*, translated by Dorothy L. Sayers and Barbara Reynolds. Harmondsworth: Penguin, 1950–1962.

_____. *La Vita Nuova (Poems of Youth)*, translated by Barbara Reynolds. Middlesex: Penguin, 1969.

Davies, Nigel. *Human Sacrifice: In History and Today*. New York: Morrow, 1981.

Dawson, David. *Flesh Becomes Word: A Lexicography of the Scapegoat or, The History of an Idea*. East Lansing: Michigan State University Press, 2013.

Dizdar, Drasko. *Sheer Grace: Living the Mystery of God*. New York: Paulist Press, 2008.

Doniger, Wendy: *The Bedtrick: Tales of Sex and Masquerade*. Chicago: University of Chicago Press, 2000.

Dostoevsky, Fyodor. *The Brothers Karamazov*, translated by Richard Pevear and Larissa Volokhonsky. San Francisco: North Point Press, 1990.

Dumouchel, Paul. *The Ambivalence of Scarcity and Other Essays*. East Lansing: Michigan State University Press, 2014.

_____*The Barren Sacrifice: An Essay on Political Violence*, translated by Mary Baker. East Lansing: Michigan State University Press, 2015.

Dupuy, Jean-Pierre. *The Mark of the Sacred*. Stanford: Stanford University Press, 2013.

_____*Economy and the Future: A Crisis of Faith*. East Lansing: Michigan State University Press: 2014.

Dylan, Bob. *Lyrics, 1962–2001*. New York: Simon and Schuster, 2004.

Farneti, Roberto. *Mimetic Politics: Dyadic Patterns in Global Politics*. East Lansing: Michigan State University Press, 2015.

Flood, Derek. *Disarming Scripture: Cherry-Picking Liberals, Violence-Loving Conservatives, and Why we all Need to Learn to Read the Bible Like Jesus did*. San Francisco: Metanoia Books, 2014.

Francis de Sales, Saint. *The Complete Introduction to the Devout Life*, translated by Father John-Julian, OJN. Brewster: Paraclete Press, 2013.

Friedman, Edwin H. *Generation to Generation: Family Process in Church and Synagogue*. New York: Guildford Press, 1985.

Garrels, Scott R., ed.: *Mimesis and Science: Empirical Research on Imitation and the Mimetic Theory of Culture and Religion*. East Lansing: Michigan State University Press, 2011.

Gibson, Jeffrey B. *The Temptations of Jesus in Early Christianity*. London: T & T Clark, 1995.

Girard, René. *Deceit, Desire and the Novel: Self and Other in Literary Structure*, translated by Yvonne Freccero. Baltimore: Johns Hopkins University Press, 1965.

_____. *Violence and the Sacred*, translated by Patrick Gregory. Baltimore: Johns Hopkins University Press, 1977.

_____. *"To Double Business Bound": Essays on Literature, Mimesis and Anthropology*. Baltimore: Johns Hopkins University Press, 1978.

_____. *The Scapegoat*, translated by Yvonne Freccero. Baltimore: Johns Hopkins University Press, 1986.

_____. *Things Hidden Since the Foundation of the World: Research*

Undertaken in Collaboration with Jean-Michel Oughourlian and Guy Lefort, translated by Stephen Bann and Michael Metteer. Stanford: Stanford University Press, 1987.

————. *Job: The Victim of His People*, translated by Yvonne Freccero. Stanford: Stanford University Press, 1987.

————. *A Theater of Envy: William Shakespeare*. New York: Oxford University Press, 1991.

————. "Are the Gospels Mythical?" *First Things* 62 (April 1996), 27–31.

————. *The Girard Reader*, edited by James G. Williams. New York: Crossroad, 1996.

————. *Resurrection from the Underground: Feodor Dostoevsky*, translated by James G. Williams. New York: Crossroad, 1997.

————. *I See Satan Fall like Lightning*, translated by James G. Williams. Maryknoll: Orbis, 2001.

————. *Oedipus Unbound: Selected Writings on Rivalry and Desire*, edited by Mark Anspach. Stanford: Stanford University Press, 2004.

————. *Evolution and Conversion: Dialogues on the Origins of Culture*, with Pierpaolo Antonello and João Cezar de Castro Rocha. London: T & T Clark/Continuum, 2007.

————. *Battling to the End: Conversations with Benoît Chantre*. East Lansing: Michigan State University Press, 2010.

————. *Sacrifice*, translated by Matthew Pattillo and David Dawson. East Lansing: Michigan State University Press, 2011.

————. *The One by Whom Scandal Comes*, translated by Malcolm B. DeBevoise. East Lansing: Michigan State University Press, 2014.

Golsan, Richard J. *René Girard and Myth: An Introduction*. New York: Routledge, 2001.

Grande, Per Bjørnar. *Mimesis and Desire: An Analysis of the Religious Nature of Mimesis and Desire in the Work of René Girard*. Cologne: Lambert Academic Publishing, 2009.

Goodhart, Sandor. *Sacrificing Commentary: Reading the End of Literature*. Baltimore: Johns Hopkins University Press, 1996.

_____. *The Prophetic Law: Essays in Judaism, Girardianism, Literary Studies, and the Ethical.* East Lansing: Michigan State University Press, 2014.

Grote, Jim, and John McGeeney. *Clever as Serpents: Business Ethics and Office Politics.* Collegeville: The Liturgical Press, 1997.

Hamerton-Kelly, Robert G., ed. *Violent Origins: Walter Burkert, René Girard, and Jonathan Z. Smith on Ritual Killing and Cultural Formation.* Stanford: Stanford University Press, 1987.

Hamerton-Kelly, Robert. *Sacred Violence: Paul's Hermeneutic of the Cross.* Minneapolis: Fortress Press, 1992.

_____. *The Gospel and the Sacred: Poetics of Violence in Mark.* Minneapolis: Fortress Press, 1994.

_____, ed. *Politics & Apocalypse.* East Lansing: Michigan State University Press, 2007.

Hardin, Michael, and Ted Grimsrud, eds. *Compassionate Eschatology: The Future as a Friend.* Eugene, OR: Cascade Books, 2011.

Hardin, Michael. *The Jesus-Driven Life: Reconnecting Humanity with Jesus.* Lancaster: JDL Press, 2013.

Heim, S. Mark. *Saved from Sacrifice: A Theology of the Cross.* Grand Rapids: Eerdmans, 2006.

Hickock, Gregory. *The Myth of Mirror Neurons: The Real Neuroscience of Communication and Cognition.* New York: Norton, 2014.

Hughes, Carl S. *Kierkegaard and the Staging of Desire: Rhetoric and Performance in a Theology of Eros.* New York: Fordham University Press, 2014.

Hyde, Lewis. *The Gift: Imagination and the Erotic Life of Property.* New York: Vintage, 1983.

Iacoboni, Marco. *Mirroring People: The New Science of How We Connect with Others.* New York: Farrar, Straus & Giroux, 2008.

Ignatius of Loyola, Saint, *The Spiritual Exercises and Selected Works*, edited by George E. Gans, S.J. New York: Paulist Press, 1991.

Jackson, Shirley. *The Lottery and Other Stories.* New York: Farrar, Straus & Giroux, 1991.

Jersak, Bradley. *Her Gates Will Never Be Shut: Hope, Hell, and the New Jerusalem*. Eugene, OR: Wipf and Stock, 2009.

Julian of Norwich. *Showings*, translated by Edmund Colledge, OSA, and James Walsh, S. J. New York: Paulist Press, 1978.

Keating, Thomas. *Open Mind, Open Heart: The Contemplative Dimension of the Gospel*. New York: Amity House, 1986.

Keysers, Christian: *The Empathic Brain: How the Discovery of Mirror Neurons Changes our Understanding of Human Nature*. Lexington: Social Brain Press, 2011.

Kierkegaard, Søren. *Works of Love*, translated by Howard and Edna Hong. New York: Harper & Row, 1962.

_____. *The Sickness Unto Death: a Christian Psychological Exposition for Upbuilding and Awakening*, edited and translated by Howard and Edna Hong. Princeton: Princeton University Press, 1980.

_____. *Fear and Trembling* and *Repetition*, edited and translated by Edna Hatlestad Hong and Howard Vincent Hong. Princeton: Princeton University Press, 1983.

Kirk-Duggan, Cheryl A. *Refiner's Fire: A Religious Engagement with Violence*. Minneapolis: Fortress Press, 2001.

Kirwan, Michael. *Girard and Theology*. London: T & T Clark; New York: Continuum, 2009.

LaPlante, Eve. *Salem Witch Judge: the Life and Repentance of Samuel Sewall*. New York: HarperOne, 2007.

Laycock, Joseph P. *Dangerous Games: What the Moral Panic Over Role-Playing Games Says about Play, Religion, and Imagined Worlds*. Oakland: University of California Press, 2015.

Lewis, C. S. *Surprised by Joy: The Shape of My Early Life*. New York: Harcourt, Brace, 1955.

_____. *The Four Loves*. New York: Harcourt, Brace, 1960.

Lowry, Lois. *The Giver*. New York: Delacorte Press, 2006.

MacDonald, George. *Creation in Christ*, edited by Rolland Hein. Wheaton: Howard Shaw, 1975.

McKenna, Andrew. *Violence and Difference*. Chicago: University of Illinois Press, 1992.

McLaren, Brian. *Why did Jesus, Moses, the Buddha, and Mohammed Cross the Road?: Christian Identity in a Multi-Faith World*. New York: Jericho Books, 2012.

McNeill, William. *Keeping Together in Time: Dance and Drill in Human History*. Cambridge, MA: Harvard University Press, 1995.

Main, John. *Word into Silence*. New York: Paulist Press, 1981.

Maritain, Raïssa. *Raïssa's Journal,* presented by Jacques Maritain. Albany: Magi Books, 1974.

Marr, Andrew. *Tools for Peace: The Spiritual Craft of St. Benedict and René Girard*. New York: iUniverse, 2007.

Marshall, Christopher D. *Beyond Retribution: A New Testament Vision for Justice, Crime, and Punishment*. Grand Rapids: Eerdmans, 2001.

May, Gerald G. *Will and Spirit: a Contemplative Psychology*. San Francisco: Harper & Row, 1983.

Merton, Thomas. *New Seeds of Contemplation*. New York: New Directions, 1961.

_____. *The Inner Experience: Notes on Contemplation*. San Francisco: HarperCollins, 2003.

Merton, Thomas and John Wu, *Merton & the Tao: Dialogues with John Wu and the Ancient Sages,* edited by Cristobal Serrán-Pagán y Fuentes. Louisville: Fons Vitae, 2013.

Meszaros, Julia, and Johannes Zachhuber, eds. *Sacrifice and Modern Thought*. Oxford: Oxford University Press, 2013.

Moore, Brenna. *Sacred Dread: Raïssa Maritain, the Allure of Suffering, and the French Catholic Revival*. Notre Dame: University of Notre Dame Press, 2013.

Nuechterlein, Paul. "Girardian Reflections on the Lectionary." http://girardianlectionary.net/, 2016.

Orléan, André. *The Empire of Value: A New Foundation for Economics*. Cambridge, MA: MIT Press, 2014.

Oughourlian, Jean-Michel. *The Puppet of Desire: The Psychology of Hysteria,*

Possession, and Hypnosis, translated by Eugene Webb. Stanford: Stanford University Press, 1991.

_____. *The Genesis of Desire*, translated by Eugene Webb. East Lansing: Michigan State University Press, 2010.

_____. *Pscyhopolitics: Conversations with Trevor Cribben Merrill*, translated by Trevor Cribben Merrill. East Lansing: Michigan State University Press, 2012.

Pahl, Jon. *Empire of Sacrifice: The Religious Origins of American Violence.* New York: NYU Press, 2010.

Palaver, Wolfgang. *René Girard's Mimetic Theory.* East Lansing: Michigan State University Press, 2013.

Pennington, Basil. *Centering Prayer: Renewing an Ancient Christian Prayer Form.* Garden City: Doubleday, 1980.

Pfeil, Margaret R., and Tobias Winright, eds. *Violence, Transformation, and the Sacred: "They Shall be Called Children of God."* Maryknoll: Orbis, 2011.

Prejean, Helen. *Dead Man Walking.* New York: Vintage, 1994.

_____. *The Death of Innocents.* New York: Random House, 2005.

Pyszczynski, Tom, Sheldon Solomon, and Jeff Greenberg. *In the Wake of 9/11: The Psychology of Terror.* Washington, D.C.: American Psychological Association, 2003.

Rabe, André. *Desire Found Me: Exploring the Unconscious Movements of Desire — How They Form us, Connect Us, Shape our Greatest Ideas, Mold Our Societies, Influence Human History and Ultimately, How They are Unveiled.* S.l: André Rabe Publishing, 2014.

Redekop, Vern Neufeld. *From Violence to Blessing: How an Understanding of Deep-rooted Conflict Can Open Paths to Reconciliation.* Ottawa: Novalis, 2002.

Redekop, Vern Neufeld, and Thomas Ryba, eds. *René Girard and Creative Mimesis.* Lanham: Lexington Books, 2014.

Reineke, Martha Jane. *Intimate Domain: Desire, Trauma, and Mimetic Theory.* East Lansing: Michigan State University Press, 2014.

Robinette, Brian D. *Grammars of Resurrection: A Christian Theology of Presence and Absence.* New York: Crossroad. 2009.

Rolf, Veronica Mary. *Julian's Gospel: Illuminating the Life & Revelations of Julian of Norwich.* Maryknoll: Orbis, 2013.

Ross, Suzanne. *The Wicked Truth about Love: The Tangles of Desire.* Chicago: Raven Foundation, 2009.

Sagan, Eli. *At the Dawn of Tyranny: The Origins of Individualism, Political Oppression, and the State.* London: Faber and Faber, 1985.

Schneiders, Sandra Marie. *Jesus Risen in our Midst: Essays on the Resurrection of Jesus in the Fourth Gospel.* Collegeville: Liturgical Press, 2013.

Schwager, Raymund. *Must There Be Scapegoats?: Violence and Redemption in the Bible.* San Francisco: HarperCollins, 1978.

_____. *Jesus in the Drama of Salvation: Toward a Biblical Doctrine of Redemption.* New York: Crossroad, 1999.

_____. *Banished from Eden: Original Sin and Evolutionary Theory in the Drama of Salvation.* Leominster: Gracewing, *2006.*

Scripture of the Lotus Blossom of the Fine Dharma (The Lotus Sutra), translated by Leon Hurvitz. New York: Columbia University Press. 1976.

Sendak, Maurice. *Where the Wild Things Are.* New York: Harper & Row, 1963.

Serres, Michel. "Ego Credo." in *Contagion: Journal of Violence, Mimesis, and Culture.* 12–13 (2005–2006), 1–11.

Shakespeare, William. *The Complete Works*, edited by Hardin Craig. Chicago: Scott, Foresman, 1951.

Swartley, Willard M., editor. *Violence Renounced: René Girard, Biblical Studies, and Peacemaking.* Telford: Pandora Press, 2000.

Swartley, Willard M. *Covenant of Peace: The Missing Peace in New Testament Theology and Ethics.* Grand Rapids: Eerdmans, 2006.

Tolkien, J. R. R. "On Fairy-Stories," *in The Monsters and the Critics and Other Essays, edited by Christopher Tolkien.* Boston: Houghton Mifflin, 1984.

Tomelleri, Stefano. *Ressentiment: Reflections on Mimetic Desire and Society.* East Lansing: Michigan State University Press, 2015.

Tutu, Desmond and Mpho Tutu. *The Book of Forgiving: The Fourfold Path for Healing Ourselves and Our World.* New York: HarperOne, 2014.

Tyrrell, William Blake. *The Sacrifice of Socrates: Athens, Plato, Girard.* East Lansing: Michigan State University Press, 2012.

Ware, Timothy (Kallistos). Introduction to *The Art of Prayer: An Orthodox Anthology,* compiled by Igumen Chariton of Valamo. London: Faber and Faber, 1966.

Wallace, Mark and Theophus H. Smith, eds. *Curing Violence: Essays on René Girard.* Sonoma: Polebridge Press, 1994.

Warren, James. *Compassion or Apocalypse?: A Comprehensible Guide to the Thought of René Girard.* Winchester: Christian Alternative, 2013.

Weaver, J. Denny. *The Nonviolent Atonement.* Grand Rapids: Eerdmans, 2001.

Williams, James G. *The Bible, Violence, and the Sacred: Liberation from the Myth of Sanctioned Violence.* San Francisco: HarperCollins, 1991; Valley Forge, PA: Trinity Press International, 1995.

_____. *Girardians: The Colloquium on Violence and Religion, 1990–2010.* Zürich: Lit Verlag, 2012.

Wink, Walter. *The Powers.* 3 vols. Minneapolis: Fortress Press. 1984–1992.

GENERAL INDEX

as creator, 2, 64, 65, 69, 84, 147, 206, 215, 308

desire(s), 1–3, 27, 40, 41, 43, 45, 59, 63, 73, 80, 81, 82, 141–142, 147, 148, 157, 159, 164, 165–166, 167, 168, 171, 174, 178, 199, 201, 215, 216, 218, 219–220, 231, 233, 262, 263, 271, 273, 274, 276, 278, 287, 290, 294, 295, 298, 306, 308, 319, 320

fatherhood, 157–58. *See also* Abba.

forgiveness, 241, 255, 256, 257, 259. *See also* forgiveness of sins.

generosity, 41, 56, 64, 83–84, 130, 210

image of, 216, 229, 278, 287

love, 21, 43, 91, 94, 129, 158, 167, 193, 194, 211, 216–217, 220, 225, 233, 255, 260, 266, 269–270, 272, 275–276, 286, 287, 290, 293, 294, 296

mercy, 116, 210, 212, 243, 260

presence of, 159, 174, 211, 215, 231, 232, 254, 275, 277, 278, 308, 309, 320

vulnerablity, 91, 92, 216

will, 1, 5, 6, 134–135, 271

wrath, 6–7, 9–10, 62, 128, 131, 134, 162, 189, 212, 213, 217, 260, 261

Goethe, Johann Wolfgang von, 49, 284

"The Sorcerer's Apprentice," 284

The Sorrows of Young Werther, 69

Golding, Sir William Gerald. *Lord of the Flies,* 29

Goodhart, Sandor, 86

goodness, 14, 250, 261

Gospel, the, 21, 23, 27, 160, 161, 197, 228

grace, 78, 84, 116, 148, 167, 200, 209, 217–219, 255, 303, 307, 308, 309, 316

Grande, Per Bjørnar, 42–43

gratitude, 171, 172, 233. *See also* thanksgiving.

Greece & Greek culture, 17, 155, 184, 207

Gregory I, Pope, Saint, 152, 300

Gregory of Nazianzus, Saint, 308

habit(s), 222, 236, 257, 281

Hamerton-Kelly, Robert Gerald, 13, 29, 131, 312

Hamor, 243, 244

healing(s), 95–98, 100, 117, 125, 126, 157, 168, 251, 252, 253, 259, 292, 308

Heaven, 175, 296, 299, 300, 308, 311. *See also* Kingdom of God.

Hell, 59, 118, 122, 249, 308

Herod the Great, 91, 93, 112, 113

Herod Antipas, 6, 110, 187

heroism, 205, 206

Hezekiah, 299

Hickock, Gregory Scott, 33

Hinduism, 56, 87, 91–92, 93, 202, 311

Parsons, Donald James, 164

Paschal Mystery. *See under* Jesus Christ.

Passover, 6, 133, 194, 195, 196

Paul the Apostle, 14, 19, 61, 68, 72, 77, 81, 82, 84, 116, 129, 136, 147, 153, 155, 156, 159, 160, 161, 179, 186, 190, 192, 193, 194, 198, 199–200, 206–207, 208, 209, 213, 216, 217, 240, 249, 258, 262–263, 264, 266, 267, 271, 281, 293, 294, 297, 301, 314, 316

peace, 79, 89, 93, 117, 127, 139, 166, 300, 315

Péguy, Charles Pierre, 20

penitence, 168–171, 184, 187, 208, 257. *See also* confession; repentance.

Pentecost, 4, 27, 80, 139

persecution, 9, 19, 20, 27, 32, 77, 79, 98, 103, 109, 118, 139, 140, 145, 146, 147, 148, 159, 176, 192, 193, 205, 209, 241, 246, 310, 319

Peter the Apostle, 4, 7, 8, 18, 116, 118, 119, 121, 124, 125, 139–140, 156, 171, 191-192, 207, 214, 318

petition (prayer), 164–166, 168, 169, 171, 273

Pharisees, 6, 19, 20, 80, 90, 101, 105, 167, 251, 260, 297, 298

pharmakoi, 17–18

Pilate, Pontius, 6, 86, 110, 127, 135, 151, 232, 237

positive mimesis. *See under* mimetic desire.

possession, 12, 27, 43, 99, 100, 106, 248, 275–276, 307, 315

Pound, Ezra Weston Loomis, 22

poverty & the poor, 20, 26, 76, 93, 104, 112, 113, 114, 129, 146, 148, 212, 218, 293

power, 38–39, 151, 172, 211, 213, 216, 227, 237

praise. *See* adoration.

prayer, 1, 3, 147, 149, 163, 164–175, 187, 219, 220, 227, 276–294, 315. *See also* centering prayer.
contemplative, 3, 174, 202, 276, 277–278, 279, 287, 290, 292, 293, 294, 305, 311
unanswered, 165, 168

Prejean, Helen. *Dead Man Walking,* 23

pride, 170, 182, 226, 233, 258, 265, 285

primitive sacred, 18, 20, 21, 22, 23, 25, 26–27, 71, 316, 317

"principalities and powers," 77–80, 83, 84, 85, 93, 94, 100, 113, 148, 149, 171, 212, 240, 258, 263, 316

process theology, 216

prohibition, 12, 16–17, 316

prophet(s), 70, 84, 88, 108, 116, 127, 128–129, 140, 187, 207, 211, 241, 260, 316

Proust, Marcel, 47

Purusha, 13, 16

Twain, Mark (Samuel Langhorne
Clemens) "The United States of
Lyncherdom," 22–23
twins, 16
Tyrrell, William Blake, 86

unconscious, 41–43, 320
Underhill, Evelyn, 186
unity, 142, 153, 162, 179, 241, 314.
See also Church, disunity.
Universalism, 308, 309
Uriah the Hittite, 241

vainglory, 170, 233–235
Vedic society, 16–17, 85
vengeance & vengefulness, 52, 62,
116, 118, 119–120, 121, 122,
139, 162, 213-214, 240, 241–
242, 247, 250, 260. See also
revenge.
victim(s), 6, 9, 11, 12, 13, 15, 16,
18, 19, 24, 26, 27, 61, 70, 75,
79, 99-100, 108, 112, 113, 123,
129, 140, 148, 151, 176, 182,
183, 185, 190, 191, 192, 215,
226, 236, 240, 246, 247, 250,
255, 256, 258, 265, 319. See
also scapegoat.
deification of, 11
intelligence of, 98, 102, 310
Victoria, Tomás Luis de, 203
violence, 25, 32, 65, 67, 112, 130,
133, 135, 136, 137, 139, 149,
151, 158, 160, 181, 187, 190,
191, 192, 212, 215, 217, 241,

244, 250, 254, 260, 265, 272,
297, 300, 305, 318
collective, 5, 6, 8–27 passim, 42,
52, 68, 70, 71, 78, 80, 84, 86,
100, 102, 116, 125, 129, 131,
155, 160, 170, 176, 177, 185,
192, 206, 237, 243, 244, 247,
304-305, 314, 318, 319. See
also mimetic violence.

war(s) & warfare, 10, 15, 23, 32, 79,
89, 166, 178, 214, 241, 250,
256, 265, 297
Ware, Timothy (Kallistos), 290–291
wealth, 76
Weldon, Thomas Dewar, 14
Where the Wild Things Are (Sendak),
43
Wilberforce, William, 158–159
will, 1, 2, 35, 102, 166, 203–204,
217, 219, 288, 290, 291, 307.
See also under God.
Wink, Walter Philip, 78
witchcraft trials, 21
Woden, 13
women, 70, 79, 117, 136, 137–138,
161, 242, 247, 251
Word, the, 59, 60, 90–91, 109, 178,
184, 188. See also Jesus Christ.
Works of Love (Kierkegaard), 272–
273, 296
worship, 60, 147, 148–149, 179,
183–184, 185, 186, 187, 224,
231, 278, 292, 304. See also
liturgy.

SCRIPTURE INDEX

****

Rule of St. Benedict

CPSIA information can be obtained
at www.ICGtesting.com
Printed in the USA
FSHW021941130619
59053FS